李　杜　著

世界的假設——

裴柏與西方的形而上學

臺灣學生書局印行

自 序

裴柏（S.C. Pepper）是現代美國有名的哲學家。但我在讀大學時並沒有讀過他的著作。

我知道有裴柏這個人是在讀研究所時一次學術演講中聽到。一九五七年美國密西根大學教授 Abraham Kaplan 來香港新亞書院講裴柏的哲學。我參加了聽講。聽過後我大致地了解到裴柏是一個不同意現代的邏輯實證論者與語言哲學家完全否定西方傳統的形而上學的人。但當時我對形而上學雖然有興趣，但多限於中國傳統的形而上學，對西方傳統的形而上學，現代的語言哲學及邏輯實證論都了解不多。故聽過了演講之後並沒有引起我的興趣去對裴柏的哲學作進一步的探討。

一九六〇年我開始在新亞書院哲教系教書，教的是宋明理學；六二年我往美國芝加哥大學研究，用心的是英國的經驗主義，尤其是休謨的哲學及蒯因的邏輯學；六三年我往臺灣中國文化學院，即現在的中國文化大學哲學系任教，教的是哲學概論、邏輯、中國哲學史等課，故皆沒有注意及裴柏的哲學。我注意裴柏的哲學是於一九六五年到香港中文大學教書時開始。但當時的注意亦僅是在教西方的哲學史的課程中以他爲現代脈絡論者的一代表人物而已，並未深入去探討。我深入去研究裴柏的哲學是在一九七〇年到美國南伊利諾大學去深造時在裴柏的嫡傳大弟子 Lewis E. Hahan 教授的指導下去讀他的專著。在細讀他的著作之後，我了解到他的哲學的重要性，及其在現代的西方的哲學與西方的哲學史中應有的地位。當時我曾用英文寫成了一篇

"S.C. Pepper's Concept of Metaphysics as the Theory of World Hypothesis"（現收入本書為附錄）。在該文中我給予裴柏由世界的假設上以了解形而上學高的評價。但亦有批評。主要的批評是他以形而上學僅為由世界的假設的觀點上去了解的學問，亦即只由經驗的層次上去了解世界，而不承認有超經驗層次的形而上學。事實上西方的形而上學除由世界的假設的觀點去了解之外，另有不是世界的假設所能了解的一面。

一九七五年我開始在中大教形而上學。裴柏的世界的假設對我的教學有重要的幫助，但我不是完全依照他的觀點去講形而上學。依我在前面所已提及的了解，形而上學除了裴氏的了解的一面之外，另有其他的一面。後來我稱此兩個不同的面相為：超越論的形而上學與存有論的形而上學（Transcendentalism and Ontology or Science of Beings）。裴柏的世界的假設應屬於後者，儘管他的講法，亦即世界的假設的講法不同於其他的存有論者對存有的講法。

由上面對形而上學兩面性的了解，我即開始試行寫一本包括有關所說的兩面性的西方的形而上學的書，並定名為《裴柏的世界的假設與西方的形而上學》。此書由一九七九年開始寫，分為四部份：⑴概述；⑵西方形而上學中的超越論；⑶西方形而上學中的存有論；⑷裴柏的世界的假設。在⑴中是總論西方由古希臘至現代的超越論的形而上學；⑵是論述西方的形而上學的性質、方法、分類，與由世界的假設去了解西方的形而上學等；⑶是論述西方由古希臘至現代的存有論的形而上學；⑷是論述裴柏的世界的假設。

由七九年終開始至八四年初，我寫成了三十多萬字的初稿。但在初稿剛寫成之後，我即不幸患上了嚴重的疾病。患病後固然沒有精神去修改已寫成的初稿，在中大教書的工作亦要停止。在疾病最痛苦中，我曾對着初稿飲泣，以為此稿將成為一堆廢紙，沒有面世的日子了！但後來

我竟能逃離病災，大病不死。在健康漸漸好轉之後，我恢復了教書的工作，亦再提起精神開始修改書稿。我按上面所列的次序修改。在教學之餘暇，經一年多時間，我竟能將前面所說的(1)與(2)修改好。正要着手修改(3)時，我忽然起了新的意念，認爲此書應分別爲兩本：一爲《西方形而上學中的超越論與存有論》；一爲《裴柏的世界的假設》❶，而不必合成一本累贅的大書。此一意念經多次考慮而決定了之後，我即先修改《裴柏的世界的假設》，再修改《西方形而上學中的超越論與存有論》的「存有論」那部份。現在前者已修改好準備付印，故寫此序言略述我撰寫此書的經過。

由假設的進路而了解世界所涵有的新意義，應由讀者看過本書或看過裴柏有關的原著之後去了解。我在此要說的只是由假設的方式以探求事物的知識在近代主要是科學家的事。在裴柏之前似乎沒有哲學家以其所建立的哲學系統來看這假設的哲學系統。假設是需要經驗的證明的，如果一假設沒有經驗的證明，則此假設即爲無效的。故由假設以了解世界是屬於經驗層次中的事，而不涉及超經驗的世界爲何。故我在前面所說對裴柏由世界的假設以了解世界的批評只是不同意他不承認有超經驗層次的形而上學的一面，而不是不同意他純由經驗層次以說世界的假設。世界的假設是可以有多個的（裴柏即分別提出了五個不同的世界的假設），對每一世界的假設是否可以接受。要看其是否對世界有適切的解釋及對所解釋有好的證明，而不是獨斷地以其一定是對的。對世界的假設的證明是一種依於經驗而來的結構性或系統性的證明，而不是重複性的科學式的證明。裴柏以爲西方傳統的哲學只有四個相對地適切的有效的世界的假設，而他則另依現代西方的哲學與科學的知識而提出了一個。所謂「相對地適切」是說他所提的五個世界的假設都可以彼此相對地而對世界作適切的結構性與系統性的解釋，而在五個世界的假設

中，沒有那一個是絕對地對的。因從不同的假設可以對世界有不同的了解，而不能以某一個相對地適切的世界的假設的了解去排斥其他的相對地適切的世界的假設的了解。

世界是怎樣的世界，除依世界的假設而說其是怎樣的之外，不能有離開假設而說其為何的說法。因如你離開裴柏所提出的世界的假設而說世界為何，你的說法亦應是一種假設的說法。你的說法是否對，要看你依你的說法而對世界的了解怎樣，是否有很好的結構性與系統性的說明？你的說法是否比其他的說法更好？此可以作比較的了解，而不能獨斷地說其為何。

由假說的方式所建立的科學的知識有其客觀性，而不是獨斷地說其為何。對整個世界作假設式的了解，亦有其客觀性，而去除了過去有些哲學對世界作獨斷式的了解，對整個世界作假設式的了解的價值亦應逐步為人設式的了解，其價值已明顯地為人所了解，對整個世界作假設式的了解到。

西方的哲學在過去如前面所已提及的沒有人以其哲學的了解是假設的了解。中國的哲學更是如此。但西方傳統的哲學如裴柏所提出的實涵有不同的假設的了解。中國的哲學依我在本書附錄中所提出的 "An Understanding of Chinese Philosophy from the Theory of World Hypothesis" 的了解亦應可以作世界的假設式的了解❷。

假設式的探求在近代普遍地為人所採用，可說此為近代學術的精神路向。人依此路向而從事學術的探求可使人的聰明盡量表現出來，依人所有的不同的經驗與不同的理解去尋求知識，而去除人的蔽塞，但很可惜在現在的中國大陸卻仍獨斷地堅持馬列主義與毛澤東思想為唯一的真理而不許人有別的了解，其蔽塞中國人的智慧，為禍炎黃後裔，不必等待將來而現在已明顯可見。

堅持某一信念不是不可以的。但此必是超越的信念，而屬於宗教形而上學的事，而不是屬

於經驗層次上依於人的理性與經驗而理解的事。此在本書的第一章及作者將要出版的《西方形

而上學中的超越論與存有論》的「超越論」方面將有所說明。

李　杜

序於香港大埔康樂園二十街三六號寓所

一九八九年八月七日

註　釋

❶ 現改名為《世界的假設——裴柏與西方的形而上學》。

❷ 在中國傳統的哲學中沒有世界的假設的說法。但我們如不談世界的假設的了解方式，而僅就其對世界可以
有不同的了解上說，此則甚近似中國哲學所說的世界觀。不同的世界的假設即不同的世界觀。中國哲學或
東方哲學有不同的世界觀是沒有問題的，如儒家的世界觀、道家的世界觀、佛學的世界觀等。裴柏所說的
五個相對地適切的世界的假設，依他的了解即為整個西方哲學在經驗層次上所表現的五種不同的世界觀。
故我們對裴柏的五個世界的假設的了解，可說為對整個西方哲學中由經驗層次上對世界作相對地適切的五
種不同的了解。

世界的假設：裴柏與西方的形而上學　目　次

第一章 導 論

裴柏（S. C. Pepper 1891-1972）是一位現代美國有名的哲學家。哈佛大學哲學博士。曾任加州巴克萊大學藝術系系主任和哲學系系主任。他年青時曾喜歡唯心論（Idealism），但不久即由唯心論轉而喜歡唯物論（Materialism）。在受到皮耳士（Charles S. Peirce）、詹姆士（William James）與杜威（John Dewey）等人的哲學影響之後，再由唯物論轉而喜歡實驗主義（Pragmatism），並由實驗主義而發展出脈絡論（Contextualism），並被稱爲脈絡論者（Contextualist）❶。但在晚年他修改脈絡論而另建立他的選擇論（Selectivism）的哲學系統。他的美學或藝術哲學亦很有名，發表了重要的專書❷。《概念與性質——一個世界的假設》（Concept and Quality: A World Hypothesis）是表達他的晚年的選擇論的哲學系統的書。此書是由保羅卡拉斯（Paul Carus）的演講稿修改而成，一九六七年出版❸。但此書雖是表達他的晚年的選擇論的哲學系統的書，選擇論的了解方式則早在一九四二年出版的《世界的假設》（World Hypotheses）一書中已確定❹。他的成名作亦是《世界的假設》。選擇論只是他由世界的假設的觀點上，依現代西方哲學與科學的知識，而對世界作一不同於西方傳統的哲學對世界的了解，而建立的新的世界的理論。因此介述裴柏的哲學應以《世界的假設》一書所表達的世界的假設的理論爲中心。由對世界的假設的理論的了解，而了解他由此理論而論述西方傳統的哲學由不同的世界的假設的觀點上以了解世界，而再進而

・1・

了解他由選擇論的觀點上以了解世界。本書即是如此做。

「世界的假設」是屬於整個哲學中的形而上學的部份。但它亦如其他的形而上學一樣可以概括其他的哲學問題。依西方哲學對形而上學的了解，形而上學可分別爲超越論（Tr-anscendentalism）與存有論（Ontology or Science of Beings）的不同❺。世界的假設是屬於存有論而不是超越論。

世界的假設是屬於存有論而不是超越論，是就它對世界作存有論的了解而不是超越論的了解上說的，而不是以它爲某一種存有論。因它不是某一種存有論。它與其他的存有論的不同，不在於它對存有有不同的了解，如杜威的實驗的自然主義（Pragmatic Naturalism）對存有的了解，不同於羅素（Bertrand Russell）的邏輯的原子論（Logical Atomism）對存有的了解一樣❻，而是它對存有的了解方式不同於其他的存有論。它是一種假設的了解方式，而不是定然的了解方式。由假設的方式以了解世界，是假設世界是一個怎樣的世界，然後給與此假設一結構性與系統性的證明，而不是定然地說世界一定是怎樣的。世界的假設既是一種假設地了解世界的方式，而不是定然地了解世界爲何，故可以有多種假設的了解而不限於一種。依裴柏的了解，在西方傳統的哲學中有四種相對地適切而有效的世界的假設對世界作假設的了解。此即形式論（Formism）、機械論（Mechanism）、脈絡論（Contextualism）與機體論（Organicism）❼，而他自己則依西方現代的哲學與科學的知識而提出了另一相對地適切而有效的選擇論的世界的理論對世界作不同的假設的了解❽。

裴柏要對世界作假設的了解，而不是定然的了解，無疑是受到近代的科學由假設的方式以了解其所研究的問題的影響。但在西方哲學中有不同的哲學對世界作不同的了解，而此不同的了

解皆可以並存於西方哲學的傳統中，亦有以每一哲學對世界的了解只為一種假設的了解，而不是定然的了解的涵義。裴柏即由此而說西方傳統的哲學對世界的不同了解是一種假設的了解，而不是一種定然的了解。並說明此假設的了解的模式是怎樣的 ❾，雖然在西方傳統的哲學上沒有人以其對世界的了解為一種假設的了解，而不是定然的了解。

對世界既可作假設的了解，世界的假設的理論與傳統哲學中的極端的懷疑論（utter sk-epticism）即不相容。因後者要懷疑一切而沒有可為我們了解的對象，而世界的假設則以世界的存在為先在的，且是不容置疑的。我們只可以相對地疑問此存在的世界是一個怎樣的世界，而不能極端地懷疑世界的存在 ❿。又對世界既只是作假設的了解，我們即不可以說世界一定是如何如何的。故世界的假設的理論與傳統的哲學中的獨斷論（dogmatism）亦不相容。因後者以世界一定是如何如何的，而前者則只以世界可能是怎樣怎樣的。假設的了解既與獨斷的了解不相容，故肯定其一即去除另一 ⓫。

近代的科學由假設而推理而經驗的證明所建立的經驗科學的知識的效用是明顯的。；對整個世界作假設的了解是否亦增加了對世界的了解的知識呢？由裴柏所介述不同的世界的假設對世界作不同的了解去回答此問題，答案亦應是肯定的。故由假設的方式以了解問題，是人類對問題的了解的進步的表現。

科學的假設要經過推理，而對推理所得要有經驗的證明才是真。它的方式是：假設──推理──檢證（hypothesis-deduction-verification）。世界的假設對世界的了解亦要有經驗上的證明。但它的證明的方式則不同於科學的證明的方式，它的假設的性質亦不同於科學的假設的性質 ⓬。

由假設以了解問題是近代人類了解問題的進步表現。但此表現並不否認人可以有不屬於由假設所了解的問題。我們在前面曾說，依西方哲學對形而上學的了解，形而上學可分別為超越論與存有論的不同，世界的假設則是屬於存有論。

世界的假設既是屬於存有論，它對存有論作假設的了解是進步的表現。但屬於超越論的問題則並不是如此。因對超越論的問題的了解不是一種假設的了解，而是一種超越的嚮往或超越的想像的肯定。人有此嚮往或此肯定是確實的。此如人在宗教信仰上對所信的對象的超越的嚮往或超越的想像的肯定。中國儒家對天帝的肯定；佛教對涅槃境界的肯定；基督教對上帝的肯定；其他的宗教對在人之上的神靈的肯定。在哲學上亦有由哲學理論的極限而對上帝的肯定。柏拉圖（Plato）理型的最高層級而對上帝的肯定；亞里士多德（Aristotle）由純現實或第一因而對上帝的肯定；康德（Kant）由人的實踐的理性的要求而對上帝的肯定；雅斯培（Jaspers）由人的存在的究竟歸向而對上帝的肯定；田立克（Tillich）由人的終極關懷而對上帝的肯定；懷海特（Whitehead）由宇宙進化歷程的終極目的而對上帝的肯定等。各人所肯定的上帝的涵義並不完全相同。

由對人的超越的嚮往或哲學理論的極限而可以有不同的超越的肯定或所肯定的涵義的彼此不同的觀點上說，所說的肯定似亦可以說是一種假設，雖從事此肯定者不以其所肯定的為一種假設。但假設要求有經驗的證明，超越的嚮往或超越的想像的肯定則不需要有經驗的證明，亦不能有經驗的證明，而是直以其為超越的真實。此真實是超經驗的的，亦為非經驗的知識的。裴柏大概即由於我們不能建立有關超越論的經驗的知識，而以其為不是屬於世界的限度表現。因世界的假設需要有經驗的證明，建立有關對世界的了解的經驗的知識。

裴柏以超越論所肯定的不是屬於世界的假設所要建立的經驗的知識是對的，但不能因此而以其爲不是屬於形而上學的事，只是其不是屬於爲世界的假設所了解的存有論的形而上學的事，而是屬於超越論的事。超越論與存有論不同。世界的假設如限於了解存有論，其即不是超越論，而亦不能由其所了解的以排斥超越論，此應是明顯的。但裴柏對形而上學的了解，並論述西方傳統哲學中爲世界的假設所了解的存有論之外另承認有超越論的形而上學，雖然在西方哲學中有存有論的傳統，亦有超越論的傳統。因此在本書正文中所說的形而上學，若沒有另加以說明，皆是爲世界的假設所了解的存有論的形而上學，而不是超越論的形而上學。

我們在本章介述裴柏的世界的假設所討論者只是形而上學中有關存有論的問題而已。

本書在正文討論裴柏的世界的假設時將由兩方面去介述：(1)是介述世界的假設所依以建立的基本的概念；此將分爲：世界的假設所依以建立的基本的概念(上)，世界的假設的基本概念(下)兩章；(2)是介述應用世界的假設的理論以了解世界，亦即是不同的世界的假設所了解的世界；此將分爲：形式論(上)，形式論(下)，機械論(上)，機械論(下)，脈絡論，機體論(上)，機體論(下)，選擇論(上)，選擇論(中)，選擇論(下)，共十章。在(2)中前八章所論述的是有關《世界的假設》一書所論述西方傳統的哲學由世界的假設的理論以了解世界的大要；後三章所論述的則爲《概念與性質：一個世界的假設》

於世界的假設所論述的存有論的超越論，而並不是在本書中對超越論有所論述。有關西方哲學中的超越論的問題，作者將在另外一本名爲《西方形而上學中的超越論與存有論》的書中去論述❸，在此只是提及以表明世界的假設所討論者只是形而上學中有關存有論的問題而已。

本書在正文討論裴柏的世界的假設時特別提及超越論。此主要是表明在西方哲學中有不同

在結構，亦即是世界的假設所依以建立的基本的概念；此將分爲：世界的假設所依以建立的基本概念(上)，

一書所展示的裴柏依西方現代的**哲**學與科學知識而來的對世界作假設的新了解，亦即對裴柏的選擇論的哲學的系統的論述。

註釋

❶ F. Thilly and L. Wood, *A History of Philosophy*. (New York: Holt, Rinehart and Winston, 1957, p. 654.)

❷ 裴柏有關美學的專書：

Pepper, S. C. *Aesthetic Quality: A Contextualistic Theory of Beauty*. (New York: Charles Scribner's Sons, 1937).

Pepper. *The Basis of Criticism in the Arts*. (Cambridge, Mass.: Harvard Univ. Press, 1945.)

Pepper. *Principles of Arts Appreciation*. (New York: Harcourt, Brace and World, Inc., 1949.)

Pepper. *The Work of Art*. (Bloomington: Indiana Univ. Press, 1955.)

❸ Pepper, S. C. *Concept and Quality: A World Hypothesis*. (La Salle, Illinois: Open Court Publishing Co., 1967.).

❹ Pepper. *World Hypotheses*. (Berkeley and Los Angels: Univ. of California Press, 1942.)

❺ 有關西方的形而上學可分為超越論與存有論及二者的不同，作者在將要出版的《西方形而上學中的超越論與存有論》一書中的第一章將有較詳細的說明。

❻ 有關杜威的實驗的自然主義與羅素的邏輯原子論在註❺所說的作者將要出版的書中將有分章的介述。

⑦ 有關形式論、機械論、脈絡論與機體論的涵義請參閱本書第四章至第十一章；並參閱裴柏的 *World Hypo-theses* 第九章至第十一章。

⑧ 有關選擇論的涵義請參閱本書第十二章至第十四章；並參閱裴柏的 *Concept and Quality:A World Hypothesis*。

⑨ 有關世界的假設的了解模式請參閱本書第三章；並參閱裴柏的 *"World Hypotheses"* 第二章和第三章。

⑩ 有關裴柏對懷疑論的駁斥請參閱本書第二章，「三」；並參閱裴柏的 *"World Hypotheses"* 第一章。

⑪ 有關裴柏對獨斷論的駁斥請參閱本書第二章，「三」；並參閱裴柏的 *"World Hypotheses"* 第一章。

⑫ 有關世界的假設不同於科學的假設和對世界的假設的證明不同於科學的假設的證明，請參閱本書第三章；並參閱裴柏的 *"World Hypotheses"* 第四章與第五章。

⑬ 此書的初稿已完全寫好，有關導論與超越論的部份並已修改好。只要將有關存有論的部份加以改定即可付印。

第二章　世界的假設的基本概念（上）

一、小　引

「世界的假設」包括了如下的基本概念：(1)形而上學與科學的不同；(2)對極端的懷疑論與獨斷論的駁斥；(3)兩種不同的確證——重複的確證與結構的確證；(4)兩種不同的假設——約定的假設與結構的假設；(5)根源的譬喻。此等基本的概念在「世界的假設」的理論中都表現了不同的功用。裴柏藉著它們為我們提出了一新的形而上學的了解方式，亦即假設的了解方式。在後面我們將對所說的基本概念作分節的介紹與討論。

二、形而上學與科學的不同

世界的假設是對世界作假設的了解，或如上章所提及的是對形而上學的存有論作假設的了解。因此它分辨形而上學與科學的不同即是分辨世界的假設與科學的不同，或分辨存有論的形而上學與科學的不同，而不是分辨超越論的形而上學與科學的不同。由超越論以分辨形而上學與科學的不同，如上章所已提及的，是以形而上學是屬於依於人的超越的嚮往，或依於一哲學

· 9 ·

理論的極限所在，而對宇宙的究竟的真實作超越的想像的肯定，而即以此肯定爲真實。此真實不需要有經驗上的證明，亦不能有經驗上的證明，而爲超經驗知識的，亦爲知識的限度表現。

至於科學則爲要對我們所在的世界從事經驗上的證明，而建立可以有經驗上的證明的系統的知識。世界的假設與科學的不同既不是由超越的形而上學的觀點上說，它即要由依於經驗而建立的知識中去分辨。裴柏對世界的假設與科學的不同的分辨，即是如此的一種分辨。此一分辨不始自裴柏，杜威已是如此地了解。杜威並不以形而上學的了解是一種對於依於經驗的知識而建立的形而上學是屬於經驗知識內的事。他與裴柏一樣都不以爲我們於依於經驗的知識而建立的形而上學之外，另有依於人的超越的嚮往或超越的想像的肯定而建立的形而上學。在有關如何了解世界的問題上，杜威以爲科學的方法與形而上學的方法是完全相同的。他不以爲於科學探究之外另有任何異於科學方法的有效的形而上學的方法❶。杜威既不以爲科學的方法之外另有任何其他的有效的形而上學的方法，而以科學的方法即形而上學的方法。因此他對所說的如何了解的分辨即只限於從事學的方法，而以科學的方法即形而上學的方法。即他以爲科學家的工作與形而上學者的工作的不同上。此研究上的特殊性與一般性的不同上，即他以爲科學家的工作與形而上學者的工作的不同上。此不同在於前者所關注的是特殊的科學的問題，而後者所關注的則是存在界的一般的性質的問題。此故相對於科學來說，形而上學爲對存在界一般的性質的描述的研究的學問❷。杜威此一分辨是可以肯定的。因爲所說的「特殊性」所意指的科學家所關注的特殊的科學的問題，與「一般性」所表示的形而上學者所關注的一般的存在事物的性質的問題實不相同。

裴柏對杜威的「特殊性」與「一般性」的分辨的涵義完全接受，但說法則不同。他認爲科學的研究限在某一領域中，形而上學的研究則沒有任何領域的限制。

後述的兩本書是討論屬於一定的領域以內的知識。如果有某些事實不能適當地放進為此領域而建立的定義與假設中去時，則可以被拒絕於此領域之內。但其他的書則是從一種不受限制的方式上去討論知識的問題。我們叫這些不受限制的知識成果為世界的假設的成果。世界的假設的特點即在其不能以任何事物為不相干的而加以拒絕❸。

引文中所說的「一定的領域以內的知識」即杜威所說的特殊的科學知識，「不受限制的知識成果」則與杜威以形而上學為對存在界一般的性質的描述的涵義相同。

但除了所說的相同之外，裴柏更就所說的研究領域的不同而提出如何了解世界的不同去分辨形而上學與科學的不同。此一如何了解世界的不同，即他依世界的假設以了解世界的不同。有關二者的涵義我們在後面的四、五兩節中再作介述和討論。在了解二者的涵義之前，我們將不容易了解所說的形而上學與科學的不同的確實意義。但我們在此可先略提其要點。

依裴柏的見解，一個世界的假設與一個特殊的科學的假設是不同的。此可以由兩方面去分辨：(1)一個世界的假設就是一個形而上學的假設，它是有關一個沒有限定的領域的問題，亦即是關連著「在我們經驗中任何需要解釋的東西❹。」至於一個特殊科學的假設則是被限制於某一領域之內，而只是解釋屬於此一領域內的事實。至於一個世界的假設只能是一個結構的假設，它解釋的範圍不受限制。(2)一個世界的假設只可以是一個約定的假設，由結構的確證去證明，它解釋的範圍亦只回應此一特定的問題。

並由結構的確證去證明，它解釋的範圍不受限制。至於一個科學的假設只由結構的確證去證明，它的範圍是有限的，它的假設是有關一特定的問題，設，由重複的確證或結構的確證去證明，亦可以是一個結構的假它的假設是有關一特定的問題，它的解釋亦只回應此一特定的問題。

由以上所提的要點我們約略地可見到：就形而上學與科學的假設與科學的假設的分辨的觀點上說，形而上學與科學的不同不只是研究領域的不同，而亦為研究方法的不同。這一不同對世界假設的理論來說是重要的，它應被視為一種在方法論上對科學與形而上學不同的分辨，是以形而上學具有經驗的意義，依經驗而建立，而又不只是依於科學的方法以從事對世界的了解的一種重要的成果。

三、對極端的懷疑論與獨斷論的駁斥

裴柏以為對極端的懷疑論與獨斷論的駁斥是肯定世界的假設必須的步驟，不只由理論的觀點上說是如此，從實際的觀點上說亦是一樣。因為世界的假設是由結構的確證依證據而確定，但極端的懷疑論則是一種拒絕任何真理的理論 ❺，而獨斷論則不守任何藉以建立理論的認知根據 ❻，要否認由經驗而獲得的所有證據。因此極端的懷疑論與獨斷論在理論上都與世界的假設的理論不相容。至於在實際上亦要對二者加以駁斥，則因為裴柏以為人類的知識在近世紀中雖已較前進步，但極端的懷疑論者與獨斷論者並不因此而失去了他們的地位，現代仍有不少人信賴他們的言論。因此對二者的駁斥是建立世界的假設的理論不可少的事。

1 對極端的懷疑論的駁斥

有關對極端的懷疑論的駁斥，裴柏從兩方面去進行：⑴實際信仰的根據的駁斥，⑵最終信仰的根據的駁斥。我們先說⑴。

從定義上說，一個極端的懷疑論者是「一個懷疑一切事務的人」❼。但裴柏以爲如果一個人眞正了解所說的定義的意義，則將會見到沒有人對事物可以持有此一懷疑的態度。因爲所說的定義所肯定的與說「一個人不相信一切事實」，或說「不相信一切事實的陳述」不同。因爲後者不是懷疑，而是直接地不相信，至於前者則是懷疑。因爲前者的眞正涵義是說，在我們面前出現的任何事物都是可信的而同時又是不可信的。可信與不可信的證據是相等的。因此我們不能毫無猶豫地相信任何一方面。因此，「一個人懷疑一切事物」是等於說他永不相信任何東西亦不不相信任何東西。此是一種沒有人可以一貫地持守的態度。因爲沒有人生存於此世界上而可以懷疑一切的事物。這是與我們的實際生活不相容的。

(2)的駁斥理據與(1)的理據相同，只是所討論的主題不是實際信仰的根據而是信仰的最終根據。

我們或會想雖然所說的懷疑態度在實際的生活上不可以一貫地持守，但從我們信仰的最後的根據上說時，它可能是眞的。但裴柏以爲即使從信仰的事物的最後根據上說，它仍然是有問題的。因爲依照裴柏的見解，除了依之而建立我們的信仰的事物的證據之外，還有什麼可以說是信仰的最後根據呢？如果是如此的話，則任何人要持守所說懷疑的態度，一定要假定作爲我們的信仰的任何事物的不相信任何事物的證據，與作爲我們的不相信任何事物的證據的陳述的證據，同時作爲該陳述的證據以至於無窮的追求的證據亦是一樣要完全相等的，並且如果有任何陳述的任何證據與它的相反的陳述的證據是不完全相等的，則所說的懷疑態度即不能維持。

依照裴柏的了解，有兩種方式可以肯定無窮的平衡的證據的假定。第一種方式是獨斷地去

肯定此假定，而不講求任何的證明。第二種方式就是以此爲一待證明的假設的問題。但不論我們採用任何一種方式，所說的懷疑都不能維持。因爲如果我們採取第一種方式則懷疑論變爲獨斷論。因爲「不講求任何的證明」是一種獨斷的態度，而不是一種懷疑的態度。如採用第二種方式則懷疑論不是徹底的而只是部份的。裴柏以爲持部份的懷疑論的立場與他所持的世界的假設的理論的立場並不相違，故可以接受。至於獨斷論則與世界的假設的理論不相容，而不可接受。

2 對獨斷論的駁斥

依照裴柏的了解，有兩種不同的獨斷論：(1)訴諸於沒有錯誤的權威，(2)訴諸於確定的事實。

(2)又可再分爲兩型：(a)爲訴諸於自明的原則，(b)爲訴諸於對當下不可懷疑的事實的描述。

(1) 對於權威的駁斥

裴柏用以駁斥權威的方法是指出權威不只有一個，而是可以有多個。當此等權威彼此發生衝突時，他們的衝突除了訴諸於證據之外，不能得到解決。權威既要訴諸於證據，它的絕對的地位即不能保持。裴柏指出各種不同的權威都有支持它們的各種不同的教條。支持的教條既不相同，在此等教條中難免有互相衝突而不一致的情事。當衝突發生時，除了訴諸於證據以消除它們的衝突之外，沒有其他可用的方法。因爲我們不能由任何教條而來的標準以消除由教條而來的衝突。因此，當各種權威發生衝突時，它們的不可動搖的權威性即要失落，而表現出知識的最後根據不是權威而是證據。

裴柏曾引用舊約〈創世紀〉有關上帝（God）創造亞當（Adam）和夏娃（Eve）的不一致的記述，以說明基督教的聖經如何失落了它的權威性。

依照〈創世紀〉第一章，亞當與夏娃都是上帝直接地用地上的泥土，依照他自己的形像創造的。但依照〈創世紀〉第二章，上帝是先用地上的泥土創造了亞當，然後用亞當的一條肋骨創造了夏娃。聖經此一前後不一致的記述，解經者常將前者相應於後者作解釋，以去除二者的衝突。但此種相應的解釋所依據的原則，並不是由聖經自身的記述而來，而是外加的。因此去除聖經自身的相衝突是要依賴聖經以外的某種融通的原則的。此即失落了它的權威性❾。

(2)　對於確定的事實的駁斥

(a)　對於自明的原則的駁斥

訴諸於自明的原則是第二種獨斷論的第一型。依照裴柏的了解，此一型的獨斷論在現代的思想中已逐漸失去了它的地位。因為它已不再為現代的某些科學家或哲學家所接受。有很多在過去以為是自明的原則，在現代已不能再被視為眞正的自明了。

歐幾里德的幾何學公理是歷來作為視數學原則為確定性的主要根據。旣然現代的數學家已一致地放棄此一看法，承認一個數學系統中的基本命題不是自明的眞理，而只是為演繹而有的假定，這些設定對事實或在事實上可以眞亦可以不眞，為數學原則的確定性而有的要求卽已大半被揚棄❿。

這是有關數學公理的獨斷論的失落。至於思想律，依照裝柏的見解，它們的命運亦是一樣的。思想律中的矛盾律是歷來用來支持自明原則的一條最重要的律則，因此裝柏即選取它作為討論的例子。

我回答，「至於可了解性，矛盾律的矛盾最低限度在它可被符示為『A是非A』的意義上說似是可以被了解的。至於此律則涵着一自相矛盾，再有什麼要說的呢？有可以相信它是錯的的經驗根據。但矛盾律的矛盾應涵自相矛盾的本身是一自相矛盾的說明並不表示是不平常的，亦不表示它本身有任何根據可作為視其為錯的或它的矛盾是真的。此論證似是由假定矛盾律的真而使其成為一循環的論證。再者，當我們從事去論證自明的要求時，自明即已不是自明。如果自明一定要由別處去找證據，它即不再是自明。當一個律則的真的確定只能建立於其他律則的假（它的矛盾）的確定的基礎上時，它即由它的自明的要求而退處於它的矛盾上了⓫。」

這是一個複雜而不容易了解的論證。裝柏好似並不認為矛盾律的反面的不可能是一自明的真理。因此他說「矛盾律的矛盾應涵自相矛盾的本身是一自相矛盾的說明並不表示它是不平常的，亦不表示它本身有任何根據可作為視其為錯的或它的矛盾是真的。」他並堅持說如果矛盾律需要論證，則它即不是自明的。

裝柏的論證是否可以接受，我們以為主要在於如何了解「自明」真理的涵義的問題上。裝柏在反對矛盾律為自明的真理的論證中所給與「自明」一詞的涵義，似與傳統上所說的自明真

理的意義不完全相同。因為傳統上所了解的自明真理即是直接地由我們的理性所把握而不需要

依據任何其他的證據的概念。

這一把握是我們理性的功用的表現。我們可以由反省中見到此一表現。因為由反省中我們

自覺到有兩種屬於理性的活動，那就是肯定與否定。矛盾律不是別的而正是我們理性的功用的

任何一種活動的表示。因此它的形式可以是肯定A即肯定A，或是否定A即否定A。但它不能

是同時地既肯定A而又否定A。因此是彼此矛盾的。此一矛盾是由理性的功用上見，而不須藉

著任何其他東西去證明。因此而稱為自明。

從理性的功用上說，我們不僅以矛盾律是自明的，而亦以排中律與同一律是自明的。因為

既然理性的功用是肯定與否定而不是其他，而這兩種功用是相互排斥的，那末理性的本質不是

別的而即是兩種對偶性的活動。這兩種對偶性的活動可以叫做對偶性的原則（The principle

of duality）。此原則可以符示成一公式。當它公式化之後，它即成為排中律。它的形式是

A＋－A＝1。它的確定性亦不是基於別的而只是基於理性的功用而不需關涉到任何其他的東西。那就

同一律亦是一樣。它的確定性亦只是基於理性的功用而不需關涉到任何其他的東西。那就

是說如果我們肯定A，那末A即被肯定，後一A與前一A是同一的。

由上面的解釋，我們以為思想三律的真理應被認為是自明的。所謂自明的即是可以直接地

由人的理性所把握，而不需要藉著其他任何的東西去證明。

基於上面的了解，我們以為裴柏對思想律為自明的真理的駁斥不是完全沒有問題的❷，如

果他對思想律是自明的駁斥有問題，則他以世界假設的理論是一種研究證據的理論，要排斥一

切獨斷說，以凡事待證據而確定的主張會否因此而受到損害呢？我們以為答案是否定的。因為

所說思想律的真理只是對我們的理性的功用的一種描述，由反省中去把握。這真理不能應用於任何其他的事情上，沒有任何其他的事情可以作同樣的要求。因此對此類真理的肯定為自明的，正如對理性功用的存在的肯定是一樣，而沒有超出理性自身活動的範圍以外。因此這對裴柏以世界的假設的理論為一種對證據的研究的主張並無損害。我們亦不能於此理性的自身的活動外，而獨斷地肯定其他什麼理論。

(b) 對當下的事實的描述為不可懷疑的駁斥

「直覺的內容，直接的感受，感覺料，共同感覺的東西，頑強的科學事實，或任何假定為給與的東西⓭」，都被傳統的經驗主義者（*Empiricists*）認為是不可以懷疑的事實。因為他們以為這些東西都是當下的事實，故是不可以懷疑的。但裴柏以為肯定當下的事實是不可以懷疑的正如肯定自明的原則是不可以懷疑的一樣都是獨斷的表示。理由是：

第一，對不可以懷疑的事實的描述彼此衝突。第二，對不可以懷疑的事實的描述與對為確定的證據所支持的事實的假設的描述相衝突。第三，當前面任何一種描述產生了困難因此而對不可懷疑的事實的描述發生了懷疑時，除了依確定的證據去考慮之外，沒有其他可循的途徑⓮。

裴柏曾引用普賴斯（H. H. Price）與杜威對蕃茄的描述為例去駁斥任何堅持有不可懷疑的事實的主張。因為該兩位哲學家對被同視為蕃茄的事實，描述成兩類不同的不可懷疑的事實。普賴斯描述蕃茄是「在某時某地紅而圓，而為我們不可以懷疑的東西⓯。」但杜威則不如此說，

• **18** •

而是以我們所遇到的「全體而帶有強迫性的東西⑯」為蕃茄的不可以懷疑的事實。因為依杜威，我們所遇到的事物的全體性與強迫性是處於一切分析之後者（從事任何的分析必得接受）。它們不是屬於知識中的事，而是「一種存在⑰」，故是不可以懷疑的。普賴斯對一事物如蕃茄所認為不可以懷疑的事實，與杜威所認為的既然不同，我們即不可以說所說的事實是不可以懷疑的。於他們二人之外亦沒有任何人可以說他的描述是確定而不可以懷疑的。因為任何人的描述只是於普賴斯或杜威的描述之外多加上一種，而不可以說他的描述即是不可以懷疑的事實的描述⑱。

以自明的原則與當下知覺的事實為確定不可以懷疑的，可謂由來已久，自古已然。在希臘古代的哲學中有人曾高舉人的理性，以由人的理性直接地所把握的為確定不可以懷疑的。亦有人重視感覺以為由感官所直接知覺的是確定不可以懷疑的。中古時期，哲學附屬在神學之下，此時期的哲學家多數是神學家。他們以由上帝而來的啟示的知識高於由人的理性而獲得的有關自然事物的知識。他們又以為人可以由理性思辨上證明上帝的存在，上帝是理的表現，以由理性所建立的知識是永恆不變的，確定不可移的；由經驗所獲得的知識則是變動不居的，偶然不可靠的。在近世紀中，理性主義者（Rationalists）信守重視理性的傳統，以由理性所直接把握的為確定不可疑。經驗主義者則上承唯名論（Nominalism）與經驗論（Empiricism）的觀點，以由感官知覺所直接知覺的為確定不可疑。故裴柏說「十七與十八世紀歐洲大陸的理性主義者過份依靠自明的原則；而英國的經驗主義者則依靠由感官給與的事實的不可懷疑性的⑲。」這是傳統哲學發展的一面。

另外的一面，亦如裴柏所指出的，「作為人的信仰的重要的依據，有一種規律性的轉移……

由權威而轉移至（理性的或經驗的）確定性，由（理性的或經驗的）確定性而轉移至假設或概然性。在中古時期，人的信仰的重要依據是權威；在文藝復興時期而至於現代，人所信賴的是理性的或經驗的確定性。只有在現代的少數人中才有以假設或概然性為我們可信賴的根據[20]。」

從現代的觀點上說，由後來的發展所表示的更重要。此是由現代的科學的成就而得的新了解。

現代的哲學家大多數都受科學的影響。他們以科學方法作為我們獲得知識最可靠的依據。維根斯坦（ L. Wittgenstein ）曾說所有的命題均需與自然科學相符。此是訴諸於科學方法以肯定知識的一個例子[21]。邏輯實證論者（ Logical Positivists ）要將命題分為形式的或事實的兩類命題亦是要由科學去確定知識的表示。杜威以探究論或經驗的方法為重建哲學的唯一方法則為以科學方法為建立哲學的依據。

皮耳士在他的∧信仰的決定∨[22]和∧科學的態度與有錯說∨[23]兩文中對上述的發展已有扼要的表示。他不以為我們的信心可以是一種固執不放的態度，亦不能訴諸於權威，或依於先驗的概念來決定。唯一可以作為我們信心的依據是科學的方法。因為沒有任何東西可以成為我們死守不放的真理，亦沒有任何教義或信條可以成為真理的權威。我們亦不可以信賴我們自然的喜好或先驗的概念，以它們為最可靠的。它們都不是常存不變的，而是常在變化之中。我們昨天所固執的固可以與今日所固執的不同，我們所信為權威的東西亦可以前後彼此相異。自然的喜好或先驗的概念亦可以因人而不同。因此我們不能以它們為最可靠的依據。

至於由科學方法所得的結論，皮耳士亦以為只是一種意見，不是絕對的真理。它只是去除我們的懷疑的一種意見。它可以被用作工具去擴大我們的探求。由此探求所得的結論可以與前一結論相反。此相反的結論照樣亦可以被用為工具去從事另一更進一步的探求。因此皮耳士不以

為我們在科學的研究上可以獲得絕對的真理。科學的知識是一種概然的知識，是可以有錯的。因此，為我們信心所依據的不是某一種絕對的真理，而只是科學在它的不斷的發展歷程中所發現的事實。

在沒有絕對真理的觀點上，裴柏與皮耳士的見解相同。但裴柏的世界的假設的理論所要說明的則不是科學知識的概然性的問題，亦不是某一類的科學的問題，而是整個世界。依照裴柏的見解，在有關了解整個世界的問題上，我們不能僅訴諸於特殊的科學。因特殊科學的研究是限於某一特定的領域中，世界的假設則是對整個世界作假然的了解。此了解以整個人類的經驗為依據，以整個世界為了解的對象。因此世界的假設是一種形而上學，而不是某一門特定的科學。但它對極端的懷疑論與獨斷論的不相容則與所有的特殊的科學與它們的不相容一樣。

第三章　世界的假設的基本概念（下）

四、兩種不同的確證——重複的確證與結構的確證

確證的涵義可以關連到多方面去了解，在後面我們將分為五項去介紹和討論。

1

世界的假設的理論是一種證據的研究

在西方的哲學史中具有悠久的歷史的極端的懷疑論與獨斷論一直與哲學思想緊密地連結在一起。但在近世，當人類的知識得到了進一步的發展之後，這一連結開始逐步分離。裴柏對它們的駁斥即是此一分離的表示。

當極端的懷疑論與獨斷論在哲學中被排除出去之後，我們即可以有研究的對象，而為我們所接受為真的即不再是訴諸於權威，或是訴諸於理性上的或感覺事物的確定性，而是依於證據而建立。真理是依於證據而建立是世界的假設理論的核心觀念。裴柏所說的世界的假設的理論而建立。真理是依於證據而建立是世界的假設理論的核心觀念。裴柏所說的世界的假設的理論是一種「屬於證據、事實、知識，和哲學的分辨的研究❷❹」，即主要表示此一意義。

2 證據的意義

世界的假設的理論既肯定爲一種證據的研究，對證據的意義即當有清楚的了解。裴柏分證據爲兩類：(1)未經批判的證據，(2)批判的證據。前者指要被批判的常識的事實，故稱爲應受懷疑的結果㉕。後者則指由批判而獲得的事實，它不由常識的了解的基礎上被接受，而爲一種確證的結果。依裴柏，我們可以有兩種不同的確證，一爲重複的確證，一爲結構的確證。相應於此兩種確證而有資料（data）與成素（danda）兩種不同的批判的證據，即資料爲重複的確證的證據，成素則爲結構的確證的證據。相應於不同的兩類命題，資料又可類分爲邏輯的資料與經驗的資料，即邏輯的資料被用於形式的命題所表現的資料，經驗的資料則被用於事實的命題上，或說是由事實的命題所表現的資料㉖。

以常識爲未受批判的證據的理由是因爲常識是由「我們日常閱讀報紙時所想及的事物」，或者在日常的生活中「我們見到聽到與感覺到的事物㉗」，這些事物都是沒有確定的認知的意義的。

對所說的材料企圖作任何確定而詳細的提示、描述、或說明，一般地都要使我們失去這些材料。原來是未經批判的事實立即轉變爲批判的事實。而且一般地這些材料的改變，正是由此企圖而來的結果㉘。

因此它們在認知上被認爲是不可信賴與不負責的。

24

常識既有所說的缺點，我們或要否認它是一種證據。但當它與獨斷論和批判的證據比較時，

它表示了於獨斷論和批判的證據中見不到的特殊的性質，裴柏因此而稱之爲未受批判的證據。

我們在前面曾說，獨斷論所肯定的是獨斷的說法，而不是訴諸於證據。

設的理論不相容。但常識與獨斷論不同。它是在一般人的了解上被認爲眞。因此，合乎常識即

可以被了解的和有共同了解的證據。但由於它只是一般的而未經深入去辨別的了解，此了解即

是未經批判的和不確定的。說它是證據只是從它曾爲一般人所同意或所依據的觀點上說。既爲

一般人所同意或所依據，故即不是獨斷的，而可以被視爲一種證據。

批判的證據是由確證上說，與確證不可分。因此它是批判地被建立，而與科學和哲學相關

連。但與常識相比較則顯示了它的不穩定性。因爲由A所認爲是批判的證據，可以爲B所否

認。正如前節所說，爲杜威所認爲是批判的證據的蕃茄可以爲普賴斯所否認。但對常識來說，

被視爲蕃茄的東西，在正常的情形之下，永遠不會爲A所承認而爲B所否認的。它爲一個人接

受之後，即可以同時爲其他人所接受。因此常識中的蕃茄爲杜威與普賴斯所同時接受。此即是

裴柏所說批判的證據有「認知的責任而沒有充份的安全」，至於常識則有「認知的安全而無責

任㉙」的意義。

3　確證的意義

我們在前面曾說，批判的證據由確證而獲得。若由此而說確證的意義，則可以說它是使人

獲得批判的證據的一種方式。此一說法沒有錯，但對確證的意義表示得不夠清楚。較清楚的表

達應說確證是一種使知識得以證明的方法。證據的意義一方面包涵著它是如何獲得的，另一方

面則包涵著它所證明的是什麼。因此我們在上面所討論的證據的問題與確證的問題有關，亦與後面所要討論的其他有關知識的建立的問題有關。但在我們討論其他的相關的問題之前，在此先看一下裝柏對確證的意義的描述。

有兩種不同的確證因此而有兩種不同的批判的證據。有人與人的確證，亦有事實與事實的確證。我們稱前者為「重複的確證」，後者為「結構的確證」。

假定我要知道某一椅子是否堅固可靠。我可以自己坐上去試下，我也可以幾次用不同的姿勢坐上去，並用力坐下。然後再請幾個朋友坐上去試一下。如果我們都認為這椅子穩固可坐，則我們會覺得有理由相信這是一張堅固的椅子。

或者我可以用第二種方法。我可以檢查該椅子的結構情形，查看它是用某一類木做成的，各部份的厚度如何，結構的方式如何，用那一類釘與那一種膠汁。並注意它是由一間信譽甚好的傢俬的公司所製造的，並且是要拍賣的家庭用品，而表現出磨損的痕跡，好似很多人曾坐用過而不見有問題等。將所有這些證據集合在一起之後，我會更覺得有理由相信這是一張堅固的椅子。⑳

裝柏以為對確證作如此的分別，「在常識中亦可以找得到」㉑。但我們以為明顯地肯定有此兩種不同的確證，並對二者作不同的分辨說明，實自裝柏始。他並由此進而分辨科學方法與哲學方法的不同，以此為建立他的世界假設的一個基本的概念。依裝柏，這兩種確證的不同可以從

兩方面去了解：(1)方式上的分辨，那就是重複的確證方式或結構的確證方式的分辨。這是裴柏在上引後面的兩段文中所主要表明的。此即他所說的要了解一椅子是否堅固，我們可以由所述的任何一方式去確證。(2)將每一種確證關連到不同類的假設去了解。由此一了解，我們見到重複的確證是一種關連到約定的假設去從事證明的確證，結構的確證則是一種關連到結構的假設去從事證明的確證。但此一意義在前面的引文中隱而不顯。在討論假設時，則預設有此一分別。此一預設是重要的。因為它是有關科學與形而上學的不同的分別。這一意義在將裴柏的方法論和杜威的探究論或邏輯實證論（Logical Positivism）的真理觀作比較的了解時會更清楚地見到。

4　裴柏的確證說與杜威的探究論

裴柏的確證說與杜威的探究論本質上相同。但確證說對形而上學的了解有進於探究論的地方。探究論對了解知識的問題的貢獻在於：(1)指出一個探究如何開始，(2)如何建立，(3)如何類分為不同的實施步驟，(4)如何獲得探究的成果，(5)由探究所能獲得的是什麼。杜威對探究曾作了如下的界定：「將一種不確定的情景在指導或控制之下，轉變為一種確定地統一的情景㉜。」

探究的歷程可分別為五步：(1)不確定的情景，(2)問題的建立，(3)對問題解答的決定，(4)推理，(5)證明或有保證的斷定。

從所要肯定的知識的觀點上說，裴柏的確證說所要肯定的與杜威的探究論所要肯定的相同。裴柏所認為由確證所獲得的只是概然性的結果亦與杜威所說由探究論所證明的只是一種有保證的斷定，而不是最後或絕對的真理的見解相同。

但除了以上的相同之外，二者亦有如下的不同：裴柏的確證說要由不同的假設去表示不同的確證，由對結構的確證與重複的確證的分辨以分別形而上學與科學的不同。杜威的探究論則對此沒有分辨。

杜威的探究論沒有對確證與假設作分別的研究，因而未能如裴柏一樣由方法論上以分別形而上學與科學的不同是明顯的事實。但對此一明顯的事實我們仍當有如下的釐清：(1)探究論雖沒有明顯的標示出所說的分別，但可涵有此一意義。因為依照探究論的第三步，我們可以採用任何適合於探究之用的假設。依照第五步，則只要有助於探究的工作，我們都可以採用，故任何實證的方式皆可為探究論所採用。因此，所說的兩種不同的確證，與此兩種確證相應而有的兩種不同的假設的關係，都可以為杜威的探究論所涵。(2)說探究論可以涵有裴柏的確證的意義是可以的，但我們不要因此而忽略了杜威從來都未曾注意及重複的確證與結構的確證的不同，並由此而建立不同的假設。又對杜威來說，形而上學的方法即是科學的方法。他並不於科學的方法之外，另肯定一種形而上學的問題與形而上學的問題從方法論的觀點上，對杜威來說，沒有什麼不同。二者同為探究論所研究的問題。它們只有或為屬於特殊的問題或為屬於一般性的問題的分別。因此，探究論的第三步雖然容許我們採用任何種類的假設，但杜威卻不需要肯定兩種不同的假設。同樣的，探究論的第五步雖然容許我們採用任何的實證的方式，杜威亦不需要肯定兩種不同的確證。但對裴柏來說，科學與形而上學的不同與由此而來的確證的差別。我們不能有約定的世界的假設，依裴柏，世界假設的理論只是一種結構的假設，只為結構的確證所確定。因此，從方法論的觀點上說，裴柏分別兩種不同的分別。此分別即主要地基於所說的兩種假設的不同上的分別，杜威亦不能由重複的確證去對世界的假設作證明。

的確證爲的是要肯定兩種不同的假設，肯定兩種不同的假設爲的是要對科學與形而上學的不作分辨。因此，對裴柏來說，重複的確證與結構的確證的分別是對約定的假設與結構的假設的分辨所必需的，而結構的假設的肯定是對世界的假設的理論的肯定所必需的。因結構的假設是世界的假設藉以建立的唯一的假設。有關假設的問題我們在下節將再談及。在此我們要再一次提出的是，將確證分別爲兩種是裴柏的世界的假設的理論的基本概念。由此一概念而建立不同的哲學方法去確立了解世界的不同的形而上學的方式。因此，確證說與探究論對知識的肯定上說雖本質地相同，前者亦可以爲後者所涵，但前者由對確證與假設的分辨因之而建立了解世界的不同的形而上學的方式則是後者所未曾注意及的。

5　邏輯實證論者對形而上學的挑戰和裴柏對此挑戰的回應㉝

邏輯實證論者將知識分別爲兩類：(1)由形式命題所表達的形式的知識，(2)由經驗命題所表達的經驗的知識。前者是必然的知識，因爲由命題的謂詞或後件所肯定的已被包涵於命題的主詞或前件中，而只是對已有的作再一次的肯定。故形式命題是一種重言的命題，它沒有提供我們新的報告，它的值是必然眞。邏輯的眞理和數學的眞理即是屬於此一類的知識。後者是經驗的知識，因爲由命題的謂詞或後件所肯定的沒有被包涵於主詞或前件中，它的肯定不能由主詞或前件分析出來，而是要由新的經驗所證明。故經驗命題是事實的命題，它給與我們新的報告，它的值是概然的，因爲它可以有錯。經驗科學的眞理，如化學，物理學，生物學等即屬於此一類的知識。

裴柏沒有拒絕邏輯實證論者對知識的分類說。他了解到對知識的分類有釐清知識的性質的

作用。上述邏輯實證論者所採用對知識的分類法，事實上並不是由他們所發明，而是有所繼承。

因萊布尼茲（G. W. Leibniz）即曾將知識分別爲必然的眞理與偶然的眞理[34]。所謂必然的眞理即是由理性自身所肯定而不是由經驗所證明的。此即是一種形式的肯定。所謂偶然的眞理則是有關經驗事實的知識。在萊氏稍後的英國經驗主義者休謨（David Hume）亦將知識分別爲觀念與觀念的關係的知識和事實的知識。休謨的哲學被後世了解爲純現象的經驗主義，與萊氏的理性主義不同。但就對知識類別的觀點上說，他對知識的了解實與萊氏的了解同路。在萊休二氏之後的康德（I. Kant）則將命題分別爲分析的、先驗的、後驗的、綜合的，與先驗綜合的。此一分別未完全爲邏輯實證論者所接受。因爲他們否認有先驗綜合的命題。但我們若暫時不討論先驗綜合的命題，而只言其餘的，則康德對命題的了解亦有與邏輯實證論者相同之處。邏輯實證論者在對知識的了解上曾公開承認有所繼承於萊布尼茲與休謨[35]。他們對康德的超越說有所非議，但對康德有關知識問題的分析則有所肯定。

邏輯實證論者對知識的了解既爲積集了西方近代哲學發展而來的成果，裴柏對此成果自然不會反對。他所要反對的不是邏輯實證論者全部知識論，而只是他們以上述對知識的分類爲包括了所有的知識，而要根據此一分類，獨斷地排斥形而上學於認知的範圍之內。他不以爲邏輯實證論者以形而上學既不是形式的亦不是事實的，故即是沒有意義的說法可以成立。

我們在前面曾說，康德亦以爲我們不可以建立一科學的形而上學。但在《實踐理性的批判》中他則從道德的觀點的人，亦中即從知識的觀點上去批判傳統的形而上學。凡接受康德的知識的限度的觀點的人，亦要求上，重新肯定了屬於超越論的道德的形而上學。以形而上學爲超經驗知識的。

他們亦不是要反對所有的形而上學，而是要尋求其他方法去建立

由經驗知識所不能建立的超越論的形而上學。

邏輯實證論者排除形而上學於知識範圍之內所用的方法與康德對傳統的形而上學的批判的方法不同。但在斷定我們不能建立一科學的形而上學，我們亦只能說我們不能建立科學的形而上學，形而上學應被排拒於科學範圍之內，科學不可以超出自己的領域以內的事，則科學不能排斥。因此，康德在他的《實踐理性的批判》中所建立的超越論的道德的形而上學不能為科學所排斥。從此一觀點上說，邏輯實證論者對形而上學的排斥亦不能超出康德的觀點之外。他們有時很能了解此一意義，但有時他們要超出此一界限去排斥所有的形而上學。但如前面第一章所已提及的裴柏所要肯定的不是超越論意義的形而上學，而是在經驗知識的範圍之內肯定形而上學。因此，裴柏的肯定超出了康德所要肯定的之外。裴柏此一超出可否面對邏輯實證論者的挑戰呢？形而上學，肯定有認知意義的形而上學呢？此是裴柏的世界的假設所面對的重要問題。

又如我們在前面討論科學與形而上學的不同時所指出的，杜威亦不認為科學與形而上學的不同是在於前者是具有認知的意義，而後者則是超認知的。他亦以為二者都是屬於認知之外肯定超越以內的形而上學。但杜威對科學與形而上學的不同只由特殊性與一般性上作區別，亦即只由科學論的形而上學。他亦要在認知的領域內建立不同於科學的形而上學，而不是要於認知之外肯定超越家所關注的是特殊的科學問題，此與形而上學家所關注的是特殊性與界的存在界的一般性質的不同上去作區別。杜威並認為科學與形而上學沒有方法論上的不同。科學家與形而上學家用同樣的方法去了解世界，只是科學所要了解的是特殊性的科學的問題，形而上學家所要了解的則是整個存在界的性

質的問題。

從杜威所說的觀點上說，他對知識的了解與邏輯實證論者的知識說並不相左。因此邏輯實證論者由對知識的分類以排斥形而上學於知識領域之內的主張亦不能應用於杜威對形而上學的了解上。他們只可以給予杜威的了解如下的疑難，即依杜威的說法形而上學的問題既與科學的問題沒有方法論的分別，而所研究的對象亦只有整個性與特殊性的不同，則爲杜威所認爲是屬於形而上學的知識即可以類分爲或爲屬於形式命題的知識，或爲屬於事實命題的知識。形而上學的知識的性質與知識的性質既沒有分別，則形而上學與科學雖有如杜威所說研究工作上的不同，並且可進一步說我們可以以科學研究所得的知識去對某類事物作特定的解釋，或對整個世界作一般性的解釋，以區別科學與形而上學對世界了解的不同。但若問此兩類了解是否得當時則對此一問題的評定仍是需要依於科學的結論，或需要訴諸於進一步的科學研究以決定，而不可以有外於科學而來的知識而可以對世界有新的了解。因此，此一對形而上學與科學不同的分別，從知識的觀點上說，即沒有性質上的差異。因此，在對知識的區別上亦不能有科學與形而上學的不同的劃分㊱。

形而上學與科學的知識在知識的本質上沒有差異是邏輯實證論者用以駁斥杜威對形而上學與科學的分辨的主要論據。相對於杜威的分辨，或從杜威的探究論的觀點上說，此一論據不能否認，或說杜威並不反對所說邏輯實證論者的論據。因爲對杜威來說爲科學與形而上學所探究的對象既相同，並且凡爲探究論最後一步所證明的即被認爲有保證的斷定，而沒有科學的問題與形而上學的問題的分別，則從知識的觀點上說，杜威可同意邏輯實證論者的說法。但雖有所說的同意，杜威對形而上學與科學的區分仍是重要的。因我們從事學術的活動，對世界的了解，

確有此兩方面的不同：科學家與形而上學家的工作彼此不同，我們如何運用已有的知識去了解世界亦不同。一般地說，專精於某一特殊領域之內的科學家不會對整個世界是如何的作判斷，若有此類的判斷則他超出了他的專業範圍之內，他所作的不再是專門科學家的工作，而是科學的哲學家的工作。對世界事物，我們不可以只有科學的說明，而亦要有對整個世界的說明。我們要了解整個世界是如何的，此是我們的理性活動不可少的事。

上面所述對科學與形而上學的分辨，不只為杜威所主，亦為現代的一些哲學家如摩爾（G. E.Moore），伍德橋（F.J.E.Woodbridge）等人所主㊲。但如前面第二節所指出的，更要從方法論的觀點上裴柏對科學與形而上學不同的了解，除由研究領域的不同去分辨之外，去給與此一分辨一理論上的支持。因此裴柏不能如上面所說的杜威一樣同意邏輯實證論者只有兩類不同的命題以建立兩類不同的知識，以此外別無其他的方法以確定具有認知的意義的形而上學的主張。裴柏此一意見是否有效主要的關鍵在於邏輯實證論者所說的知識是否概括了一切具有認知的意義的知識。如果邏輯實證論者所肯定的知識命題概括了一切具有認知的意義的形而上學的知識，則裴柏似不能再有有其他的方法可以肯定一具有認知的意義的形而上學。即認知的意義的知識，如只可以為邏輯實證論者所說的兩類命題所表達，知識只有所說的兩類知識，則裴柏即不能有此外的說法。因此，現在問題的要點是，到底邏輯實證論者所說的知識是否真正地與所有認知的意義相等。故裴柏要有進於上述杜威的見解而提出一新的方法，要在認知的意義上去分辨科學與形而上學的不同，則即要查考下面所說的兩個問題：(1)邏輯實證論者的知識說是否真正地學與形而上學的不同，與所有認知的意義相等；(2)如果不是，我們是否可以於認知的領域中提出另一方法以分辨形而上學與科學的不同。對第一個問題裴柏的回答是否定的，至於第二個問題的回答則是肯定的。

裴柏否認邏輯實證論者的知識說與所有認知的意義相等，主要是依於他對證據的類別。因由證據的類別中他表示了某類的認知的意義是不能為邏輯實證論者的知識說所包括的。我們在前面曾指出，裴柏分證據為非批判的與批判的兩種。常識是屬於非批判的證據，批判的證據則為由確證而來的結果。確證又分別為重複的與結構的兩種。由重複的確證所表現的為資料，由結構的確證所表現的為成素。資料再分別為經驗的與邏輯的兩類。

依裴柏，邏輯實證論者所稱為形式的命題與事實的命題的知識並不包括具有認知意義的知識的全部。它們只表示了由重複的確證所獲得的知識。形式的知識是一種由邏輯的資料而來的結果，由重複的確證所確定。經驗的知識則是由經驗的資料而來的結果，亦由重複的確證所確定。因此，依照裴柏的見解，邏輯實證論者的知識說只是由重複的確證所確定的知識的一種表示。但除了由此一表示所建立的知識之外，另有常識和科學與哲學的知識，而後者可以為結構的確證所確定，而它的證據不是資料而是成素。

對資料與成素的不同的討論，緊密地關連著對重複的確證與結構的確證的肯定，並關連著約定的假設與結構的理論問題。有關後一問題我們在下節中再討論。在此，相應於前面所已表示過的我們再總括地作如下的說明。

邏輯實證論者所認為知識的證據——邏輯的證據與經驗的證據——只是有關重複的確證上的提升的或批判的兩種證據。此兩種證據清晰而確定可成為不同的人的觀察了解的對象，亦可在不同的時間上重複地表現。因此它們是資料。

於此資料之外，有些是有關結構的確證的證明的成份。它們不是必然地可被觀察到的。它們輻輳在一起以支持一事實或一假設，由此而證明此一事實或假設為們亦不能重複地表現。

眞。因此它們被稱爲成素。

既然從結構的確證中有成素的表現，資料即不能被認爲知識上的唯一證據。因此，邏輯實證論者只由資料以建立知識的理論亦不能被認爲獨一無二的有效理論。

依照裴柏的見解，資料的應用有它的一定限度，而成素被用爲知識上的證據則是不可以否認的。這不但事實上是如此，而且從理論上說亦是不可以否認的。因爲如果邏輯實證論者想要否認此一事實，他們不能僅依於他們所接受的資料去建立論證。因爲依於資料而建立的論證不能否認有成素的存在。因爲成素不是依於資料而建立的論證所討論的對象。因此，如果任何人想要建立任何反對有成素的論證，他一定要建立一假然的論證以爲反對的依據，而此假然的論證即預設了成素的存在。依裴柏，此一對成素的否定的預設是任何反對成素的理論所不能免除的預設。因此，成素作爲知識的證據是在理論上不能否認的。如果成素必須被接受爲知識的證據，則邏輯實證論者的知識論是不完全的，他們以形而上學爲無認知意義的論斷亦失去了理論上的依據。因此，裴柏即由邏輯實證論者對知識了解不足之處而提出了其新的補充的了解，而此了解即涵有方法論上的差異，亦即於邏輯實證論者所主的兩類命題，兩類知識，及以事實知識只可以由一種證明與一種假設所建立的說法之外，而提出了兩種不同的確證，相應於不同的確證而有不同的假設，而作爲不同的假設的證據亦有不同的了解，由此而建立他在認知的範圍之內而以形而上學爲具有認知的意義而可以有不同於科學的證明的世界假設的理論。

五、兩種不同的假設——約定的假設與結構的假設

在對裴柏的確證有了上述的了解之後，現在我們可以介紹和討論他的假設。

假設在世界的假設的理論中佔有中樞性的重要地位。因為，如我們在前面所已提及的，懷

疑論既然已被駁斥，即有可以為我們研究的對象，獨斷論被排除之後，所有的知識都是依於證

據而建立。證據則可以分為未經批判的與批判的。未經批判的證據有特殊的性質，它要成為知

識的證據必需要被批判而成為批判的證據。批判的證據則為由確證而來的結果，而確證則是為

假設而工作。因此未經批判的證據，批判的證據，與確證等皆被關連到假設上去以從事知識的

建立，而使假設成為世界的假設的理論的中樞。

裴柏以為在常識上亦用假設。假設在過去曾被看作「一種猜測」或「一種預感」 ❸。但此

只是一種沒有系統性的使用。它在知識上的功用與地位不清楚。假設在人類的思想活動中，或

知識的建構上佔有重要的地位，是近代知識進步的表現，或說是人類知識在近代得到了進一步

發展之後才受到特別的重視。

在上節我們曾說每一個確證都預設有一個假設。確證是對假設從事推斷的證明。確證所要

證明的是假設，而所謂真的假設即是可為確證所證明的假設。我們不可以有沒有假設的確證，

亦不能視沒有確證的假設為真。但在日常的生活中，我們沒有明顯地自覺到此一意義，而以為

確證可以沒有假設，亦沒有明顯地要為每一確證提出一假設。例如，我們要查看一椅子是否堅

固好坐，或試用一枝鋼筆是否適手好寫時，我們都沒有自覺地先作一個「如 P 則 Q」的假設，

以椅子的堅固好坐或鋼筆的適手好寫為證明某某假設的確證。但在從事科學的研究時，則每一

確證都是對一假設的推證，沒有不立假設的確證。一個不為假設所引導的確證要被視為一種捉

迷藏的行為，不能期望好的結果。

我們在前節曾提到，裴柏將確證分別為重複的確證與結構的確證。相應於此兩種不同的確

證，他提出了兩種不同的假設，即約定的假設與結構的假設。他了解約定的假設為人用以處理所得的資料的一種人為的方案。故說約定的假設是「為了有秩序地處理資料而來的人的約定❸。」此種假設為邏輯實證論者和脈絡主義者所推重❹。依照他們的見解，「它本身沒有認知的意義」「認知的意義屬於知識的事，而我們所知的是資料。一個假設不是一種資料，它只是為對資料的安排而有的一個符號的方案，藉此方案而可以容易地找到並使用我們所知的資料❸。」「基於所用的假定與基本的概念的不同，同樣的資料常可以在不同的系統中組織起來。

至於系統的優劣的問題，那個最節省科學家的思想的即是最好的系統❹。」因此，一個約定的假設是「人為的，而且與它系統化了的證據可以有清楚的分辨。資料與重複的確證愈清楚對假設與證據的分辨亦愈不會有錯。衡量約定假設價值的最佳標準是理智的節省與簡潔優雅，而二者都不是衡定認知意義的標準❸。」

至於結構的世界的假設則不是人為的一種約定。它不是概念上的一種發明用以組織或系統化已有的證據，而是自然事物的結構的一種顯示，並為描述自然的一種工具，或者說，它是輻輳諸證明項目的一種表現，或是組織或連結各證明項目的一種方法。因此它「不是人為的，它大半與它所組織的證據沒有清楚的分別❹。」它有認知的意義。「它自身表示了認知的意義。

此認知的意義在實踐上與它所組織的證據分別不開❹。」

（1）上面所說的兩種不同的假設涵有下列幾點應特別注意的事：

從約定的假設的觀點上說，一個約定的假設為人的一種約定。因此，「創造的想像」為獲得假設的唯一方法❹。但從結構的假設的觀點上說，一個結構的假設是對自然結構的一種描述。因

此，它的根源在常識中，由常識而來，而不是一種創造的想像。裴柏在他的根源的譬喻的理論中對此有說明。

(2)既然結構的世界的假設是源於根源的譬喻，我們若有不同的根源的譬喻，即可以有不同的結構的世界的假設。這是裴柏肯定作為相對地適切的世界的假設的概念的一種依據。從哲學史的了解上說，過去的哲學既然有依於不同的根源的譬喻以描述自然事物的結構的表示，我們即可以依據此不同的描述而說不同種類的世界的假設。

(3)一個結構的假設本質地要發展為一個世界的假設。因為一個結構的假設不能被限於任何特定領域之中。故一個結構的假設為關連到所有可以連結在一起的證據上去的假設，亦即為一個沒有限制的假設。

(4)一個結構的假設的可靠性是不可避免地與它的確證的範圍與精確性成正比例，而且範圍與精確性是互相地關連著的。因為當一個結構的證據更被清楚地分辨時，與它有關的假設便更適切，而當一假設的範圍被擴大，則它即更可靠。因此，為了要使一個假設更可靠，它的範圍將會盡可能地被擴大，為了要使它更適切，它的有關證據將更精確地被分辨。這擴大與求精確的活動將不會停止，直至達到一種不受限制的範圍，並使其精確性亦達到相對地最適切的程度。

於上述四點值得注意的事之外，另有幾點疑問應在此加以釐清：(1)一個約定的假設可否被形式化為一個世界的假設？我們在前面曾指出，一個約定的假設可以或為重複的確證，或為結構的確證所推證，而一個結構的假設本質地要發展為一個世界的假設。因此，我們即要問一個約定的假設是否一樣可以被形式化為一個世界的假設？裴柏對此一問題的回答是希望可以。㊼

但他的此一希望失敗了，因為一個世界的假設不能由假定的方法去產生[48]，因為資料的應用既然只限於某一領域中，由重複的確證而推證的約定的假設即不能公式化為一個世界的假設。(2)我們可否有一個為結構的確證所推證的約定的世界的假設？我們在前面曾指出，一個約定的假設可以或為一個重複的確證所推證，或為一個結構的確證所推證。當它為一個結構的確證所推證時，它是否可以成為一個世界的假設呢？裴柏對此一問題似沒有直接地回答。但我們可以代他去考慮。我們認為如果我們能夠建立一個約定的世界的假設，而此假設是為結構的確證所推證，則我們似沒有方法或很難去分辨一個結構的世界的假設與所說的假設的不同。也許因為這原故裴柏對此一問題沒有作進一步的討論。至於由裴氏所說世界的假設只能源於根源的譬喻的觀點上說時，則所提的問題已隱約地被排拒。(3)我們是否可以用不同的重複的確證或結構的確證所假設中的任何一種？亦即是約定的假設或結構的假設是否可以任由不同的重複的確證或結構的確證所證明。就上節所引裴柏對確證的描述的意義上說，答案似是肯定的。因為裴柏曾表示，對於兩種不同的確證的分辨，部份是基於實施確證時所採用的不同的方法。但此似應被限於約定的假設可以為重複的確證所證明，亦可以為結構的確證所證明。如有關椅子是否堅固的假設，因為就裴柏對資料與成素的分別，及就資料與成素的不同的應用的觀點上說，資料既是重複的確證的結果，成素是結構的確證的結果，則資料主要是屬於約定的假設的事，而成素則是屬於結構的假設的事。因此，結構的假設不能只由重複的確證去證明。重複的確證或者資料只可以為結構的確證所引用以從事結構的假設的證明。我們不能只用重複的確證去推證結構的假設。(4)當分辨結構的確證與重複的確證的不同時，裴柏曾說後一方法「似特顯觀察的重要」，至於前一方法則是「一種假設的方法[49]」。如果我們以此一說法為對確證是否需要預設假設的分辨時，

則很容易會誤以爲只有結構的確證是爲假設所指引，至於重複的

上裴柏的意思並不是如此。他是說重複的確證是一種由「人與人」或由不同的人而得的確證，

故「似特顯觀察的重要」，至於結構的確證是一種有關「事實與事實」關連在一起而得的確

證，而爲了要從事此一結構的確證，不同的事實一定要被連結或輻輳在一假設之上，以從事推

證，而此一被推證的假設相對於整個事件來說，只是要被證明的結構的假設中的一個副假設，

而不是意指重複的確證可以不需要假設。

上面所說的對假設的了解，一方面緊密地關連著裴柏對形而上學的了解，另一方面亦緊密

地關連著他對科學的了解。有關形而上學的問題不再多說。我們在此擬說幾句有關科學的問題。

那就是只以約定的或運作的理論爲有效的理論是裴柏所不能接受的。他不否認它們在近代科學

上所表現的價值，但他不能同意只以它們爲有效的。因爲由世界的假設的理論的觀點上說，不

同的世界理論有不同的科學理論。例如，形式論有符合的眞理說，機體論有融貫的眞理說，運

作的眞理說只爲機械論與脈絡論所主。除此之外，裴柏亦不以爲運作的眞理說是完全可靠而沒

有問題的。因爲依照他的見解，「在某些形式上運作的觀點可以有正確的表現，但它亦有困難。

最明顯的是，雖然它很能適合現代科學強調『解釋』與『預測』而輕視描述的潮流，但它對爲

什麼有些運作成功而另一些則失敗沒有解釋[50]。」因此，他在他的選擇論的世界的假設中不跟

隨正統的脈絡主義者採用運作的理論作爲一種科學的理論，而是另外建立一種運作與符合合用

的名爲運作的符合理論（Operational-Correspondance Theory）[51]。

六、根源的譬喻

根源的譬喻是裴柏用來作為解答世界的假設的根源所在的一種理論。就我們所知這是用來建立世界的假設的唯一理論。

在上節的討論中我們曾說，一個結構的假設不是如約定的假設一樣是人的一種創造的想像，它不是一種發明，而是對自然事物的結構的一種顯示。我們如何可以有此一種顯示並本之而建立世界的假設呢？此即是裴柏的根源的譬喻所要解答的問題。

裴柏先在一篇論文中提出了這一理論，該論文名為《形而上學的根源理論》[53]。在《世界的假設》一書中此一理論又再一次得到了肯定[55]。從根本的義意上說，上述三處對該理論所陳述的相同，只有措辭上或解釋著重點上的差別。因此我們在後面只引述《世界的假設》一書中的記述作為討論的根據。

從原則上說，這方法是這樣的：一個人希望了解這世界，故尋找了解它的線索。他選取了某些在常識範圍中的事實，試看是否可以藉此去了解其他的範圍。這原來的範圍因此而成為他的根本的類比或根源的譬喻，他盡可能描述這一範圍中的事實的特質，或分辨它的結構。一組屬於它的結構的特質即成為他的解釋或描述的基本概念，我們叫它們為範疇，藉着這些範疇他從事去研究所有其他範圍中未經批判過或先前已經批判過的事實。他藉着這

些範疇去解釋所有的事實。由於別的事實衝擊他的範疇的結果，他或會修改和再調整那些

範疇以使這一套範疇可以共同地改變和發展。既然基本的類比或根源的譬喻正常地（而且

可能最少有一部份是必然地）由普通的常識而來，如果它們要證明對一個沒有限制的範圍

的假設是適合的，經進一步的發展與提煉而成的一套範疇是需要的。有些根源的譬喻較其

他的根源的譬喻表明了更能開展，有更大的適應的力量。因此它們乃得以生存，而產生了

相對地適切的世界的理論56。

由上面所引的話，我們可以對根源的譬喻簡單地表示如下：一個根源的譬喻即是一種基於「某

些常識領域中的事實」而成的類比解釋，要由此「去試行了解其他的領域」。這是此一理論的

關鍵所在。其他的描述即是關連到此一關鍵而來的陳述。例如，如果我們問這如何可行呢？進

一步的解釋是(1)被選擇為根源譬喻的領域將盡可能被描述，那就是這一領域的結構將盡可能被

分辨，因此(2)被描述或分辨的選擇的領域可以被肯定為解釋或描述的基本概念，亦即被視為範

疇，(3)以這些範疇去研究和解釋所有其他領域的事實，(4)在此一研究和解釋的歷程中被肯定的

範疇可以被修改與調整使其能面對新的領域的衝擊，(5)那些曾得到發展與提煉並證明對一個無

限的範圍的假設為適當的範疇即成為相對地適切的世界的假設的理論的範疇。依照裴柏早期的

見解有四種不同的理論叫做選擇論。他在他的《世界的假設》一書中討論由前四個世界的假設

立了一新的世界的理論——形式論、機械論、脈絡論、機體論。晚年他建

以了解世界。在《概念與本質——一個世界的假設》一書中則討論由他晚年所建立的世界的假

設以了解世界。

依據前面對根源的譬喻的了解，我們可以對它的涵義作進一步的分點的說明或肯定：

(1)源於普通常識的根源的譬喻既是世界的假設的本源所在，因此，我們由世界的假設所獲得的結果，雖然是經過了進一步的提煉而來的成果，但所得的成果既然是源於普通常識，我們即大致地可以說，形而上學的問題與知識的問題一樣，都是由普通常識開始而可以再歸到普通常識上去。

(2)雖然形而上學的問題或知識的問題由普通常識開始，但我們若將由結構的假設的提煉而來的結果歸到普通常識的假定上去，則是不合法的❺❼。因為普通常識是未經過批判而且是要被批判的。它是安全的，因此形而上學或知識的問題可以歸到它上面去，但它是未經過批判的，因此我們不能以它的任何假定為確定的。

(3)由根源的譬喻引伸而來的世界的假設的範疇是事實的特質的表示。事實的特質相互地連結或組合成為事實的結構。因此範疇的連結是事實的特質的連結的表示，此即是它的結構。因此一種特質可以成為另一種或所有其他的特質的證據。它們是相互地關連著而有緊密的結合。因此，如果我們只是看具體的特質，我們所見的只是一組或一套屬於事實上的特質，我們見不到任何的假設。一個假設是對事實的結構的關係的抽象的了解。因此它叫做結構的假設。

(4)既然一個結構的假設或說一個世界的假設是由對事實的結構作抽象而且亦關連著成素的了解而建立，我們即不可以由重複的確證對它作充分的證明。因為它不只關連著資料的證據而且亦關連著成素的證據。既然我們不可能由重複的確證對它作充份的證明，因此那些要藉著依於重複的確證而建立的標準去排斥它的行為即不合法❺❽。

(5)既然每一個世界的假設的範疇都是由它自己的根源的譬喻自動地引伸出來，以此去解釋

世界，我們即不可以將由一個根源的譬喻所引伸出來的範疇與由其他根源的譬喻所引伸出來的範疇結合在一起⑲，亦不可以假定某一個世界的假設的建立是由於對其他的世界的假設對世界的解顯露而來的結果。我們亦不可以用某一世界的假設的範疇去批評其他的世界的假設對世界的解釋⑳。一個世界的假設應由對它自己的範疇的擴展而建立。它的任何缺點亦應關連到它自己的精確性與所能概括的範圍而加以評定。但一個世界的假設可以與其他世界的假設相比較去看那一個較為適切。

（6）從理論上說，一個根源的譬喻的涵義可以充份地被發展，它的範疇可以充份地被了解，藉著所確定的範疇以解釋我們所在的世界。但事實上它的涵義不能在一個短暫的時間內得到充份的發展與了解。從哲學史上看，我們見到它需要很長的時間才可以得到較大的發展與了解。因此，任何一個世界的假設有它自己的發展史。它的後期發展通常是比前期的發展較為完善。但既然所說的前期與後期都是基於同一的根源的譬喻，則不論發展如何，它們是屬於同一的理論⑪。

（7）既然一個世界的假設是由一個根源的譬喻自動地發展而成，它所建立的即系統地組織在一起，它不可以接受任何由其他的世界理論而來的東西。因此，折衷主義（Eclecticism）與世界的假設理論是不相容的⑫。它在世界假設的理論上沒有地位，我們不能對它有任何的肯定。從世界假設的觀點上說，有關世界的了解的問題，我們只能就某一個結構的假設去建立了解，而不能將幾種理論結合在一起。因此，我們即不能有折衷的想法。因折衷的了解只會對世界的理論產生混淆，而不能對它所提供的有機的了解有任何的幫助。

（8）所有世界理論的範疇或概念都是對事實的結構的一種抽象的了解，存有解釋現實世界的

目的，它們不是離開世界而獨立地存在。因此，當它們被用來解釋世界時，必定要與它們的根源的譬喻相關連。任何不與根源的譬喻相關連的概念將只是一種空的抽象的表示，它將要遠離事實，失落了它原來解釋世界的功用❻❸。

⑼從原則上說，每一事實都可以成為一根源的譬喻。但實際上，只有少數的事實具有被擴展與提煉成為一個具有無限制的範圍的結構的假設的性質❻❹。其他大多數的事實只可以被用來建立有限的結構的假設，應用於某些特殊的問題上以了解有關的事實。這是有關形而上學與特殊的科學的不同的真正根源所在。

⑽既然一個結構的假設是源於一個根源的譬喻，它即與約定的假設不同。就上面的了解，特別是就⑴，⑶，⑷，⑺，⑼與⑽各點的了解，一個世界的假設與一個結構的假設，以及一個根源的譬喻的關係，好似是必然的。即我們不可能有任何結構的假設而不是源於一種根源的譬喻的，我們亦不可能有任何世界的假設不是由結構的假設發展而成。因此，雖然裴柏說根源的譬喻的理論是與結構的假設居於不同的層次❻❺，並且說一個人即使接受了結構的假設的觀點上去的了解形而上學的問題，仍可以拒絕根源的譬喻❻❻，但實際上如果一個人接受了結構的假設作為了解世界的方式，他即自然地要接受根源的譬喻的理論作為建立結構的假設的根據。因為除了根源的譬喻之外，我們不能藉著任何其他的方法可以建立一個結構的假設。並且依照裴柏的說法，如果一個人接受了假設的觀點，由此去了解形而上學的問題，他一定要接受結構的假設。因為除了結構的假設可以擴展為一個世界的假設之外，我們不能建立任何其他的世界的假設。

註

釋

❶ 請參看 John Dewey, *Experience and Nature* (La Salle, Illinois: The Open Court Publishing Co., 1958; first published in 1925), Chapter One.

❷ John Dewey, *Experience and Nature*, p. 51.

❸ S. C. Pepper, *World Hypotheses* (Berkeley and Los Angles: Univ. of California Press, 1966; first published in 1942), p. 1. 引文中所說後述的兩本書指 Euclid's *Elements* and Darwin's *The Origin of Species*; 其他的書則指 Plato's *Republic*, Aristotle's *Metaphysics*, Lucretius' *On the Nature of Things*, Descartes's *Meditations*, Spinoza's *Ehics*, Hume's *Treatise*, Kant's *Three Critiques*, Dewey's *Experience and Nature*, Whitehead's *Process and Reality*.

❹ S. C. Pepper, *Concept and Quality : A World Hypothesis*, (La Salle, Illinois: Open Court Publishing Co., 1967), p. 8.

❺ S. C. Peper, *World Hypotheses*, p. 3.

❻ Ibid., p. 11.

❼ Ibid., p. 3.

❽ Ibid., p. 7.

❾ Ibid., pp. 19-21.

❿ Ibid., p. 21.

⓫ Ibid., pp. 23-24.

⓬ 裝柏在他所著的 *Concept and Quality: A World Hypotheses*, (La Salle Illinois: Open

⑬ Court Publishing Co., 1967), 第十四章第四節中對 "logical reality is dependent for its being on the processes of actuality" 有詳細的解釋，但對所說傳統上所了解的矛盾律是自明的說法似亦未能作有效的駁斥。

⑭ S. C. Pepper, *World Hypotheses*, pp. 24-25.

⑮ Ibid., p. 25.

⑯ Ibid., pp. 26-27.

⑰ Ibid., p. 28.

⑱ 中國的莊子在二千多年前對事物沒有絕對的說法的見解，與裴柏在此所說的似有相同之處。因莊子既不同意「儒墨之是非」之爭，又曾說「既使我與若辯矣，若勝我，我不勝若，若果是也，我果非也邪？我勝若，若不吾勝，我果是也，而果非也邪？其或是也，其或非也邪？其俱是也，其俱非也邪。我與若不能相知也。則人固受其黮闇。吾誰使正之？使同乎若者正之？既與若同矣，惡能正之。使同乎我者正之？既同乎我矣，惡能正之。使異乎我與若者正之？既異乎我與若矣，惡能正之。然則我與若與人俱不能相知也而待彼也邪？」〈齊物論〉但莊子排遣是非不是如裴柏所主對事物的了解皆要依於證據以求一概然的知識。莊子要人不要執守己見而無別人之所見。故要「照之於天」，從天的觀點去了解事物，亦要從天的觀點去承認各種不同的說法。

⑲ S. C. Pepper, *World Hypotheses*, p. 25.

⑳ Ibid., pp. 17-18.

㉑ F. C. Copleston, S. J., *A History of Philosophy* (Meryland: The Newman Press, 1960), Vol. IV., pp. 57-58; 61-62.

㉒ C. S. Peirce, "The Fixation of Belief," in *The Philosophy of Peirce.* J. Buchler,

㉓ ed. (New York: Harcourt, Brace and Co., 1940), pp. 5-20.

㉔ C. S. Peirce, "The Scientific Attitude and Fallibilism," in The Philosophy of Peirce, pp. 42-59.

㉕ S. C. Pepper, The Basis of Critism in the Arts. (Cambridge, Mass.: Harvard University Press, 1965), p. 3.

㉖ S. C. Pepper, World Hypotheses, p. 47.

㉗ Ibid., pp. 51-52.

㉘ Ibid., p. 39.

㉙ Ibid., p. 40.

㉚ Ibid., p. 44.

㉛ Ibid., pp. 47-49. 裴柏在他的 "The Basis of Criticism in the Arts" 一書中亦有類似的描述。

㉜ Ibid., p. 48.

㉝ John Dewey, Logic: The Theory of Inquiry (New York: Henry Holt and Co., 1938), p. 117.

㉞ 在《世界的假設》一書中，裴柏並沒有用「邏輯實證論者」(logical positivists) 一名詞，而只用「實證論者」(positivists)。

㉟ B. Russell, A Critical Exposition of The Philosophy of Leibniz (London: George Allen & Unwin Ltd., 6 th Impression, 1964), pp. 16-17.

㊱ A. J. Ayer, ed., Logical Positivism (New York: The Free Press 1959), pp. 4, 10.

R. Carnap, "The Rejection of Metaphysics," in 20th Century Philosophy: The

37. Analytic Tradition, p. 210.

38. 請參看 G. E. Moore, Some Main Problems of Philosophy (London: The Macmillan Co., 1953), Chapter One 和 F. J. E. Woodbridge, "The Scope of Metaphysics", in A Modern Introduction to Metaphysics (eddited by D. A. Drennen), pp. 174-182.

39. S. C. Pepper, World Hypotheses, p. 71.

40. Ibid., p. 71.

41. S. C. Pepper, 'Concept and Quality : A World Hypothesis, (La Salle, Illinois: Open Court Publishing Co., 1967), p. 45.

42. S. C. Pepper, World Hypotheses, p. 71.

43. Ibid., p. 72.

44. Ibid., p. 82.

45. Ibid.

46. Ibid.

47. Ibid., p. 83.

48. C. G. Hempel, Philosophy of Natural Science (Englewood Cliffs, N. J.: Prentice-Hall, Inc., 1966), pp. 15-16.

49. S. C. Pepper, World Hypotheses, pp. 87-88.

50. Ibid., p. 89.

51. Ibid., p. 49.

S. C. Pepper, Concept and Quality : A World Hypothesis, p. 268.

Ibid., p. 269.

52 S. C. Pepper, *World Hypotheses*, p. 84.

53 S. C. Pepper, "The Root Metaphor Theory of Metaphysics," The Journal of Philosophy, Vol. 32 (1935), pp. 365-74.

54 S. C. Pepper, *World Hypotheses*, pp. 91-92.

55 S. C. Pepper, *Concept atnd Quality : A World Hypothesis*, p. 3.

56 S. C. Pepper, *World Hypotheses*, pp. 91-92.

57 Ibid., p. 102.

58 Ibid., p. 101.

59 Ibid., pp. 96, 104.

60 S. C. Pepper, *World Hypotheses*, p. 98.

61 Ibid., pp. 96-97.

62 Ibid., p. 104.

63 Ibid., pp. 113-114.

64 Ibid., p. 91.

65 Ibid., p. 84.

66 請參考 "The Root Metaphor Theory of Metaphysics," pp. 265-266.

第四章　形式論（上）

一、小·引

世界的假設如上章所已提及的是一種結構的假設，而不是一種約定的假設。結構的假設是依根源的譬喻而建立。由根源的譬喻而引伸出範疇，再以所引伸的範疇去對世界作結構性或系統性的說明。

裴柏以形式論是一個相對地適切的世界的假設。西方傳統哲學中的柏拉圖的哲學，亞里士多德的哲學，經院主義者（Scholastics）與新經院主義者（Neo-scholastics）的哲學，新實在論者（Neo-realists）與近代的劍橋實在論者（Modern Cambridge realists）的哲學，皆是形式論不符」的問題 ❷。我們應由它們所依以建立的根源的譬喻去給與它們的名稱，而同稱它們爲形式論。在後面我們將分別爲：(1)形式論的根源的譬喻與內在形式論（immanent formism）的範疇的確定；(2)對類型論（theory of types）與類的分辨；(3)超越的形式論（transcendent formism）的範疇的確定；(4)內在的形式論與超越的形式論的範疇的融會與合併；(5)具體的存在物與時空的關係；；(6)因果關係的分辨；(7)形式論的真理說等七節以介述形式論對世界作結構性與系統性的了解及其真理說的涵義。所說的七節將分別爲上下兩章，(1)至(4)及本「小引」爲上章，(5)至

❶ 傳統上曾分別稱它們爲理型論、實在論、或新實在論等。但裴柏以傳統的稱謂「有涵義與名稱

(7)爲下章。

二、形式論的根源的譬喻與內在形式論的範疇的確定

形式論的根源的譬喻爲「相同的東西」。此「相同的東西」可爲「相同的事物」或「同一的計劃」❸。因「相同的東西」有「相同的事物」與「同一的計劃」的不同，形式論者即由此而引伸出兩組不同的範疇。而發展成爲內在的形式論與越越的形式論。形式論既有內在與超越的不同，則二者到底爲範疇的不同，其既同以「相同的東西」爲根源的譬喻由之而引伸出範疇以了解世界雖有內在與超越的不同，其即應爲一種世界理論或兩種不同的世界理論應是一問題。但依裴柏的了解，二者，其即應爲一種世界理論。又內在的形式論與超越的形式論除各別地或依「相同的事物」或依「同一的計劃」引伸出不同的範疇以對世界作結構性或系統性的了解之外，所說的兩組不同的範疇可以融會與合併爲一組範疇以了解世界。兩組不同的範疇既可以融會與合併以了解世界，其即應爲一種世界理論。

作爲內在的形式論所依據的「相同的東西」爲相同的草葉、樹葉、或一套匙羮、一叠報紙、一刀白紙等。作爲超越的形式論所依據的「相同的東西」則是由人所確定的計劃，如一個工匠所確定的製造工藝品的計劃，或由自然界所表示出來的計劃，如自然世界的水晶體或橡樹所表示出來的生長的計劃等❹。

依裴柏的了解，所說的「相同的東西」都是可以由常識上見得到的。我們在日常的活動中與在自然的事物上隨時隨地都可以見到所說的「相同的東西」。形式論者以此爲根源的譬喻，如前面所已提及的，即是由所說的「相同的東西」所具有的特殊的性質而引伸出一套範疇作爲

解釋世界的依據。範疇是由根源的譬喻引伸而來，故範疇是屬於第二層次的概念，爲範疇所依的根源的譬喻則爲第一層次的概念。裴柏以內在的形式論由「相同的東西」如草葉或樹葉等所引伸出來的範疇有三個：(1)特質，(2)個別性，(3)參與❺。所說由範疇以對世界作結構性或系統性的了解，即由對各別的範疇作解釋及對其作相關性的了解以了解世界。

(1) 特質：特質爲內在的形式論的第一個範疇，因爲它是根源的譬喻——「相同的東西」所必具有的。但作爲相同的東西必具有一共同的特質。特質既爲相同的東西所必具有，其即爲由內在的形式論的根源的譬喻所引伸出來的第一個範疇。

(2) 個別性：「相同的東西」所具有的特質是彼此相同的。如同爲黃的東西，黃的特質是彼此相同的。但黃的A與黃的B爲兩個不同的個體。黃的A必爲A然後可以與黃的B同具有黃的特質而成爲其相同性，而黃的A與黃的B的本身則不同。然不同爲黃的A或黃的B所特有。此特有即爲黃的A或黃的B的個別性。故個別性爲一個個體所獨有的特質。作爲形式論的根源的譬喻的相同的東西除了具有一相同的特質而可以被引伸爲了解事物的範疇之外，亦有其自身的特殊性而可以被引伸爲了解事物的範疇。

(3) 參與：相同的東西都有相同的特質。由此相同的特質而使相同的東西爲同類。同類的東西的相同的特質是遍在類中的每一份子的。但就各份子的個體來說，此爲份子的個體的自身有其個別性。此具有個別性的個體如何可以具有共同的特質呢？此即個體的個別性參與共同的特質而使其爲個體所有。故參與爲個體的個別性與特質連結的表現。此連結是一種關係。但此關係不同於個體與個體間的關係，而是個體的個別性與其所具有的共同特質的連結關係。此種

關係是由形式論的根源的譬喻所表現出來的一種範疇與範疇之間的關係。我們由此種關係所了解及的存在界的真實是由形式論的根源的譬喻本身引伸而得。我們對此「得」不能否認。因為它有經驗的依據，它表現於經驗的認知的了解上：我們不能否認有相同的個體，此相同的個體彼此不同而有其共同的特質。

三、類型論與類的分辨

裴柏由個體的個別性與特質的連結表現的事實而駁斥實證論者（Positivists）依「類型論」而來對世界的假設的理論的批評，並由此而分辨類的意義。

裴柏以個體的個別性參與特質所表示的連結為類型論的理論根源所在。所說的連結亦由類型論的建立而更得到確定。因此實證論者要藉類型論以批評世界的假設的理論是無效的。因類型論既為由形式論所涵有的連結的關係發展而成，即不能由之而批評其所依而發展出來的世界的假設的理論。

依羅素對類型論的了解，類型論是一種邏輯理論。它主要說明類與個體的不同，類亦有層級上的分別。依它對類的概念與個體的概念不同的了解，用以分析個體概念的類概念自身不能被包涵於被分析的個體概念之中，它的圖像式的說明是一個人的眼不能反觀其自己，或一個影相機不能反影其自己 **⑥**。實證論者用此以反對世界的假設的理論是說世界的假設是以整個世界為了解的對象，但世界的假設的理論是在世界的假設所要了解之上，而不在為世界的假設的了解的層次中，故世界的假設的理論不能成立。裴柏對實證論者用類型論以反對世界的假設的

反駁，首先是由常識的觀點上指出我們的眼雖不能直接地反看其自己，但可以間接地由鏡子中見到其自己。一個照相機亦可以由另一同類的照相機以攝其形相。由此常識的分辨，我們了解到我們對於用以分析的類概念與對所分析的個體概念都可以有了解❼。但更重要的是如在上章所已指出的，世界的假設的理論不是依於重複的確證而建立，而是依於結構的確證而建立❽。因此我們不能用重複的確證的證據去否認結構的確證所要了解的。類型論正是屬於重複的確證範圍內的理論。故不可以依之以反對建立世界的假設的結構的假設。相反地，我們見到了此一理論的依據爲何。它是由形式論所具有的連結的關係發展而成。

裴柏以類爲一群特殊的事物參與一種或多種相同的特質的表現。因此所有藍的個別事物構成了藍的事物類。此是以藍一種特質爲藍的事物參與的根據。如特質多於一種作爲參與的根據，則類即相應於特質的不同而不同，如藍的花類或藍的鳥類。又特質有層級之分，故藍的花或藍的鳥類不同於藍的事物類。一般地說爲個體參與愈多的特質，類的外延愈大，爲個體參與愈少的特質，類的外延愈小。傳統上以沒有一定的特質而包涵所有個體的類爲最大類，以只有一個體所具有的個別性的類爲個體類。但就個體的個別性參與特質而成類的觀點上說，我們不能有一個「沒有一定的特質」而包括所有個體的類❾。至於個體類則是可以說的。但裴柏以爲我們對個體類常給與一專有的名詞而稱之爲某個體而不名之爲類❿。

前面對範疇的引伸及對類的了解即爲對存在事物的了解。因爲沒有存在事物不是因所說的範疇而存在而成爲類的表現。但此只是依內在的形式論的範疇對存在事物的一種了解。於此外尚可有依超越的形式論的範疇而來的對存在事物的不同的了解。

四、超越的形式論的範疇的確定

超越的形式論的根源的譬喻，如在前面所已提及的，是人所確定的計劃或自然所表現出來的計劃。由此根源的譬喻所引伸出來的範疇為：(1)模式，(2)例證模式的資料，(3)使模式具體化的例證原則⓫。

(1) 模式：超越的形式論的第一個範疇是模式。模式常容易與類混淆，故要分辨；又模式不同於為進化論所反對的定種說的種性，此亦要分辨。模式不是類。模式是一範疇。類不是範疇。模式是個體事物依之而存在的形式，類不是形式。類是具有共同特質的個體的表現，它不是事物依之而存在的範疇。

進化論者否認有一定不變的種性。他們以各類事物的種性常在變化中。進化論者的思想盛行之後，模式為事物依之而存在的形式，個體事物在變，而模式的本身則常存不變的說法即成了問題。因此，有人本進化論的觀點認為模式隨個體而改變，模式不在個體之外而是在個體事物之中。以模式不離個體事物而自存的說法，相對於柏拉圖的理型論說，即理型不離感官事物而自存。此是不為柏拉圖所接受的。但此與亞里士多德所說形式即在質料之中的意義相同。但如此一說法成立，則超越的形式論不能成立。因為若模式沒有超越的意義而是內在於事物之中則模式即成為前面所說的內在的形式論的特質。但裴柏以為就超越的形式論的根源的譬喻的觀點上說，模式為由計劃引伸而來的範疇，此計劃在人的行為表現上，及在自然事物的生長中均可見到。因此我們不能由進化論的觀點而否定它的涵義。就現代科學的觀點上說，科學家亦常

以其所要探求的律則外在於其所探求的事物之上，由歸納法以證明一律則為有效的歸納事件，只是使一律則得以證明的事件而並不是此律則。又為我們所肯定的自然律，我們明以其為超越於我們所可觀察及或實驗到的事物之上而不是內在於其中。因此模式超越事件而為其所表現的說法仍有其一定的意義 ⑫。

(2) 例證模式的資料：此如內在的形式論的個別性一樣為存在個體事物所必具的範疇。從內在的形式論說，特質不可以沒有個別性的參與而可以成為個體事物。從超越的形式論說，模式亦不可以沒有例證模式的資料而可以有個體事物。例證模式的資料既然為不可少的，故其即成為超越的形式論的第二個範疇。

(3) 使模式具體化的例證原則：此與內在的形式論的參與同功用。從內在的形式論說，特質與個別性必須通過參與而連結在一起，即後者參與前者而成為個體事物。從超越的形式論說，模式與例證模式的資料必須有使模式具體化的例證原則然後後者才可以使前者落實為具體的事物。因此其即成為存在事物不可少的因素而為超越的形式論的第三個範疇。

五、內在的形式論與超越的形式論的範疇的融會與合併

對內在的形式論的範疇的說明為由內在的形式論而來對世界的一種了解與說明；對超越的形式論的說明是由超越的形式論而來對世界的一種了解與說明；於此二種了解與說明之外，我們亦可以有融會與合併內在的形式論與超越的形式論的範疇而為超越而內在的形式論的範疇而來對世界的了解與說明。

內在的形式論與與超越的形式論的範疇之所以可以融會與合併而成爲一套超越而內在的形式論的範疇，此主要由於模式可參與特質而成爲涵有模式與特質的形式；而此形式並具有第二層次的相互參與。裴柏爲了要對此一意義加以說明，曾引用形式論者所用的「存在」（exist-ence）與「潛存」（subsistence）二詞去作解釋⑬。相對於內在的形式論的範疇的觀點上說，「存在」即任何屬於具有內在的形式論第二種範疇的個別性及此個別性所參與的任何特質結合而成而可爲我們所接觸及與知覺到的事物，所說的個別性可能只是一純抽象的東西，而不可以脫離它的參與的特質而被知覺。但由思辨上說「存在」則可以有如上的分辨；而所謂具體的事物即爲具有所說的兩種範疇而存在的事物。至於「潛存」則是沒有爲個別性所參與的內在的形式論的特質，與沒有爲質料所例證的超越的形式論的模式。柏拉圖與亞里士多德對於所說不爲個別性所參與的特質，或不爲質料所例證的超越的形式的見解彼此不同。柏拉圖以潛存的理型可以獨立存在。亞里士多德則說潛存的理型即在具體的特殊事物中。它不能離感覺事物而獨自存在。由於亞氏不同意柏氏理型獨自存在的以其說料所例證的概念具體化而來的謬誤。在形式論的世界的假設中，取代柏拉圖的理型論的地位的說法，故修改柏氏的理型論爲形式論。在形式論的世界的假設中對它們另有所知，確是一問題。特質或模式可否獨自存在，或我們可否於具體的存在事物之外對它們另有所知，確是一問題。但從形式論的世界的假設的範疇的觀點上說，特質或模式則皆可以獨立於個別性或例證模式的質料之外，而成爲抽象思想的對象，由此以研究其與個別性或例證模式的質料的關係爲何。此所說的關係即特質與個別性或例證模式的質料所表現的各種不同的參與關係。於此各種不同的關係之外，另有前面所說的模式參與特質的關係。此後一參與是第二層次的參與。此一參與的情形可由人爲的鞋的模式或自然橡樹的模式表現爲一定的形狀或一定的顏色而見到。此

形狀或顏色即爲鞋或橡樹的特質，其成爲如此的鞋或橡樹即爲模式參與特質的表現。模式既參與特質，參與特質的模式即被看作一個別性，但此一個別性是第二層次的個別性，參與亦是第二層次的參與⑭。模式既參與特質，參與特質的模式即與特質合而爲一而爲一種具有特質與模式的形式。此形式即爲超越而內在的形式論的第一個範疇⑮。

超越而內在的形式論的第二個範疇爲基本的個別性。此即爲內在的形式論的個別性與超越的形式論的例證模式的資料，此二者說法雖不同，其涵義則一樣，故可合之而名基本的個別性，而爲超越而內在的形式論的第二個範疇⑯。在此加「基本的」一詞一方面爲要限定它不是純指內在的形式論的第二個範疇，另一方面則要分辨其爲不具有任何特質的個體事物的個別性。

超越而內在的形式論的第三個範疇爲第一層次的參與或例證⑰。此二者的涵義亦是一樣，故可合之而名爲第一層次的參與或例證。此亦爲內在的形式論的參與與超越的形式論的使模式具體化的例證原則。在此加「第一層次的」一詞亦是相對於第二層次的參與或例證而說的。

如前面所已說及的，模式參與特質，特質亦可參與模式，二者可以彼此參與。一特質亦可參與另外的特質，此一參與於存在事物中亦隨處可見。又存在事物之成爲存在事物常不限於一種個別性參與一種特質而存在，而是一種個別性參與幾種特質而存在，而所參與的幾種特質亦彼此相參與而成複合的特質或樣式（Pattern）。構成複合的特質或樣式的基本成份常爲一種不可以完全分離的結合，此即爲一種形態（gestalts）。此所說的形態即爲形態心理學的依據所在⑱。方形的樣式即是一種複合的特質。此複合的特質是由四次參與一定長度的直線的特質，四次參與一定的直角的特質，一次參與一定濶度的面的特質而成。除非我們要以方形只有名言上的意義，否則即不可

以將方形分解爲只有各別的四條直線的特質，與一個平面的特質。方形的各個物並不僅因爲它們是方的而彼此相同，它們之所以同稱爲方的物，亦因爲它們都參與了一定數目的長度的直線的特質，和一個平面的特質。方形的物雖彼此有所不同，但它們所具有的形式則是可以從直覺上見到其相似性。此一由直覺上所見到的正與作爲內在的形式論與超越的形式論的根源的譬喻之可以由直覺上確定一樣。我們亦由此而接受由直覺上所確定的方形的事物爲方的，而承認此一複合的特質，以其爲具有第二層次的一種特質參與其他的特質的呈現。

特質的彼此參與亦可以由深紅、紅、與顏色的關係而了解到。因從第二層次的參與的觀點上說，深紅參與紅，紅參與顏色，而三者皆爲特質。當我們見到一個深紅的物體時，我們常以此物體爲紅色的物而不細加分辨它的深紅與紅的不同。但深紅與紅的分別仍是存在的，而且紅與顏色的不同亦可加以分別，而視深紅、紅、與顏色爲不同的特質。它們由於參與的表現而成爲一具有複合的特質的紅的物。

第五章　形式論（下）

六、具體的存在物與時空的關係

上章對內在的形式論的範疇與超越的形式論的範疇的了解，及對二者融會與合併的說明，皆為相應於存在物而說，而所說的即為存在物所依以存在或表現的方式。存在物以如此的方式表現，對如此的了解即為對存在物的了解，亦即為對世界的了解。從形式論的觀點上說，世界的事物是不能離開所說明的範疇而存在。了解或說明世界即須依所說的範疇而了解或說明，此即為形式論的世界的假設的根本意義所在。故上章對根源的譬喻的說明及對由根源的譬喻而引伸出不同的範疇的說明，以及對兩組範疇的融會與合併的說明，即為從形式論的觀點上去對世界所作的說明。但裴柏除上述的說明外，另專由具體的存在物而說明形式論者對時空的了解，並說明具體的存在物皆表現於時空之中而不能離時空而獨存。

由常識上說一切具體的存在物皆表現於時間與空間之中，不能離時空而獨自存在。但有些哲學家對此一問題有不同的見解。例如桑地耶拿（George Santayana）[19]。此所說的「本質的直覺」（intuition of essence）即說我們可以有「本質的直覺」（intuition of essence）。此所說的「本質」可以有特殊的直覺。如依前一解釋，一為我們可以直覺一些特殊的特質；一為我們對本質可以有特殊的直覺。如依前一解釋，桑氏似主我們於覺知為一事物的個別性所參與的特質之外另有所覺知。此所覺知的特質為何？

很不易了解，如依後一解釋，則桑氏似主我們可以於時空之外直覺一些本質。桑氏之所以持此

一說法或許以為我們對一些和音如：do-mi-sol，或一數學方程式如：5＋7＝12，可以不

在時空形式之內被直覺到。但事實上，這樣了解是錯誤的。因為和音的音調需要有持續的時間

以表現，而數學方程式亦需要寫出來，即符示化於空間之中。故它們皆需要憑藉時間或空間而

表現，而不能全離時空而自存。我們對此一了解或仍有爭議，而說音調或數的關係可不表現於

任何的時空之中，超所有時空的形式而自存。正如具體事物的個別性不參與任何特質而被抽象

地了解一樣。但即使我們承認此點，為我們所覺知到的音調與數學方程式皆存在於時空形式之

下則是不能否認的。

具體的事物不可以離時空而自存。為事物所依而表現的時間即必有其持續性而可以連結起

來而成為一無限延伸的「物理的時間」（physical time）形式⑳，而且此「物理的時間」形

式即為一種自然律，所有具體的存在於物皆存在於此自然律中，亦即皆參與此一自然律。我們由

此參與的持續表現而說過去、現在、與未來。我們對整個未來是如何的不能先有所知，但我們

相信有未來，我們並可確定地說公元後三千年、一萬年、或十萬年等。

具體的事物不可以離時間而存在是確定的。但其是否可以離空間而存在似有疑問。因為我

們好似可以有不屬於任何空間之內的事物。例如在我們專注於某一抽象思想，或欣賞某一樂曲

時，我們可以不知身在何處，亦不問所欣賞的樂曲是由何處而來。因此我們以為雖然我們不能

離開時間而對具體的事物有所知，但可以超出於空間之外而有所覺。被覺的聲音可以沒有空間

的屬性，而思想的表現亦不為空間所限。

依時間的持續性而有「物理的時間」的確定。由對空間廣濶性的經驗，我們亦可將所經驗的

各別空間組成一整體的「物理的空間」（physical space）形式㉑。物理的空間形式作爲節制具體存在於事物的普遍律亦正如物理的時間形式一樣。由觀察上所見空間形式對存在事物普遍的節制，我們可推論它不僅節制可觀察及的事物，而亦要節制一切在觀察之外的具體存在事物。

由此一意義上說，有關是否有離空間的具體事物而自存的問題，則即使我們承認當我們專注於某一思想，或專心於聆聽某一樂曲時，我們有忘記或不知覺到我們身在何處或一樂曲由何處而來的情景，但我們的思想或樂曲仍有它們呈現的空間所在，只是不爲我們所注意及罷了。

由以上的分辨，我們可以說所有具體的存在於事物，不論其參與其他何種的形式而存在，皆參與自然的時空的律則，亦即皆存在於時空之中。由於此一事實，亦即由於物理的時空律則的普遍在性，具體的事物不能與時空分離，有些形式論者即主物理的時空與「基本的個別性」爲同一的東西，亦即是將超越而內在的形式論的第二個範疇與物理的時空合而爲一。此一主張雖有其一定的理據。但從形式論的根源的譬喻的觀點上說，此是不合法的。此並是一種不必要的對範疇的混淆。此會使形式論的形式失去了它的獨立的意義，而破壞了整個形式論的特性而趨於與後面第六章和第七章所要介述的機械論混合爲一。故形式論者應注意此一破壞性，而要以經驗爲依據，而以所有具體的存在於事物皆實際上參與物理的時空律則以成爲具體的存在。亦即以每一具體的存在於事物皆存在於一定的時間上與一定的空間中，而不因時空常與事物並存而將其與事物的「基本的個別性」合而爲一。

七、因果關係的分辨

一切具體的存在事物皆存在於時空之中。若有具體的存在事物不受時空的節制，它即可自由活動超出因果律則之外，而為偶然的存在事物。就形式論來說，此是可能的。但形式論者不強調此一偶然性，而是重視事物在時空上的因果關係。依照形式論的了解，因果律即是事物在時空上參與形式、模式、或律則的決定。萬有引力律（the law of gravitation）對一鉛球由高處下墜至地面上的解釋正可以對此一意義加以說明。

地球上存有眾多的具體存在物和所說的鉛球。它們被時空分隔而分別存在。它們參與萬有引力律。萬物依萬有引力律而相互吸引。故鉛球以一特殊的速度向地球作直線的移動。隨着鉛球移動而出現新的時空關係——新的日子——距離與速度——亦受此律則節制而使鉛球下墜的每一階段都相應於所說的一定的時空關係中。鉛球的一切變動依從此律則而得以決定。

因此所謂因果律實為：(1)具有某些特質的一個（或一組）基本的個別性，(2)這些具有某些特質的其他基本個別性在律則上所產生的基本個別性在時空中參與一律則，(3)具有其他特質的其他基本個別性對具有某種特質的基本個別性在律則中引生的決定；而所說的律則即成為由具有某些特質的一個或一組基本的個別性到具有其他特質的另一組的基本的個別性的通道。由此通道而一組的特質與其他組的特質互相影響。

所說的律則是屬於自然事物的真正結構。但它們不可以與任何特殊的事物合而為一，亦不可與任何一組事物合而為一。因為一個律則不是一個事物的基本個別性，亦不是整個具體存在的特殊物（即不是例證此律則的一個個體存在物），亦不是一群具體的存在特殊物（即不是一個類）。一律則是一形式，它的位份是屬於超越而內在的形式論的第一個範疇。

依照柏拉圖的哲學觀點說，律則即使永遠未爲其體的存在物所例證，仍然是潛存着。但由

亞里士多德的哲學觀點說，相對於物體的個別性而說形式時，律則是潛存着，但所說的潛存的

律則不能離表現它的事物而獨自存在。形式論的世界的假設並不主律則與具體的物質結合爲一。

此一見解不因柏拉圖的事物說與亞里士多德的哲學有所不同而不同。對一個形式論者來說，一個

律則即是一個形式。這是形式論與後面所要介述的機械論基本不同的所在。

一個律則可藉着特殊化的特質而參與存在事物。此參與存在事物的律則並與存在物參與其

他的自然律而受其規限。鉛球在下墜之前被握在手裡的情形即表明了此一規限的要義。就形式

論者的了解說，參與事物的律則雖然受到其他的律則的規限，但仍不失其自身的作用，如鉛球

所有的重量或向下墜的壓力即爲其自身作用的繼續表現。但它要受另外的律則的干涉。其之所

以要受另外的律則的干涉，因鉛球參與另外的律則，例如衝擊律（the law of impact）。

鉛球是一個固體。因此它參與衝擊律。由於此參與而可有鉛球與執持鉛球的手的肌肉與骨格的

緊張表現。

存在物參與自然律則所產生律則的相互干涉爲形式論所要說明的自然現象。此一現象除了

以上的分辨外，更可以以環繞太陽旋轉的行星軌道爲例，或以橡樹的生長歷程爲例去說明。在

環繞太陽旋轉的行星軌道中，萬有引力律是要以直線的加速度吸引某一行星到太陽上去的。

但慣性定律（inertial law）則要以直線的慣常的速度引此行星到太空外去。所說的被吸引

的行星爲一物體，在一定的時空中。所說的二律皆爲此一行星物體所參與。結果是此一行星物

體在此兩種律則的吸引中而產生了衝突。衝突的結果是出現了在兩直線運行的歪曲而成橢圓形

的旋轉。故橢圓形的旋轉是由所說的二律與行星所成的多種關係而來的決定，亦即是橢圓的出

現是由慣性力與萬有引力對所說的行星物體所產生的吸引的結果。

橡樹有一定的模式。植物學者或園藝學家都能對橡樹生長的形式有了解。一棵橡樹如得到適當的泥土、水份、陽光、肥料，並不受到其他植物的干擾，或昆蟲的侵害，則它的正常的模式將會於生長中呈現，它的律則亦將於此具體的存在於橡樹中表現出來。此正如萬有引力律要在鉛球的下墜中表現出來一樣。但如果所說的橡樹被種植於貧瘠的土壤中，或被種植於受狂風吹襲的山端上，或被種植於密集的森林中，則它正常的生長將受到歪曲。此亦正如上說的行星在萬有引力軌道上運行時受到歪曲一樣。因此所說的歪曲正是橡樹所參與的其他律則所表現的力量與其自己生長律的力量所發生衝突的結果。

同樣的歪曲將以同樣的理由發生於人和其他動物或人類社會的模式中。人或人類社會的模式為形式論的倫理學的依據。在具體的存在上，或在較複雜的存在於形式中。人或人類社會的模式表現為人或人類社會的平衡。如此平衡有歪曲即帶來人或人類社會的不安。為要保持平衡而去除不安，故柏拉圖要建立理想國，亞里士多德要尋求中庸之道。近代的人要由各種模式的文化，或由一文化所表現的不同的階段上以尋求出一完全的社會結構，亦如柏拉圖、亞里士多德二氏要尋求一平衡的社會模式一樣。三者皆預設了形式論的範疇。因為沒有其他世界的假設以模式為律則而此律則決定具體存在的表現歷程。

八、形式論的眞理說

形式論的眞理說是符合說（The correspondence theory of truth）。依照此說，所

謂真理是二物中的一物與另一物相似，如第一物為某物則第二物即相似於某物。或象物中的一物與其他物的相似，如某物與某箱中的蘋果相似則它亦為蘋果。

由物與物的相似而說其真為符合說的原初意義。但在知識的建立上則不限於此一原初的用法。而所說的相似並不是指謂者與被指謂者的完全相似，而只是與它們的形式相符合。例如我們說一畫像真是某人，亦只說它刻畫出某人的形式，而並不是說所描述的與被描述的各方面都符合。

以指謂者符合被指謂者的形式即為被指謂者，則被指謂者對指謂者的描述可僅為符號的描述，而符號更可由象物符而發展為會意符。後者可為純語言或數學方程式的描述。因此被描述的對象即物與描述的表達方式大不相同。但雖然如此，形式論者以為人不要因此而以為語言或數學方程式的描述沒有真正表達被描述的對象。一個可以由一張圖畫所描述的對象所表達其與對象的相似性，亦可以由一句句子或一個數學方程式的描述去表達。如果有人以為一個畫於紙上的圓圈與所畫的圓球的形狀相似，但不承認對此球的描述的一個數學方程式與此球的相似，此會使一位形式論者感到困擾。但此「以為」是不能成立的，因為一個方程式或一句句子雖不是一種直接的描述，我們通過了對文字或符號的約定使用是可以用之以代替圖畫的描述的。

由以上的分辨我們可以見到形式論者對描述雖有不同的說法，但符合真理說實為一種對對象具有某種程度的相似性的相似。在大小黑白不同的限度內，一幅炭畫確實地表現了被畫者的形狀，在所說的限度內，炭畫的形狀正是人的形狀。此一以炭畫對人的形狀的描述亦可為文字或其他的符號所代替，而同可表現描述與被描述者的相似。而以相似為真的確定則為依於形式論對事物相同性的分析而建立的範疇所保證，亦即為對事物的特質、模式、或形式的確定而得到

保證。

描述者與被描述者的相似爲符合說的核心所在。但所說的相似則可以分別爲由於指涉的對象的不同而有歷史的眞理與科學的眞理的區別。前者是相應於「潛存」而有的對事物所依的模式與律則的描述。如果他發現所發生的事件有因果關係，他描述此關係內在於所描述的事件中而爲其一部份。他的興趣是事件的特質，而不是爲事件所例證的律則。

至於科學家的根本興趣是自然律。他之所以留心事件只因爲事件可以例證自然律。科學的歸納法是研究特殊事件的一種方法。科學家藉此方法以證明爲事件所例證的律則。形式論者承認有兩種歸納法：(1)對在經驗上表現爲一致性的事物的描述，(2)對產生自然律則的描述❷。第一種僅是陳述對具體存在事物所觀察到的互相關聯，而並不說明此互相關聯爲什麼會恆常地如此發生。第二種是對眞正自然律則的陳述。此陳述被視爲對某種互相關聯之所以恆常地如此發生的解釋。

在經驗上可見到很多恆常地表現着互相關連的事例。例如由地球上所見到的晝夜相從，月光的圓缺相隨，海潮的漲退依時等。這些都是可靠的恆常現象。我們可以對它們加以預測而不知其爲什麼如此。但當我們發現了萬有引力律、慣性定律、傳播律（The law of propaga-tion）、與反射律（the law of reflection of light）之後，我們了解到那恆常現象之所以如此表現的理由。那恆常現象的表現被了解爲基本的物理定律的例證。

在經驗上表現爲一致性的事物的描述是居於歷史的陳述與科學的陳述之間。以其作爲對所

觀察到的具體存在事物的陳述，此即為一種事實的陳述。此陳述即本質地為歷史的。但如以其作為對所觀察到的事實的恆常性的表現的陳述則有科學的涵義，由於其不能表示出那恆常性的表現之所以如此表現的理由，故其不完全是科學的。

從一個形式論者的觀點上說，經驗的一致性的陳述只是與真理有關的陳述。真理的全部涵義是陳述與所發生的事實確切地相符合；或陳述與所表現的律則相符合。因為如果我們知道事件的全部真相，我們應知那恆常性必然如此表現的律則為何。或相反地我們應知道所說的一致性不是必然的而只是歷史的偶合。此偶合錯誤地被普遍化，而並不能由之而作科學的預測。

如果大多數我們稱為科學知識的僅僅是對經驗一致性的描述，此可能是錯誤的。但此並不妨礙真正科學知識的獲得。因為當科學向前發展時對自然恆常性的描述會變為更可靠，而成為自然的必然性。故繼續接近可靠性可視為一科學原則。此即由一系列對自然的恆常性的描述而繼續地接近到自然所潛存的實際必然律，此一原則是正確的，因我們可以由科學的發展史上得到證明。

註釋

❶ S. C. Pepper, *World Hypotheses*, p. 191.

❷ Ibid.

❸ Ibid., p. 151.

❹ Ibid., p. 162.

❺ Ibid., p. 154.

❻ 有關《類型論》的要義請參看羅素著的 *"The Principles of Mathematics"* Appendix B, Cambridge, 1903. 作者在將要出版的《西方形而上學中的超越論與存有論》討論羅素的存有論時亦有介紹。

❼ 裴柏在此隱涵了解者可客觀化所了解的對象而常超越於其上的意義。

❽ 請參看上章，「五」。

❾ 邏輯上所說的全類是由 A ＋ ～ A ＝ 1 而成，而不是由個體的個別性參與一共同的特質而建立。

❿ Ibid., p. 161.

⓫ Ibid., p. 163.

⓬ Ibid., pp. 166-167.

⓭ Ibid., p. 167.

⓮ 我們對於所說的模式參與特質的第二層次的參與或不容易了解。但我們如果想模式不僅可以作為抽象的了解對象，而亦可為表現於某一形狀或某一顏色的特質上而被了解的對象，即可見模式參與特質而成為了解的對象的意義。

⓯ Ibid., ❶, p. 170.

⑯ Ibid.

⑰ Ibid.

⑱ Ibid., p. 169.

⑲ Ibid., p. 171.

⑳ Ibid., p. 172.

㉑ Ibid., p. 173.

㉒ Ibid., p. 176.

㉓ Ibid., p. 182.

第六章 機械論（上）

一、小引

機械論亦爲依根源的譬喻而建立的一個相對地適切的世界的假設的理論。它所依以建立的根源的譬喻不同於形式論的根源的譬喻。因此它由所依的根源的譬喻而引伸出來的範疇對世界作結構性或系統性的說明亦不同於形式論。但由根源的譬喻而引伸出範疇再以所引伸的範疇去說明世界的程序則二者相同。

依裴柏的了解，西方哲學中的德莫克脫斯（Democritus）、留克里撒斯（Lucre-tius）、伽利略（Galileo）、笛卡兒（Descartes）、霍布斯（Hobbes）、洛克（Locke）、巴克萊（Berkeley）、休謨（Hume）、黎昌巴（Reichenbach）等人的哲學皆爲機械論❶。此諸人的哲學皆由同一的根源的譬喻而建立。在後面我們將分別爲：(1)機械論的根源的譬喻與範疇的確定；(2)分立的機械論（discrete mechanism）及其與統一的機械論（con-solidated mechanism）的不同；(3)分立的機械論對世界的了解；(4)統一的機械論對世界的了解；(5)第二組範疇的意義及其與第一組範疇的連結問題；(6)機械論的眞理說等六節去介述機械論對世界作結構性或系統性的說明，及其眞理說的涵義。所說的六節將分別爲上下兩章，(1)至(3)及本「小引」爲上章，(4)至(6)爲下章。

二、機械論的根源的譬喻與範疇的確定

機械論的根源的譬喻是機器。它可以是一個手錶，或一個發電機，或一條槓桿，或其他同類的東西❷。傳統的機械論皆由此一根源的譬喻而建立。但物理學發展至近代，對於物質的理解已由槓桿的觀點而轉移爲電力的觀點，對物體究極的描述亦由槓桿式而轉移爲電磁場式。此一轉變使人對物理世界開展了新的了解。但依裴柏的了解，機械論的基本觀念並沒有因此而改變。它仍是以機器爲根源的譬喻由之而引伸出一套範疇以解釋世界。因機械論的世界理論與機械的物質論並不同。槓桿的物質論與電磁場的原理以了解世界的不同，機械論亦相應而分別發展爲分立的機械論與統一的機械論。前者以原子論（Atomism）的理論爲代表，後者則以電磁場（electromagnetic field）的理論爲代表。

分立與統一的不同是基於對物質的不同了解而來的分別。但依世界的假設的觀點上說，二者同可由可肯定的範疇而得到解釋。此亦爲二者之所以同視爲機械論的原故。但機械論除由所依據的根源的譬喻而引伸出另一組範疇而對世界作機械式的了解外，亦可以依根源的譬喻而引伸出另一組範疇而對世界作感官性的了解。此二了解如何結合，爲機械論自身內在須謀求解答的問題。此一問題在後面第六節將談及。

裴柏以槓桿作爲說明機械論的根源的譬喻。因由槓桿較爲容易說明由機械所表現的關係的涵義。

槓桿為將一條桿置於一支撐物之上的簡單機器。我們對此一機器的作用的了解，可以用力壓低桿的一端以竪起桿的另一端。此一活動涵着嚴密的量化的因果關係。此關係由桿的兩端與桿的支撐點的距離為何而確定；由對桿的長度而計算出來。桿的兩端如何得到平衡的表現，一端與另一端的輕重關係為何，皆可以由支撐點與兩端的距離與兩端所持有的各別重量為何而確定。此一確定為量化的。故由槓桿的作用可以表現出一簡單的動力因的結構關係。此關係表明了機械論的基本範疇的涵義。裴柏即由此一表現而先討論分立的機械論的意義，再進而過渡到對統一的機械論的說明。

機械論者由槓桿引伸出兩組不同的範疇。第一組稱為主要的範疇：(1)場所，(2)第一性質，(3)結合第一性質於場所中的律則（第一律則）；第二組稱次要的範疇：(4)第二性質，(5)聯結第二性質與主要範疇的原則，(6)規範第二性質的律則（第二律則）❸。

(1)場所：場所之所以成為機械論的第一個範疇，因為它是構成槓桿所不可少的成份。若以世上萬物皆為機械的存在物，則構成槓桿的場所即為了解萬物的基本範疇。槓桿是定於某一位置的桿與支撐桿的架座的組合。桿可以長短不同，但當其成為某一特定的槓桿的構成部份時，其即有確定的長度。若其長度為三公尺或三百公分，用力壓低的一端所在處的力點為零，另一端的盡頭處的重點即為三百公分。若支撐點的所在處的支點為距離零端的三份二，則支點的所在位置即為二百公分點。支撐點所在的位置確定後，槓桿的功用為何，亦即其力點與重點的關係為何亦得而確定。作為槓桿所確定的位置即為場所。

(2)第一性質：第一性質是指槓桿的物質性。此物質性不是指物的色澤、紋路、香味等，而是指物的重量。物的重量全由計量器衡定，以確定量與量的關係，而不問表示此重量的物為

何。

(3) 第一律則：第一律則是指由槓桿所表現的規律；是槓桿的機能的作用。此作用表現了槓桿或任何的機器在活動時各部份的互相關係。例如，如一個槓桿的結構如我們在前面所說的槓桿的長爲三百公分，它的支點是距力點二百公分，則只需要二十五公斤即可舉起在重點上的五十公斤重量。由此可見槓桿的支點、力點、重點的相互關係是表現了一定的規律的，而第一律則正是表示機器結構的機能作用。

(4) 第二性質：第二性質是指構成槓桿的物質的色澤、紋路、香味等。此與槓桿的機能表現無關。但它們是屬於槓桿的一部份，而在槓桿之中。它們是感覺的對象，槓桿藉它們而被感覺到。

(5) 聯結第二性質與主要範疇的原則：聯結第二性質與主要範疇的原則是指第二性質與前述構成槓桿的主要範疇相聯結的原則。第二性質與槓桿的機能無直接的關係。但一個槓桿不能沒有第二性質，而二者的關係似有某些原則可說。

(6) 第二律則：第二律則是指第二律則。一個細心地描述一個機器的所有性質的人，會注意以上爲對以槓桿爲根源的譬喻所引伸出來的兩組範疇作簡略的說明。依照裝柏的了解，機械論者以世界爲一機器，故對世界的了解即爲由一機器，例如槓桿所引伸出來的範疇去對世界作結構性或系統性的說明。此一說明是否適當即在它是否可以由所引伸出來的範疇對所有存在的事物作解釋。依照機械論者的了解，任何存在的事物都

第二性質中亦可能有第二律則。故在第二性質中有第一律則。如前面所指出的，在第一性質中有第一

依上述的範疇而存在，故任何世界現象都可以由上述的範疇而加以說明。

機械論者以世界是一機器的觀點是一致的。但機械的涵義為何則可以因人的了解不同而不同。我們可以對一機器作分立的了解，亦可以作統一的了解。以世界為一分立的機械表現與以之為一統一的機械表現，二者雖同為機械的，但彼此很不相同。但雖不相同因同為機械的故可以由依一機器而引伸出來的範疇去說明。在後面我們先介述分立的機械論的一般意義，及其與統一的機械論的不同。

三、分立的機械論及其與統一的機械論的不同

從分立的機械論的觀點上說，自然宇宙的結構只是一種鬆弛而外在地相關連的結構。故時間與空間彼此分立，第一性質亦與場所分立。每一第一性質亦可以與其他的第一性質分立，或每一原子均有其自己的獨立性而與其他的原子分立；每一自然律如慣性律或反作用律亦與其他的自然律分立，而更與場所及分佈於場所中的原子不同。

分立的機械論者以為時間可以被確定地描述而不需要與空間連結；一個空間點可以確定地被描述而不需要與任何其他的空間點連結。一個原子的形狀、組織、質量可以確定地被描述而不需要涉及時間與地點；一個原子D不需要關連到任何其他的原子上去，自然律D亦不需要關連到遵守自然律的原子上去；反過來說亦是一樣，原子亦不需要關連到自然律上去。此是一種分立的機械論的宇宙觀。在此一理論的宇宙中，任何東西可以彼此不同，因為任何東西可以獨立於其他的東西之外。如果此一原子在另一時空中出現，它即可以不為另一原子所撞擊。並且

為什麼會如此沒有必然的理由可說。又如物體所受的不是慣性律而是加速律（the law of acceleration）或減速律（the law of deceleration），原子的撞擊亦可不發生[4]。此亦不是不可能的。但由於此一原子事實上是在此一空間和此一時間中出現，而遵守着慣性律，所以不可避免地產生了撞擊。因此在分立的機械論中同存有偶然與必然彼此不同的奇異現象。但此一現象不是不可以理解的。我們可以說原子、時空與律之所以如此分立是偶然的。但當其如此分立之後其彼此間的關係即成為事實上不可避免的必然。因此，此一偶然與必然的奇異對立即歸到宇宙的根本結構上去。宇宙之所以如此結構是偶然而非理性的，但當其表現為如此結構之後即有必然而不可避免的事實關係。統一的機械論對所說的偶然與必然的分別，沒有不同的說法。但其對於所說的必然性則有不同的了解。因它不由分立中去說每一事件的必然性與不可避免性，而是以分立的機械論所說的分立不是真的分立，而是彼此關連。因此在統一的機械論中每一事件都與其他的事件彼此相關而相互決定而不是彼此分立。

四、分立的機械論對世界的了解

此即是以第一組範疇去對世界作分立的解釋。

(1)塲所：機械論者以宇宙間所有的事物不能離塲所而說，故塲所為機械論的第一個範疇。機械論者以事物之定位於一定空間之中為事物之得稱為真實之所在；以凡是未能定位的東西其意義為不明確的。此並不是說一東西的真實只在於它的定位，而與其他的範疇無關，而只是說任何東西如果它的位置不能確定則不可以被認為真實。此亦即是說機械論者以事物的定位為使

事物成爲眞實的必要條件而不是充足條件。

由場所一範疇而說定以確定事物的眞實爲機械論與形式論對於存在的了解一主要不同所在。形式論者以超越的形式亦爲眞實的存在。但機械論者則以眞實的存在只限於特殊的事物上。而此所說的特殊事物與形式論的基本的個別性亦不同，因它是結合了時空在一起的特殊事物。形式論的基本的形式亦是超越而內在的形式論的第二個範疇。此被結合的時空則不是所說的形式。因形式論的形式是超越而內在的的形式論的第一個範疇。

眞實的存在定位於時空上亦與形式論的形式內在於質料的意義不同。因形式論的形式如前面所已說的可以不內在於質料而獨立存在，此爲事物所定的時空則不可以獨立自存。故我們不可以將機械論的時空與形式論的形式相等同，如將時空等同於形式即有使機械論解體而轉變爲形式論的危險。

早期的機械論者曾將場所與空間同一。空間被想成爲一立體而無限地向四面延伸的宇宙。場所即在此一無限的空間中。一物之成爲一物即表現於一特定的場所上。此爲物所表現的場所可分別爲點、線、途徑、或立體等。確定一物的特定場所是不易的事。我們或者以爲在房子的各物是個別而靜止地繼續佔有一單一的特殊場所。但事實上並不是如此。我們只要留心觀察地球與太陽的關係，即會發現到所謂靜止只是相對地靜止，事實上所說的各單一的特殊場所都在移動。那就是說它們在一段時間內所佔有的是一段場所，而不是單一的場所。但此一錯誤只是限於以事物僅佔一單一的場所上的錯誤，至於以事物皆在一定的時間上佔有一定的場所則是沒有錯的。

此正與前面所說不能離開事物的場所而說事物的存在的觀點相符。一物體所在的空間原先是被了解爲一無限的立體形式，亦即三度空間說或牛頓（Newton）

的絕對空間說。並以物體與其塲所的關係爲一種外在的關係。一物體所在的塲所沒有使該物體本身產生任何的改變。由此而認爲塲所自身在地亦沒有彼此的不同。因此，即使有廣濶的塲所在宇宙中某一區域上消失亦不會使在宇宙中的其他塲所受到影響，而所損失的塲所僅被設想爲不會再有物體在該失去了的塲所上顯現。

相應於絕對的空間說而有絕對的時間說。絕對的時間說視時間爲外在地連結所有日子在一起的一無限直線形式。此直線的時間與立體的空間分立爲二。故空間被了解爲如在時間之流上航行的船。我們可以在不同的時間上佔有同一的空間塲所。空間雖然要由一個時間轉移到另一時間上，它是獨立於時間之外而不變的。

但正當上述的時空概念廣泛地被描述時，一新的概念隨之而出現。在此一新的概念了解中，時間不再被看成爲獨立於空間之外，而是以之爲塲所的一部份，爲塲所的第四度，即所謂第四度空間說；亦即是說一個塲所不僅由所說的三度空間而建立，而是包括了時間在內。此一新的了解很重要。因它將時空結合在一起。存在的特殊事物成爲在時空中的特殊事物，在一定的時間與空間之上，而不僅在空間之中。此一了解正是一種由分立的機械觀而轉向統一的機械觀的了解。

(2)　第一性質：傳統的分立的機械論即是原子論，亦即一主張有無數的基本的微粒或原子分佈於空間之中的理論。微粒之所以說爲基本的，因爲它們爲物質中最微小的東西。物質要最後分解爲此等微粒。現代的物理哲學家曾從現代科學的觀點去論證此等微粒的真實性❺。

物質要最後分解爲此等微粒。現代的物理哲學家曾從現代科學的觀點去論證此等微粒的真實性❺。在傳統的原子論中原子或微粒被假定爲永恆而不可毀滅的。故在時間的軌道上由無限的過去存在至無限的未來。但從機械論的觀點上說，此一假定是不必要的。因機械論的範疇並不要

求此一假定。最近曾有一些電子學說要假定究竟的微粒活動的軌道是不連續的。電子在原子核中的活動被描述爲由一軌道跳躍到另一軌道而不需經過中間的空間塲所。電子的內在性質不受跳躍的影響❻。此一了解與傳統的原子論的假定不同。但此一不同並不越出機械論的範疇架構。相反地，而可使人對究竟的物質微粒的了解獲得更大的自由。由此我們更可以說只要原子與塲所的結構相合，它在其塲所中突然顯現與突然消失亦不違背機械論的原理，而是由分立的觀點上去了解原子在其塲所上可說明的。我們如不同意此一說法，並不表示此一說法有問題，而是我們未由分立的觀點上去了解此問題。

原子或基本的微粒與塲所有質的不同。如果沒有此不同，於塲所的物質與塲所即完全不能分辨。每一塲所將會與其他的塲所混合。宇宙將成爲虛無的宇宙，即時空的軌道亦不能說。如果只有物質而沒有塲所爲物質所展現，亦不能有各別的個體物。故塲所與物質相互補足而彼此對立。設定其中的一個即要設定其中的另一個，以此二者去描述和解釋我們所在的世界。

傳統上以物的第一性質爲物的大小、形狀、移動、堅固性、質量、數。此一了解開始自古希臘原子論者（Atomists）德謨克里脫斯經留克里撒斯而至伽利略，繼而爲文藝復興時期及近代的科學家與自然主義的哲學家所承傳。他們以這些第一性質爲存在物所具有。並且除了依照某些基本的物理律則而改變其所在的位置外，它們沒有其他的改變而繼續存在。由機械的物質論改變爲電子的物質論之後，亦只以電量去代替質量或加電量於質量之上，及隨着第一性質的詳細應用而來的一些修改。此等修改進一步發展即促使分立的機械論走上統一的機械論的道路，而並不危害及已確定了的範疇。

以上所說爲傳統上所肯定的第一性質表現了很特殊的現象。即除了質量（或重量）之外，

其他的都是有關形體的性質，亦即是與場所相連結的性質。例如大小是表現不同的體別，形狀是表現不同的結構，移動是表現變位，堅固性是去除其內在的分別，數是對不同的場所的分辨。它們並不是完全離開場所而另具有其自身的獨特性。因此以它們是單一而分立的概念是有問題的。

以電量代替質量對第一性質的分辨了解的情形仍是一樣。有些第一性質與場所相連結，有些則不同於場所。從機械論的了解上說，到底有多少性質與那些性質可被視為第一性質可有不同的說法，但不論第一性質的數量如何，被接受為第一性質的諸性質仍將可分為兩組：(1)與場所相結合的性質，(2)不同於場所而有分別性的性質。

(1)所說的性質與場所是互相結合的，但(2)所說的分別性是否真正的分立呢？就前面了解所及的確是如此。質量與電量或任何其他的的分別的性質都是分立的。一粒原子有一定的質量和其他的性質如親和力原子價，這些性質並不內在於它們的場所中而只是出現於它們的場所上；它們不是場所的結構特質，故不與場所結合。電子與電力亦是一樣。在它們呈現於場所時雖然歸到場所的結構上去，但與場所的結構性質彼此不同，互相分立。

從前面所已論及的說，分立的機械論的觀點是可以成立的，但在進而討論第三個範疇時，此一觀點是否仍可說則似是一問題。

(3) 結合第一性質於場所的律則：從機械論的了解上說，律則是機器的一特徵。機器之所以如此地引起我們的注意，之所以能成為一世界的假設的根源的譬喻，正在於由律則而來的有效的說明使然。

從來好似沒有人嘗試建立一種沒有律則的機械論。相反地，以在時空場所上的結構為嚴格

地完全被決定的概念成為機械論的普遍的見解。在現代尤其是如此。這正是此一理論最吸引人的地方，而對科學家的吸引更大。他們的信念是任何在物理世界中所發生的事都有它的律則。

因此他們不斷地從事律則的探求。形式論沒有給人如此的信念。即使是一個機械論者，如果他不覺悟到他所持的理論有統一性的趨向，亦將缺少此一信念。惟有一個完全地統一的機械論才是一個以宇宙為完全內在地決定而機械化的宇宙。這正是機械論所肯定的範疇所具有的趨向。

此一趨向是有它的理論上的根據的。但我們如只從表面上看，則此一趨向似是不必要的。因為我們或會以為充塞宇宙中的每一時空場所不必為嚴格地被決定的場所。為什麼在某些時空之中不可以出現一些偶然的事物或混沌不定呢？早期的機械論者即以為在早期的宇宙中確有混沌的事。秩序與律則是因某一偶然的機會由混沌中出現。

混沌與偶然並可不限於早期。即在現今為什麼某些最後的自然律則不可以有伸縮性，而必需為必然的決定律呢？為什麼不可以是一種有偶然性的統計律（statistical laws）呢'?'表面地說，我們好似沒有理由說為機械論者所了解的宇宙的究竟律則不可以是統計律，或以我們所在的宇宙只是部份決定的。但從基本上說，後一說法確有問題。故機械論的物理學家與哲學家要持守完全決定論的信念。

拉普拉斯（Laplace）即是主張完全決定的宇宙的著名的天文學家和數學家。他以為如果我們知道任何時期整個宇宙的物質的結構和物質定律，或者說如果我們知道兩個不同時期的物質結構和由之而推出由一個時期的物質結構過渡到另一個時期的物質結構的律則，則我們即可以推定任何時期的物質結構。他在他的《世界的系統》（Exposition du systeme du monde）第三冊開始時說：

由天上和地下一個連續地繼承了另一個的無限殊異的現象中，我們了解到為物質所跟隨而移動的一些普遍的律則。自然界的每一東西都服從它們；每一東西必然地由它們而引生，正如四時不斷地在交替。好似被風偶然吹襲而成的微塵中的曲線，其受律則的控制正如行星在軌道上旋轉所受到的控制一樣。❼

此是以宇宙為完全系統化的說法。此一說法與牛頓的運動三律及萬有引力律的了解相應。牛頓所發現的律則正是‧駕御所有物質，而自然界的每一東西都服從它們的律則。拉氏的完全決定說亦正是依牛頓的了解而說的。牛頓的運動三律：

運動第一律（慣性定律）：如果不是受外力迫使，則一切物體靜者恆靜，動者恆依直線方向等速移動，永無止境。

第二律（力的定律）：物體動量對時間的變化率與所受力成正比；動量變化的方向與所受力的方向相同。

第三律：有作用力必有反作用力，其大小相同，方向相反。❽

牛頓的萬有引力律：

兩物體的相吸與它們的質量成正比例，與它們的距離成反比例，乘以恆常的萬有引力❾。

由此等律則所描述的宇宙是決定的宇宙。其與場所及第一性質共構成機械論的宇宙觀。律則構成了機械的宇宙動態的因素。場所自身是靜態而無分別的。即使在場所上有質量，它們缺少效力。

自然動態的結構由律則而來。律則將質量結合起來引使它們由一種結構到另一種結構。

機械論以場所，第一性質與律則去說明自然宇宙。但由分立的機械論的觀點上說，除了確定律則為組成機械論的基本的範疇之外，尚要了解其與其他的範疇的關係。此正如拉普拉斯所說的：「讓我知道於任何時間上在空間場所中的質量結構，和在這些質量上選作的律則，我將說明任何其他的時間（過去或現在）場所中的質量的結構⑩。」依此一說法律則是分立而與場所中的質量分離的。它們在場所之外而對場所與質量產生規限的作用。

但如律則真的與場所與質量分離而在其外，而涵有潛存的意義，則律則將成為一種形式，而潛存的分離亦將不限於律則。因為由分立的觀點上去了解場所與第一性質，二者皆可被了解為彼此對立而分離，而各別地潛存着而為律則所結合與顯現，但若如此地了解，則機械論即要轉變而為形式論，機械論的範疇功用將要消失而為形式論的範疇所代替。如我們在前面所已提及的，此是形式論對機械論的一種威脅。

要免除所說的威脅，第一性質與律則即要緊密地與時空場所相結合，只以在一定的時空之上的事物為真，惟有特殊者存在。此一原則即永不能放棄。若放棄此一原則機械論即要解體。因此分立的機械論是有問題的。其問題不僅要使律則變為形式，而其以律則、場所，第一性質彼此轉變的說法亦有問題。故機械論除了以律則與場所及第一性質相結合之外，對相似的了解亦要由物體的基本成份與物體的結構而說其相似。一滴水與另一滴水相似因為二者都是由同樣的

氫氧原子所結合。二者既同為氫二氧一的結合物故其結構相似。此一以水滴的相似而歸到原子的

相似與原子結構的相似即為將相似歸到基本成份上去的了解。人若問原子的相似與原子結構的

相似又怎樣說呢？對此一問題的回答，最後是要歸到時空的場所的究極的結構上去的。機械論

者對抽象與形式是不重視的。他們重視具體，要立足於時空場所之具體上。他們不信任任何不

是具體的東西。但要達到此一目的他們必需結合他們的範疇。第一性質與律則必需成為時空場

所的獨特結構。並與其密切連結正如空間之長潤厚各度密切連結在一起一樣。一物與一物之相

似因此而歸到場所的結構中，而不要遊離到潛存的形式上。

我們如了解以上的說法，即見到機械論者對自然的了解不能有其他的選擇。因此從究竟的

觀點上說，統計律亦不能成為自然律，而只是人所杜撰出來的律則。它在某一程度上亦能說明

自然間的關係，但它並不是自然律。

第七章　機械論（下）

五、統一的機械論對世界的了解

分立的機械論向着統一的機械論發展。以世界爲如一組組分散的星群，或如彼此不相黏結的泥團的圖像轉而爲以世界爲如一個具有錯綜複雜的內在地相結合的結晶體的圖像所代替。時空的軌道代替了分立的微粒，宇宙的幾何學（cosmic geometry）代替了分立的機械律（discrete laws of mechanics）。由宇宙的幾何學所展示的宇宙向我們表現了時空整體的獨特結構。

我們之所以對統一的機械論有更高的信念，因爲現代的科學正向此一方向穩步地發展。十八、九世紀的正宗科學理論是分立的機械論。但今日的科學理論則正環繞着統一的機械論開展。現代推動向統一機械論發展的主要動力是相對論（theory of relativity），因它對時空的場所有新的了解。它去除了以時間與空間彼此分立的想法，而使時間歸併到空間上去，場所由此而得以統一。

但最重要的是相對論的普遍理論。它結合了萬有引力場與時空場。萬有引力是質量亦即第一性質的現象。此現象表現爲萬有引力場。因此萬有引力律即與第一範疇亦即場所相結合。而此場所不再僅是時空場所，而是時空的萬有引力的場所，而使場所第一性質與律則相結合而成

統一的表現。此一表現對統一的機械論是甚為重要的，因它使統一的機械論由原來的純由思辨

的肯定，而進而得到了在物理學上最前進的理論支持。

又現代對電磁場（electromagnetic field）的使用亦使統一的機械論得到了進一步的證

據。作為物質的基本概念上說，電磁場與萬有引力場甚類似。電力的性質與磁力的性質均被收

歸到電磁場律上，而電磁場律則直接地在時空場上運作。因此一個電磁場不是別的而是電磁

力在時空場上的表現。由此一了解即有人嘗試將此一結合推進一步要將電磁場的律則消解到基

本的場所的幾何學上去。

由以上的了解，就已有的物理學證據來說，統一的機械論不只是一種想像，而已成為理解

自然世界最可信的理論。現代對電子、陽電子、中子等的了解與留克里撒斯對原子的了解已完

全不同。它們不是相對於場所而分立存在，而是被了解為時空場的結構模式。此模式可以依一

定的規律而加以符示。嚴格地說，在統一的機械論中亦沒有律則，而只有時空場所中的結構模

式，亦沒有第一性質，因為已被消解到場所律則上去，而律則則被消解到場所的結構上去。

由以上的了解，我們可以說普遍的東西已被消除而只有特殊。一切歸到特殊上去。此一特

殊即統一的時空萬有引力電磁場。此場可以不是完全無限的而仍有所限。但它是完全決定的。

拉普拉斯以世界為完全決定的想法，可以更充份地在此一理論上表現。在拉氏所了解的機械的

世界中，質量的結構和律則之間的關係是否完全是決定的仍有問題。但在統一的機械論的世界

中，律則與質量是場所自身的結構，而場所自身即是此一結構。由此一了解上說，前面所說過

的統計律在統一的機械論的世界中更沒有地位。它只可以被視為了解場所結構的一種方便符號，

而並不表現場所的根本性質。不論我們如何去了解它，場所的結構是確定的。一個機械論者如

不接受統一的機械觀，則只能接受分立的機械觀了。但分立的機械觀正向統一的方向發展。就機械論的觀點來說，統一說應是最適切的一種理論。但從對整個世界作解釋上說，它仍有欠缺。要補足此一欠缺便要靠着第二組範疇而來對世界的了解。它的應用範圍有限制。

六、第二組範疇的涵義及其與第一組範疇的連結問題

第二組範疇所要解釋的是所有不能為第一組範疇所解釋的性質。如前面所已提及的此組範疇亦有三個：(1)第二性質，(2)聯結第二性質與主要範疇的原則，(3)規範第二性質的律則（第二律則）⑪。

機械論發展得越精密即越遠離人對宇宙的一般性的了解。我們所了解及的廣濶的空間。持續的時間與所說的宇宙塲的時空結構並不一樣。對時空了解如有錯是常以鐘尺為準則去改正。進而可以以數學公式去衡定。但此均不是對世界作宇宙塲的了解。對時空如此，對第一性質如重量、質量等亦是如此。我們所經驗到的只是第二性質，依此去推測宇宙的機械結構。

所說的機械結構與第二組範疇中聯結第二性質與主要的範疇的原則所要解答的。此一範疇在近來對「突現」（emergence）的了解上受到了很大的注意。第一性質與第二性質到底如何聯結起來的呢？傳統上對此有三種不同的理論：(1)同一說，(2)因果關係說，(3)相互的關係說⑫。現在雖然仍有人相信同一說，但此一說法很容易被排斥。因為我們絕不能說顏色或聲音即是電磁或空氣的震動，亦不即是人的神經中樞的活動。它們與電磁或空氣的震動或人的神經中樞的活動並不相同，而不能將前者歸化到後者上去。因果關係說亦要被排

斥。因為我們很難說明第一組範疇與第二性質的有效的因果關係。電磁場律中的運動律（the laws of motion）對質量與電荷是有所說明的。但此一說明並不能應用到顏色或聲音上。(1)

與(2)既被排斥，剩下來的便只有(3)相互的關係說了。此一說法的大要如下：當我們看到某一結構的物體呈現出來某些相狀的，此等相狀並不能歸到物體的性質上去，亦不能歸到結構的性質上去，而只能以所呈現出來的相狀時一相狀，用以狀述此一相互關聯的呈現。

所說的第二種性質在自然中到底可以伸展多遠是一不容易確定的事。它們可能伸展很遠。此一信念已由層級的突現理論（the theories of levels of emergence）所顯示的得以證明。為我們感覺到的顏色或聲音與第一性質中的物體的結構其間差異如此之大，好似可以容許很多中間的層級不斷地突現出第二性質。因此我們由最初的電子、陽電子、中子等過到原子、分子、晶體、氨基酸、細胞、體素、有機體，在每一層級中新的性質好似突然顯現。新突現的性質不能歸化到低層級的結構性質上。前者亦不能由後者所預測。不管突現的說法是否成立，但在人感官上出現了突現的感覺性質是沒有問題的。而此與人的某些神經的結構有相互的關係亦是可說的。

當物理學家、化學家、生理學家建立了以宇宙為一機器的理論後，感官的突現與宇宙的機器的關係的問題即成為近三世紀以來的哲學家所關注的重要問題。這是一個可怕的心物關係的問題。我們如何處理這些對宇宙的機器好似是多餘的感覺的性質呢？對此一問題的回答好似只能說：「無他，只要注意它們與物質的結構所成的相互關係即可。如果物質的結構能明確地被決定，而與它們相互關連的第二性質被注意，那末我們有可能預測那相互關連的第二性質的突現。於此外，仍能有什麼期待呢 ⑬？」但雖然如此，機械論仍是感到有困難。此一困難是不能有好

的解答的統一機械論中的分立問題。

　　由以上所討論及的我們已大致上見到第二性質的特徵，它是指感覺的性質，而所謂感覺的性質普通上是以其爲由心靈內省而得的知覺料；只有當它們在我們個人內心上出現時我們才能明顯地知覺到它們。在與別人交談時我們亦可以間接地知道別人亦各別地有此感覺的性質。我們甚至可以由其他動物的某種表現而推測牠們亦有類似的感覺性質。但對它們直接的證據則是個人私下的。

　　從心理學上說，我們見到機械論者對心理的了解亦有分立的與統一的不同。在分立的說法中，複合的心靈狀態被認爲可完全分析爲細微的各類心靈成素，如聲、色、香、味的感覺，各種觸覺及好惡等。這些成素常與化學的成素作類比的了解。因此此類心理學有時被稱爲「心靈的化學（mental chemistry）⑭。」聯想律（the laws of association）即有時被認爲心靈的律則，將所說的成素連結成爲複雜的心靈表現。如果此一說法是可接受的話，此所說的律則即當爲機械論的第六範疇。但聯想律常常被視爲生理律則的內省表現。此表現可被看成爲機械律的一種複雜的作用。因此，第二性質的有效面即外在地被關連到物理世界上去，亦即關連到以宇宙爲一機器的基本範疇上去。這種依於心靈成素而建立的心理學是最簡潔與最得到理智上的滿足的心理學。故一經洛克提出後即不斷地得到發展而廣泛地被接受。

　　但有些現象是此一心理學所不能解答的。故它亦受到一些人包括機械論者的非議。在現代的心理學家中尤其是此即是如此。形態心理學家（Psychologists of Gestalt）是對此一理論極爲反對的。他們中有些人即是機械論者。柯勒（Köhler）更是一個典型的代表人物。他以爲心靈的實質是一種結構、模式或形態。此不能被分析爲心靈的成素⑮。在機械論的術語中形態一概

念是較模糊的。它只有在與帶有想像性電磁場相互關連時才得到相應的了解。在此一關連的了解

中，這些心靈現象被看成爲生理上的連結。因此形態心理學由依第二組範疇而來的了解通過統

一塲的關連而與第一組範疇所論謂的有類比的了解。但有關統一的問題在所說的事件上仍顯著

地留有不妥協的現象。此即第二組範疇不能與第一組範疇統一。此一不妥協的分立再以形式論

的方式威脅着機械論。在衆多複雜的心靈現象上一組基本的心靈的原子同一地重複表現，以形

式論的方式對機械論的威脅是很明顯的。這些原子是什麼呢？豈不是形式論所依以建立的形式

嗎？從機械論的觀點去了解即使是心理形態仍是一種重複而要求一潛存的範疇。這是機械論所

潛存着的大困難，要消除此一困難只了有了解此一宇宙大機器爲一高度的結構塲所；而此塲所的

任何部份嚴格地說不存有任何程度上的重覆。並且所說的突現的性質永遠不重覆表現，它們將永不能被預測。

但如此了解將產生另一問題，即如果所說的突現的性質亦沒有完全的重覆表現。

因此而不能說它們與機器的結構有任何相互的關係。此是一嚴重的問題。因爲很明顯的惟有藉

着所說的相互關係我們才可以有由我們主觀上所知覺到的以對此宇宙機器作推理的了解。並假

定宇宙的機器爲我們提供了所說的相互關係。如果沒有物理的結構與心靈的狀態之間可靠的相

互關係，則不僅我們不能由物理的結構預測或推斷心靈的狀態，而且我們亦不能由心靈的狀態

去推斷物理的結構。這將是一很不好的結果。因爲我們對有關物理結構的知識只能依於我們的

心靈狀態的證據而加以推斷。若去除了此一相互關係，知識即無從建立。因此機械論者對於心

物的問題的害怕是有根據的。它表明了有關機械論的完整性的憂慮。

七、機械論的眞理說

由知識的建立的問題我們說到機械論的眞理說。由對此一問題的討論我們將見到機械論的另一困難。如我們在前節所已注意到的，所有有關知識的直接的證據都是通過對第二性質的感受而得到⑯。再者這種證據是與每一個各別的人的活動互相關連。只有每一個各別的人才可以直接地知覺到。因此所有直接的證據是爲每一個各別的人所私有的。既然如此，我們對外在的世界的知識只可以有符示與推理的知識了。此符示爲推理的知識如何可以建立呢？

舊的機械論者曾嘗試以符合的眞理說去回答此一問題。但如在前面第五章所已說及的，符合的眞理說是形式論的眞理說。因此我們可以預見此一理論與機械論的範疇不能有好的結合。它預設了形式論的相似性。於不同的特殊事物中肯定了同一的形式。符合說之所以對舊的機械論者甚至對某些新近的機械論者有吸引力，部份的原因是由於繼承了經院哲學的觀點。另外是由於分立的機械論的性質。因分立的機械論不能去除在機械場中最後的同一形式。再則由於他們不能爲眞理說提出更好的說法。

舊的機械論以眞理爲感覺觀念與外物相符合。心中的觀念被了解爲鏡中的影像，或畫像或地圖。它們肖似地表現了爲其所反映的對象。觀念之眞是相對於爲其所表現的對象的確切性而說的。

此一理論在以觀念與對象二者皆爲個人的直接精神現象時是相應的。但如觀念與對象都是屬於個人內在自覺上的事，符合只由內在的心靈狀態上說，則對外在的世界的了解即得不到保

證。因為此所說的符合或眞只是屬於第二性質。它由個人的神經中樞突現。它在各個人之內而成為個人的。此一情形曾被視為自我中心的境況。此境況所表現的是觀念與對象皆在個人的心靈中而可以為個人作直接的比較。但如對象不是內在於個人，而是外在於個人，個人即不能對它有自覺。因此，如所有直接的經驗都是由個人內在的神經中樞所突現，而知識的對象又是在個人之外，它即不能被知覺，亦不能將之與個人內在的觀念作直接的比較。因此外在世界的知識即不能建立。

巴克萊是第一個充份了解到此一結果的哲學家。他亦毫不遲疑地接受此一結果。他否認有外於感覺觀念而存在的世界。從機械論的觀點上說，即否認有不為我們感覺到的物質結構。他否認前面依第一組範疇而說明的宇宙機器。他只肯定由第二組範疇所述說的世界存在，即是只有心靈及為心靈所顯現的內容存在。有關外在的世界存在的問題，他仍是從被知覺上說，而主「存在即被知覺」（to be is to be perceived）的說法。我們若說有不為人知覺的世界存在，或世界不是由人的知覺而存在的，則他以上帝去解釋，以世界永為上帝所知覺而得以存在。從機械論的觀點上說，我們若不說上帝知覺的問題，此一理論是有缺陷的。但它以所有被知覺的不論是常識的或科學的問題皆是私下的或個人的，此正符合機械論依第二性質而來的了解。至於不論是第一性質及第一組其他範疇所了解的都無直接的證據而是由推理而得，或說是思辨的結果。

巴克萊的說法或依機械論第二組範疇而來的說法是很有說服力的。如果所有被知覺的材料都是私下的和心靈上的，而機械論者所說的物質如永不屬於任何人所知覺的材料，並且眞理如是一個觀念與它的對象符合，則有關物質的眞理永遠不可能建立起來的說法是很清楚的事。如果是如此，所說的物質是否要成為沒有意義而應該放棄呢？

我們如果接受巴克萊的說法，或者說我們如只能由第二組的範疇去了解問題，並以其與第一組範疇爲分離的，則對上一問題的答案似是肯定的；但如果我們問此一說法的依據所在時，我們即見它以觀念、證據、材料都是私下的說法的依據是有問題的。因它對人作了分離的了解。此一了解預設了在人的有機體中的物質結構可分隔開人的心靈而獨存。事實上巴克萊的心靈正預設了機械論的意義的物質。由機械論的觀點說，雖然我們所能有的證據不能離開第二組範疇而說，但第二組範疇預設了第一組範疇。因此巴克萊的說法從究竟義上說是有問題的。

因此觀念與對象的關係不能依巴氏的觀點說，而應另有解答，批判的機械論者即因此而排斥樸素的符合眞理說，而代之以符號的符合說。他們轉化觀念爲一句一句子或一個科學公式中的一組符號。因此如此組符號與對象的特徵符合，而且符示關係與對象中的關係符合，則這個句子或公式即是眞的。但此一了解只是將問題技術化而並不能消除前面所說的困難。即我們既然對物質對象不能有知覺，如何去比較爲我們自覺到而屬於第二性質的符號與屬於第一性質的物質對象的特徵呢？

對此一問題符號的符合說雖不能解答，但很多現代的機械論者卻由此而主張符合說的重要性不在於一句子或一公式的眞正符合，而在於一句子或一公式所具有的預測能力，由之而產生所期待的結果。一公式之眞在於它之有效。但此一對眞理的了解，不是機械論的特色。此是以眞理爲可運作的運作論，是屬於後面第八章要討論的脈絡論的眞理說。此一眞理說包含了對符號的指涉解釋，而對此一解釋追求至極會招來對機械論的範疇的修改而使機械論變爲脈絡論。

有一點值得我們注意的事在此應稍爲一提。那就是喜歡運作的眞理說亦即脈絡論的眞理說的人，都是對機械論作一統一的解釋。至於分立的機械論者則傾向於符合的眞理說亦即形式論

的真理說。二者皆沒有建立起獨立的理論。 因此，前面所說機械論存有不穩定的情形在真理說

一問題上亦表現了出來。

機械論者是否不能有自己的真理說呢？此是一值得探求的問題。在機械論中實有可以建立

適當的真理說的原則。機械論者常以唯名論者見稱，唯名論對抽象與普遍的名詞的理論正是機

械論者可用以對形式論者以形式為實在，並主張有潛存的範疇的攻擊工具。傳統的機械論者與

唯名論者一樣都以藍的形式或藍的鳥的形式只不過是用來表示一些對象的名詞。這些名詞我們

自小即學會用以指謂一些物理對象而稱之為藍物或藍的鳥。於這些名詞與所指謂的物理對象外，

並沒有藍物或藍的鳥的形式。藍物或藍的鳥之所以被團聚成類亦只是由於它們都為藍一名詞或

藍的鳥一名詞所指謂。

以上這種排斥形式的唯名說法，並不能使人完全信服。 因為我們可以問為什麼一名稱被用

以指謂某些物理對象而不可以指謂另一些。是否因為某些物理對象事實上具有共同的藍顏色或

某種共同的羽毛的性質而另一些物理對象則沒有呢？唯名論者只有名言而無形式的說法若不能

回答此一問題，某類物有共同形式的說法將不能否定。

因此機械論者要克服上述的困難即不能停留於唯名論者有關名的使用的樸素說法上，而要

就自己的範疇去對名作新的解釋。事實上他們是可以有其自己的解釋的。從機械論的觀點上說，

名稱不是別的，而只是人在某一特殊環境之下對其所受到的刺激的積極反應的特殊回應。刺激不同回應亦不

同。而此不同可以有積極與消極的分別。如我們對食物的積極反應與對釘尖的消極反應。此反

應與刺激物彼此相應。所說的分別皆可以有生理學的解釋，而生理學的解釋可轉為生化學的解

釋，而生化學則可以與時空塲相結合而為第一組範疇所解釋。

名稱既爲表示人對環境的回應，從生理學的了解上說，一句子或一科學公式不是別的而只是所說反應的表現。而整個反應表示了一因果關係而可以作因果的解釋，而所謂眞的只是合乎因果關係的陳述。

由以上的說明，我們可以說機械論可以有其自己的眞理說。在此一眞理說中不涵有形式的同一問題。它亦不是一種如脈絡論所說的運作的眞理說；而是述說一種環境的刺激與一個有機體的回應的因果連結系統。一個有機體由於某種物理的刺激而發展出一套反應的態度，或說發展出一套生理的反應集，而所謂眞理即述說此等反應。

眞理既爲表示一個有機體對環境的回應的生理活動的名稱，故有人稱此爲「身體的適應性」（the aptness of the body）⑰。

因果眞理說要說明的因果關係既由生理而及於生化而至時空塲，故機械論的第二組範與第一組範疇所表示的差異即可有如下的解答：第二性質與生理的結構相互關連。生理的結構在有效的時空萬有引力的磁塲中，它們是宇宙塲的一部份，因此直接地反映了宇宙塲的結構。故宇宙塲的結構即直接地由與生理的結構相互關連的第二性質所反映。因此我們藉着一種探究的工作而得知有關此一宇宙大機器的結構，亦即我們由注意我們私下的第二性質的變化而可推斷它們與在我們的有機體中的生理的結構的相互關係。由此而推斷包圍着塲所的結構的性質。由它的結果而推斷我們有機體的結構。例如我們想要知道世上有沒有一種紅翼的黑鳥，我們可先在心中形成一紅翼黑鳥的形像，或用語言表明此一意義。當我們如此做時即知覺到一種屬於第二性質的觀念。我們以此觀念與我們有機體中的生理結構相互關連，推動我們的有機體在周圍環境中去尋找是否有任何東西直接地刺激我們的生理結構而在我們的知覺上顯現出相互關連的顏

色與形狀。如果我們能找到，我們會以我們的觀念或語句是眞的，若不能，而且我們以爲有足夠的證據支持我們相信所說的觀念或語句永遠不會得到如此外來的刺激，我們即以我們的觀念或語句爲假的。

因果的眞理說相應於機械論的觀點而有其特質應可以了解。但它是否能成功地避免符合的眞理說或運作的眞理說的威脅呢？所說的生理態度對環境的刺激的推斷是否預設一種態度與環境的結構的符合呢？在分立的機械論中可能會如此。但在統一的機械論中那推斷將僅爲一種因果的或幾何學的連結表現而不涵有重複於其中。

但生理的態度與其假定地相互關連的第二性質則有重複的問題。我們由什麼的意義上可以說機械論中的相互關係呢？如我們在前面所已說及的，爲了要由一邊推斷到另一邊我們要建立起兩邊中的一種連結。這一連結不能是同一的，亦不能是因果關係的，而只能是相互關連的；而此相互關連好似即隱涵有形式論的同一性的意義。

因果關係的眞理說好似成功地克服了第二性質與第一性質的分隔，但它似不能去除存於相互關係的觀念中作爲第一組範疇與第二組範疇連結環節的形式論的相似性的涵義。我們也許會想有別的解決辦法，例如我們不要相互的關係而用唯名論的符號的指謂，即用一名去指謂一對象。但唯名論的整個觀點是要以機械論的因果關係去解釋符號的指謂，而因果關係則已被排斥作爲連結第二性質與第一性質的橋樑。因此第一組與第二組範疇的分隔仍是機械論的一主要的問題所在。

註 釋

① S. C. Pepper, *World Hypotheses*, p. 141.

② Ibid., p. 186.

③ Ibid., pp. 193-194.

④ Ibid., p. 196.

⑤ Hans Reichenbach, *Atom and Cosmos*, Trens, E. S. Allen (New York: Macmillan, 1933), pp. 194-196.

⑥ S. C. Pepper, *World Hypotheses*, pp. 201-202.

⑦ Ibid., pp. 208-209.

⑧ Ibid., **①**, p. 203.

⑨ Isaac Newton, *Mathematical Principles*, ed. Florian Cojori (Berkeley: University of California Press, 1934) p. 13.

⑩ Ibid., p. 209.

⑪ Ibid., **①**, p. 210.

⑫ Ibid., **③**.

⑬ Ibid., p. 216.

⑭ Ibid., pp. 217-218.

⑮ Ibid., p. 219.

⑯ Ibid., **⑭**.

⑰ Ibid., ❶, p. 228.

⑯ 所有為第一性質所顯示的究竟指謂，如電子與宇宙塲都不是為我們所直接知覺的對象。

第八章　脈絡論

一、小引

脈絡論為依根源的譬喻而建立的另一個相對地適切的世界的假設的理論。它主要為展示現代西方的哲學家皮耳士·詹姆士（Wiliam James）、柏格森（Henri Bergson）、杜威、米德（George H. Mead）的哲學，亦與古希臘哲學家普洛塔哥拉斯（Protagoras）的哲學有關❶。在現代西方哲學史家中亦有人以裴柏為一脈絡主義者❷。但依我們的了解，裴柏並不以自己為一脈絡主義者。在他寫《世界的假設》一書時，他是較為喜好脈絡論的理論，但在他後來完成了《概念與性質——一個世界的假設》一書之後，他對脈絡論有所修改，而成為一選擇論者❸。在後面我們將分別為：(1)脈絡論的根源的譬喻與範疇的確定；(2)由對附屬範疇的說明以了解世界；(3)運作的真理說等三節以介述脈絡論對世界作結構性與系統性的說明及其真理說的涵義。

二、脈絡論的根源的譬喻與範疇的確定

脈絡論的根源的譬喻是「歷史的事件」❹。此所說「歷史的」一詞不僅限於已過去了的事，而是包涵了現在與未來的事，而且可為人所知覺的。故歷史的事件是可為人所知覺而連續地呈現的事件。

以歷史的事件是可為人所知覺而連續地呈現的事件為脈絡論者對歷史的事件的主要了解，他們由此而說在知覺以外的事件是如何的，不能有確定的說法。其所能確定的是凡可呈現於知覺之前的事件都是連續地呈現的事件。他們並以事件與事件之間所構成的前後關係是可變的。故他們不肯定事件為永恆不變的，而是相反地預設了變遷的可能性；不否定「有」可以由「無」而出。；而承認有異乎尋常的事❺。但「有」由「無」而出而異乎尋常的事雖為他們所預設，就由經驗所了解及的事件上說，所呈現的事件表現了事件與事件中的共同性。而此共同性即為脈絡論依以了解世界的範疇。

什麼是歷史的事件的共同性呢？依脈絡論者的了解，歷史的事件的共同性即歷史的事件的性質與結構。故性質與結構為脈絡論者由歷史的事件引伸出來以了解世界的主要範疇❻。此所說的性質是指一事件的整個意義·；結構則是指一事件是怎樣構成的。一事件的性質不能離開結構而說其為何。因一事件的性質即由結構而顯現，而不是於結構之外另有性質。結構亦不能離開性質而說。因結構不能離開性質而另有所呈現。性質與結構共同表現了一事件的整體性。但性質與結構雖表現一事件的整體性，我們對一事件的了解則並不限於對性質與結構二者的整體的了解，而可以對二者再作整體性，亦沒有無結構的性質。由分別的了解中而更了解到一事件的涵義為何。

所謂由對性質與結構再作分別的了解而更了解到一事件的涵義為何，依裴柏的說法，此一

再分別的了解即爲對脈絡論的附屬範疇的確定的了解，亦爲對據以說明一事件的分別的細目的了解。此了解就性質一範疇來說，可進而作三種不同而彼此相關聯以說明。此即爲對屬於性質一範疇之下的三個附屬範疇的了解。它們是：：(1)延展，(2)變遷，(3)融合。就結構一範疇來說，亦可進而作三種不同而彼此關聯的了解，亦即爲對屬於結構一範疇的三個附屬範疇的了解。它們是：：(1)股份，(2)脈絡，(3)指涉。對於此所列的(3)指涉可以更進而有四種不同而彼此相關的說明：：(a)直線的指涉，(b)輻輳的指涉，(c)阻礙，(d)工具的指涉❼。在後面我們即由對所說的附屬範疇作分別的說明以了解脈絡論對世界所作結構性或系統性的說明。

三、由對附屬範疇的分別說明以了解世界

對附屬範疇的分別說明即爲依各附屬範疇而展示以世界爲事件的涵義，亦即由事件以說明世界爲何的意義。現分別依次說明如後。

(1) 延展：：延展是屬於性質的附屬範疇。我們由它而可以更了解一事件的意義。但此一意義亦只是一方面的，因爲延展只是性質的一個附屬範疇，於此外另有變遷與融合二範疇。所謂延展是指由知覺所了解的事件的連續表現。此連續表現被了解爲一個表現。因爲由其表現的性質是連結着事件的過去、現在與未來而成爲一個意義。故延展又被名爲「似真的現在」（spe-cioue present）❽。其之所以有如此的稱謂，因其所呈現的不是純現在，而是結合了過去與未來而成爲一事件，以顯示一意義。舉例來說，我現在書寫「延展」兩字是一事件。我「舉

頭向窗外望」亦是一事件。此兩事件皆有其延展性。分析地說當我寫「延展」時經歷了一段時間。「延」字先於「展」字而寫成。「舉頭望窗外」亦經歷了一段時間，先有「舉頭」的動作而後有「向窗外望」的動作。「延」字的一撇「丿」亦先於一直「—」而寫成，而「舉頭」一動作更可以有進一步的生理活動的先後分析。故每一活動皆包涵了「過去」、「現在」與「未來」而成為一事件。若以此所了解的事件只是一「現在」即為「似真的現在」。但脈絡論者不以為有純現在，故沒有「似真的現在」，而是以現在應由其所肯定的範疇去了解，亦即由「延展」去了解而見所謂現在均是涵有過去與未來的事件。脈絡論者並不否認我們可以從別的觀點上對「延展」加以了解，例如由直線圖式的時間觀念而說「延展」是「似真的現在」，而另以直線圖式的分析去說明依直線圖式所了解的現在為何。但脈絡論者並不以對「延展」作直線圖式的分析而可以認識一事件的真象為何。相反地，他們以為如此的分析是歪曲了事件的真實性。故脈絡論者雖不否認直線圖式的了解亦有其意義，但以其有違於脈絡論的範疇涵義，而不是即範疇而了解事件而適切地認識其真實性質為何。

(2) 變遷：變遷是由性質引伸而來的另一附屬範疇，而表明了性質的另一涵義。所謂變遷是指一事件所表現的性質的不斷改變。如以前面所舉的書寫「延展」一事件為例，則此一書寫常在變遷中。由書寫「延」字至「展」字固表示了一改變，而書寫「延」字或「展」字的每一筆畫莫不為一改變。事件既表現了變遷，由變遷而說事件的性質則性質的意義亦在改變中。所舉的書寫的事件是如此，此外其他任何的事件亦莫不然。脈絡論者以整個世界為事件的呈現，故整個世界即常在變遷中，而沒有絕對而不變的事物，亦沒有絕對獨立於事物之外而不變的永恆。一切皆為事件，事件在連續地不停表現，亦不停變遷，永不停止。

(3)　融合：融合亦是由性質而來的附屬範疇。它亦表明了性質的一種涵義。此涵義是因結構的和合表現而顯。最能表達此一涵義的事例為由味覺所感受的滋味，或由聽覺所感受的和音。詹姆士曾以檸檬露為例去說明融和的意義。構成檸檬露的成份為檸檬、糖與水。但檸檬露的滋味則是由三者融合表現而成。此一融合表現使三者各別的味道隱而不顯❾。又音樂上的和音亦是由幾種不同的樂器共同表現而成。但各樂器所發出的聲音彼此融合而共同呈現一律韻，使聽者只注意此一律韻之高低抑揚表現，而不分辨其各別的聲音為何，為由何種樂器所發出的聲音構造而成。於所說的檸檬露與音樂的和音外，我們日常所經驗到的其他事物亦有相似的融合性質。如看書，我們所注意到的只是書中所說的整個意義為何，而常不理會構成一書的各別的章、節、段、句，或一句中所用的不同的字所表達的各別意義為何。又如我們看窗外的大紅花，我們所注意的是花的形狀為何，顏色為何，姿態為何。由此而得到一種美的感覺。此感覺為由花的整個融合表現而成，而即以此花為一朵花，而不去分辨其各別的花瓣為何，花蕊為何。因此融合呈現於我們所感知的每一事物中，而為一事物性質的意義所在。事物的表現有差別，感知亦有大小之分，融合亦隨之而異。前面所提到的檸檬露雖在味覺上有融合的表現，但我如專注於其構成份的各別不同，亦可有分別的感覺。音樂的和音亦一樣。若我們所注意的不是整個律韻，而是各別樂器所發出的聲音，我們即對演奏的融合表現作各別的分辨，而可有不同的感覺。所說的讀書亦是一樣，而可以由對全書意義的了解而轉而對一書中的一章、一節、或一句、一字的了解，而分解了其由全書所共同表現的融合性。看花亦是一樣。我們可不注意花的整個形狀為何，顏色為何，姿態為何，而分辨花瓣或花蕊的彼此異同，而不注意全花的共同融合表現。但依照脈絡論者的了解，我們雖然可以對我們所感知的事物作分別的了解，而改變了合表現。

其原初所呈現的融和性。但事物的融和性並不因此而消失，只是相對於我們所改變的注意力而隱而不現。但爲我們所分解注意及的事物仍是以融合的姿態出現，只是此出現的融合異於前者而已。前面所舉的每一分別的了解皆是如此。檸檬、糖與水相對於檸檬露說時各爲構成檸檬露的融合的成份，而此每一成份的本身亦爲一融合表現。其他如和音中每一聲音的表現，書中每一章、節或句、字，一朵花的每一花瓣或花蕊莫不如此，只是其作爲一份子所表現的融合層級與其自己所呈現的層級不同而已。因此，依脈絡論者的了解，融合是事物性質的範疇表現，其有種種層級的不同。但不可以將融合去除而以其爲不真實，爲含混，或爲姿態的事。融合並不只是一種主觀上的感覺，而有其客觀存在的意義。在我們感知的事物中無物不表現了某一程度上的融合。至於若問究竟有沒有最簡單的事物如電子或質子。脈絡論者的回答將是：：那只是分解的概念。我們可以有如此的理解。但在我們感知的事物中則皆表現了不同層級的融合性，而此實即爲事物的性質所在。

(4) 由結構一範疇的了解而引伸出的三個附屬範疇中，股份與脈絡可以作配合的說明。

股份與脈絡：結構、股份與脈絡三者緊密地相關聯。結構是由股份所構成而表現在脈絡之中。股份與脈絡不能有截然的劃分。因脈絡乃由股份聯結而成，而脈絡在很大的程度上決定了股份的性質。但爲了對它們的意義作界定的說明，我們可以說股份是直接地就一結構的表現而呈現其性質上說，而脈絡則爲就結構的前後聯結上說。

結構、股份與脈絡不但緊密地相關聯，而且有相對的涵義。一事件的股份可爲另一事件的結構，而一視爲結構的事件亦可成爲另一更大事件的股份。脈絡亦相對而有不同的了解。作爲一事件的脈絡可成爲另一更大事件的股份，而一事件的股份亦可轉爲另一結構的脈絡。舉例來

說，一個簡單句子表現了一結構。它的股份即為構成此一句子的每一個字，而其脈絡則為與此句子連結在一起的前後句子。成為一句子的每一個字亦可被了解為一結構。它的股份則為構成此字的形聲，而與此字在一起共同構成一句子的其他字即為它的脈絡。句子可如此了解，為我們所經驗到的任何事物亦可以為此了解。如前面所說的大紅花是一結構的表現。它的股份即為花蕚、花瓣與花蕊，而其脈絡則為花托與花柄。花蕊亦為一結構，其股份則為大蕊與小蕊，而其脈絡則為花蕚與花瓣。我們所經驗的事物既皆表現為結構、股份與脈絡的相對呈現，故脈絡論者以為我們對事物的了解即應與此相應而了解其為結構、股份與脈絡式的存在。我們若不理會事物的存在本質為何而純從事非本質的分析而找尋其成素為何，我們即會曲解事物的存在真相。因此脈絡論者對形式論與機械論所說的分析表示了反對的態度。因它們皆以為被分析的結構以獲取其最後構成的成素。故他們以為水可以完全被分解為原子、電子或其他成素。但脈絡論者對此一「以為」並不承認而以其犯了範疇上，亦即本質上的謬誤。就脈絡論的範疇上說，我們不能對任何事物作完全而徹底的分析。理由是凡被分析的事物都是一事件。我們要對一事件從事分析必要顯示它的結構為何，而要顯示一事件的結構即要分辨它的股份，而要對股份作充份的分辨即要顯示被分析而與股份相聯的脈絡中的結構，因為被分析的結構的股份與其他結構相關聯以形成其性質。因此在對任何事件作深入的分析時，我們即見到我們的分析與被分析的脈絡不能分。因此而由一事件至另一事件而可永無已止。

一事件的性質為構成該事件的眾股份的性質的融合表現；而股份的性質表現於其脈絡中；而其脈絡則有超出該事件之外而與其他事件相交織的。此為由脈絡論的觀點去了解對一事件作分析所得的結果。由此一結果我們見到當我們見到一結構的構成成份時，我們即發現我們所見

到的是與原先所見到的結構有所不同，而進入了與其他結構相關的脈絡中。我們對事件的分析

結果既有股份與結構，結構與其他結構，股份與脈絡，脈絡與其他結構不能完全分離的事實，

脈絡論者即不重視只為分析而分析的做法。他們以為此一做法沒有甚麼意義。我們只有為實際

的需要而作分析的了解時才是有意義。此是一種以實用的觀點去說分析的說法。例如，我們如

先有一個想法要由一個結構作分析的了解進而了解另一結構，則此一分析即有一定的目的和一

定的方向。在分析的過程中會見到有些股份與此一目的相干，有些則不相干，而要選擇作為分

析的股份即與此一目的相關聯而每一階段可不同。若一分析不存有任何目的，而是純為分析而

分析，則不會有所說的了解，而要成為沒有特定的意義的事了。

由以上的了解，我們亦見到相對於其他的世界理論上說，脈絡論是一種橫觀世界的理論，

其他的理論則是直觀世界的理論。脈絡論者的世界沒有直線的上下兩端，而只有橫線的彼此關

聯。依照形式論、機械論或機體論的觀點上說，我們可以用某一方式去分析宇宙事物，而可以得到

其底蘊為何，或究極所在，但脈絡論者不如此觀。他們不以為我們可以對宇宙中的事物從事分

析，而可以發現整個宇宙的真理為何，或事物的究極性質所在。他們更以為我們並不需要尋求

那遙遠的宇宙真理。因為每一當下的事件，表現了其所具有的充份的意義。要了解宇宙的真理

為何，我們所要做的，不是去探求遙遠的宇宙究極意義，而是了解當下每一事物所表現出來的

性質為何。任何事物其所表現出來的任何性質，其意義為宇宙的與究竟的，正如為牛頓的萬有

引力律所說明的為宇宙的與究竟的一樣。萬有引力律對更多人有用的事實，並不使其更成為

真實。

(5)

股份的指涉：指涉是結構一範疇的第三個附屬範疇。由此可以對股份的意義作更貼切

的了解。　故名之曰股份的指涉。此可作如下分別的了解。

(a)　直線的指涉：直線的指涉是就一股份的直線延伸的指向所涉及者而說。此一涉及可分

別為始點，中間的指向，以及終點。而此分別並不是確定不移的，而是相應於一股份的選定上

說。例如我們如以某一句話為某一段文章的一股份，而該段文章為由若干句（亦即若干股份）

而形成的結構，則所說直線指涉的始點，中間的指向與終點即相應於各句話的構成的不同而不

同，其相同的是作為股份的每一句話皆由其始點經中間點而指涉及終點。以一句話為股份如此，

以其他任何可經驗的事物為股份亦是如此。在此要特別注意的是中間指向的前後指涉意義。有

些實驗主義者特別強調向前指涉的重要性，而忽略了向後指涉的同樣重要。忽略了直線指涉的

向前與向後，未來與過去，開始與終結的兩頭表現。此兩頭表現為作為結構的脈絡論的歷史事件亦即

「似真的現在」的各範疇所涵。由此兩頭表現所具的兩度向而構成結構的延伸以及延伸的當下

涵義。我們如去除了向後指涉的意義將使結構收縮到一點上去而不能有所確指。

(b)　輻輳的指涉：輻輳的指涉是一種複合的直線指涉。此可以為由幾個始點而輻輳到一終

點上，亦可以為由一個始點而分指向幾個終點上。脈絡論者即由此而說明從普通經驗上所說的

相同。我們仍然以一個句子為例去說明：「然人之所以必於此實際經驗之草木開花之事實之外

設定一先經驗之功能之存在。」在此一句子中共用了六個「之」字。我們對此諸「之」字很少

特別加以注意。但當我們注意及它們時，此六個「之」字即同時向我們呈現。呈現的方式有二：

一為如果我們有意去找尋它們，則我們的「有意」即為始點，由此一始點而向六個

「之」字上，而六個「之」字即成為分別指向的終點。但如我們不是有意去尋找它們，而是它

們自然地向我們呈現，則它們即同時呈現在我們注意之前而成為由六個不同始點輻輳於我們注

意之終點上。對一個句子所用的相同字如此的了解，對其他相同的事物亦可如此了解。要特別注

意的是，就脈絡論者來說，所謂「相同」不是由事物的本身上而說相同，而是由其所表現的輻

轊的共同意義上說。故如事物不受注意到，亦即無輻轊的共同意義，或無輻轊的指涉可說時，

即無相同可說。又如上面所說一個句子中的六個「之」字，如就字形上說，六者並不完全相同，

用手寫的更是如此。但在指涉的表現上，則六者彼此相同。六個「之」字是如此，世上所有的

事物皆是如此。櫃前的水滴，前一滴不同於後一滴；同一棵樹的兩片葉子亦彼此不同，惟有在輻

轊的指涉上我們才可以說有相同的事物。兩個五磅重的鉛球，二者並不是本質地相同，惟有當

其在天秤上使指針表現了同一的指向，我們才說其重量相同。從輻轊於天秤上表現了相同的重

量的意義上說，不但兩個鉛球各表現了五磅的重量，而以之為相同，任何其他的東西只要其表現

了同一的重量即皆輻轊地表現出同一的事實，而以之為相同。由於我們所謂物質的東西都表現

了所說的輻轊的指涉——重量、體積、或溫度。因此脈絡論者以為物質沒有恆常不變的性質，

而只有可為人所預測的輻轊的指涉性質。

(c) 阻塞：嚴格地說阻塞並不是一指涉，而是指涉的障礙。當直線的指涉或輻轊的指涉不

能由其始點而經中間指向而達於終點時，即有了障礙。當此情形出現時，我們可以即以此障礙

為指涉的終點，而不求於此障礙之外另有終點而為指涉要達到的目的。但脈絡論者不如此說，

他們以為指涉有其自始的指向。他們以障礙為股份受到了阻塞不能由其始點而順利地指向其終

點的內在事實。他們以順利的指向為股份合乎秩序的呈現，不順利的指向為反秩序的呈現，而

為異常的事。由股份的指涉上說障礙是一種新奇的突現。

我們可以在一股份的指涉上所出現的障礙為受另一股份的干擾。當一個股份干擾了另一股

份，或者當一行為妨礙了另一行為時，干擾的股份或妨礙的行為是意外的，而為奇異的出現。

但此奇異是相對的，只相對於某一股份或行為是奇異，而其自身則為自然的表現。因此，當一

股份或一行為與另一股份或另一行為衝突而對其有一障礙的事情發生時，我們可以尋求各

股份或各行為自身的歷史所在。由此而對障礙獲得解釋。但亦有得不到解釋的障礙。此不能得

到解釋的障礙可能由遠處的脈絡的侵入而產生。但脈絡論者只探求障礙的所在而不作如此的假

定。一股份可絕對地被阻塞而得不到解釋。脈絡論者稱此為突現的奇異。

由一事件的性質上說，每一事件的性質是明顯的事。脈絡論者很注意此一事實。

當我們向窗外望時，向窗外望此一事件的性質即突然呈現。在我們由看窗外而轉看房間時另一

看房間不同事件的性質隨之而突現。又由一結構的本質去了解，我們所見到的一結構是包涵有

股份而在一脈絡中。結構與脈絡之結合甚為複雜而經常可改變，很少有完全重複的表現。故每

一結構所表現的性質即為一新的突現或結構上新的突現。因此由脈絡論的觀點去了解事件的性質或

其結構所常見有性質上新的性質即為一種突現。

所說性質上或結構上的新奇可作分析的了解，而尋其源始於其他脈絡之中。正如上面所

說的入侵的新奇一樣。因此等新奇皆是相對的，即相對於我們所注意及的情景而說。但於所說

的新奇之外是否尚有其他新奇呢？

當我們見到一受到了阻塞的股份得不到順通時，好似出現了一絕對的終結。相應於此絕對

的終結而說的事件好似完全停止或消失了。但事情並非完全如此。當我們對一終結作分析的了

解時，我們見到在一完全阻塞中被摧毀的只是受阻塞的整體。此整體的成素是被分解了，但不

是被摧毀，而是在另一脈絡中仍可尋到它們。此正如一被打敗了的軍隊，人都死了、或被驅散

了。但此死了或被驅散了的份子仍然存在。在另一情景或另一地方中再可見到。消失了的只是此一部隊。此一部隊的結構的整體性，它的融合或性質是失落了。在此宇宙中不再有它們而完全消失了。它們的失落與一突現的結構所出現的新奇相對顯。但二者的或成為整體或解體仍可以由其構成的股份作分析的了解，而見到構成的股份的分別表現。

由以上的了解，所有的新奇好似都是相對的。但於此外是否有完全的新奇或終結呢？即整個結構或股份是否可以完全消失而不留有痕跡，或突然出現而無任何的朕兆呢？此完全的新奇或終結是否可說呢？是否有任何支持此一說法的證據呢？

如我們所了解到的，此一種新奇或終結很不易說，或很易被忽略。正如路易士（C. I. Lewis）在他的《心靈與世界秩序》（Mind and the World Order）一書所一再指出的⑩，我們在實際上和理解上都為那些可以作預測，並可以有系統分析的規律，以及有連續性的事物所吸引，而集中我們的注意力於其上。我們並沒有適當的名稱用以指謂完全的新奇和終結。因用以指謂一結構的真正的名稱是相應於該結構的存在而說。由定義上說，一完全的終結表示一股份停止與現實，而至於將來的事件任何的因果連結。要對此一終結命名，也許只能以一完全沒有意義的名去表示。如果我們有理由以如此說的。至於對完全的新奇，我們則必要找出證明在其突現之前無任何事件與它相關，它的出現是絕對的而不是任何其他股份的融合和整體的表現。落而在世上不再有痕跡可尋。

如在前面曾說及的，在事物的本質上，或由脈絡論的範疇上說，我們並不能排斥它們的存在。在實際上和理解上我們都注意該系統、規律與連續性而不注意完全的新奇與完全的終結。但從事物的實際表現如一稱阻塞，或一種如欠缺證據而不知其來源的意外事件。當我們在各別特殊的事件上其表現

不能找出一事件的根源時，我們一般地假定有關它的證據受到了阻塞。但原則上是可以尋得到的，只是暫時不知其所在而已。由於我們常能找出我們一時以為不能尋找得到的證據，因此而形成了一種對事件的證據可尋找性的假定的普遍信念。但正如路易士所提示的，在整個經驗的領域中，我們的成功只限於很小的範圍內，而此很小的範圍可能是由於其合適性而小心地加以選擇。可能有很多完全的新奇，它們並可能即在我們所有的事件中。

前面所說的結構性或成為整體性的新奇性正近於完全的新奇。它由融合而構成了新的股份，它具有新的因果潛能。此潛能由回溯上而得到分析的了解，但沒有可預測的性質。其後果亦不可以由預測上得到。因此脈絡論者懷疑水的性質可以由氧與氫的性質作預測。一工業組織的結果亦不可以由個人的心理和經濟的需要而加以預測。

(d)　工具的指涉：工具的指涉隨着阻礙而顯現。此一指涉為自稱為工具主義的脈絡論者所特別重視。但從以性質與結構為脈絡論的主要範疇的觀點上說，工具的指涉只可以視之為完成其目的時的一種表現。因此工具的行為是先有前面所說直線的指涉受到阻礙後而來的一種去除阻礙的次一活動。所謂工具即此一去除阻礙活動的整個表現。在此一表現中的指涉表示即為工具的指涉表示。因此工具的指涉包括三種主要因素：(1)它自身是一具有始點與終點的直線指涉；(2)但此一指涉表現在另一原先的指涉上而成為其工具的作用，而使其與原先的指涉連結在一起；(3)它是一對受阻礙的股份所表現的指涉[11]。

上述以指涉為一附屬範疇的諸指涉中的一個項目。

工具的行為是在一行為受到了阻礙而不能達到其預先所期待的目的而要藉工具的協助以完成其目的的一種表現。因此工具的行為是先有前面所說直線的指涉受到阻礙而來的一種去除阻礙的次一活動。所謂工具即此一去除阻礙活動的整個表現。

由所說的三種主要因素看，一工具的行為有其自己的結構表現與自己的行為為目的。此表現

與目的為另一在前面受到了阻礙而具有一定的目標的行為所引導，而二者彼此結合互相補足而成為一個結構。在此一結構中原先的阻礙不再為外來的行動，而是與原先的行為結合為一複合的行為。後面的例子可以對此一工具的指涉作說明。

有一獵人要到一草原上去打獵，中途為一小溪所攔阻，他打獵的事受到了妨礙。他可以放棄此一打獵的活動。但他不願意如此而要繼續往草原上去。他找到了一條枯乾了的木幹與一根竹竿。此木幹與竹竿幫助他渡過了小溪。此一事件之所以在此時出現是由於小溪阻礙了他要到草原上去的目的。此尋找與渡小溪的行為與原先要到草原上去的行為可以清楚地分開為二，前者只為後者的一外加行為。但當獵人打完了獵由草原上歸來時，因他已知道如何去渡過小溪，故渡小溪的行為即不再有如去時的不同感覺。此後如他再常往草原上去，則渡小溪會成為他整個行程中的一部份，與行程中的上山落坡打成一片，而不再成為一特殊問題。

由上面的例子我們可以清楚見到工具的行為與原先的行為的相互關係。工具的指涉如何轉變為直線指涉的一部份，脈絡論者特別注視此一意義。尤其在倫理的問題上，他們更注意要將目的與手段截然劃分所可能存有的問題。

這一問題在尋求了解一行為的性質時亦甚為明顯。當一行為僅被視為一工具的行為時，為此一工具的行為的對付的阻礙顯示得特別清楚。工具的活動因此而被視為一種分別的表現。工具的行為與原先的行為結合而成為整個表現的一部份，其即與整個行為結構融合。能使這一意義的了解將會更為親切。在剛開始學車時，每一動作都是分立的，但在熟練了之後，整個開車的行為即連在一起而忘記了原先剛學車時各動作的分別表現情形。

工具的指涉是隨障礙而說，故其意義常由行為上顯。但亦可以說明事件的工具結構。我們如由工具的指涉去了解事件，則我們即見到工具的事件結構比當下所了解的事件結構為廣。它超出了一事件在當下所呈現的範圍，而與多數事件貫串與連結在一起而成為一大的結構，而更可覺悟到結構與結續表現的相互連結的結構。

由工具的指涉所連結在一起的大事件仍可稱之為結構。但為了分辨其與只呈現在感覺中的結構的不同，脈絡論者稱之為個體的結構。任何一給與的事件的結構是由其融合的範圍而確定。由工具而獲至的整但如前面所指出的藉著工具的指涉而完成的事件是超出了給與事件的限度。由工具而獲至的整體經驗是超出了任何給與的現在。它們不呈現於任何的現在上。它們表現在連續的事實上而成其秩序性，而使歷史的過程成為有順序而可預測的過程。故個體的結構是由當下給與的結構而伸延至整個廣袤的宇宙中，於其中無數給與的事件交織在一起而向著未來伸展。

有別於只呈現於當下感覺中的結構是依脈絡論的副範疇工具的指涉而來對事件的了解。由脈絡論的觀點上說，所有範疇都是由事件分解而得。我們所在的世界即依所分解而得的範疇而呈現，而不須要加以推知。脈絡論者以為我們任何個人私下的事件都與公共的世界相聯結，個人私下事件的結構與其他結構交織，二者互相結合交織而延伸至其結構之外。

由脈絡論的範疇去了解，人類社會亦因人的合作而表現了一互相貫穿與聯結的社會結構。不但由人的合作行為組成的社會如此，人的一般的知覺行為亦是如此。在我所見到的一張怡中，即有兩個或多於兩個繼續地相連結的結構。屬於物質性的枱與其所在的環境常有因果性的交互作用，因此而表現出個體結構的連續性。因此我們不可能以表現於視覺之前的一張怡是完全新奇的。個人的物質身體亦有結構上的連續性而表現於其所在的時空環境的脈絡上。在我們分析某

些光線與空間的情形時，二者的各別的連續性是可以有分別的了解，而後顯出其成爲一甚多複雜的結構。此一結構的性質包括顏色和形狀。當此等顏色和形狀被知覺時，其成爲結構的與性質的顯現。那就是說，在枱的連續的結構的股份與身體的有機體的股份交結之前，沒有顏色與形狀的存在可說。顏色與形狀是由性質的與整合的顯現而來的新的出現，由股份的結構而生起。如果我轉移視線，所說的知覺的結構即分解而其性質亦消失。如我再回看原物，其即再結合，其性質亦重新出現。在此應特別注意的是，由結構的整合而呈現的性質既不只屬於我所有，亦不只屬於枱所有，而是屬於一共同的結構所有。

如果我們問：當枱不與人的知覺交感時，枱是如何的。脈絡論者的回答是它是具有適當的性質的個體的連續結構。但我們對它所有的知識於知覺之外即爲關係的。作爲一結構，一物質的連續有它複合的性質，正如一句子的結構或一曲調的結構有它的複合的性質一樣。於知覺之外這些性質是如何的，我們是無所知的，因我們只能由知覺去直覺一物質的連續性。但雖然我們不能於知覺之外直覺物質的連續性的性質爲何，我們可以推論於知覺之外的結構或關係的連結爲何。

不能爲我們直覺到的結構的關係的知識的性質是怎樣的呢？它表現成爲一種方案（或計劃）的關係，而可以爲我們所預測。所謂方案如地圖、圖表、公式、函數方程式和符號系統等。它們的本身有其持續性，而爲預測的工具。人們依過去的社會經驗而發展出所說的諸方案。它們在人類文化中的地位有些類似人的社會組織。正如一國的憲法是一種管制社會事務的工具，依過去的經驗而建立，是過去社會經驗的一種總結，亦是將來經驗的指導。所說的諸方案亦是如此，它們成爲所謂一個時期的「科學」，隨着不同的時期而改變。有些實驗主義者誇稱此等方

案改變的涵義，而以之與物質世界的結構相應為說。以每一時代的物質世界結構的不同由於每一時代的「科學」不同。不同時代的物理世界可能有所不同。但脈絡論者沒有理由將一時期的自然的結構與該一時期的「科學」相等同。因為我們不可能將樹木的進化與鋸斧的進步相等同。

物質的結構與控制它們的方案的結構雖然並不是一回事，但我們是以控制物質結構的假設中的關係結構歸到物質上去的。這並不是說汽油機的結構可以完全與控制它的生產或表明機器各部份的配置情形與活動模式的圖表的結構同一，但圖表是涵有一參證的系統，依此而可以相應地了解機器的結構則是事實。

四、運作的眞理說

依裴柏的了解，脈絡論是依據一眞理說而產生。他曾注意到早期的脈絡論者如皮耳士與詹姆士曾說此一眞理說與世界的理論無關。他們以為實驗主義只是一種方法論。它不預設或涵蘊着任何東西。它是純經驗的，只注意人獲得一結論而稱之為眞時實際上如何行⑫。此一方法即現代所說的運作說。所說早期的實驗主義者的觀點亦為很多現代的運作論者所贊同。他們亦以運作的眞理說是沒有預設的。

但裴柏以為運作的眞理說由開始提倡至現在，時間雖很短暫，在此短暫的過程中已表現上一說法有問題。所說的方法已形成為一種主張而發展為一世界的理論。他並以為前面對脈絡論對世界了解的說明是逆其發展的順序而介述。即由其所發展為一世界理論開始而說到此一理論所依而建立的眞理說。

運作的真理說既發展成為脈絡的世界理論，我們即可由對脈絡論的解釋以了解其形而上學

的涵義。從脈絡論的觀點上說，真理的問題是由股份的受阻塞而引生。股份既受阻塞，即求對

此阻塞有所通達。用普通的話說即一問題出現了之後，我們即求對該問題有所解答。我們要能

有所解答，即要分析出問題的情形以尋求解答此一問題的假設。此分析包涵了尋求出在受

阻塞事件中的各股份的阻塞情形，如果此是一複雜的問題。此一分析將要導引我們至不同的相

關的計劃上。這些計劃要對受阻塞的股份從事研究，由此而暫時建立一假設。此假設是一種工

具具有引導實證的行為表現其指涉的作用。指涉得到了表現，行為即成為對假設的實證。如果

假設有阻礙，原來受阻塞的股份即得不到通達，尋求指涉的運作即被視為假的，而整個分析的

歷程，假設的建立與實證的表現即要重新開始。但是如果假設的進行受到阻塞的股份得到了

滿足的通達，問題得到了解答，則整個運作即被視為真的。因此，真理即為一種工具表現的結

果。此結果去除了阻塞而使一有限度的股份結構得以顯明。

以上是相應於脈絡論的涵義而對運作的真理說所作的陳述。此陳述並未能將運作的真理涵

義充份展示。因此，脈絡論者再進而作三種分別的說明。此三種說明依裝柏的了解亦大致地表

示了實驗主義發展的三階段。

(1) 成功的行為表現。此說以真理即為成功的或有實效的行為表現。什麼是成功的或有實效

的行為表現呢？此可以以前面所說的獵人到草原上去打獵的事為例作說明。獵人由家裡到草原

上去。中途受到了溪流攔阻。此一受阻若以整個打獵的事件為一股份上說，即為股份受到了阻塞、

若依照普通表達的方式上說，是往草原去打獵的事出現了問題，要使股份得到順利的展現，或

要使所遇到的問題得到解答，獵人即視察其所遇到的情景，運用他與此有關連的已有知識，去

尋求解決此問題的方法，亦即提出此一問題可行的假設。此方法或假設具有落實可行性而引生一系列的連續行為（如尋找一枯樹幹與竹竿，撐樹幹渡溪流等），而使其過渡到溪流的彼岸，而繼續其往草原打獵的行程。

所說的獵人的成功的行為，從成功的行為說的理論上說，此行為即為真。相反地，如所說的行為不成功而失敗了，則此行為為假。故真理為有效的或成功的表現，而此亦即為行為的目的。當一老鼠在迷宮裡從事多次走出迷宮的嘗試而未能達目的時，它的嘗試失敗了，它的行為為假的。但當它達到了目的，尋找到了真正的出路，它成功的行為即為真的，而失敗了的行為則為假的。此與所說的獵人的行為是相似的。獵人與老鼠的不同，是獵人能由思想上去分析與判斷真與假而老鼠則不能，而只能由行為上不斷去嘗試以求出真假。

以成功的行為為真而失敗為假的說法曾為某些實驗主義者所主張，但後來受到了反對。反對的主要理由為：(a)此一說法並未對真與假加以界定，而只是指出了有些行為是成功的而達到了目的，有些行為則沒有成功而不能達到目的的存在事實。此與說有些行為是敏捷的而有些則遲鈍的，有些行為是可喜的而有些則是痛苦的，有些行為為社會所讚許，有些則不為社會所讚許的說法同類。他說：「真的即是我們以為有利的。……我們要依我們現在所能獲得的真理而生活。今日以為是真的，明天可以視之為假。托勒密的天文學，歐幾里德的空間說，亞里士多德的邏輯，經院學派的形而上學，對過去幾世代的人是有利的，但人類的經驗已超出了這些學問的界限，現在我們視它們為相對地真，或說在那些的經驗範圍內為真⑬。」詹氏此一「我們以為有利的」為真的說法，後來更說成為：當托勒密的天文學可以對天象加以說明，當它為社會大眾所讚許，當它滿足了了人的要求而相信它時，它即是

真的。此一對真的說法自然與常識的了解有距離。

(b)⑭

此一說法對假設的重要性不能肯定。從成功的行為說的觀點上說，假設被建立而未有運作前無所謂真亦無所謂假。因其既未表現成功亦未表現失敗。但當其被運作而表明了成功之後，假設亦不能被稱為真，因其已經過去而不再是一假設。因此由成功的行為去說真假，假設即無真假可說，而被排除於真理之內。但假設在脈絡論中是一主要部份，真與假是依假設而說。去除了假設的脈絡論的真理說是不能將真理納於脈絡論的範疇中的。故成功的行為說即不能表達脈絡論的真理涵義。事實上，成功的行為說不但對假設沒有正視，對指涉的功用亦沒有注意。而此二者皆為脈絡論所不能忽略的。當假設與指涉被認定為運作真理說的不可忽略的要素時，脈絡論者即由成功的行為說而進於實證的假設理論。

(2)

實證的假設。由實證的假設去說運作的真理說，真理即為實證的真理。依照此一說法，所謂真，不是成功的行為是真，而是引導到成功的行為的假設為真。當沒有假設時即無真假可說，而只有成功與不成功的行為。對假設的證明的運作如其結果為成功的則此假設為真，否則為假。由此一意義上說，真理不只為成功的行為，而是較成功的行為更為複雜的表現。真理是一假設與其可能發生的事件的關係的整個表現。

在一個實證的行為中最少包涵了如下三階段：一、符號結構的形構（一假設可僅表示一態度，但亦可開展為一文字或符號的陳述）；二、符號的指涉的求證（運作）；三、指涉得到了滿意的結果或受到阻塞（實證）。成功的行為說只表示了最後一階段的意義，而有以前面二階段為多餘的涵義。實證的假設說則表明了前二階段的意義，如實證成功亦具有了後一階段的意義。

依照成功的行為說，嘗試錯誤的行為表現了真假的判斷。但實證的假設說則不如此說。一個胡亂地嘗試迷宮裡不同途徑的老鼠會表現出成功或失敗的行為。依照成功的行為說，這些行為可以之為真的或假的行為。但實證的假設說不如此說。而只是以如果老鼠表示出一種預測的態度，而它的行為是要證明它的預測，則它的不成功的行為即表明它的態度為錯的，而成功的行為則表明了它的態度為真的。此一了解是與常識較多相合，亦與其他世界理論的真理說較為相合，並可去除一些有關實驗主義或運作的真理說的吊詭說法。

由以上的了解我們即可以說一個尚未被實證的假設為真理，它的假設是潛在地真或潛在地假。我們可以提出間接的證據以增進或減低它在直接實證中所存有的概然性。例如，前面所說及的獵人如確定地見到他不可能越過那溪流，他將不會去嘗試那不可能的假定。他了解溪流的假定的根據是間接的，只是依於過去對溪水的經驗，但我們會同意他以他的假定為真。但此只是概然的真。此真只是一種可靠的信賴。因為尚未有實際的證明。無疑地，很多科學的知識亦是屬於此一類的知識。其中有一大部份是不可以證明的。實證的假設的理論不忽視要給與具有間接的證據而不能證明的假設高度的信賴。但亦注意到所說的假設所存有的危險性，特別是對此帶有誇張的說法。

此一理論亦強調了一實用的吊詭。那就是它以為真的假設對於自然的真正性質無所見。它強調說，一符號的陳述或一圖表或一模式只是控制自然的工具，它並不是如符合真理說的反映了自然，亦不是如融貫的真理論所說的以此為有機的自然整體的一部份。因此，此一理論的說明者以為一個人不能由運作的假設以洞見或直覺自然的性質。假設的結構是一件事，證明此假設的成功行為是另一件事。其間的指涉關係只是運作地相結在一起。但裴柏以為此一說法有過

份將自然的性質與假設劃分開的涵義。作為反對傳統的符合說與融貫說對自然性質所涵蘊的洞見理論，

運作說作如此的強調是可以了解的。但是涵蘊此一理論而又為此一理論的經驗所涵蘊的脈絡論

的範疇並不要使一真的假設的性質與為其所表達為真的事件的性質有極端的分割。為了要釐清

成功的行為說理論的意義脈絡論者要由成功說而轉到實證的假設說，同樣地現在為了要去除實

證的假設說所涵有的困惑，脈絡論者亦要進而討論性質的肯定說。

(3) 性質的肯定說。此一理論只是強調脈絡論的基本原則，即符號的意義是由其所指示的

性質見到，一股份的性質結合了其所在的脈絡的性質。依照脈絡論的觀點一完滿展現的結構的

性質將要預示一性質的完滿表現。事實上由檢查知覺結構的事上我們見到實證行為（此即一知

覺）的結構一定會部份地由知覺者的活動所構成。當此活動為證明一假設的運作時，這運作明

顯地即成為運作者所給與證明的結構的成份。由此可見它們即表現於成功的實證行為上。（但

它們不會在一個失敗了的實證行為上出現）因此，一真的假設的指涉結構是經歷了一系列的運

作表現而進於為其所指向的事件的建構上成為其成功的實證。

假定前面所說的獵人在了解他所面對的情景後，即作如下的明顯的陳述：「如我取用該竹

竿而置身於該木幹之上，撐離此岸，將可達於彼岸。」我們如以此作為一有意義的句子，則此

句子已是一個顯示了指涉的結構，這指涉是運作的開始，表現於我們的觀念中，這開始的指涉

或觀念在取竹竿置身木幹上，平衡身體撐開木幹而達於彼岸等運作中其體地表現了出來。這些

運作的行為即為對假設的實證行為，獵人現在所經驗到的性質，就是那為語言的陳述而

要從事證明的事件的性質。但這些性質亦正是那為語言所指涉的結構的性質，而為溪流、空氣、

竹竿的粗糙、木幹的轉動等的實際環境所加強。實證事件的建構是不同的貢獻而成的整體表現。

部份來於獵人的運作，部份來於連續的物質組織，而運作即在其中進行。為我們直覺到的性質即為此一整體結構的性質。此結構滿足了獵人的期待，結合了始於語言陳述的指涉結構。由句子的結構所作為一系列的開始的指涉而在其指謂上得到了真正的實現。因此，對該結構的直覺正是對於該句子所指謂的事件的結構的部份的或預示的直覺。因此，一真正的假設在其結構與性質上能對於其所指謂而加以實證的事件的結構與性質有所洞見。

因此，在某一意義上，一真正的假設與其所要實證的事件相符合。因為指涉繼續地貫徹於實證的事件上。在另一意義上，一真正的假設與其所要實證的事件相融貫。因為它的指涉不是受到阻礙，而是得到了完成。脈絡論者說此即為符合真理說與融貫真理說所要表達的一些真正的意義。他並進一步說，符合說以為可以不需要動進的運作交滙而有符合則是錯誤的；融貫說先於融合的行為而可以有任何融貫的表現亦為錯誤的。符合說與融貫說皆有以真理可以是一種獨立於實證的行為之外的說法，依運作真理說的了解，此實為錯誤的說法。

因此運作的理論由性質的肯定說而極成其說。此一理論並以為由科學與哲學所持有的假設為我們提供了對於自然的建構甚大的洞見。在假設可直接地實證時我們不僅對假設所要實證的事件的結構有所洞見，對其性質亦然。在假設不可以直接實證時我們只知道一些關於假設所指涉的事件的結構，我們可以清楚知道有如此的事件，但我們對它們的性質為何則無所知。我們知道它們有性質正如知道有不可以直接地證明的事物一樣。脈絡論由當下的事件開始了解。它對廣大的世界建構的確定性則逐步減當下的事件甚確定，由此而及於其所關連的周圍事件，但對廣大的世界建構作思辨的了解，但在受到反駁時將退歸當下可以實證的少。它是願意去對有關廣大的世界建構作思辨的了解，但在受到反駁時將退歸當下可以實證的事件上。

但脈絡論者可否依於其自己的原則而被逼承認有某些獨立於實證行為之外的事件結構呢？

對當下事件的假設的眞或假豈不是不可以直接地實證的嗎？脈絡論的範疇豈不是表示了他的假設的結構與其他世界的結構的符合或內在的完整嗎？要而言之，是否對運作的眞理說進一步的釐清將不可避免地會歸到符合說或因果的調整說或融貫說上去而要使脈絡論者承認一些更確定的建構理論呢？

此是脈絡論要面對的問題。脈絡論者對此一問題最好的回答是說：你們如有本事可以由此去攻擊脈絡論。但由脈絡論的前提上說是無法對它攻擊的，因它常常堅持直接的證明，即由運作而表現的證明。對其所持的前提所引生的問題是，如脈絡論如將其說限於可直接的證明中，則其即不能被認爲一可適切地解釋整個世界的理論。因此脈絡論即要面對一兩難的問題：或限其說於直接的證明中，如此則其理論即缺少廣度性；或承認間接證明的有效以開展其理論，如此則必需承認自然有其確定的結構。脈絡論者不論採用任何一說法皆將陷於同時肯定與否定自然結構的矛盾。對此一矛盾，脈絡論者最後的回答可能是：你們如何知道自然不是內在地常在改變而充滿了奇異呢？

註 釋

❶ S. C. Pepper, *World Hypotheses* (Berkeley and Los Augels: Univ. of California Press, 1966; first published in 1942), p. 141.

❷ F. Thilly and Ledger Wood, *A History of Philosophy* (New York: Holt, Rinehart and Winston, 1957), p. 654.

❸ S. C. Pepper, *Concept and Quality: A World Hypothesis* (La Salle, Illinois: Open Court Publishing Co., 1967), pp. 2-3.

❹ S. C. Pepper, *World Hypotheses*, p. 232.

❺ Ibid., pp. 235-36, 243.

❻ Ibid., p. 236.

❼ Ibid., p. 236.

❽ Ibid., p. 236.

❾ Ibid., p. 243.

❿ Ibid., p. 258.

⓫ Ibid., p. 261.

⓬ Ibid., p. 268.

⓭ William James, *Pragmatism* (New York: Longmans, Green, 1922), pp. 222-23.

⓮ S. C. Pepper, *World Hypotheses*, p. 271.

第九章　機體論（萬物一體論）（上）

一、小引

機體論亦爲依根源的譬喻而建立的一個相對地適切的世界的假設的理論。依裴柏的了解，西方近代哲學中的席林（Schelling）、黑格爾（Hegel）、格林（Green）、布萊德雷（Bradley）、包桑奎（Bosanquet）、羅哀斯（Royce）等人的哲學皆是機體論❶。在後面我們將分別爲：⑴機體論的根源的譬喻與範疇的確定，⑵舉例說明，⑶應用範疇以了解世界，⑷融貫的真理說等四節以介述機體論對世界作結構性與系統性的說明及其真理說的涵義，所說的四節將分別爲上下兩章，⑴與⑵及本「小引」爲上章，⑶與⑷爲下章。

二、機體論的根源的譬喻與範疇的確定

機體論的根源的譬喻是「合各部份爲一整體的表現」，可簡稱爲整體的或合一的表現❷。「有機」比「機體」一名在常識上較爲適用。故裴柏似應以「有機論」（Organism）一名去稱謂他由「合各部份爲一整體的表現」的根源的譬喻所建立的世界的假設的理論。但他以「有機論」一名是生物學上的名詞，有生物學的專門涵義，而並不能適當地表達由所說的根源

的譬喻所涵有的意義。故他仍以一較不常用的「機體論」一名去稱謂此一世界理論❸。從中文譯名來說，Organicism 一名最好譯為「萬物一體論」。但由於前面三個世界理論的譯名都是三個字，為了一致起見，故仍以「機體論」一名為主譯，而附以「萬物一體論」一名於括弧之中。

由「合各部份為一整體的表現」的根源的譬喻而引伸出來的範疇有七個，但此七個範疇並不是絕對而不能有增減的。增減的決定將相應於對此一理論的要求詳細或簡略的解釋而定。七個範疇是：(1)經驗的片斷，此片斷隨(2)連鎖或連結而表現，由此一表現的加劇而引至(3)矛盾、缺口、相反、或反作用，而自然地再引生(4)在一個有機的整體中的消融，而見及此消融(5)隱潛於所說的經驗的片斷中，而由一個融貫的整體去超越先前的矛盾，此整體(7)保存了原來所有經驗的片斷而沒有任何的失落❹。

以上所說的七個範疇可分為兩組：第一組為前進組，第二組為理想組。範疇(1)在(4)為前進組，(4)至(7)為理想組。(4)之所以既屬於前進組而又屬於理想組二者之中。它是前進組範疇的目的和最後階段，是理想組範疇的明確表示的所在。因此範疇(1)至(4)相容地構成了前進組，而範疇(4)至(7)則相容地構成了理想組❺。

「所有事實都被機體論者了解為隱潛着的有機的歷程。「因此，他（機體論者）相信對世界中任何現實的歷程的一種小心的審查會顯示它的有機的結構，雖然有些為我們一般地熟悉的歷程較其他的歷程更清楚而明顯地顯示了有機的結構❻。」為了要適切地表現此一了解或此一信念，所說的七個範疇一方面應表示包括在有機的歷程的諸步驟中——此是第一組的範疇企圖要

做的，另一方面則應表示在有機的結構中最後所獲得或實現的主要特色——此是第二組的範疇所朝向的目的。既然第一組範疇的主要功用是表示每一事件如何朝向最後的合一，它顯示了前進的作用，因此而被稱為前進組的範疇。至於第二組範疇的主要功用是表示每一事件如何獲得或實現了它的最後的合一，並表明了那最後或那理想的目的，因此這一組範疇即被稱為理想組的範疇。

三、舉例說明

前面所說的範疇的涵義可以先用例子去說明。裴柏即舉了天文學的發展史為說明的例子。天文學始於人對散佈於天空中的光體的驚奇。天空的光體放射出不同的光芒，依不同的方

所說的前進組的範疇與理想組的範疇存有對立性。此一對立性是此一世界理論不可以去除的對立，而亦為它所要對付的。理想地說，如機體論只有理想組的範疇而沒有前進組的範疇是最理想的。但果真是如此，則機體論將要收縮到一很小的範圍內。相反地，如機體論只有前進組的範疇而沒有理想組的範疇，則前進組的範疇要被改變，而機體論的根源的譬喻亦要被揚棄，而使機體論轉為脈絡論。

有些機體論者曾以前進組的範疇與理想組的範疇的對立，為「現象」（Appearance）與「真實」（Reality）的對立❼，但裴柏不以為如此的了解為合適的，他不以為前進組的範疇所指謂的僅為現象，而理想組的範疇所指謂的則為本體。因依機體論的理論說，所說的現象實同為事物的真實所在，而此所在即為由前進組的範疇所展示。

式而移動。此依不同的方式而移動的光體表現了一種彼此互相關連的現象。古代的人注意到此一現象而由此進而尋求更大的關連，而將諸關連的現象組織起來。起初天上諸現象與地上諸現象如枱桌、樹木、山川、河流等彼此分離，沒有連結。將天上諸現象與地上諸事物關連在一起是後來的事。

亞諾諸曼尼斯（Anaximenes）以地球好似圓的盤一樣，浮於空氣中。太陽、月亮與諸行星好似火盤一樣浮於天空中。星星如透明的水晶球一樣散佈於穹窿上。它們都在地球的上面旋轉好似人的帽子在人的頭上旋轉，或好似磨石的上蓋罩在磨盤上旋轉一樣。位於地球北緣的高山在晚上遮蓋了太陽使地球由光明轉爲黑暗。

在亞氏的了解中，諸現象散殊而片斷地呈現。每早昇起一個新的太陽。雜亂的星星散亂地往來移動。行星無目的地遊蕩。由星星的運動而來的預測與行星的運動相衝突。因太陽西沉而來永遠黑暗的期待與新出的陽光所呈現的光明相衝突。依陽光而來對事物確定的預測因陽光的消失而改變。對永恆的規律的期待爲變化與不規則所抵銷。對無常與不規則的期待又爲永恆與規律所抵銷。人好似永遠存在於不確定的世界中。但由於對所說的諸現象的繼續觀察，以及對其他類似的現象的觀察的組合，而使所說的諸衝突與抵銷逐步去除，而使北緣的高山，如磨石的上蓋，以及無數新出現的太陽成爲一可預測的系統。日與夜不再矛盾而是彼此一貫而互不相違。白天與晚上以及每一時刻亦是如此。行星、月亮與太陽以及其他的衆星星，不僅浮在空中或布列於穹窿上，亦移動於一定的軌道中。一種對天上諸現象的組織使其他的現象得以解釋。預見了先前所未能注意及的事，進而建立一個融貫的天文學系統而去除了其中存有的矛盾。在此需要特別強調的是，此一融貫系統的建立，是由觀察而達到，建基於觀察的了解上，而不是

出於幻想或由任意的杜撰而成。

但亞氏由對天象的了解所建立的系統，並不能免除幻想與杜撰的弊病。對亞氏的系統進一步的觀察即見其所存有的矛盾。爲了去除亞氏的矛盾他的系統即轉成爲後來的系統中的片斷資料，北緣的高山和如圓的盤一樣的地球，或似火盤一樣的諸行星的說法被揚棄。但透明如水晶的球體觀被保留，並增加了它們的數目。他的繼承者視恆星、行星、月亮和太陽皆爲透明的球。

並以它們各有一特殊的軌道環繞地球而旋轉。當一個行星的軌道太過複雜而不可以由一個星球加以解釋時，即增加其他沒有發光的球體進去作解釋。這些不發光的球體朝着一個或多個方向運動與發光的星球相混合而產生可見的不規則的軌道。此一系統保存了亞氏所有的觀察，並增加了很多他所未曾見及的，而使天文學隱存的矛盾得以消除。初看起來行星的移動好似是無目的的。但依照此一系統的了解，其所存的規律性實際上是較在風中吹動的樹葉所具有的規律性更大。此一水晶式的天象系統即是亞里士多德的天文學。

但當人們從事更多的觀察而獲得更多有關天象的資料時，即見到有關行星的軌道的複雜現象，不是任何已有的天文學系統所能解釋的。由更多的觀察所見的與星球可能的移動相衝突。由增加圓周式運動的不同速率和方向，設立一些離心的旋轉運動，並肯定於第一個圓周運動的周圍上有第二個圓周的運動，即可以更細微地描述所觀察到的任何天體的軌道。此即托勒密的系統（Ptalency's system）。

但上述的解釋是很複雜的。觀察愈精細解釋愈複雜。每增加一個新的觀察所及的行星離軌的運動，即要增加另一個圓周的運動以作解釋。尤有甚者，一個軌道或一個球體與另一軌道或

球體之間彼此不相涵，而沒有連結。每一軌道相對於其他的軌道都是孤立而分離的，皆可爲托氏的圓周所描述，故皆爲片斷的。由球體至球體或由軌道至軌道不能有所預測。任何歸到其自己去的軌道在托勒密的系統中，皆可由繁複的圓周的軌道去描述。

在托勒密的系統中每樣東西都是可能的，沒有任何東西是被決定或被解釋了的。此與現象的規律性與依此規律性而從事預測與希望獲得決定性的期待相反。托勒密的圓周越多越表示了過份的任意、虛構與抽象。它們好似不是緊密地依隨觀察而有，或爲二者不可缺少的相互涵蘊或連結。它們好似僅爲一種方便的法門。對軌道越來越複雜的解釋成爲一任意的連結。此連結與觀察所及的現象無關，正如亞諾諸曼尼斯的高山與火似的盤浮於空中脫離了觀察與觀察無關一樣。

哥白尼（Copernicus）以地球爲行星之一，各行星皆環繞太陽旋轉的以太陽爲中心的理論（heliocentric theory）大大地簡化了托勒密的說法。此一簡化預示了一可由觀察而建立的更大的涵蘊系統，而即在此一方向上建立了由觀察而顯現的內在的連結基礎。

克卜勒（Kepler）以諸行星環繞太陽作橢圓形的旋轉說，以及由觀察所得而設定天體運動三律說，更進一步結合了由對各別行星觀察所得的相互涵蘊的意義。

望遠鏡的發明增進了觀察的精確性，擴大了觀察範圍，並使觀察的工作可以大量進行。波拉（Brahe）從事了大量不大嚴密而鬆弛地相關連的觀察，在一定的限度內而可以作出預測與彼此相涵蘊的解釋。但在所說的限度之外，其他方面仍是彼此不關連而爲片斷的資料。已有的系統與大量新的觀察資料未能連成一系統，它們要求進一步的系統化，它們等待着更大的完成。

由牛頓此一更大的完成得以實現。牛頓所完成了的不限於天文學上，而是使天文學與機械

學結合爲一而成一互相包涵的系統。在當時所了解的機械學被涵納於天文學系統之內。克卜勒對天文學現象所觀察得到的片斷的系統化被確定，而連結於牛頓的運動三律和萬有引力律中。運動三律與萬有引力律亦由於包括了大量對天文觀察所得到的事實而更得以肯定與加強。通過所建立的運動三律使天文的觀察獲得了決定的涵義而爲托氏的系統所不能獲得的。

但如我們現在所知道的，即使是牛頓的系統亦內存有矛盾，而使愛恩斯坦（Einstein）提出了新的說法。但作爲舉例的說明，裴柏以爲前面所說的已足夠。他亦表明所說的繼續向前系統化的表現於愛恩斯坦之後仍在進行。他並以爲機體論者相信只要有矛盾或缺口仍然出現則此一向前系統化的表現即不會停止 ❽。

第十章　機體論（萬物一體論）（下）

四、應用範疇以了解世界

(1)

片斷：在說明範疇的應用時，裴柏特別指出，上章第三節所舉的例子不是應用機體論的範疇的一個例子，而是一系列的應用表現。同樣的表現，亦即不斷完成的歷程一再在進行，並朝着一個方向進行，即朝着進一步完成的方向進行。

此一事實表示作爲完成的資料常與先前已有的完成相對。換句話說即是片斷是相對於某一已完成的階段而說的。對亞諾諸曼尼斯來說，片斷即爲天空中的光體及它們分立的運動；對克卜勒來說，片斷爲圓周的系統運動；對牛頓來說，片斷則爲克卜勒的律則。因此，片斷一範疇是一消極的範疇。它是由一已完成的階段所表現出那尚未完成的限度，亦即片斷是任何尚未達到整體化的東西。

片斷的特殊性由整體去確定。在整體中片斷不再爲片斷。在亞諾諸曼尼斯達到系統化的圓周的運動之前，光體或分立的運動是什麼他自己亦不能說。在達到系統化之後，他即能確定光體或分立的運動爲圓周運動的部份表現。此圓周的運動使所說的光體或分立的運動組合爲一體，而成爲此一體的材料。依照機體論者的觀點，所有被組合的材料在被組合之前都是不確定的。一孤立的材料，或在系統被建立之前，沒有任何科學家能確定地知道他所處理的材料是什麼。

一片斷惟有在它被納入一融貫的系統中去而與其他的材料結合在一起時，它的意義才清楚。

片斷雖然是一消極的概念，但在它的意義確定了之後，它表示如下的積極性：它是第一給與，它不是虛構的。天空中發光的現象是如實地如此呈現，即使我們在其被系統化之前不清楚它們是什麼。在使部份成爲整體的進程中，每一階段必需以在其前的片斷或部份的完成爲它的材料。在此一意義下，片斷常爲整體的材料，每一片斷都是眞實的。不眞實的不是片斷而是片斷表現的方式。此方式是相對於一整體或一系統而說，故機體論者不以其爲眞實的方式。

片斷是消極的概念，但是積極的現象。只是此現象不能由片斷本身上說，而要由整體上說，亦即由整體上將其融貫組合而爲整體的一部份上說。

(2) 連結：片斷內具有整體性的趨向。此趨向即爲第二範疇連結。

依機體論者的了解，事物的組織表現不是有一外來的東西在組織它們，而是事物自己在組織自己。科學家與哲學家的活動亦是自發的，亦如材料自己在表現其內在所具有的形式一樣。故不是亞諾諸曼尼斯、亞里士多德、托勒密、哥白尼、克卜勒與牛頓發明了天文學，而是天文學藉着他們而表現其自己。他們的天才不是別的，而只是彰顯其受干預越少，表現即會越好。故不是由人的偏見而來的蔽塞，使事實得以展現其自己的連結。連結未嘗離開事物而了事實，去除了由人的偏見而來的蔽塞，使事實得以展現其自己的連結。連結未嘗離開事物而不內在於其中。在克卜勒的片斷中所具有牛頓的整體性，在牛頓將其顯明之前與事後是一樣的。所有的東西都在那裡，除了任由其依其自己而表現外，沒有其他可做的。牛頓最大的識見即在他如實地見到了事物的眞正性質。如果他對事物了解不夠，或干預了事物，將不能對事物有他所作的綜合的了解，那就是說他所作的綜合的了解不由他而顯現，而是另有所待。但卻不可避免地總要顯現。此即片斷所具有不可避免的連結表現，亦即片斷所具有的整體性的涵蘊表現。

機體論論者相信每一片斷、現象、材料、事實、都內存有連結。他們以為任何人要尋找此連結都可由觀察中尋找得到。但最好的證據則是由知識的發展史上見到。它是在逐步的經驗積累中所呈現出整體性的發展的表示。

(3) 矛盾·連結由片斷伸展出去如觸角一樣。觸角遇到了抗拒，片斷即產生矛盾。整體的進展並不是常常順利而連續的，而是一個片斷與另一個片斷互相抗拒，而產生衝突與矛盾。此衝突與矛盾只能在一個整體中消解。

早期的機體論論者如黑格爾，以事物只有一個發展的途徑。由最小的片斷至最終的整體。他的書敘述了此一唯一而不可避免的發展的悲喜劇。這是一喜劇，因為最後的快樂結局是不可避免的，亦是一悲劇，因所經的道路是衝突的。人類經歷不斷的鬥爭但永不能達到最後的目的。

正——反——合是他的戲劇中一幕幕一再呈現的模式。一片斷在孤立與抽象的景況中不停地為它的連結所驅使而至另一相反與矛盾中去。此等相反的片斷不可避免地連結着，並不可避免地敵對着。每一片斷需要其他的片斷，包涵着其他的片斷以完成其自己。一片斷亦與其他的片斷相矛盾與相摧殘。正與反既相生相需而又相反相克，衝突最後消解於一整體中，一更高層級的綜合中，此綜合涵攝了每一片斷，並超越它們，在一更豐富而具體的整體。它的連結驅使它到特殊的對立上調和。但此一整體隨即表示出其相對性而要尋求更大的整體。它的連結驅使它到特殊的對立上去。這兩個較前更豐富的片斷再彼此相涵與彼此矛盾，彼此吸引與彼此排斥，彼此要求亦彼此互相毀滅，直至獲得一新的與更高和更具體的綜合。在獲得了之後，同樣的衝突又再出現。如此地一再發生，由一階段至另一階段。在每一階段中片斷都豐富了其內涵而幾至於完全，而其向前發展預示了其所向的目的。在此目的上所有片斷互相結合與互相調和而彼此涵蘊而沒有遺漏。

因此在該全體中每一片斷獲得了其完全。在那完全中沒有相對，不再有片斷，不再有鬆弛地飛馳着尋求滿足的連結。所有都結合在一個絕對而具體的有機而融貫的整體中，此即黑格爾的絕對⑨。

對後來的機體論者來說，此一戲劇是對真實的一種拙劣的描述。通向宇宙真理的道路不是唯一的，使片斷的材料得到最後的完成亦不是唯一的。每一片斷亦非只表現出一種單一的不可避免的對立。天文學可以循着不同的途徑發展。由錯誤走向真理有很多道路。對開始的事物或片斷的認識愈薄弱，愈抽象，愈孤立，愈含糊，或愈混淆，對其解釋的可能方式亦愈多。當了解片斷的涵義增加了之後，可解釋的方式即相對地減少。對任何事物知道的愈少，可能用以了解的方式即愈多。對亞諾諸曼尼斯觀察所及的天象，可以提出千百個可能的假設作解釋。但對牛頓所具有的資料，則大概只能有一個可能的綜合。

後來的機體論者以黑格爾所說的認識不可避免地朝向一最後的綜合，一切矛盾在其中不再存在是對的；他由觀察所見一片斷的連結趨向於其他的片斷因而產生矛盾，矛盾要求融貫的合一亦是對的；他以爲片斷所具有的連結對已結合在一起而有頑強的抗拒的相關的事實有特殊的吸引力亦是對的；天皇星（Uranus）在它的軌道上所出現的差異，那些頑強的資料不服從牛頓的律則，特別引起了天文學家的注意，而引至對海王星（Neptune）的發現。黑格爾以上的說法可以說都是對的。但他以事物的發展任意而怪誕地限於一個路向上，由此而招至對機體論的非議，則是錯的⑩。

片斷的連結表現不能受限制，其表現的數目亦不能限定，其遭遇到的矛盾亦不能預定，幾種表現的路向可以同時進行。例如阿里斯塔克斯（Aristachus）在哥白尼之前已提出了太陽

為中心的天文學說。阿氏的提議太早，有違於當時希臘流行的物理學說，以地球為物質展現的不變所在。但阿里斯塔克斯的理論仍然是出現了。天文學的歷史亦可沿着阿里斯塔克斯的見解發展，而不必出現亞里士多德的說法。但發展的路向雖然可以不同，而牛頓的天文學則是二者所要共同達到的目的所在。即目的要為事物的發展的結構所預定。但到達目的的特殊路向則並不預定。

後來的機體論者即由於此一了解而對有機的發展的描述比其前輩更具伸縮性。他們注意到現象是被給與的，並注意到被給與的現象所涵蘊着與其他的現象所產生的矛盾，以及這些矛盾在系統上被消解而融貫地互相結合。他們並不規定知識的路向。他們亦不相信他們可以規定任何東西；他們只是指出在世上的事物是怎樣地發展。他們的論述完全是闡釋的，而要人看由天文學所顯示出來的事實是否是如他們所說的一樣地在表現。

那帶着連結的矛盾向事實不斷求結合以滿足它的要求如前面所指出的，到底是什麼呢？對此一問題的回答，很顯明地，機體論者並不以其即為邏輯上「p與非p合取的否定」的矛盾。他們雖然以此形式上的矛盾是最抽象的，並以此是片斷的，表達了他們所謂矛盾的一種說法，但他們並不以他們所要說的矛盾即為形式的矛盾，他們以他們所說的矛盾所具有的意義不僅僅是表示一種符號上的涵蘊關係，而是表示了事物的真正衝突。例如由亞諾諾曼尼斯所觀察到的太陽即涵蘊有既為一個而又不是一個太陽的矛盾。每日的太陽，一日間由東至西的連續現象，顯示了其為一個而又不是一個對象。但如果太陽為一個對象而在西方的彼此相似，它將會由西方再興起，如一個人在一洞中消失再由洞中出現一樣。但太陽恆常地由東邊興起。因此每日應有一新的太陽。但太陽不能既是一個而又不是一個。由觀察地球的結構而發現到太陽可以在山邊的背後繞到北邊去而轉到東邊出現，而使這些現象所表現出的衝突得到解決。他們指出，一種矛盾是常

基於事實上的衝突。因此，有多少不同的片斷顯現出不能解決的現象即有多少不同的矛盾⓫。

例如，一孤立的現象是與其未表達的連結相矛盾，或說孤立的概念本身是自相矛盾的。因為一現象常是某物的現象而有它的連結。在此一意義上說，所有形式主義者的特色是抽象的與自相矛盾的。黃色永不會完全孤立地呈現，它與某人或某物或某人與某物二者相連結，即它要有所附托。因此以黃色為孤立的是與它所具有的連結性及它的附托相矛盾。

又不確定亦是自相矛盾的。此正是托勒密系統的主要困難所在。用以說明行星軌道所增加的圓周不是由觀察所及的行星位置所確定涵有。曾有人以為托勒密的系統從來未被否證過。但機體論者以為事實上是此一系統從來未被證明過。將由對行星觀察所不可確定的圓周包括進去，正如將以為是推動行星旋轉的精靈包括進去一樣。機體論者以為此一包括事實上是將一確定的系統包括進去，而此一系統則與托勒密的系統相矛盾，因為他的系統並不確定⓬。

又如脈絡論者所說的融合亦是自相矛盾的。因融合既肯定了事物的獨立性而又否定它的獨立性。此是另一形式的不確定。要消除此一矛盾我們即要對融合所隱存着的結構有了解，亦要對由包涵於結構中的資料而來的組織所引生融合的相對獨立性有了解，並要對結構所涵的脈絡有了解。

又衝突的材料如亞諾諸曼尼斯所觀察到的太陽是矛盾的，此等材料涵有一組合的可能性，亦涵有一否認此一組合的可能性。有時如亞諾諸曼尼斯所見的，一些新的觀察彌縫了已有的裂痕，而可以得到一種綜合；又有時如亞里士多德所見的，新的觀察排除了不相干的東西，而使這些被排除的東西在別處得到了關連，使其餘的得到另一更確定與完全的組合。當托勒密排除了亞里士多德的透明的球體時，亦表現了同樣的情形。

片斷可能有的矛盾方式是多的。此正如世界有不同的衝突、游離、混淆、雜亂等一樣。但片斷中的連結如容許其循其所涵蘊的而達於整體時，則所說的不同的矛盾皆得以自己消融。

(4)　有機的整體：消融常為衝突的片斷的一整合。此整合由一階段而進於另一階段。如果我們查看這些階段，如在天文學史上所表現的，我們將見到消融的進展表現了三個特徵：(a)逐步的包涵，(b)逐步的確定，與(c)逐步的組合❸。

在將天文學與機械學合而為一。此一合一使大量互相涵蘊與互相肯定的材料得以結合。組合了的材料得到逐步的·確定標示了天文學的發展。確定只是包涵的一面，更大的確定即更大的包涵。增加了觀察的精確性即增加了可觀察到的事實，望遠鏡不僅增加了觀察的精確性，亦增加了可觀察的對象，但確定性所要求的則不僅是對與一個對象有關的事實要注意，而更要了解構成對象的細微的組織為何，以探求其確切的性質所在。

為亞諾諸曼尼斯所組合現象比較少，所以被包涵在他的系統中的事物也較少。但由於天文學所觀察及的資料日漸增加，組織資料的方式亦因此而逐步地增加。牛頓的一個大的貢獻，即在將天文學與機械學合而為一。

但若只有包涵性或只有確定性則不足以解釋天文學的發展。觀察在逐步完成。此一完成的趨向表現在更大的組織上。有兩種組織原則，就其表現上說此兩原則不完全相同。但二者最後皆輻輳於同樣的事實上。依據第一原則，一個有機的整體即是一個以整體中每一成份皆涵蘊着其他的成份的系統。依據第二原則，一個整體是任何一個成份被改變或被移去，即會改變其他的成份或者甚至要毀滅了整個有機體的系統❹。

由以上所說的原則，我們可以對有機性的程度作如下的分辨：一系統中的某些部份可能有高度的涵蘊性，其他的部份則不是如此。又一系統中某一成份的改變可能對有些部份有嚴重的

後果，對其他的部份則不如此。但雖然如此，只要一系統對其所有的成份具有某一程度上結合的性質，或者只要作為一系統的部份對其他的部份有影響的表現，其即具有某種程度上的有機性。

現代的機體論者即以知識的進展（如天文學的進展）是朝着更大的包涵性、確定性、與有機性上走。他們引用已有的歷史知識作為證據。例如，我們為什麼無疑問地以牛頓的天文學較亞諾諾曼尼斯的天文學為優越呢？機體論者的回答是，因為前者包涵了更多的材料；；因為這些材料更確定；，並且因為這些材料是如此緊密地表現了整體性的結合。它們在很大的程度上互相涵蘊或彼此因果關連。若涵蘊或關連有所改變，則其整體性亦要改變。例如，若太陽的質量有所減少，則牛頓的計算即無效。愛恩斯坦的相對論之所以較牛頓的理論優越，即因其能使要解釋的材料具有更確定性，並能更穩定地建立起一互相涵蘊與互相倚賴的有機整體。

機體論者特別指出，以上所說的天文學知識正是我們現在所能有的有關宇宙結構的知識。

但天文學的事實是什麼呢？它為什麼正如牛頓或愛恩斯坦的系統所表現的呢？無疑的在愛恩斯坦的系統中會有錯誤，正如在牛頓的系統中有錯誤一樣。但錯誤是如何地被發現與改正的呢？

豈不是正如近代的物理學者與天文學家改正牛頓的系統所表現的一樣嗎？藉着尋求到的新材料，找出其中矛盾所在，求出其整體性所在，由此而去除其中的矛盾。當我們增加、補充並組合這些材料時，我們即逐步見到事物的真相所在。說至此，我們或者要問，我們可以假定事物的真相是怎樣的嗎？機體論者的回答是，事物的真相不是別的，而即是經過了一系列的探求所顯示的極限所在。此極限清楚地為系統的探求所界定。由界定所見它是一互相涵蘊或因果地彼此倚賴，完全包涵與完全決定的系統。在極限上，涵蘊與因果關係會合併，因邏輯的必然性要與

最後的事實合一。此一對極限所認識的即爲絕對的事實，亦即機體論者通常所簡稱的絕對。

此一絕對爲機體論者的統體所在。每一事物皆歸到其上去，亦由其中出來。如我們所已說過的，它是前進的範疇的目的，亦爲理想的範疇所要展現的所在。我們已攀過了前進的範疇的高峰。現在我們將抵達目的地，以觀看此目的地的景況爲何。

我們在此要注意的是機體論中的純事實即是它的理想。純事實即爲極限。因爲純事實即是絕對，此一絕對永遠不能由我們所熟習的部份的完整中得到。此極限由我們所依而開始的相對地不純的事實去接近。此是一理想，此理想是眞實的事物。初看起來此好似是一吊詭。但我們隨即會覺悟到，除了機體論者將它完全普遍化之外，其實它只是一普通的觀念。對機械論者來說，宇宙的大機器自然亦爲一理想的事實。但我們永遠不能接觸到此一大機器。它的時空架構，它的陰陽電子等都是機械論者的基本事實，但在認知上這些完全是屬於知識中理想層次上的事，而永不能爲我們所感覺到。機體論者在此一點上不同於機械論者，他們要由部份的證據而見到至最後事實的連接通道。但機體論者則永遠不能見到他們的理想事實。因此，以事實爲理想的並不新奇，新奇的是機體論者要展示爲機械論者所不能達到的目的。

機體論者由各別事物的矛盾中找到了最後的事實融貫的證據。如果有一個孤立而不相矛盾的事實，則機體論者即不能建立起在絕對中所有事物彼此有機關連的論證。是否一切事實都是自相矛盾的呢？此並不能有確定的回答。因此除了絕對外，機體論者要以所有經驗事實內具有矛盾的說法似是獨斷的。

但他們並不訴諸於獨斷，而是提出了強而有力的論據，他們的論據是強而有力的，因爲由對證據的分析，我們見到：任何材料都是一具有連結性的片斷，由此連結而引生矛盾，此矛盾

將在一整體中消融。此一歷程在片斷中自然出現而成爲連結的眞正活動，由對證據不斷分析，我們不斷見到機體論者的論據的可信性，由此而引向對世界最後的結構的了解。

依據外在的證據而從事推演的論證是外在的形式的論證。在如此的論證中，凡可用的證據必全部採用。但機體論者由融貫上以建立的論證是一種內在的眞價論證。在此一論證中，使部份成爲整體的活動的證據在一有機體的事實中尋求它不可避免的目的，而消融一切矛盾。對此一論證唯一可反對的是否認它評析證據的合法性。但在所積累可靠性的證據的面前，此一否認是很難成立的。我們曾見到脈絡論者曾如何試行否認此使部份成爲整體的趨向，而肯定蔽塞、新奇、混融等爲事物的最後所在。各種否定整全的力量，或否認認知的不滿足的要求，或內在的矛盾的嘗試，惟有在最後的失敗中才能見到我們不能分辨自然的特殊的結構的困難所在。對其他的世界的理論來說，它們內在的矛盾只有我們肯定了機體論者對證據的評析。如果根本的矛盾不會在其他的世界的理論中發生，則他們將是勝利者。因他們能調和絕對的事實有機的結構與不是絕對地有機的事實。但他們果眞能作如此的調和嗎？答案無疑是否定的。

再徹底了解機體論者對所說的有關的問題的是否得當，要進而了解其所說的理想的範疇爲何。理想的範疇是表明有機的整體的特色所在，亦是絕對的表現所在。機體論者希望由理想的範疇去解釋自然內在的有限性不存在。他們希望表明在宇宙中現在、過去與未來都不會有任何眞的片斷或有限的事物。

(5) 涵蘊：片斷被涵蘊於整體中成爲整體的一部份。機體論者在此上要說明的是當我們見到有機整體中的片斷的矛盾被消融時，我們即承認這些片斷在整體中始終都是整體的分別表現。它們表面上的片斷性只是一種錯覺或幻像。支持機體論者此一說法的證據有二：(a)片斷中的連

結由所遇到的矛盾而導引我們以片斷事實上為屬於全體的片斷，(b)當整體已經達到後，在回顧的了解中我們承認事實上，由始至終，片斷皆為整體的片斷。地球確實是始終都在太陽的萬有引力場中。當牛頓顯示了萬有引力的關係時，我們見到這些關係始終隱涵在由亞諾諸曼尼斯至卜克勒的觀察中，而不是另有所在，只是他們見不到其所在而已。觀察所得的永不會內在地相矛盾。此一說法可由它們皆於牛頓的系統中而得到融貫的表現上得到證明⑮。

但若果是如此，片斷所遇到的矛盾本身又如何說呢？

(b)　超越：機體論者以矛盾在整體中得到超越。矛盾不是真實的，因為它們並非真實的存在。支持此一見解的有力的證明在當整體達到後矛盾即消失。整體中的各部份在其脫離了有機的關係而成為一片斷時，好似出現了種種的矛盾。但部份事實上永不會脫離整體而自存。當我們僅由片斷而了解片斷的錯誤被去除而見到其在有機的關係中的純粹事實的意義時，它的矛盾即自動地消失。在包涵著各部份的有機的整體中是沒有各別的矛盾的。此一意義可以在我們所達到的相對的完整中見到。我們見到所說的完整如何逐步地顯示為純事實。由此而見到完全的完整或者見到絕對，即絕對的純事實。在絕對的純事實中沒有矛盾，因為在絕對的純事實中矛盾已完全被超越。

但此一說法與人的一般的經驗不相應，作為有限的人的本身更不是絕對。人事實上有矛盾的感覺。

(7)　保存：人的矛盾的感覺是人依一般的經驗而有的事實。但此事實可以被超越。機體論者以此事實內在於絕對中。並且不僅是此事實，而是一切的事實皆存在於絕對中而不會有遺失。在絕對中一切事實皆不會有遺失的涵義，由我們所達到的相對的完整中即可以見到。在牛

頓之前所觀察及的天文事實不是皆為牛頓的整體所探納嗎？所有為亞諾諸曼尼斯、亞里士多德、亞里斯塔克斯、托勒密、哥白尼、波拉、克卜勒等所收集的有關的事實，都可以於牛頓的系統中佔上一定的位置。在牛頓的系統中它們彼此間的缺陷得以彌縫，相互之間的涵蘊的關係得以展現。沒有任何積極的東西失落。所有矛盾在這些事實連結的表現中消失。

沒有任何積極的東西失落。但毫無疑問的某些不是積極的東西，或不相干的事物則被排除了。如亞諾諸曼尼斯的圓盤與高山，亞里士多德的結晶的球體，托勒密的圓周與離心圈。這些不相干的東西與牛頓的系統不相容。但事實上如牛頓的系統所表示的，它們並不眞正地為天文學所觀察及的事實。它們是我們慣常所說的「心理學的解釋」⑯。心理學的解釋自然亦是一種事實，但心理學的解釋在天文學上不佔地位。它只在心理學的系統上相干。故很多屬於心理學上的事實，在天文學的發展上被揚棄。但正如天文學一樣，心理學在其自身的不斷發展史中亦趨向一絕對的最後完成。儘管心理學的系統仍未能如天文學的系統一樣達到一定程度的完整。但可以預測心理學的系統是可以與天文學的系統結合而成為一更大的系統。依機體論者對證據的分析所顯示的此兩系統的資料涵蘊着此一眞正的結合。

由以上的了解我們見到由逐步整合表現而成的天文學所捨棄以為不相干的材料，並不是完全不相干，而只是由一個不為其所歸屬的系統轉到另一為其所歸屬的系統上去。它們與排斥它們的系統中的其他的材料所具有的內在連結，最後在一整合為一的系統中表現其相互的關係。因此在機體論者的整體的材料中沒有東西失落：所有的材料不會失落，因為它們不歸到一系統中去將在別的系統中存在；連結亦不會失落，因為當一個充份概括的整體性結合表現達到後，所有眞

正存在的連結將會顯示出來。至於矛盾的感覺則為心理學上的事實。此是天文學家為其所得到的資料而尋找其內在的律則失敗後所表現出來的外在的反應。但由心理表現的內在脈絡上看，矛盾的感覺是沒有矛盾的。

因此，機體論者歸結說：既然絕對涵於所有片斷中，而在絕對中所有的矛盾與片斷性的證明被超越，在絕對的本身上沒有任何遺失。所以在絕對的事實中亦沒有片斷可說。

五、融貫的真理說

在展示機體論者的範疇的涵義時，我們已涉及它的真理說。因每一片斷都是指涉事實的判斷，而指涉則為連結所表示。要對一判斷作形式的表達要藉着語言或約定的符號，但判斷本身不是語言或約定的符號。形式的表達只是真正的判斷的代替，而真正的判斷是由語言或約定的符號所表示的片斷，一個具體的片斷和它的連結可以用主謂式的句子去表達。例如，亞諾諸曼尼斯對他由觀察太陽所得來的部份系統化的片斷可以總括為：「太陽是一單一的連續體。」此一句子的主詞是指謂事件中的真正事實，亦即是指謂亞氏由觀察太陽所得到的事實。句子的謂詞則指謂他以為與主詞相關的事實，他將謂詞所表達相關的事實歸到主詞中去。如謂詞所肯定的事實與主詞所具有的相符合，則此句子即是真的。但此所說的真本質地不是說句子真，而是說句子所意指的判斷真。句子只是用來表達或符示判斷。如果判斷不真，句子亦不能真。因此，機體論者對語言的邏輯（即由命題、或句子、主詞、謂詞、p項與q項等所表達的邏輯）持保留的態度，而喜歡直接地說判斷。

如在前面所已說及的，一判斷即是一片斷與它的連結。一判斷的真即在於一片斷藉着連結而達到的全體其中不存有矛盾。當亞諾諸曼尼斯見到太陽繞着地球經過了高山而至北邊時，他證明了他有關太陽的判斷。他的觀察與他的理論相合，進一步的觀察更確定了他的判斷。他由此而獲得一較高層級的判斷。但如我們所已知道的，此一較高層級亦被證明為一具有連結的片斷而等待着完成。因此，真理有層級的不同，每一層級的整體表現在它以下各層級所存有的矛盾，去除了其中的錯誤。每一層級皆使判斷有所改進，每一層級藉着事實所得到更大的整體表現而表現了更多的真理。有關事實的真理，在托勒密的系統中所表現的較亞諾諸曼尼斯的系統為多，在克卜勒的系統中所表現的較托勒密的系統為多，在牛頓的系統中所表現的較克卜勒的系統為多。由此一了解上，我們即見到所謂真理的標準即為機體論的範疇所表現的概括性、決定性與有機性，而理想的真理即為絕對自身。

此一真理說被了解為融貫的真理說（ the coherence theory of truth ）。很明顯的此一真理說是被包涵於機體論的範疇中，而它亦預設了該等範疇。我們如不由機體論的觀點上而是由其他理論的觀點上說，融貫的真理說只可被視為一種真理的標準，而並不是真理的本質所在。事實上除脈絡論者之外，其他的哲學家曾將融貫說與一致說（ the theory of consistency ）混淆。但就我們所了解的，一致說只是融貫說的形式影子。因為一致說只是融貫說的形式上的不矛盾，而融貫說則指事物本身的有機連結。因此，反對機體論者以我們可以有很多的自相一致的邏輯系統，故不能以一致為真理的最後標準的說法是不能成立的。機體論者不是以形式上的一致而是以事物的融貫為真理之所在。由他們的範疇的依據上說，此似甚為確定的，他們的範疇與他們對證據的分析可以有可議的地方，但當其被接受之後，對絕對的肯定是不可以

避免的，亦是確定不移而沒有其他的說法可以代替的，因爲絕對即爲事物自己是完全而有機的。

融貫的眞理說的特點有三：⑴眞理不是語言符號與事物的關係，或一事物（如一影像）與另一事物的關係，它不是表示所說的關係，而是表示事物所達到的程度；⑵因此眞理因事物所達到的不同的程度而有不同的層級；⑶因此事物的全體或絕對即是眞，事物的全體或絕對亦是眞理的極限或眞理的最後的準則⓱。

註釋

❶ S. C. Pepper, *World Hypotheses*, pp. 141–142.

❷ Ibid., pp. 280–281.

❸ Ibid.

❹ Ibid., p. 283.

❺ Ibid.

❻ Ibid., p. 281.

❼ Ibid., p. 282.

❽ 請參閱 :S. C. Pepper, *World Hypotheses*, pp. 283–289.

❾ Ibid., pp. 293–294.

❿ Ibid., pp. 294–295.

⓫ Ibid., pp. 295–296.

⓬ Ibid., p. 297.

⓭ Ibid., pp. 298–299.

⓮ Ibid., pp. 299–300.

⓯ Ibid., pp. 304–305.

⓰ Ibid., p. 306.

⓱ Ibid., p. 311.

第十一章　選擇論（上）

一、小　引

選擇論是裴柏繼承形式論、機械論、脈絡論與機體論而來的另一個世界的理論。但前四者是裴氏在他的《世界的假設》一書中第二部份依傳統的西方的哲學而寫成的四種不同的世界的理論。選擇論則不是依傳統的西方的哲學而寫成的理論，而是對現代西方的哲學與現代的科學作系統的了解而寫成的世界的理論。

現代的科學開展了人類對世界的新了解；現代的西方的哲學相應於此新了解而有種種的討論，而顯示了一與傳統的哲學對世界不同的了解。但裴柏不限於任何已有的現代的西方的哲學的了解，而是依他所建立的世界的假設的理論，藉現代的科學的知識與現代的哲學所討論的問題而對世界作一新的假設的了解，而建立一不同於前面所介述的四個依傳統的哲學而建立的世界假設的理論。

選擇論的建立在時間上較前面四個世界的理論晚出約二十五年。在這期間，歐洲大陸出現了存在主義的學派（school of existentialists），英國則由牛津的語言分析學家（Oxford linguistic analysts）而引起了一分析哲學的運動。裴柏對此兩派哲學各別的貢獻

皆有所肯定。但對它們對傳統的形而上學的否定則不能同意❶。依裴柏的了解，西方的傳統的形而上學由世界的假設的進路而對整個世界所作的結構性與系統性的了解，如他在論述前面四個世界的假設時所展示的，是不可以否定的。因此他要在他的《概念與性質：一個世界的假設》一書中仍本其「世界的假設」的進路而藉現代的科學的知識與哲學所討論的問題而對世界作另一新的假設的了解❷。

選擇論既是繼承其所已建立的世界的理論而來的藉現代的科學的知識與哲學的討論而建立的一新的世界的理論，其所採用以表達此理論的方式即與前面所已介述的四個世界的假設的方式相同，亦即是先確定一根源的譬喻，由根源的譬喻而引伸出範疇，再本範疇而對整個世界作建構性和系統性的說明。此一方式為每一世界的假設的理論所藉以了解世界的範疇，於確定了所引伸出的範疇設對世界的解釋都是由根源的譬喻的確定以引伸出了解世界的範疇，於確定了所引伸出的範疇之後，再對每一範疇作解釋，並由對每一範疇的解釋中以說明某一世界的假設的理論對整個世界的了解為何。以機體論為例，當其確定了「合各部份為一整體的表現」為根源的譬喻，並由此根源的譬喻而引伸出前進組與理想組七個範疇之後，即對每一範疇的涵義作解釋；由「片斷」而至「保存」由此而說明機體論所了解的世界的涵義為何。但選擇論依世界的假設的方式以了解世界是：(1)確定「有目的的行為」為根源的譬面所已介述的四個世界的假設不同。它不是由對每一個世界的範疇逐一作解釋以說明世界的涵義為何，而是採取另一不同的說明方式。由《概念與性質：一個世界的假設》一書所論述的，我們見到選擇論依世界的假設的方式以了解世界是：(1)確定「有目的的行為」為根源的譬喻而引伸出性質組與概念組兩組不同的範疇之後❸，即論述此兩組範疇所指謂的是同一的問題。

在說明了兩組範疇所指謂的是同一的問題之後，再進而就所引伸出的範疇去討論現代的科學的知識與現代的西方哲學所關注的問題。由此而說明世界的涵義為何，而不是如前面四個世界的假設一樣，依對所已引伸出的範疇的解釋而解釋世界。故《概念與性質》一書在(2)說明了性質與概念的指謂同一，亦即神經中樞的同一理論之後，(3)即討論意向的問題。此一問題之所以先被討論，除了其是現代的哲學所重視的一問題之外，亦為選擇論所依以了解世界的範疇的依據的根源的譬喻的一基本性質，即有機組織的一基本性質。由對它作詳細的討論可以進而了解「有目的的行為」的主要涵義，以及有關建立知識活動的依據所在，故此它先受到注意，由對它得到了一定的了解之後，再進而依建立知識問題的順序及存有的涵義而分別討論；(4)知覺的活動；(5)知覺的對象；(6)對人的知覺；(7)科學的對象；(8)時空歷史與現前；(9)因果的關係；(10)現實歷程中的相似性；(11)形式的相似性等問題，以及(12)價值與(13)美學問題。

以上所說的程序是《概念與性質·一個世界的假設》一書所論述的程序。此等程序所表示的問題，若只分別就其自身上看是裴柏對現代的西方的哲學所探討的知識論、存有論、價值論與美學諸問題的討論。此討論涉及現代的哲學的專門性的問題。但我們若在諸分別的討論中而注意裴氏對此諸問題的最後歸向所在時，則見其皆歸到依「有目的的行為」的根源的譬喻而引伸出的兩組範疇中去。在此一歸向中一方面說明了性質的指謂的指謂同一的意義；另一方面或說其中心的意旨則在輻輳所說的諸問題而成其選擇論的世界的假設的理論。

裴柏以為依現代的知識以了解世界，不能不歸到其所確定的範疇中去。故相應於現代的科學知識與現代的**哲學**的問題而建立的新的世界的假設理論即在將此諸問題關連到依「有目的的

「行為」所引伸出的範疇上去了解。故此一了解與前面四個世界的假設對世界的了解雖不同,但以所確定的範疇或依傳統的哲學理論而說明世界的本質為何則是一樣的。在後面我們將依上引論述的程序而分(上)、(中)、(下)三章去介述。(上)章包括本「小引」及(1)至(4)五節,(中)章包括(5)至(7)三節,(下)章則包括(8)至(11)四節,至於(12)與(13)有關價值與美學問題則略而不論。

二、選擇論的根源的譬喻與範疇的確定及其與傳統的目的論的不同

1 小引

如前面所已提及的,為裴柏所採用作為選擇論的根源的譬喻為「有目的的行為」。此一行為是人人所共有而為常識上所可肯定的。但如裴柏所指出的,此一行為雖是人人所共有而為常識上所可肯定的,但它的涵義在過去並未得到深入的了解。故在西方傳統的哲學中並沒有人依此而建立一世界的假設的理論,但隨著現代學術的發展,「有目的的行為」得到了新的了解。在此新的了解中可見到其內涵可作為一新的世界假設的理論的根源的譬喻❹。

「有目的的行為」為一有機體或人依其有機性而求達到一目的的活動。裴柏以一個人在夜裏忽然感到口渴而求水飲的活動為例去說明。一個人在夜裏感到口渴而起來開燈到廚房取水飲以解渴為一有目的的行為。我們如對此表現作分析的了解,可分別為始點、中間經過與終點。始點為感到口渴或一有機體的欠缺表現,中間經

過爲起來開燈行到廚房取水飲的過程，終點則爲獲得水飲之後而口渴得以解除❺。此只是一個有目的的行爲的例子。在日常生活中，我們有各種不同的有目的的行爲。但行爲的目的雖不同，其性質都是一樣——要達到某一目的。所有要達到某一目的的行爲都有始點、中間過程與終點。並且每一中間過程都是爲達到目的的過渡或是爲達到目的的工具作用。因中間過程是過渡或工具作用，故有選擇和有對或錯的可能，亦即有可以幫助達到最後的目的和不可以幫助達到最後的目的的可能。

所說「有目的的行爲」及其經過的過程，在常識上是沒有問題的。但裴柏要以其爲一個世界的假設的根源的譬喻，故他即不能限於常識的了解，而是要依近代科學的知識而指出對此一行爲可以有兩種不同的進路。所謂兩種不同的進路的了解，即此一行爲可以爲表現此一行爲者的內在反省的了解，亦即常識上所依據的了解；亦可爲行爲心理學家由外在觀察此一行爲而作的概念描述的了解。由前一了解我們可以清楚地反省到上述取水飲以解渴的行爲過程；由後一了解則可以有對此一行爲事件經過的客觀的描述。故裴柏稱前者爲由內在的質的了解，亦即直覺的反省的了解；後者爲外在的量的了解，亦即概念的描述的了解。此兩種了解所指謂的均爲同一的事件。但了解的進路或方式以及表達了解的說法則不同。裴柏由此方式與說法的不同，而引伸出兩組不同的範疇，以作爲選擇論了解世界的依據。

2 性質的範疇與概念的範疇

所說的兩組範疇第一組稱爲性質的範疇，第二組稱爲概念的範疇。

(1) 性質的範疇

性質的範疇分為下列三項：

(A) 單獨的性質的股份的範疇：

1. 為行為而有的動力要求的感覺性質。

2. 性質的持續，持續的性質的股份。

3. 由動態的活動所感覺到性質的強度。

4. 在動態的性質中所感到的對目的的指涉。

5. 由周圍的股份而生的蔽塞。

6. 動態的指涉分裂為可達到工具的目的的工具股份，此股份趨於達到由欲望而來的目的。

7. 為達到最後的目的而選擇的工具股份。

8. 達到目的行為中的積極的滿足感（與在蔽塞時的消極的不滿足感）。

(B) 脈絡的性質股份的範疇：

1. 不同股份的同時存在。

2. 在成為一全體行為中連續股份的顯示。

3. 為行為而有的感覺意向的期待與恐懼。

4. 融和 —— 不同股份的性質的融合由之而構成其自己的性質的股份。

5. 似真的現在 —— 或當下的範圍。

• 156 •

(C) 性質的界限的範疇：

1.
 (a) 現實的現在——包括在行為中似真的現在的整個界限。
 (b) 過去——是真實的但不是現實，曾經是現實但現在不是現實。
 (c) 將來——是真實，潛存著現實但尚不是現實。

2. 控制環境的股份——任何在行為中的性質股份——情景中的現實性與真實性。

(2) **概念的範疇**

概念的範疇亦相應於性質的範疇而分為下列三項：

(A) 用客觀的名詞表達的簡單而完全的有目的的行為的範疇：

1. 由內在身體的改變或環境的刺激（精力的衝動）而引生的身體上的活動與緊張的形式。

2. 經歷一段時間的連續性。

3. 可量度的能量，如在明顯的行為中所見到的運動能力，或在身體的緊張狀態中所感覺到的潛存能力。

4. 身體能力的向量性，隨著身體的情形的改變而使能力分散或身體在穩定的情景下而維持能力的顯現。

5. 與環境的活動力的交互影響。

6. 由與環境的交互影響而生的向量的改變，與為了最後的發放能力或為了維持穩定的情狀由回應的機構通過最短的渠道而運送精力。

7. 為發放能力或維持穩定的情狀回應的機構的選擇。

8. 因為精力的衝動而減低其能力而得的安靜狀態。

(B) 物理結構的範疇：

1. 有機體。

2. 在一整體表現中有機行為的顯示。

3. 動的意向如在適當的刺激下可引出的生理機能表現。

4.

5.

(C) 物理環境的範疇·

1. 時空。

2. 在時空中的物質形狀❻。

以上兩組範疇除了第一組的(B)4.與(B)5.在第二組的(B)4.與(B)5.中仍沒有相應的範疇外，其餘的範疇都彼此相應。裴柏以為第二組的(B)4.與(B)5.仍沒有與第一組的(B)4.與(B)5.的相應的範疇，只是現實上是如此，而並不是原則上不可以發展出與「融和」及「似真的現在」相對應的概念的範疇。

3 選擇論與傳統的目的論的不同

如前面所了解的，「有目的的行為」應為一高度的有機的表現。但此一表現亦如前面所已提及的在過去並未得到深入的了解，故沒有人本此行為以建立一世界的假設的理論。但依現代

的了解，「有目的的行為」實可以作為一新的世界的假設的理論的依據。由此依據所建立的世界的理論以了解世界，我們即見到世界到處表現了有目的的行為。由所見到的到處表現的有目的的行為，我們可進而推論出那不可見的，即尚未經驗到的有目的的行為。由此而以世界的本質即為一有目的的行為事件的表現。此是選擇論以「有目的的行為」為根源的譬喻以建立一世界的假設的理論所可肯定的。

以世界的存在為一有目的的存在。世界的一切事物最後皆向一究極的目的而發展，而顯現出一和諧的宇宙，在西方的傳統的哲學家中的亞里士多德與黑格爾及黑氏的後學皆曾有如此的想法，並依此想法而建立了傳統的目的論。但此目的論與以「有目的的行為」為根源的譬喻所建立的選擇論並不相同。此不同的主要所在，在於所說的目的論是先驗地肯定整個世界事物共同表現一終極的目的。選擇論則不作此先驗的肯定，而只是以「有目的的行為」為根源的譬喻，由此根源的譬喻所引伸出的前面所述的範疇以了解世界。於此了解中並無必然的歸結的肯定，而只是說明各別事物的有目的的表現。被說明的事物可能共同表現一終極的目的，但此只是可能的表現而並不是選擇論依其根源的譬喻而引伸出來的範疇的必然的肯定。如所說的「可能」被證明是真的，其即為選擇論所具有的內容。但它所重視的是分別依範疇而對世界諸事物的有目的的表現逐一加以說明，而不是於說明之前先作一先驗的肯定。又依上列的範疇去了解世界目的的表現才能顯現其目的為何的事物，亦即是說它的目的的不是由直接的了解的了解可見，而是要透過其他的相關連的了解才能顯現出來。不管「有目的的行為」由直接的了解所見或間接的了解所見，選擇論的特別處都在於它依所確定的範疇而顯示各事物的有目的的表現，而不是先了解所見，肯定一宇宙的究極的目的為何？故選擇論不同於傳統的哲學的目的論。若以其與前面所已介述

三、神經中樞的同一說

1 小引

如前面所已提及的，作為根源的譬喻「有目的的行為」可以有兩種不同進路的了解，一為內在反省的了解，一為外在概念的描述的了解，而此兩種了解同為指謂同一的「有目的的行為」。此一情形又如在前面所已說及的，在常識上亦可以見到，我們對此「見到」可以再舉例加以說明：例如一個醫生診斷病人時對病人的痛苦有描述的了解，此對病人的痛苦的描述的了解，即病人所感覺到的痛苦的了解；又如一小孩在為某一事而感到害怕時，他的害怕的感受可為其父母由他所表現的神態而察覺到。但此一為選擇論所肯定為同一而同為常識上所認可的事實，在西方近代的哲學上卻不能有相應的了解，而相反地引起了不同的爭論。此一爭論由笛卡兒的心物二元論的建立開始。笛氏在他所建立的心物二元論中以心物為不同性質的兩種存有。心與物既不同而彼此異質，則由心靈內所呈現的感覺即與由身體上所顯示的情狀不是指謂同一的兩種事件。則前面所說病人所感覺的痛苦與醫生對痛苦的描述；或小孩所感受到的害怕與其父母所察覺到小孩的面部所表現的神態即不是同一的事件。選擇論由「有目的

曾以選擇論為脈絡論的一種修正的理論❼。

的四個世界的理論相比較，則它近似於脈絡論而遠離於機體論。因機體論的特色在顯示整個宇宙的有機表現為何，而脈絡論的特色則在分別說明各別的事物的脈絡為何。正因為如此裴柏

・160・

的行為」的兩種不同進路的了解亦不是同一的事件，而是所有所說的都是心物的分別不同的表現。

笛卡兒的心物二元論的學說流行之後，對心與物是否為異質的存有，或心與物只是同一本體的不同表現，以及二者的關係為何，即成為西方近代的哲學所爭論不已的事。於此爭論中：(1)有主心與物為不同的本體，二者的關係乃由於偶然的原因使然者；(2)有主心與物為不同的本體，二者並無相互的因果關係，而只是相互的平行表現者；(3)有主心與物不是本體而只一本體的不同屬性的表現者；(4)有主物只為心的現象表現，究竟地說只有物而無心者，而以對物的了解則為對物理語言的了解，至於對心的了解則為對精神的語言或現象的語言的表現，而只談表達語言的不同而不談心物為何。

以上所引有關對心物不同的了解，皆是對心物的問題的一種解答，並且除了語言的哲學家的說法外，皆是各別不同的形而上學的解答。笛卡兒的心物二元論是一種形而上學，其他的對心物或二者的關係的不同說法，亦是各別不同的形而上學。唯有現代的語言的哲學家是要由語言的觀點上去談此問題，而否定上面所說的形而上學的了解❽。

2 選擇論的心物同一說

選擇論對心物問題的了解不同於笛卡兒的心物二元論的了解，亦不同於所說其他的形而上學的說法，如現代的語言的哲學家一樣，而只是對形而上學從事學的了解。但它並不是要否定形而上學，如現代的語言的哲學家一樣，而只是對形而上學從事

不同的了解，即與世界的假設的了解。

由選擇論以「有目的的行為」為根源的譬喻而建立的世界的假設的理論的觀點上說，由根源的譬喻而引伸出來的兩組不同的範疇所指謂的「有目的的行為」既是同一的事件，如由內省所了解的為心，由外在概念的描述所了解的為物，心與物是同一的。但僅由此而說同一，則所說的同一似仍是不很確定的。若要有較確定的了解，應對心物同一的交滙點有進一步的說明。心物既同一其同一的交滙點在什麼地方呢？對此問題的回答，選擇論者不可以有先驗的答案，而須由經驗的了解中去確定。由經驗的了解上對此一問題的回答可以有。(1)此同一的交滙表現在人依其感官所感覺及的外物中。此即以人依其身體而生的生理感覺所覺及的客觀的對象即為人心靈了解之所在。此所在亦即為心靈與感官的物質表現的交滙處。(2)此一同一的交滙處亦可不在外在的對象上，而在人的有機的感官中，如在人的視覺的視膜中，或聽覺的耳鼓中，或在人的其他的有機的組織的部位上。心物同一的交滙點究竟何在？是過去的哲學家與近代的科學家所不斷探求的問題。據近代生理學所了解的，則此一交滙點不是在前面所說的(1)所指示的地方，亦不是在前面所說的(2)所指示的地方，而是在人的腦神經中。選擇論亦由此而說神經中樞同一。此說正與它所肯定的兩組不同的範疇為指謂同一的事件的說法相應。

3 神經中樞同一說不同於斯賓諾塞的一元論

依神經中樞同一說，傳統的哲學所謂心實即為對腦神經的內省的自覺，而所謂物即為由觀察所見到的腦神經構成的物質成素。去除了所說由觀察所見的物質成素不能有內省的心靈的了解；去除了由內省的心靈的了解亦不能有對所說的物質成素的觀察與描述。故心與物實為人的

腦神經的兩面的表現，而對此兩面的表現的了解是人類學術發展至現代才獲得的了解。此一對傳統的哲學所說的心與物的新了解，即為由選擇論所說的內省與外在的描述為同一的指謂的了解。但此一了解與斯賓諾塞所建立的心與物的一元論的了解有不同。就同一心物而以心物只為所指謂的不同的表現上說，此與斯氏的心物二元論的觀點有相同的地方。但斯氏以心物同為一絕對的本體的不同的屬性，於心物二屬性之外，此絕對的本體尚有其他無數多的屬性，並且本體與屬性有體用上的不同的功能，此則與神經中樞同一說所說的心物同一的涵義不同。神經中樞所顯現的同一一並無體用的分別。並且此同一除了由內省與外觀上顯示其為同一而相應於傳統不同的心物的不同了解外，再沒有其他可能的了解，亦即此同一除了由心物二進路所了解為同一外，沒有另外屬於本體性的潛存，而是常為一現實的事件，常在現實表現中，而分別為所說的兩種不同的了解：其為內省所見者可名之為心，為外觀所描述者可稱之為物。

4 神經中樞同一說的科學的證明

依選擇論所肯定的神經中樞同一說的觀點上說，世界不是別的而即是可為內省的了解與外觀的描述的了解的表現；亦即是依內省的規律與外觀的描述的規律所不斷生起而有一定的目的的活動事件。此事件顯現於心的領域內或於內省的了解內，既為一時的隨意的感覺，亦可表現為文學、藝術、道德與宗教有規律的展示；事實上人的文學、藝術、道德與宗教體驗即為一內省的體驗。此事件顯現於物的領域內或於外觀的描述了解內亦不僅為一時的無律則的描述；而可表現為科學的有規律的展示；事實上人的科學的探求即為一外觀的探求。但所說的體驗與探求雖有所不同，同為指向此一不斷生起而有一定的目的活動的事件上。表現所說的事件可有內

省的與外觀的兩種不同的了解，而此兩種了解的交滙點即爲人的腦神經。以人的腦神經爲交滙

點如前面所已說及的可以有經驗的證明。此經驗的證明再可依現代科學研究所得而有後面三點

不同的證明方法：⑴追求在感官受到刺激時即傳到腦上去由腦表現對所受刺激的有機的反應，

而再傳到肌肉上去所表現的事實；⑵橫切所說傳達的通道，或移去腦的一部份然後觀察其情形；

⑶使病人局部痲醉將腦部暴露然後對腦的各部份加以刺激，以看病人由內省上所表現的反應。

用此三種不同的方法對上面所說的心物交滙或內省加以了解與外觀的描述所指向在人的腦

神經的說法即可得到進一步的了解，而肯定腦神經中樞同一的理論。依此理論，由所說的第一

種方法我們可以見到內省的表現是在腦而不是在與腦連接的其他部份；由所說的第二種方

法割除人的腦的某一部份其人即跟著而失去某種相應的感覺反應；由此可見知覺反應主要在腦

而不是在與腦相應的感官；由所說的第三種方法我們可更確定的知道腦是各感官的中樞。對其

某一部份加以刺激即相應而有某一回應，由此而知視、聽等感官的根本反應不在眼膜或耳膜

而在腦神經。因此現代生物學家了解腦如一備有良好的分隔的線路的電話總機一樣，分別輸送

與接收由不同的線路而來的訊息；又由其運作與傳達的表現而以其好似是一結構完美而表現了

一整體性的電磁場，人的種種感覺活動皆爲此磁場所收攝，亦發自此磁場。生理學家與醫學家

曾從實驗中一再證明：對暴露著腦髓的病人的腦所作的刺激所產生的可觀察的反應現象，與病

人由內省而來的回答常相應，即對暴露著腦髓的病人Ａ所作的某一刺激其反應的現象爲ｘ，病

人由反省而來的回答爲ｙ，對暴露著腦髓的病人Ｂ所作的同樣的刺激，其反應的現象與由內省

而來的回答與病人Ａ的反應亦相同。由此而證明ｘ現象與ｙ的回答爲指謂同一的事件，亦即腦

神經的某一事件表現可同有內省的直覺的了解與外在的觀察的了解。由此而得以證明內省與觀

察所指的爲同一事件。

5　對神經中樞同一說的疑問及回答

選擇論由範疇的確定而引證生理學與醫學的證明，以說腦神經的同一，而肯定內省與外觀同爲指謂同一的現實而有目的的活動事件，似是清楚而可確定的。但此一確定並非全無疑問。

疑問之所在：從範疇的確定上說，選擇論由所肯定的範疇而確定腦神經中樞同一說，是否要比機械論由所肯定的範疇而以精神與物質爲不同的眞實，因此而作不同的相應的了解要好呢？從世界假設的理論的觀點上說，對此一問題並無必然的答案。因選擇論與機械論同爲相對地適切的世界的理論。故持機械論的觀點者可以以精神事件與物理事件而不可以混同。又由科學的觀點上說，亦無必要以爲由外觀所描述的腦神經現象即爲病人內省所了解的同一現象，而可以以二者只是彼此相關連而不必以之爲同一。於此外，亦可以由其他的觀點而加以反對腦神經同一說。例如主張我們對外在的事物可以有直接知覺的人，可以說我們對暴露的腦髓的知覺與向內反省而有的知覺不同。並以由外觀的了解而獲得的物理知識較由內省而了解而獲得的知識更爲確定，而主張我們應充份運用外觀的知識以了解世界，至於由內省的了解而獲得的知識只應作爲外觀的知識的附屬的東西，而可以對其不加以理會，或將其剔除。又由語言的觀點上說，物理的語言與精神的語言或現象的語言雖同指謂一相同的存在的事件，但由語言的觀點上說，物理的語言或現象的語言更清楚確定而有效，因此我們即應運用奧坎刀以去除精神的語言或現象的語言，以符合經濟的原則。又由邏輯的觀點上說，如由內省的了解與外觀的概念的了解同爲指謂一相同的對象，則二了解的意義是相同的，但邏輯上說二了解的意義並不

相同。凡此種種反對對腦神經中樞同一理論的說法，皆有其一定的根據。但亦皆不是絕對的而是可以受到批評的。批評可以成為細微的有關理論的分析問題。但我們在此不深入細微而只求其

大意以作回答。由大意上說，除了由內省上我們可以有直接的知覺之外，外觀的知覺皆為因果關係的知覺，故不能以內省的知覺與外觀的知覺的不同以反對腦神經中樞同一說。又對世界作

物理的概念的解釋雖較內省的現象的解釋為確定，但並不能因此而取消內省。因對存在著的事實我們不能任意加以取消；對以物理的語言或現象的語言為清楚、確定而有效，因此而要取消精神的語言或現象的語言，以符合經濟的原則的說法亦可以同樣的理由以回答。至於內省與外觀在邏輯上的意義同一的問題，從內涵上說，內省的了解與外觀的了解是不同的，而不能以二者為同一，但同一除了內涵的相同之外，亦可以由外延或外指上說，而腦神經中樞同一說所用以證立的證據正是由內省與外觀的指謂同一上說的，亦即由邏輯上的外延或外指上說的。從世界假設的觀點上亦不能絕對地以機械論的世界假設以否定由選擇論的世界假設所建立的理論，因兩種世界假設都是相對地適切的。

6 由神經中樞同一說所了解的世界及此一了解的進一步肯定

反對神經中樞同一的理論的理由不是絕對的，對反對的回答亦不是絕對的。因此我們是否可以由上面對理論的肯定與對反對此理論的回答而建立同一論應仍是一開放而可繼續討論的問題，而不要以為此一理論已建立。但若果我們接受此一理論則我們由內省與外觀所指謂的同一涵義上即可說由此一理論所肯定的世界為何。世界是怎樣的呢？從此理論上說，我們不能離開內省與外觀的了解而有所說。依此一理論的了解，外觀的了解最後必歸於內省的肯定上。由外

觀的了解上，我們可以開展為各種概念式的描述、假設、推論、證明等科學了解的程序。此程序不是由直接的內省所能獲得。說其最後歸於內省是以一切知識始於內在的感覺與歸結於內在的感覺而不問其歷程為何上說的。

又就知識的對象上說，此對象可被分解為不同的具體的經驗與不同的抽象的律則、原理、公式、符號等。但此等在知識上成為認知的分解對象如收歸到內省的感覺上，則可通稱之為內省的感覺性質。此內省的感覺性質在神經中樞的同一理論上說，只有在腦神經所表現的內省上顯現，而與由外觀而了解對腦的活動表現為同一的事件。但此同一只為由腦神經內省而呈現的現實活動的事件，不限於由內省所見的腦神經中，而是遍在一切的事件上，而成此一世界理論所主的感覺性質的現實事件，為世界的真正本質所在的說法。此說法與其他的世界的理論或以世界的究竟為形式與質料的結合呈現，如形式論所主；或以世界為一脈絡的表現，如脈絡論所主；或以世界為一機械律則的呈現附以第二性質的質料，如機械論所主；或以世界為一整體的表現，如機體論所主不同。

以上所說的以世界為感覺性質的現實事件的說法是否可以進一步證立呢？

進一步證立的方法在於依自然科學所展現的自然宇宙的連續性表現，以及現代學術對由融合的了解而作的推概的肯定上。

所謂自然科學所展現的自然連續性是指現代自然科學所顯現的生物學與化學，化學與物理學的連續關係。此連續關係由後面的被了解而見：生物的有機體被了解為生物的細胞形狀，生物的細胞形狀被了解為化學的原子形狀，化學的原子形狀被了解為次原子的原素形狀。在所說的各了解中有一物理的相關的律則關連貫串於所了解的對象中，而呈現其中的連續性。整個自

然界不分有機與無機物既表現一連續性，我們可以推定爲選擇論所肯定的感覺性雖只由內省的了解中而見其爲一現實的事件，而此性質其不限於可由內省了解而見的感覺中，而有其通貫於不爲內省所感覺到的諸階層之中，而遍及於所有的可由內省，而成爲每一了解的最後歸結的事件的本質所在；亦即神經中樞同一的理論所說的同一遍及於各階層而爲連續性所肯定的。於由連續性而來的推論外，由融合說亦可以有相同的推論。依融合說，爲我們清楚而明白地所感覺及的並不是最簡單的性質，而是融合的呈現。此正如詹姆士所指出的，我們所味覺到的檸檬水不是一單一的味覺，而是融合了糖、檸檬與水的味道而爲一的味覺。構成檸檬水的糖，或檸檬，或水的味道亦爲一融合的表現而可以再分解❾。屬於味覺的檸檬水如此，其他屬於聽覺或視覺的對象亦是如此，亦皆爲一融合的表現，而可以對之作分解。如音樂中的某一和音，或繪畫中的某一景色。構成和音的某基音或景色的某一色素亦皆爲一融合的表現而可以再分解。從再分解中我們可以顯示出我們感覺的限度。此即爲感覺所限而只能依感覺的能力而呈現的仍不是事物的最簡單的性質，而可爲一融合的表現，而可以再作概念的分解以求進一步的了解。人的感覺是有限度的，此一限度可由與其他動物的感覺作比較而見到。如人的嗅覺能力不如狗；人對紅外線無所感，但蟻則有所感。

　由人所感覺的是一融合的表現，而此表現的性質與其他的性質有連續性的關連上說，則在人的內省直覺上所呈現的感覺性質，在內省的直覺上所見的雖僅限於某一程度，但此一定的程度的呈現既與其前後上下有連續性而爲一融合的呈現，我們即可以推論地確定未爲內省直覺上所見的，在層次上亦應有內省直覺上所見的感覺性質。此即爲由融合關連於連續性而說由內省的直覺上所見的性質遍在的主要意義。由此一意義上說，內省的直覺上與外觀的描述上的同一

即不限於僅可由內省的直覺所見的事件上，而可以擴及於各階層，而使外觀的描述與內省的直覺有完全的對應，而了解到由感覺所見的融合的對象涵有爲概念了解的事件的細微成份，而此成份可以由科學的分析而來的理解所決定。

四、意向的分析

1 小引

從普通常識上說，意向一詞只適用於人或有意志活動的動物上。但選擇論在此所說的意向則不受此限制而可應用於所有的存在物上。故此所謂意向可說爲存在物的性質。但此所謂存在物的性質有它的特定的意義，即不是泛說而是依選擇論的根源的譬喻，亦即是依「有目的的行爲」事件所具有的性質上說。意向既是指謂爲根源的譬喻所表示的事件的性質，它在選擇論中即屬於範疇的地位。故在前面「第二節、2.」所列的範疇表中它分別出現於性質的範疇與概念的範疇的(A)4.上。

由神經中樞的同一理論既肯定了內省的直覺與外觀的描述的「有目的的行爲」事件在腦神經中同一意義，而此一行爲事件可分別爲性質的範疇與概念的範疇所表達，則進一步的說明當爲論述此一事件的性質爲何。對意向的分析即爲對根源的譬喻的「有目的的行爲」的性質爲何的論述。所論述的既是由根源的譬喻而引伸出來的範疇所肯定的，而分別表現於兩組範疇中，故論述的進略亦可以爲內省的或外觀的描述的。

意向既是「有目的的行為」事件的性質，它即與此一行為事件不可分，而屬於此一行為事件。但我們不能說意向即是此一行為事件。通常我們不說意向即是行為，而是說行為是意向的表現。意向是行為的依據。依據與實際的行為表現既在同一活動的事件歷程中，亦可不將其分離為二。

以上是以意向相對於行為上說。若只就意向本身上說，我們可分別意向為意向之所在與所在而來的表現所顯示的性質的不同。我們若仍以前面所說及的某一個人在晚上起來取水飲以解渴的「有目的的行為」為例去說明意向的所在，則此「所在」不能在別處而只在於該個人的有機體中。依此而來的行為的表現所顯示的性質，則為依意向的驅使而起來取水以解渴的整個表現。又由意向所在而來的行為亦可以有連續的或間斷的的不同。但行為雖可以有連續的或間斷的的不同，行為的意向既發於同一有機體，則此意向即可被視為一個意向，屬於一個有機體的整個性的一連串的表現。

2 積極的意向與消極的意向

意向亦可以有積極的意向或動態的意向與消極的意向或被動的意向的分別。積極的意向具有下面的成份：(1)所在；(2)表現的性質；(3)作為表現的固有的潛能；(4)實現的條件❿。(1)與(2)在前面「小引」已說及。至於(3)是就一意向所內涵有的驅動力而使其所趨向得以表現上說的。由於此一驅動力是內在的而不是外來的，故說為固有的潛能。(4)是兼內外而說一意向之所以成為一意向的整個條件。

積極的意向具有以上所說的四種成份。

至於消極的意向則不全具有所說的四種成份，而是

缺少了⑶。此缺少了⑶的消極的意向實為一物被他物接觸或排拒時只顯示一物的消極的承受而不表示它的積極的活動的性質。我們若仍以前面所一再舉過的有目的的取水以解渴的行為為例去分辨積極的意向與消極的意向的不同，則此有目的的取水以解渴的行為即為一積極的意向，有滿足解渴的要求的水即為一消極的意向。此一消極的意向有被積極的意向所獲得的性質。但它並沒有一積極的趨向以表現其自己。它雖沒有一積極的趨向以表現其自己，它有可以被獲得或得以接觸的條件，有被表現的性質，並有它的所在。只是沒有作為表現的內在或固有的潛能而已。故它缺少了上面所列積極的意向的四種成份的⑶。所說的「有目的的行為」與被取以解渴的水只是用以說明積極的意向與消極的意向的不同的一個例子。於此外，其他存在的事物沒有不可以由所說的積極的意向或消極的意向以了解它的性質為何。一切的事物均依此兩種意向而存在，亦皆表現了此兩種意向的性質。故所說的兩種意向有其普遍性而為此一世界的理論藉以了解世界為何的範疇所在。

除前面所已說的外，積極的意向所具有不同於消極的意向的特別成份——固有的潛能，為意向所表現的驅動力所在，與科學知識的建立及對科學理論的了解有密切的關係，故我們將進一步加以分析。

3 對積極的意向所具有的固有的潛能進一步的了解

要進一步了解固有的潛能應對「潛能」的意義先有所說明。潛能的意義涵有：⑴一生長的情景，亦即一存在物或事件所涵有的生長性或發展性；⑵所要生長成或發展成的目的；⑶連結生長物至其所要達到的目的生長律則⓫。我們若以一橡樹為例作說明，則橡樹子即為有生長性

的存在物。橡樹爲它所要達到的目的。至於生長律則即爲橡樹子所依而生長爲橡樹的規律。此是以自然物爲例。於此外，其他事件都具有潛能的意義，亦即具有由潛能而發展爲其所要達到的目的，或由潛能成爲現實的意義。如再以一學生到大學讀書爲例作說明，則學生到大學去讀書爲前面所說(1)生長的情景；完成學業得到學位則爲(2)所要完成的目的；至於(3)則爲學校的章程，學生必依此章程而達到其所要達到的目的。由選擇論的觀點上說，整個世界即在一潛能表現的歷程中。此表現依照著各別不同的律則而表現，此律則有爲自然規律，有爲社會法則，有爲遊戲規則等。每一規律、法則或規則皆有它的客觀性，而有它的眞實的意義。選擇論在此要特別說的是有關自然的律則，亦即自然律的眞實性。

4 自然的律則及展示此律則的語言符號

我們可以以自然律爲一套符號，如物理學教科書中的方程式；亦可以以自然律爲指謂在自然歷程中所顯示的規律性與秩序性。前者可以等同於後者，而以之爲指謂後者，但前者亦可以獨立於後者之外，而只在語言符號的層次上說自然律則的結構爲何。若以前者爲指謂後者，則其對錯將依其是否眞能表達後者而定，而不是於自然界的眞實表現之外對自然律另有所說。但由於我們要對自然律有所說明，故必需將其表現於語言符號中。因此亦有只就語言符號的結構、用法與意指爲何而說自然律的。至於從後者上說，它是自然界的眞實表現，不管我們用什麼語言符號去表示它，或如何表示它，它仍然是如此地在表現而呈現它的一定的歷程，展示它的一定的律則。但若就對此一展示的表達而成爲知識層次上說，它一定要藉一定的語言符號依一定的方式而後得以呈現。但雖然如此，自然律的呈現與表示此一呈現的語言符號仍是有所不同。

並且此不同不僅是名言或概念上的分別，而有真實上的不同，即自然律是指謂自然歷程中的規律性或秩序性。

語言符號要具有自然律的意義必為表達此一自然歷程中的事而相應而有對錯，而不能只屬於語言符號本身的結構、用法或意指的事。此一分別為選擇論所堅持，而自別於以僅對語言符號的釐清即可以解答自然律為何的語言哲學家的觀點；或以科學規律只有運作意義的運作論者的說法。選擇論以為僅限於語言符號的釐清與分辨的表現只是屬於語言符號層次上的事。

自然律則為其所指謂的事。相對於運作論來說，則為那些有效運作的事，其之所以能成為有效的運作必為其表示了其所運作所指涉的自然的真實性。故若以前面「3.」所曾舉過的例子作說明，則自然律即為橡子所依循而成為橡樹的律則，自然律為此一真實的表現。語言符號的說明必歸到此一真實的表現上。又若以在夜裏起來取水飲以解渴為例作說明，此取水飲的行為的內在的潛能表現，即為一有機體的缺乏水份而引生一驅動力而經歷所說的歷程而取得水飲以解渴。此一潛能的表現或有機的驅動力的活動歷程即顯示了一潛能表現或因驅動力而行為的律則。此律則可為由外觀的概念的描述藉語言符號以表達的符式，亦可為由內省的感覺所知所顯示的歷程。此二者所表示的方式不同，但同為指謂此一真實的意向表現。因此由選擇論所了解的自然律的意義上說，依自然律而從事的科學預測以建立科學知識，不僅是語言符號層次上運作的事，而亦是預測自然本身的真實表現的。自然本身有真實的表現，語言符號的本身宜有一套聯結或相關而為預測的依據。

故預測不僅是表現一種概念上相互關係。語言符號的本身為語言與概念層次上的事，則必將其關連於自然的本身上以確定其相應性。因此選擇論是不能同意英國的經驗主義者以我們所知的只是觀念上的事的說法，尤其不能同意休讀以觀念是分立的，其間沒有任何的聯結的說法，而與概念間的關係亦自有其聯結的方式。但若要其不僅為屬於語言與概念層次上的事，則必將其關連於自然的本身上以確定其相應性。

5　對賴勞的批評

選擇論除了對英國的經驗主義者，尤其對休謨的觀念分立而無關連的說法不能同意之外，其對賴勞（Gilbert Ryle）以意向僅為一種語言的結構的說法更明顯地加以批評。賴氏的說法見於他反對笛卡兒的心物二元論的評論中。賴氏以笛卡兒在心物二元論中所說的心為神奇不可知的。依賴氏的了解，我們所謂心知的活動僅為意向的表現，而意向只可以有行為為心理學式的了解，亦即前面所已說的外觀的概念描述的了解，而不可有內省的感覺式的了解。意向既有所表現而對其表現有所知，對意向亦應有所知。但賴氏卻以為所說的意向是不可以由觀察得到並論證其存在的，可觀察與可證明的只是由意向所表現的行為。意向既不可以觀察亦不可以證明，如何可說其有呢？賴氏以為其有不是由笛卡兒的形而上學的方式說其有，亦不是由內省感覺上說其有，而是由語言的分辨上以明其為一種不同的說法。所說的語言分辨上不同的說法，即是我們對可觀察可證明存在的事物，是用表示的陳述的句子加以紋述；對於不可以觀察不可以證明其存在但可以由其而引導到獲得觀察與證明的結果的律則，原理則不用表示的陳述的句子而是用假然的句子加以表達。此一種分別，賴氏以為已普遍地被接受而不當再有問題。但表示意向的句子不應說是完全假然的律則句子，而是一種半假然的意向句子，例如，張三有吸烟的意向，當你給他一枝烟時他會接受❸。

從選擇論的觀點上說，要對意向與表示意向的行為作一種語言上的分辨是可以的。但不能

· 174 ·

因可以有此語言上的分辨而即以其僅爲語言結構上的事。因語言符號一定有所指謂，而指謂不應只以其爲停留在語言層次上的事，而可以以其對自然眞實有所指涉。故對意向的了解可以最後歸到自然的眞實上。從自然的眞實上說意向，即有前面「2.」所說的積極的意向與消極的意向的不同。由積極的意向上說，即有內在的潛能的意義，而由此以了解自然律，則科學依賴自然律而從事的預測即爲指涉自然本身的眞實，而不能離此眞實而自限於語言符號的層次上，故最氏只由語言的不同表達的層次上以分別意向與表示意向的行爲的不同，而不說意向的眞實爲何是不夠的⑭。

五、知覺的活動

1 小引

我們都有知覺。但什麼是知覺？知覺的涵義爲何？則很不清楚。傳統的哲學對知覺有不同的了解，各依其不同的了解而建立了不同的知識論。選擇論對知覺的了解是依由其根源的譬喻而引伸出來的範疇，並相應於現代的科學知識而來的了解以建立一與它的中心觀念相應的知覺理論。於此一理論中顯示了以下的主要意義：知覺爲「有目的的行爲」活動的一種表現，故應由選擇論所肯定的根源的譬喻所引伸出來的範疇去解釋，藉以顯示選擇論的世界理論的一特色；知覺活動雖屬於「有目的的行爲」活動，但後者不限於前者，而另有其他有目的的活動，故在此可分辨由知覺活動而來的知覺指涉與意向指涉的不同，知覺指涉與思想指涉的不同；知覺既

2 由選擇論以說知覺的進一步說明

從選擇論為一種世界的假設的理論的觀點上說，知覺活動可由其所確定的根源的譬喻而引伸出來的範疇作解釋。以知覺為「有目的的行為」活動的一種表現即為依此一世界的假設的理論的觀點而來的解釋。如前面所已說及的，「有目的的行為」是一依自動的意向而表現的行為，亦即一固有的潛能的本質性的表現，而知覺即在此表現中呈現，而不是於此外另有知覺。但知覺雖為「有目的的行動」的意向的表現，亦如前面所已說及的，此僅為意向的一種表現。意向表現是在於達到一定的目的。此目的可為滿足某一由意向而來的對產生此意向的人或有機體的傷害。此二者合稱為意向的活動，或有目的的行為。在此行為中有知覺表現，亦有其他的表現，如感覺、想像、思想等。

依選擇論的了解，知覺與感覺不同，亦與想像或思想不同。知覺主要是一有機體對一外於其所在的客觀對象的活動表現。此一表現是藉感官對外物的知覺而顯現，如由視覺而見到一物的形象或顏色，或由聽覺而聽到一聲音，或由觸覺而觸及一物的堅固性等。此被知覺的對象是獨立於知覺者之外而有其客觀的獨立性的，並對知覺者產生感官上的刺激作用。知覺者的知覺對此

有指涉，所指涉的為客觀的存在，故知覺的指涉即為客觀的指涉。此客觀的指涉為知覺活動的一種特性。此特性使其與沒有客觀指涉的想像、幻覺、以及主客不分的感覺分別開。知覺活動既為「有目的的行為」的一種活動，其即為一種主動的活動，為意向或內在潛能的一種表現。此與傳統上以知覺為被動的接受的說法不同。故如何回答以知覺活動不常是主動的，而是被動的接受的說法成為建立選擇論的知覺理論的一問題。

被知覺的外物有一客觀的指涉。我們如以知覺者的知覺爲能知，外物爲所知，則當知知所知時，能知不只限於其自己的活動而是對所知有所指涉而關連及於所知。感覺的涵義則與知覺不同。它並不一定對外在的客觀對象有所指涉，而只是自己有所感。能感與所感混合而不分，如一個人或一有機體感到痛苦或寒冷，痛苦與寒冷皆不獨立於感覺之外成爲一客觀的對象而爲能感所指涉，而是所感與能感同時呈現融合而爲一。想像如爲幻想，則能幻與所幻亦不分，並且於幻者的活動之外沒有與之相應的客觀事物。如想像不是幻想而是一種思想，則思想可有被思想及的客觀對象，而可以有客觀的指涉。但思想的客觀指涉與知覺的指涉不完全相同。此不完全相同主要在於知覺所對的爲具體的事物，而思想所對的則常爲觀念或語言符號。觀念可指具體的事物，語言符號亦可指具體的事物。但觀念與語言符號本身不是具體的事物，故其與被知覺的客觀具體的事物不同。

「有目的的行爲」有知覺以外的感覺、幻想、想像、思想等活動，而此等活動不同於知覺活動。故知覺活動只是「有目的的行爲」的一種活動，而此活動在整個「有目的的行爲」中常因求取對目的的達到，亦即要使意向的指涉及於被指涉者而顯現。例如晚上起來取水飲以解渴是一「有目的的行爲」，其意向的指涉即爲水，其知覺的指涉則爲對幫助獲得水的工具的運用。在此運用中先對工具有所知，如對開燈、到廚房去、取水壺等有所知，然後以所知以幫助對水的獲得，亦即使意向得以完成。又知覺既是爲使意向的達到而顯現，故其即爲一主動的知的表現，而不是被動的接受某一可知的對象。故主動地要對幫助達到意向所指涉的目的的工具有所知，而不是被動的接受某一可知的對象。故說其爲意向或固有潛能的自動表現。

3 傳統的哲學對知覺的了解

以知覺為「有目的的行為」的一種表現，為選擇論依其根源的譬喻引伸出來的範疇以解釋世界的一種說法。此一說法是從選擇論的觀點上說的。但如不從選擇論的觀點上說，而從傳統的哲學的觀點上說又如何呢？對此一問題可略作如後的介述。

傳統的代表觀念論或英國的經驗論者，以我們所知的只是觀念，而不能於觀念之外另有所知，亦即不能於依於經驗而有的觀念之外另有客觀的指涉。至於如何知覺觀念的問題，洛克以為由外在的感覺而來的簡單的觀念皆是被動地接受，由內在的反省而生的簡單的觀念亦是被動地覺及。唯有複合的觀念才是由心靈主動地結合簡單的觀念而成。洛克並以為物之初性亦是其固有的性質以刺激人，而使人生起與之相應的觀念；物之次性則有一種力量刺激人而使人生起與之不相應的觀念。但不論相應與不相應為心靈所知的只是觀念，而心靈的知覺活動皆是被動的。

此一所知限於人的觀念與知覺被動性的說法為巴克萊與休謨所繼承。巴克萊極力主張於為人所知覺的觀念之外沒有外物。「存在即被知覺」；被知覺的不是物而是觀念。休謨以觀念為印象的傲本，而印象為被動地接受，為人所接受的印象而成的觀念為人唯一可知的對象。此對象彼此孤立分離。它們間的關係完全不可知。我們只可以根據對它們已有的經驗而說它們可能有的關係為何，而不能離開已有的經驗而說它們的客觀的關係為何。我們會根據已有的經驗而習慣地說某一觀念與另一觀念有某種關係。但既是習慣地說，此只有個人的主觀習慣的根據，而沒有客觀的根據。故事物的客觀的關係不可說。既不可說故沒有一定的因果關係。因果關係不能依事物的客觀性而建立，而只有主觀心理上的習慣的根據。休謨以後的英國經驗論者大致地繼

承了休謨所發展的經驗主義的傳統，而對於知覺的客觀指涉與知覺的主動表現皆不能適切地了解。

理性主義者笛卡兒曾由思想的我的存在，以證明上帝的存在。因外物與思想的我亦即外物與心靈為異質，故客觀的外物的存在並不能由心靈所確定，而要靠誠實無欺的上帝的保證它的存在才能確定。康德在能知與所知的關係的問題上有哥白尼式的革命。他以為不是人的心靈依外物而有所知，而是外物依人的感性的先驗時空形式與知性的先驗範疇而被知。在此感性與知性充份表現了先在性。但對於所知的外物仍是被動地接受。

4　選擇論受杜威及近代科學的影響

依選擇論的了解，有關知覺的客觀的指涉的問題，是英國的經驗論者以及其他的傳統的西方的哲學家所未能解決的問題。經驗論者對知覺的主動性表現的誤解更甚。對此二問題的解答與糾正，在現代的哲學家中主要為杜威。杜威的哲學亦重視經驗，但他反對由經驗而說觀念，以知識限於觀念中，而對外物無所知的代表經驗論者的見解；亦反對休謨以觀念為分立隔離而彼此沒有關連的說法；而是以知覺不只是被動地接受，並以經驗中充份表現了事物的彼此關連。是主動地對外物有所知，而不僅是被動地接受；而是知覺不只是限於觀念中，而是對外物有所知，有所指涉；知覺並選擇論以知覺有客觀的指涉與知覺的自動表現的見解，當受杜威的說法的影響。但它除了受杜威的影響之外，同時亦綜合了近代的科學對此二問題的了解而將此了解與其由根源的譬喻而引伸出來的範疇相結合而形成其理論。

近代的科學以知覺有客觀的指涉原是一假定。但它由此一假定而獲得的成果使它的假定成

為不可置疑的事實。故無論為一物理學家或一行為心理學者為他們所知覺而描述的物理現象或心理現象皆有在他們的知覺之外的客觀的事實而為他們所描述，而從此等描述的恆常的表現中而得出各別的規律。

5 知覺的自動表現的困擾及解答

前面所說的知覺的自動表現的說法，並不是說我們的一切知覺活動皆如根源的譬喻所表示的為「有目的的行為」表現，而只是說所有知覺活動可歸到此上去了解。最使知覺的自動表現感到困擾的是外物對我們強迫的刺激，如窗外傳來的雷聲或電光，它們好似都是主動地向我們而呈現，又如我們外出時沿途所見的房子、樹木、花草或行人等，我們好似都是被動地接受。我們則好似好像被動地接受它們的呈現。此等事實即常識上以知覺為被動的接受的根據，而有「人心如白紙」（tabularasa）的譬喻，而以簡單的觀念全是被動的知覺的觀念，而以白紙的文字為被寫上的，人心中的觀念是由被動地接受而有的。前面所說的經驗論者對知覺的了解大概亦即是由此根據所作進一步的解釋而來的了解。

由常識及經驗論者的了解上說，我們的知覺活動好似不是一種「有目的的行為」表現，亦即知覺不是一種有目的的順求，而是一種無目的的順受。

選擇論由其根源的譬喻去說知覺的涵義既不是要以所有的知覺皆是自覺的「有目的的行為」表現，則所說的知覺主動性又是怎樣說的呢？選擇論所說的知覺主動性主要是要說明知覺的自主性的活動此一事實。知覺有自主性又是可以由我們日常自動地去求知覺此一事實見到。如我們自動地去注視某一顏色，或某一形狀，或自動地去傾聽某一聲音，或自動地去觸摸某一外物等。

此等知覺活動都是主動的「有目的的行爲」表現，而不是被動地接受某一刺激。此一主動的知覺表現，不但對外在的事物是如此，對內在的意念活動亦是一樣。例如我們從事某一思想活動，或從事某一回憶，或從事某一想像，或甚至從事某一幻想時，皆是一主動的知覺活動。此等活動可以有知覺的客觀指涉，亦可以沒有。但其具有主動性則一樣。此是由普通的經驗事實可以說明的知覺的主動性。於此等事實的說明之外，從理論上說，知覺活動亦不可能是完全無所主而是被動的。故以「人心如白紙」白紙上的字是寫上的，知覺即是被動地接受的說法是有問題的。因即使我們承認「人心如白紙」，白紙亦應有受寫字的功能，然後可寫字於其上，若白紙沒有受寫字的功能，字是寫不上去的。故以「人心如白紙」心亦必有接受的活動，然後對觀念有所知覺，若不是如此，心亦留不下所接受的觀念的。據近代生理學研究的結果，心不僅有接受的活動而不全是被動的，知覺對任何的刺激皆有選擇的表現，而不全是被動的接受，此與中國古人所說「心不在焉，視而不見，聽而不聞，食而不知其味」的注視心的主動性的說法正相合。

此所說的心應即生理學家所說的人的神經系統。依近代生理學家的了解，人的神經系統如一個常轉動不停的磨盤一樣，即使是一個甚爲簡單的感官刺激都要經過甚爲細微的神經活動的持續表現歷程，和要經過無數的內在的修改活動，然後才抵達腦神經中樞。在抵達腦神經中樞之後，再由腦神經中樞而傳達至它的有機的結構上。由此可見知覺對任何一細微的刺激在其由刺激而顯現爲觀念時不只是一種被動地接受刺激，而是主動地轉化了刺激而爲一觀念。因刺激可以是無數的多，但爲知覺所注意的不是無數的多，而是於無數的多中只選擇爲它所注意的而表現爲知覺的已被接受的刺激而表現的活動。在此接受之前，知覺實先有一選擇表現。因刺激可以是無數的多，但爲知覺所注意的不是無數的多，而是於無數的多中只選擇爲它所注意的而表現爲知覺的活動。此選擇即是「有目的的行爲」的一種表現，亦爲內在的潛能的自動表現。

6 知覺的確定表現與肯定知覺主動性的價値

以上所說的知覺自主性與選擇的表現亦可以由知覺的確定表現而得以證明。所謂知覺的確定表現即爲對一對象的知覺保持其恆常性，而不因被知覺的對象的距離遠近，或環境有所改變而改變。若知覺純爲被動的，它應因環境時空距離等的不同而隨時相應於不同的刺激而改變其所知的對象。但我們的知覺活動並不是如此，而是對知覺的對象有所知後即持守它的所知，而以它常是如此。此見於常識上爲我們對我們熟知的事物皆保持它的恆常性。唯有在特別的變動後才再有新的選擇與自動的認知表現。

以知覺爲主動的有選擇的表現是選擇論依它的根源的譬喩引伸出來的範疇而對知覺活動的肯定。此一肯定的價値在其能與近代的生理學與心理學對知覺了解相應。由此相應的了解而去除了傳統的哲學與現代的科學相違異的說法，而釐清了知覺的本質，並使它成爲選擇論的世界的理論不可少的一環節。

第十二章　選擇論（中）

六、知覺的對象

1　小引

相應於上章「五、」所說的「知覺的活動」來說，知覺的對象即為知覺的活動中的知覺的客觀的指涉。知覺不同於幻覺或感覺。它不僅為一種主觀上的感知而是在主觀的感知中同時相應地而有客觀的指涉。我們如何由客觀的指涉而說明知覺的對象呢？從選擇論上說，此要由「有目的的行為」的活動表現上去說明。此可分別由視覺、聽覺、或觸覺依預期的表現而說明知覺的對象在此不同的知覺中如何相應而呈現。由此呈現而分別概念的指涉與知覺的暗示的不同，以及對知識的對象的直接知覺與間接指向的疑難的釐清，並可去除傳統的哲學由觀念的靜態的涵義而了解知識問題所引生的困難，並進而了解選擇論為何以簡單的符合的真理說或運作的真理說為不足，而要建立一符合的真理說與運作的真理說相結合的理論。

2　由「有目的的行為」以說客觀的知覺的對象

「有目的的行為」為選擇論的根源的譬喻。由它以說明知覺的客觀的對象即由它所引伸出來的範疇以說明知覺的客觀的對象。「有目的的行為」是有要達到的目的的。此目的的既為要達到的，故其即成為一外在的對象。此對象不隨主觀的願望而改變。故為客觀的對象。但此客觀的對象是相應於「有目的的行為」而說，故其為「有目的的行為」的對象，而不能即稱其為知覺的對象。故由「有目的的行為」進而說知覺，此中表示了一分化的活動表現，即由整個「有目的的行為」活動中而特別注視它的知覺的活動表現。於此知覺的活動表現外向有欲望、情緒、幻覺或意志等不同的表現。

就整個「有目的的行為」上說，知覺的活動表現是一分化的活動表現，亦即一特別注視整個行為中的一方面的活動表現。就知覺本身是一對視覺、聽覺與觸覺等的共同稱謂上說，所說的分化的活動表現或一特別注視整個行為中的一方面的活動表現亦只是一種比較上的說法，而不是究竟的。因我們若要具體地或事例地依知覺的活動而說知覺的指涉，由此而顯示知覺的對象，不能以具有共同稱謂的知覺去說明，而要分別由視覺或聽覺或觸覺去說明。後面我們即主要以視覺為例去從事說明。

3 以視覺為例去說明知覺的對象

每一「有目的的行為」的活動，活動者皆將其整個活動置於一預期的系列中而逐步加以實現。知覺活動中的視覺亦是如此。視覺者亦將其所要知的對象置於其預期的系列中而逐步使其依次呈現。我們如以視覺所要知的對象為可以獲得水飲的水龍頭為例作說明，其大要情形將如後。

從「有目的的行為」活動上說，可獲得水飲的水龍頭為要取得水以解渴的「有目的的行動」的活動對象。此取得水飲以解渴的行為有視覺的活動。如僅就此視覺的活動上說，作為獲得水飲的「有目的的行為」對象即為視覺所要求有所知的客觀的指涉對象。此對象從視覺上說是先以一概念形式呈現於為視覺所預期的了解中。但由概念的預期了解了而並不能確定所說的視覺的客觀指涉。它只在視覺中表現預期的了解。要由預期的引導而達到經驗上的證明，則必須由概念的引導而至視覺的經驗引導，亦即依視覺而展現的預期的系列依次而逐步達於視覺的對象——視覺所指涉的水龍頭。在此依次而逐步達於視覺的對象的過程中，可出現由對象而起的不同的視覺暗示，即由對象而來的對視覺的不同的刺激。由此刺激而生起的現象亦為視覺而生起的對象。但其與因視覺而要見到的究竟的對象則有不同。我們若以此由究竟的對象與其所要達到的究竟的對象的距離，以及其他的環境因素而來的不同。其不同是由於視覺與環境的關係而生的刺激現象為視覺所直接把握的對象，則為視覺所最後要達到的對象即為超直覺的間接對象。前者又可稱為近似的對象，而後者則為究竟的對象。但此二者並不分離為二，而是要由前者以導至於後者；由後者以呈現前者。但既有此前後的分別，我們即不能只由依刺激而來的直覺而說視覺的對象只有前者而無後者，或只由究竟的所見而只說後者而否認前者；亦不能如傳統的哲學所主以後者為本體，以前者為現象；以為概念所指向的為真實，呈現於視覺刺激之前的為幻像。其實二者的不同只是視覺者依預期的系列而進行對對象的接觸所呈現出的不同的階段。此為選擇論依其所確定的故為概念所指向的與呈現於視覺之前而被知覺的沒有本質上的不同。由此一說法對動進的特別肯定，我們即可以去除傳統的哲學由對觀念「有目的的行為」的根源的譬喻而來的由一動進的預期的系列以說知覺的客觀的指涉，以及客觀的對象的特別的說法。

的不正確的了解所產生的困難。因依傳統的哲學的說法，我們對一對象有所知是一已有的觀念與此觀念所指謂的對象的符合表現。但一靜止的觀念如何可以符合其所指謂的對象呢？此是不能有所說明的。又依傳統的哲學的說法，知覺與對象亦無所謂符合。因知覺只是一對所知的對象的認知活動，在此認知活動中沒有對所知的對象符合的問題。要說符合必須於知覺活動中以一觀念去指謂其所知的對象而有其是否符合其所知覺的指涉活動，而不是以知覺為一純粹沒有指謂的表現。若其是有指謂的表現，則其從事的知覺指謂活動即為一動進的，如前面所說的一有預期的表現，而不能說僅是一靜止的觀念與其所指謂的對象間的符合的事。

4 運作的符合真理說

由前面「3.」的了解以說知覺的真理，則選擇論即以傳統的符合真理說與現代所倡言的運作的真理說皆有所不足。知覺真理應為既是運作的而又是符合的表現。

符合的真理說的不足，如依前面「3.」所說的是缺少了動進的行為表現，而只說靜態的觀念與其所指的對象的相符合，而靜態的觀念如何可說與其所指的對象相符合是不能有所說明的。

至於運作的真理說的不足則由於其以真理只是由運作而來的決定，對於為什麼有些運作得當而可行，有些運作則不得當而不可行，不能有所解答。由此可見一事的真不能只由運作上說，而亦要由其有所符合而可運作上說。由於符合說或運作說各有所不及，我們即見結合此二說而成的運作的符合真理說的要點是：由知覺上去說真理，此知覺中的能知必對所知的對象有所預期，而此預期必與其所要求知的對象有所符合然後能說真。然而此符合則不是一種靜態的觀念與其所指的對象的符合，而是此預期動態地依其一定的程序，亦即預

期者依預期的系列而逐步以達至其預期的對象。在此依預期的系列而走向預期的對象中即有運作的表現。由運作的表現而達到預期的對象，此為得當而可行的運作，亦即符合了預期的對象的運作；而以此為真，則此真即既為運作的而又符合於對象的真，故此一真理說為運作的符合真理說。

七、對他人的知覺

1 小引

對他人的知覺是由前面「五」知覺的活動及「六」知覺的對象的說明進而專就如何知覺他人，特別是如何知覺他人的心的問題作專門性的討論。裴柏在作此討論時注意到奧士丁（Austin）對他心的說法，而以奧氏對他心的了解與他的選擇論對此一問題的了解作比較的討論，以指出二者的異同⑮。在異同的了解中，裴氏除了指出奧氏的說法的缺點外，並進而依選擇論的觀點去對「對他人的知覺」作說明，並由此說明而肯定作為被了解的他人的最後對象──感覺性質，在通過神經中樞同一說而有其客觀性，而可以互相交感而彼此認知。此一交感與認知有其一定的共同性。由此而批評以不同的人對同一顏色，A可以之為紅而B以之為藍的說法的不能成立。再進而指出由對被知覺的他人的最後對象──感覺性質的了解，而推論其他動物如狗、貓、馬等，以及無生物如車、船等的感覺性質的被知覺，以及對其他的物質所具有的感覺性質的推論。

2 奧士丁的他心說及他對語言的了解問題

由前面「六」論述知覺的對象的了解上說，知覺的對象即由知覺的指涉依預期系列所達到的客觀對象。此對象可以爲物亦可以爲人。因此人是可以被知覺的。一個人知有他人的存在是由知覺所確定。選擇論此一對他人的知覺的了解甚合乎常識，而亦與奧士丁由知覺以說明「他心」的存在的意旨相合。由知覺而知有他人或他心的存在與奧氏的說法雖與選擇論的意旨相合，但裴柏認爲奧氏在論述知有「他心」時對「知」的分析所強調的實有問題。他的問題在於(1)對語言的過份強調而不能確切把握其限度所在；(2)對感覺性質不能有正確的肯定⑯。

奧士丁以知有「他心」正如知有公園中的金翅雀一樣。此一對知有他心的說法是現代英國哲學由對笛卡兒的心物二元論的駁斥而來的說法。笛卡兒氏以物爲客觀的知覺對象，而心則爲主觀的個人的反省對象。個人只可以反省地知道自己的心而對他人的心則不能有反省的知。他心既不能有反省的知，故對他心不可以有直接的知，而只可以由類比推理中去推知。笛卡兒氏此是依他以心與物有不同的本體而來的說法。英國現代的哲學家如賴勞與奧斯丁等則否認心與物有不同的本體。心與物既沒有不同的本體，故對心與物亦沒有不同的知覺。笛氏如前面所已說及的以心只可以有由個人自己的反省而來的知，對於他心不能有所知，而只可以有類比的推論上說。但奧氏以類比的推論只是一種推論而不是知，知只可以依感官知覺而說，而不能由類比推知。故對他心的知即不能由推論上說，而只能由知覺上說。既由知覺上說，則其與知有公園中的金翅雀的知爲同樣的事。

確定了類比推論不是知而是推論，我們要對他心有所知只能由知覺上說而不能由推論上說。

奧氏即要問我們如何知公園中的某一存在物爲金翅雀。對此「如何」的回答是我們見到此一存在物所表現出的形狀與活動，例如其形狀是如何的，其發出的聲音是如何的，食某種東西等。依過去的經驗我們知有如此的形狀與具有如此的活動的存在物爲金翅雀，現在由知覺觀察所見其表現亦是如此的。故我們可知其亦爲一金翅雀。我們知一存在物爲金翅雀是由其所表現出而爲我們所知覺及的形狀與活動上說。知有他心亦是一樣。我們亦是由一對象表現了某種形狀與某種活動而說他心，例如由某一對象爲圓頭方趾的，表現了喜、怒、哀、樂等情感，與表現了與他人交談、爭論、或關注別人的事業活動而說他心。他心既由某一對象所表現的某些形狀與某些活動上說，其即不能於某一對象的形狀與活動之外而另說他心。故心與物不是二元，而是同一的知覺對象。

　去除心物二元的分別而由知覺以說知有客觀的事物與他心，此是奧氏論他心的主要點，而亦爲選擇論所同意的。但當奧氏對「知」作分別了解而以我們不能離開語言有所知，我們只可以由語言表現而有對「什麼」的回答的知，而不能有對「那是什麼」的回答的知，或用羅素的術語說我們只可以有描述的知識而不可以有接觸的知識時[17]，其即過份強調了語言的功用而忽略了對直接的感覺性質的了解。

　以語言與思想不能分離爲二，我們不能於語言之外另有思想，在英國經驗主義的傳統中是由霍布斯（Hobbes）以來所強調的事。奧斯丁在討論他心的問題時雖然注意到我們有許多知覺活動是沒有適當的語言加以表達的，但他亦以我們不能離開語言而有所知。他對語言的功用與語言與知覺或思想的關係沒有加以分辨。依選擇論的了解，我們的知覺需要語言去表達，而所用的語言需合乎社會上對此一語言的用法。並要對語意語法語用等有所了解。但語言與知覺

3 選擇論對內省的知與概念的知的了解

從選擇論的了解上說，對感覺性質的內省的知與概念的描述的知自有不同。但不是只有後者而沒有前者，而是二者為兩種不同性質的知。所謂不同性質，即是後者是由概念描述而呈現，藉語言以表達而可以客觀化的知；前者則是由內省直覺而顯現的個人當下的體會的知。此知是個人的感覺性質，而不是由外在的觀察所描述。故其為感覺性的而不是概念化的，是內省的而不是行為主義式的外現的。但依選擇論的神經中樞同一說的理論，此兩種知有其同一的指謂，

究竟為二事。知覺所指涉的為所知的客觀對象，而不是語言。知覺的對與錯以其能否對其所知的對象有所運作而符合其所知的對象上說，而不是對語言而說。語言的功用只是表達知覺所依循的預期系列的活動表現，而使其客觀化與公共化，而不即是知覺與其所知的活動自身。故以語言的表達等同於知覺活動，並以於語言表達之外無所知，是將知覺與語言的各別指謂混淆的說法。由此混淆而來的弊害是以知覺只限於對語言的了解中，而不見於語言了解之外另有對其所要求知的客觀對象的活動表現。

由語言的功用與知覺的活動合而為一的弊害而有以知覺只為概念所傳達的有關描述所了解的事，而忽略了直接的接觸的知，而以此為屬於心靈內省的直覺，而不可以有概念上的傳達。因此直接的接觸的知即與由內省而知的感覺性質同被排除。奧士丁在討論「他心」時本是肯定個人有其自己的內在的知覺活動的，但由於他以此知覺活動不能為他人所知，故以其不是屬於可知覺的範圍內，而不能分辨其與可作概念的描述的知有層次上的不同，而即加以排斥。因此他對感覺性質的意義即不能了解。

而是對所知的兩種不同進路的知覺。內省的知可轉化爲外觀的概念的描述的知，而外觀的概念描述的知需要歸到內省的依據上。此是將心物二元的隔核化爲一事的兩面。但不是由於去除二元的相隔而否認傳統哲學上所表現的屬於心靈上的內在的感覺性質。此內在的感覺性質是有機組織本身，即人的自然表現，由內省的顯示與由外觀而作的概念的了解所見者不同，但我們不能由由概念描述的所見或以此所見的確定性而可以從事證明，而忽視了由內省所顯示的感覺性質，亦不能由反對心物二元論的說法而以感覺性質爲屬於所謂心的內容而加以否認。

4　選擇論對他心的了解與奧士丁說的不同

奧斯丁由「他心」的討論所表現的對語言功用的強調與對感覺性質的忽視雖有流弊，他的知覺有人與知覺有物，物與人皆由知覺而知其存在的說法則應是確定不移的。但人與物雖由知覺而知其存在，對二者知覺的歷程與相互的反應則有所不同。對此一不同所特別要注意的是對人的知覺不限於外觀所見的形狀與活動，而是要及於其內在的感覺性質。傳統的說法是知其心。奧氏以他心只能由所知的人的形狀與活動上說，而不能於此外說他心。他以我們既不能對他人的感覺有所內省，因此而去除了只能由個人自己所見的感覺性質。但選擇論雖不說我們對只爲個人自己才可以內省而見及的他人的感覺性質有直接的知，而是仍然有所知，而對他人的知的最後歸向是要及於其內省所見的感覺性質上。此如何可能呢？此可能不在於依傳統所主的類比推理上說，而是依於選擇論所肯定的神經中樞的同一上說。由此後一說而知我們對所知的他人的概念描述的知是指向於其內在的感覺性質的知上。　概念描述的知有可被證明的客觀性。故與此知相應而其有同一指謂的感覺性質亦有其客觀性。　此客觀性在對人的知覺時並可以爲互相交

八、科學的對象

1 小引

從知覺上說,科學的對象即是為知覺所指涉的客觀的對象。科學的對象既為知覺所指涉的客觀的對象,其即與前面「六」所說的知覺的對象為同一的對象,既為同一的對象為何又有不同的說法呢?其之所以有不同的說法,因二者雖皆為知覺所指涉的客觀的對象,其如何指涉實

感而彼此認知的事。此事有其一定的共同性。因此以人的認知是彼此完全殊異的,對某一顏色A可以以之為紅而B可以以之為藍的說法是不能成立的。其之所以不能成立,除所說人的交感認知有一定的共同性外,更可以由對不同的人對同一顏色的認知作外觀的概念的描述以求在經驗上的證明。

由以上的說明我們或許以為只有人才有感覺性質。但事實上感覺性質不限於人中。由交感認知上以知此感覺性質亦不限於人中。人對狗、貓、馬或其他的家畜在與其交感中,亦可知其各別的心意。故常識上說狗、貓有人性,而馬亦懂主人的意向而常與主人互相配合而跳躍奔騰。此所謂「心意」、「人性」、「懂」即其所顯示而可以與人感應的感覺性質。不但狗、貓、馬如此,無生命而有機械性能的車、船之外的其他的無生物所具的感覺性質。於車、船或人有某種程度上的相互感應的表現,而顯示了某一程度上的感覺性質。但可以依前面「三」論神經中樞同一說時所說的連續律與融合說而作推論的確定。

有發展性的不同或方式上的分別。既有此不同或分別，我們即要對二者有所分辨而各別加以論述以顯示人的知覺活動如何由前者而發展爲後者，或後一方式如何異於前一方式，以展現一同爲知覺活動所指涉而不同於一般所說的知覺的對象的科學的對象。

科學的對象與知覺的對象的不同既在於由知覺活動所指涉的發展性或所表現的知覺的程序，的不同，在認知的本質上二者即沒有差異。因此由知覺活動而呈現的一般的知覺的對象的程序，與由知覺活動而呈現的科學的對象的程序有其相同的地方，而對二者可作類比的了解。由知覺活動而呈現的一般所謂知覺的對象的程序爲：以一預期指向所知而引生由對象而來的刺激而呈現近似的對象，再由對近似的對象的了解而獲得一最後的對象，而此最後的對象即爲對象的內在的性質（感覺性質）。由知覺活動而呈現的科學的對象的程序則爲：以一預測的科學的假設以指向所知而引生由對象而來的刺激而呈現近似的科學的對象，由近似的科學的對象的了解而進於最後的科學的對象，而此最後的科學的對象亦爲對象的內在的性質（感覺性質）。由於知覺的對象與科學的對象皆由近似的對象而進於最後的對象，而呈現對象的內在的性質，從選擇論所肯定的神經中樞同一的理論上說，此即由對一般的知覺活動所得到的說明而進於由科學理論的了解而得到的說明。隨著此一說明我們即見到世界的眞實即爲由一般的認知與科學的認知所追求了解的對象。對此對象了解的發展與了解的方式可有不同，但不是只有了解的發展與方式而無對象，如現代的約定主義者或運作主義者所主；亦不是有一對象但此對象完全不可以爲我們所知，我們所知的只是由對象所呈現出來的現象，如康德所主的一樣。

2 科學的對象的發展經過

科學的對象是由知覺活動經歷了長遠的發展之後而來的不同於一般的認知活動所顯現的對象。它的發展的經過可大略述說如後。

對象是相對於人的知覺而說。一對象稱為客觀的而不僅是主觀心境上的現象。知覺是指人所具有的覺知官能，涵有與現的對象有客觀的指涉，而不僅為主觀內省的感知不同。與外物相接而有所知的意義。此與感覺只作內省的感知不同。知覺是指人所具有的覺知官能，涵有與外物相接而有所知的知覺主要為所視覺、聽覺、觸覺。故所謂知覺的對象亦主要為與此三覺中的任何一覺有所接觸的外物而為所知的對象，如與視覺接觸而為人所知的外物的形狀、顏色與所在的位置，或與聽覺接觸而為人所知的外來的聲音，或與觸覺接觸而為人所指涉成為直接的認知的對象，而有所說的不同的性象。此等對象皆依知覺而顯現，而為知覺所指涉成為直接的認知的對象，而有所說的不同的性質的呈現。此呈現為知覺的對象的特殊表現。依人的普通的知覺而知的世界即為一具有如此不同的性質的殊異性的世界。

科學的對象與為前面所說的普通的知覺所呈現的對象的不同，即首在於人的知覺不循前面所說的普通的自然接觸而知，而是對知有所專注。由對知的專注而注視被知的物的規律。由規律的注視而使不同的物皆歸於一規律中，而顯現其相互間的關係，而求各物彼此相同的地方，或各物的彼此的關係所在，而去除其彼此的殊異性。此即為對物的量化與類化的了解。

所謂量化的了解，此即對所了解的物只求知其量的多少，而不問其性質為何。此一量化的了解在人的知覺活動中很早已出現。其初應只為相應於人的生活實用上的需要，或生活上的方便而來的表現，而並無以世界僅為一量的不同配合的存在的形而上的觀念。形而上學的觀念應是由生活實用上的表現所啓發而來的了解。人生日用上對度、量、衡的使用即為人的知覺活動

由性質的分別了解，而轉爲量化的了解的初步表現。但人依自然的知覺以知物，物的大小、多寡、輕重與其所具有的性質爲何是同時被知覺的，而對具有一尺長的竹竿與一尺長的布料，一

斗穀與一斗麥，一斤菜與一斤肉要作分別的看待。但純由量化的觀點以知物上說，物的性質爲何是不重要的。故不問所量的物爲竹竿或爲布料，爲穀或爲麥，而只問其長短多寡輕重爲何。並且常將由他覺所知的對象轉到視覺上去，如輕重本爲觸覺所知，當其轉化爲衡時，其即通過槓竿的原理而表現爲視覺上的事。如前面所已說過的，此一對量的重視起初只是因日常生活上的需要，或日常生活上的方便而來的重視，而沒有任何形而上學的假設。但由生活實用上需要或方便的對量化的不斷發展，而終於出現了依此而對世界作量化的了解的形而上的假定。

由度、量、衡以量化物是最原始與最基本的。但人並不停留於此最原始與最基本的階段中，而有後來進一步的發展。由進一步的量化發展，而有溫度計、記音器、辨色器、計時器與電流計等的設計與製造。此等量化的表現與已說的度、量、衡的表現，皆爲視覺的對象。氣溫的冷暖本爲觸覺上的事。冷暖更可依隨著不同的性質的物而表現。但當水銀或其他的物體所表現的

恆常伸縮性被用以製成溫度計後，由溫度計所發出不同氣溫的物體在量化的了解中即不再受注視，而只注視其所發的溫度爲何。此一注視亦使由觸覺所感受到的冷暖的性質轉化爲由視覺所能分辨的溫度的度數。記音器則將人由聽覺所知覺到的聲音量化爲由視覺所能分辨的高低音

視，而只注視其所發的高低音爲何。顏色本爲視覺的對象。但通過辨色器後所顯示的色澤亦使原來具有性質上的分辨的了解轉爲純粹量的度數的分別。時間可能爲人對太陽的昇降移動而生的觀念，亦可爲對其他事物的變

遷或對人內在的觀念的持續等而生的觀念，而此不同的觀念可各依其所生而有不同的性質。但

當其量化爲計時器或鐘錶時，其不同的性質亦退隱而純顯示了一量化的時間表。電原非人所能直覺知的，但通過電流計的發明亦將原來不爲人所覺知的電顯示成爲在視覺可覺知的流動度數。於量化了解對所知的對象的量化了解爲科學的對象與一般的知覺的對象一重要不同所在。於量化了解之外，另一不同所在則爲將對象類化。相應於人的一般的知覺活動而呈現的知覺的對象，本常是各別的個體。此個體彼此不同而分別地被知覺到。個體與個體之間有其相似處，亦有其相異處。我們可由其相似處而說其爲相同，以凡具有某一相似處的個體爲同類；亦可以不注視其相似處而只注視其相異處而說其爲異類。在一般的知覺活動中被知的事物常是以各別的姿態呈現而成爲各別的個體，表現爲一散殊的世界。由散殊的個體中而求其相似處而團聚成類爲知覺活動的一抽象表現。此一表現先於各別的個體中求出其相同的地方，而以此標準以團聚成類爲凡具有此一標準者爲一類，而使散殊的個體成類。純從知覺的活動的本身上說，此一抽象活動可不受拘限而可任意選擇不同的個體的相同的地方，而作客觀類性的了解，求知一類的客觀的事擇則不是任意的，而是受存在的個體本身的規限，以此去了解存在界。此一了解即使原來一般性的了解進物的共同性而了解其共同的規律，以此去了解存在界。此一了解即使原來一般性的了解進展爲科學性的類化的了解，而使一般性的知覺對象成爲科學的對象，而對此對象作科學性的陳述，亦即用命題或方程式加以敍述與說明。此敍述與說明可以有類性的普遍應用，而不限於某一特殊的個體中。此即相應於科學的類化的對象而有科學的假設與陳述而求此假設與陳述得以證明。

此得以證明的陳述，其之所以得以證明因其符合了上面所說的類性或客觀的律則。由此而表現了陳述的客觀性。此具有客觀性的陳述是由某一個人而提出。其提出時可能只爲個人的一

種假設。此假設原來是沒有的。故其提出此一假設的事為一「創造的想像」（creative im-
agination）❽。當此創造的想像的假設被證明時即成為一具有客觀性的陳述或律則。此陳
述或律則始於個人。但可以為眾人所了解，即合乎眾人的理解而可以為眾人所接受。此所說的
眾人的理解與接受，即各人去除了其各別的私意，亦即去除僅屬於個人的心理欲望或生理情緒
而本於一人人所共有的理解而加以接受。此即中國荀子於他的解蔽篇所說的去除個人的蔽塞而
顯示一大清明的心知的表現；亦即英國經驗主義者培根所說的破除偶像而提煉出一客觀的認知
心的表現。由此一表現而在殊異的個體中顯現了一共同的客觀的認知的依據。此認知的
依據是從認知的個人而說，故其相對於被認知的對象可說是主觀的。但其不限於某一個人，而
在眾人中有共同性，故可就此共同性上而說其為客觀的。此客觀自與被認知的對象有共同的類
性或規律性的客觀的意義不完全相同。但雖不完全相同，而仍可說其各具有客觀的共同性。並
可由此二共同性進而說科學活動的社會性。由科學活動的社會性的了解而再進一步了解科學的
對象與一般所說的知覺的對象的不同。

3　科學活動的社會性

科學活動的社會性可說為依於前面所說的眾人的共同理解與接受而來的表現。但由現代科
學活動的社會性表現的特別意義上說，科學活動的社會性不由上面所說的一般性的共同理解與
接受上說，而是由所說的共同理解與接受而作進一步的深度化、專業化與組織化的表現上說。
此三化的出現次序首為對所說的共同理解的深度化。以某一類的問題為何，本為人本其所有的
共同理解而說其為何。但當此理解進一步發展之後，即表現了其深度化而不再為每一個人所能

了解，而成爲專門研究此一類問題的人所了解的事。既爲專門研究此一類問題的人所了解的事，此了解即由一般性而深度化。由深度化而專業化，此即對深度化的問題只有專門研究的人才能了解。專業化的問題出現了之後，從事此一專業工作的人即成爲一特殊的群體。他們所從事研究的問題在此群體中彼此交流，交換研究所得，彼此互相承認研究所得。他們將所研究的問題與所得的結果寫成專文或專書，而使此文、書成爲他們所探討的問題的專門學問。此學問不斷在發展，前有所承後有所開，自成統緒，有關此一專門的學問的客觀性的學統即由此而建立，而成爲此一專門學問的客觀的共同性的表現所在。

以上所說的科學活動的社會性的表現與其他學術的社會性的表現亦有相似的地方。例如在科學興起之前在西方古代的柏拉圖學派，或亞里士多德學派，或在近代的理性主義學派，或經驗主義學派，或在中國先秦的儒家思想，或道家思想等皆有類似的社會性的活動表現。又宗教思想與現代的所謂某一主義，亦有類似的社會性的活動表現，而後者的社會性的活動表現更強。大凡人依據人類所具有的某一共同性而建立的學術思想、宗教信仰、或政治信念皆有其共同性或社會性的活動表現，而有一定遵循的規律，有一定了解的路向，其與人生社會有一定的關連性，而有學統、教統或政統的建立。

科學活動的社會性與其他的學術、宗教或政治的活動的社會性，雖有相同的地方，作爲科學的活動依據與其他的學術、宗教或政治的活動依據則不完全相同。科學必依於人的理性的了解。此了解必對事物有所指涉而有經驗上的證明。其他的學術、宗教或政治所探討的問題則不必皆如此，而宗教更是超越人的理性的了解與經驗的證明而爲一純粹的心靈歸向上的事。

4 科學對象的進一步的發展

前面所說的理性的了解要對事物有所指涉而有經驗的證明，此即為理性對客觀的存在事物作描述的了解。此一了解為近代科學的本質所在。此亦即伽利略由亞里士多德要以「為什麼」（why）去探求世界而轉以「是怎樣」（how）去了解事物的，而建立了近代科學的知識。此所開啟的近代科學能適切地描述所要了解的事物，而建立了近代科學的知識。此所建立的近代科學知識當其充份開展了類概念的普遍性的律則與類概念的系統性與邏輯關連性之後，原先以科學為對事物從事描述而求其知識的目標，即被威普勞（Hempel）了解為：「經驗科學有兩個主要的目標：描述世界上特殊的現象和建立普遍的原則，藉此原則以解釋和預測諸特殊的現象[19]。」納格爾（Nagel）亦說：「由於希望對有事實證明其為系統的，而可以加以控制的事物得到解釋而產生科學；科學的特殊的目的即在於依於解釋的原則而對知識加以組織與分類[20]。」杜爾文（Toulmin）對於自然歷史與物理科學亦作嚴格的劃分。前者只是對散殊而沒有組織的規律性的尋求，只是蒐集而沒有洞見。後者則是具有洞見的組織，使所組織的有系統而表現為一定的模式，由此而可以從事廣度的邏輯推理。因此他說：「物理型的科學的解釋與所有平常所說的描述是多大的不同。」又說：「對於自然律來說，『真』『可能』和同類的字是沒有應用的。」「自然律與其他的律則、規則、條例相似。雖然有關它們應用的界限的陳述可以有真和假，它們自己沒有真和假[21]。」

近數十年來以科學為命題的邏輯系統，由一套的基本的假定藉邏輯的推論引伸而得的見解，由於於歐幾里德的幾何學之外而有其他的自相一致的非歐幾里德的幾何學的發現，而得到了鼓

勵。當人們發現到非歐幾里德的幾何學對相對論中某些問題的解釋更爲適合時，上述對科學的觀點更得到了信任。古典機械學已成功地得到了公理化。其他的科學亦朝此而發展。烏德格（Woodger）對生物學，哈爾（Hull）對心理學，紐曼（Neumann）和摩根斯坦（Mor-genstein）對經濟學即分別從事此一公理化的努力㉒。由此一發展威普勞乃說：「科學理論可以了解爲涵著一未經解釋演繹地發展的系統，並涵著一種給與所說的系統的名詞與語句的經驗意義的解釋㉓。」他並依此而對科學的了解作一圖像式的描述：

一科學理論因此可以比喻爲一複雜的空間網。它的名詞可爲網結所代表；至於連結網結的線索部份可相應於定義，部份可相應於涵在理論中的基本的和引伸的假設。整個系統浮於觀察的平面上，而由解釋的規則所穩繫。此規則可被看爲繩索，但不可以其爲網的一部份，而是將網的某些要點與觀察面的某些特殊的地方相連結。藉着那些可解釋的繩索我們可上昇至理論以表現出科學理論的功用：由某些觀察所得的材料通過一可解釋的繩索的連結，那網可的網的某點，由此而通過定義與假設可達於其他的點。由那裡藉着另一可解釋的繩索而下降至觀察平面中㉔。

咸普勞作了如此描述之後即提醒我們說，表現爲公理化形式的科學理論是一種理想化。此是爲了邏輯上的釐清與理性上的重建。但對經驗科學理論的公式化的眞正嘗試直到現在仍然不是很多。但雖然如此，經咸氏此一對現代的科學的了解的描述之後，「科學的邏輯網」（nomo-logical network）㉕成爲討論科學的哲學一普遍地承認的名詞。

此一由以科學的對象爲知覺的對象至概念的科學的邏輯網的了解可簡別爲以下六階段：(1)依知覺所及而對對象的性質作如其所呈現的小心的描述；(2)爲了精密起見而藉著相關的媒介物而使觀察的對象量化而成爲一種指針的標示，如以磅表示重量，溫度計表示熱度，鐘錶表示時間等；(3)量化的概念被引伸而超出了感官知覺範圍之內，由此而創生了概念的建構；(4)將觀察所得普遍化而成爲經驗律則與假設的系統；(5)要求科學的觀察要有普遍的承認，由此而使科學發展爲一超個人的社會組織；(6)提昇科學程序組織化的結果到邏輯地不解釋的公理化系統，此系統可藉著符號或解釋的律則轉爲科學的假設，此即科學的邏輯網❷⑥。

以上是陳述人藉其最可信賴的知覺觀察以了解所在的環境，進而逐步發展出一極爲複雜在結構上高度概念化的科學的邏輯網。由此發展去看現代的科學理論，若有人以科學的程序對事實的描述沒有任何的關連，應不是奇怪的事。故約定主義者以科學的假設僅爲組織科學材料的方便的概念設計。運作主義者以科學的假設僅爲預測的工具，不表示任何描述或顯示事實的作用。假如其在控制人的經驗的事上能預測地引導到人所期待的結果，則假設是有認知的意義的。但約定主義者與運作主義者對科學的假設的了解都是對概念的結構與現實的性質與現實的歷程的結構的相互連結關係不加以理會的。

運作主義是與脈絡論相結合的一種理論。二者尤其是後者對現代的思想甚有吸引力。現代有不少的思想家要藉著它們以解釋現階段的科學發展。運作主義者的觀點如我們在前面「六」所已說及的，在某一形式上所表現的是對的。但其所存有的明顯的困難是它雖然很符合現代的科學強調解釋與預測的意義，但忽視了描述的需要。它對爲什麼有些運作表現成功而有些則失敗的事實無法解釋。對於描述論者來說，如果他能尋找得到連結概念的科學的假設與現實的性

5 科學的假設與科學的對象

從知識論的觀點上說，科學的假設是一種能知要對所知有所指向的活動，亦即能知活動提出了一如何如何的假設而指向於所知而要求此如何如何的假設與所知相符合。而使其得以證明以建立知識。故科學的假設不是科學的對象，而是相對於對象而求對其有所知的求知活動。此被相對而求有所知的對象，即依求知的活動方式亦即假設而顯現的事物的性質。但此性質常不能全部顯現，而是依假設而表現了部份的意義，或作間接的呈現。故所知的對象應分別為近似的對象與最後的對象。近似的對象即對假設有所符合而為感覺有所知的對象；最後的對象則為假設因近似的對象所呈現的證明而指向最後的現實結構，亦即現實事物的性質。此是對科學的假設與科學的對象所作最扼要的了解。此一了解符合了實際科學活動的表現，亦為選擇論依其範疇而開展出來的一種了解。但此一了解在近代西方的科學的哲學中卻產生了問題。問題之所以產生主要是在於由科學的假設與其所指向的對象的不同產生了混淆。

科學的假設既是一種能知要對所知有所指向的所知對象，照理不應與其所要指向的所知對象相混淆。但當其由個人的創造的想像而提出來而成為求知的方式，此方式為眾人所接受因而具有客觀性與共同性，並表現了組織化與系統化之後，其即成為從事科學研究的人所注意的對象。

質與現實的歷程的表現方法，此一問題是容易解釋的。因為選擇論依它的根源的譬喻而引伸了兩組平行的範疇，即性質的範疇與概念的範疇，以描述同一有目的的結構。因此選擇論是主張一種描述的科學理論，並對真理了解為某一形式的符合表現，而稱之為運作的符合說。

此連結與表現涵於選擇論的根源的譬喻中。

象所在，而有以其即為科學的對象的。任何一有效的特殊的假設一經提出之後，其即不是限於個人的，而是從事該特殊的科學研究的所有人所接受，而要從事證明以求成果，並要與其他已接受的假設相關連，而歸於一系統的假設理論之中，而成為一公共了解的對象而有其客觀性。既有此客觀性不限於某一個人的了解中，而是為一群體所共同了解，而有群體的繼承與發展，但雖然重要我們不可以以其即為科學的對象，或即是科學，其只是科學家所藉以研究科學的對象的方式，而其自身並不是科學。此學統在近代的科學的研究中甚為重要，其即成為一學統而有群體的傳承，但群體的繼承與發展，其即為一公共了解的對象而有其客觀性。

另一使人誤解科學的假設即為科學的對象的為科學的假設經由個人提出，而發展出其公共性與客觀性之後，其求證的活動成為一社會的目的與社會的要求。因此而使此假設增加了其動力。有一社會群體的動力在催促其指向其所指涉的對象而求證。從事證明的仍是各別的個人。但因有此社會群體的要求，而使所說的假設更表現了它的動性。具有如此的動性的假設自與傳統上以觀念為靜態的，一觀念的真在其是否與其所指的對象相符合的符合真理說的靜態觀念說不同。但由假設所具的動性而求對其所指向的對象作運作的證明，由此而說假設所具所指向的對象即對對象從事運作的證明的動態的運作方式仍是有問題的。此正如我們不能以月球的大小、形狀、質量與化學的結構即是科學家對其所作的徵查與測量一樣。運作論依假設所具的動性而表現其假設在科學的活動中自有其價值。但若以依假設的動性而從事對假設求運作的證明本身即現其涵義在科學的活動中自有其價值。但若以依假設的動性而從事對假設求運作的證明本身即其所要求證明的證明者，即有以科學的假設即為科學的對象的為科學的對象的謬誤。

再一使人誤以科學的假設即為科學的對象的假設由個人提出而建立了其公共性與客觀性之後，由假設對其所指向所作的預測與解釋即發展為一種系統性與合乎邏輯的陳述，而

有人即以此陳述爲科學的對象。對假設與由假設而對其所指向的對象所作的預測，或對其預測的解釋所作的陳述的求合乎邏輯而有系統性，或以最理想的語言符號以表達所提出的假設，是假設之得以清楚表現而可以盡其功能的要求。此要求在近代的科學或哲學的研究中表現了重要的價值。但其所表現的重要價值亦只限於問題的釐清上，而不能即以此釐清即爲科學的探求，或以所釐清的即爲科學的對象。此一以對科學的假設或對科學的問題所作的陳述，或對假設所作的邏輯架構的展示，或所作合乎語言規律的展示即爲科學，或即爲科學的對象，在現代的科學的哲學中常有如此的說法。但此說法明顯地是將科學所研究的對象與其所藉以表達的有關理想的語言，或合乎邏輯的陳述相混淆，而誤以合乎邏輯或爲理想的語言所表達的本身即爲科學的對象。因爲他們以爲我們不能於語言所表達之外另有所知。唯名論者以邏輯或理想的語言爲了解的對象。此一誤解可分別爲唯名論式與形式論式的不同。故其將語言的結構或理想邏輯的結構等同於世界的結構，而不以爲於前者之外另有後者。科學所了解的既不能超出語言邏輯之外。故科學的對象即爲理想的語言系統或邏輯的系統，而不以理想的語言系統或邏輯系統只是表現科學所要探求的世界而不是世界自身。形式論者有以理想的語言或邏輯概念所表達的不僅是言說概念上的事，而即表現了存在事物的形式。語言的結構所表達的即爲形式的結構，由形式的結構所展示的即爲世界的真實。如我們在前面第三章與第四章論述「形式論」中所指出的。此一了解表示了一相對地適切的世界理論。但亦有形式論者只以形式的結構即爲一理想的語言或邏輯的結構的事的。此一對形式的了解，即是以表達科學的假設本身，或由之而作的預測與解釋的陳述即爲科學的對象本身。將由對科學的假設所表達的邏輯結構與物理世界的結構相等同，正如將一描述句子的文法結構與其所描述的對象的結構相等同一樣同爲有問題的。

6 科學的近似的對象與科學的最後對象

每一科學的假設都是人要求對某一特殊的對象有所知而來的創造的想像的方式。近似的科學對象即為由此了解方式而呈現的部份證明。近似的科學對象對科學與最後的科學對象皆為假設所指向而求了解以建立科學知識的對象。近似的科學對象對科學的假設所呈現的證明只是部份的。

從以科學的假設為一種描述的理論的觀點上說，其對對象所作的描述亦只是部份的而不是全部的。因此其所能肯定的即不能超越其所對的近似的科學對象之外，若要對最後的科學對象有所接觸，須要有進一步的發展。所說的對對象作部份的接觸與進一步的發展正為分別近似的科學的對象與最後的科學的對象的依據所在。但雖然如此，假設指向近似的科學的對象與最後的科學的對象的顯現以及對假設本身的肯定上，而是同時顯示了對最後的科學的對象的指向而幫助人對最後的科學的對象作肯定，亦即由科學的假設的指向所顯示的證據呈現了近似的科學的對象而引向最後的科學的對象。

科學的假設與近似的科學的對象皆表現了一對最後的科學的對象的趨向。但此為假設與近似的科學的對象所趨向的最後的科學的對象是什麼呢？從科學的假設的指涉與近似的科學的對象所呈現的證據所顯示的去了解，每一最後的科學的對象皆有其活動的意向或性質，科學上有關連續性、內在的變遷與對其他的對象所產生的影響的預測皆由其活動的意向或性質而得以解釋。

最後的科學的對象的活動的意向或性質，在科學的假設的指涉上是否可以得到確定的說明呢？有關此一問題的回答是肯定的。傳統的科學提供了兩種說明的方式。選擇論增加了另一種

說明的方式。

　傳統的科學的第一個說明的方式是以表現為科學的假設的近似的科學的對象的證據皆有其遠源而不是止於其自己。故近似的科學的對象的證據必指向使其如此表現的最後的對象上。若以對遠方的知覺對象為例去說明，則我們可以說我們對遠距離的對象所感覺到的對象的大小、形狀、結構等不是完全可靠的，但其表現了此對象所在的位置、形狀與變遷的情形，而為感覺刺激的本源所在。又如以由科學所發展出來的指針標示為例去說明，則作為近似的科學的對象的指針標示，如溫度計、或天秤等，它們皆不只是表示了其自身的現象，而是顯示了一使其如此的本源所在。

　傳統的科學第二個說明的方式是以作為構造成整個科學的假設理論的一成份的模式的建構代表了最後的科學對象的活動的性質的結構。模式的功用是為抽象的理論提供一可解釋具體的經驗事物的方式。因此其常以類比的方式依具體的事物所呈現的情形而作想像的提示。故模式的表現即為最後的科學對象的顯示。

　選擇論所增加的說明的方式即為對其所確定的兩組範疇的了解而對最後的科學的對象作肯定的方式。如前面第二節所說明的，兩組範疇同為由「有目的的行為」的根源的譬喻所引伸而來。一為性質的範疇由內省的知覺而確定；一為概念的範疇由行為主義心理學的外觀描述的方式而確定。兩組的範疇雖不同，但它們所了解的對象則同為所知的對象的最後的性質所在。以前面第二節所已舉過的有目的的飲水的行為為例去說明，由內省所見的固表示了此一飲水的行為的性質所在，由外在的觀察所見的亦表示了此一行為的性質為何。若從事觀察者為一行為主義的心理學家，其所藉以顯示其所觀察的行為的概念、假設與陳述符合其所要求知的行為，

而呈現出一近似的了解對象。但此近似的了解對象最後的指向正是為內省的了解所見的行為自身，即所謂感覺性質。此感覺性質為所說有目的的行為的自身，亦為由所說的兩組不同的範疇所要共同指向的在動進地表現其自己的現實。此現實是一性質的結構，亦為動進不已的歷程，為最後的知覺的對象與最後的科學的對象所指向的滙合所在。此即前面第三節神經中樞同一論所已展示的。由此展示所表現的真實，可為由概念的範疇所表示的科學的假設所了解。但其自身不是概念的。因概念只是真實的性質的一種表達。此一真實的性質除了在人的層次外，亦即的了解同為指向此一真實的性質外，在對其他的對象的了解中則沒有如此清楚的表現。但由知覺的對象與科學的對象的探求而顯示了近似的對象與最後的對象的了解上。我們可以知道由近似而過渡到最後，而在對有目的的行為的內省上可對感覺性質有所確定，故在其他的了解中亦可以由近似的對象而指向最後的對象，而最後的對象的涵義即得以確定。此一確定與前面所說為指針標示的有淵源的所在，模式的構造表示了最後的科學的對象的活動性質的結構雖不完全相同，而後者亦可以幫助對最後的對象的真實性的了解。

選擇論對科學的對象的了解，與西方現代或過去很多的哲學家的了解並不相同。例如早期的邏輯實證論者以科學的對象為由基原句子所陳述的感覺料，以此感覺料為最後的精神的成素；後來的邏輯實證論者則以科學的程序在於對科學的陳述作邏輯的系統化，及對為實驗所獲得的散殊的觀察材料作規則的解釋；約定主義者以科學的理論所要做的是簡便地使觀察所得的資料系統化；運作主義者則以科學的假設只有預測與解釋的作用而不注意描述的意義。故他們對科學的了解皆與選擇論的了解不同。

傳統的哲學家多以知覺的對象具有第一性質與第二性質的不同，而只以第一性質爲科學的對象。從世界的假設的觀點上說，以物的第一性質爲科學的對象即爲機械論的科學的對象說。機械論是將物的性質皆量化而成爲指針所標示的。物既皆量化而無質的分別而以此爲科學的最後的對象，此自與以科學的最後的對象爲一種活動的意向或性質而非純量化的選擇論的了解不同。

傳統的哲學的另一說法是以於科學中我們只了解及自然對象間的概念上的關係。而對其性質無所知。此爲代表觀念論的說法。此一說法對機械論所了解的第一性質只是重視它們的相互的關係，故它不是機械論。但它以概念間的關係爲了解的對象亦與選擇論對科學的最後的對象的了解不同。

康德有物之體的說法，並以所有現象皆由物之體所呈現。我們只可以對現象有所知，而對物之體則無所知。因此，如以科學的最後的對象爲所知的事物的最後的依據，則此依據是不可知的。選擇論不採康德的現象與本體絕對地劃分的說法，而只有近似的對象與最後的對象的分別。由近似的對象所呈現的證據，指向對最後的對象的了解。故最後的對象即爲眞實的現實，其活動、變化與彼此間的相互作用與相互影響皆爲科學的假設所求知的對象，而不是不可知的本體。此爲科學所求知的對象即爲眞實的性質，亦即是科學的最後的對象，而不僅是現象，於此外另有本體。

第十三章　選擇論（下）

九、時空歷史與現前

1　小引

有關時空歷史與現前的探討將分別爲後面六分節去論述：(1)物理時空的意義；(2)對歷史的事件的了解；(3)傳統的西方哲學對歷史事件與歷史時間的不同解釋；(4)選擇論對歷史事件與歷史時間的了解；(5)對現前的了解；(6)選擇論對物理時空歷史時間與現前的總括了解。於此分節的論述中，我們先一般地說明時空的意義，歷史事件的意義，歷史時間的意義，現前的意義，再專門地介述選擇論對此諸意義的了解，及此諸意義的互相關連的問題。

2　物理時空的意義

物理時空的意義可先由常識的觀點開始逐步加以了解。我們先說空間。常識上所謂空間是指地面上可容納各物的位置及不爲物所佔有的空虛。其爲視覺的對象，亦可爲人所感觸及。其既容納各物爲各物所在的位置，故各物不能離空間而存在。空間與各物相結合而遍在各物中。

此是人依其感覺而來對空間的了解。此一了解後來與幾何學與機械力學相結合而發展出抽象的純理建構的空間說。抽象的純理建構的空間說，在古希臘已形成，而在後代有不同的建構的系統出現。此即由對幾何學與物理學不同的理解逐步發展而來的表現。

幾何學原為古埃及人測量尼羅河兩岸的土地的技術。尼羅河每年氾濫一次。每經一次氾濫後其兩岸土地的分界、疆畛、或田塍即被冲走，而要重新加以量定，以回復其原來所有的分界、疆畛、或田塍的直角、灣角、或其他角度與點、線為何，而從事新的點、線、面與不同的角度的確定。此等確定本為對實際的土地的劃分的事。但此一對實際的土地的劃分，傳至希臘，即被希臘人作純抽象的了解。對實際的土地上點、線、面及不同的角度皆抽象成為純粹的概念，而建立一純形量的概念與概念間的關係而可推演的幾何學。開始從事此一純推演的幾何學的建立大概是畢達哥拉斯（Pythagoras）及其弟子，經柏拉圖至歐幾里德（Euclid）而得以完成。

歐氏的幾何學系統建立後，即是依人的理性自明的原則而建立。它可以被用以解釋經驗的事物，或說經驗的事物必需依它而了解。但它與現實的經驗無關。此是以幾何學為純理的形式科學而來的了解。但於此一了解之外，亦有以幾何學本身雖是純理的，其原理的依據是經驗的。即其原理是由衆多的經驗事實歸納而得㉗，或在人的後天的不同依據所在的說法，與傳統的哲學對知識的本源所在，在人的先天的理性？此兩種有關幾何學不同依據所在的說法有關。

此一不同的說法在傳統的哲學中是重要的。因傳統的哲學的理性主義者只以由理性所建立的知識即是真的必然的知識，亦即依理性而建立的知識。又如果我們對世界的了解不能離開幾何學而了解，幾何學為依人的理性而建立，則世界的存在即為合乎人的理性的。

但經驗主義者則不以我們對世界的了解是純粹

理性的，而是須依於經驗的。由經驗所了解的事物不是不合乎理性的，而是合乎理性的，只是不是全由理性上所作的先驗的確定，而須要經驗上的證明。由幾何學對世界的了解是合理的，但此合理的了解並不必然地以其純粹為依理性而建立，而可為由對經驗的抽象的理性的運用而建立。

此一先天的理性與後天的經驗的不同的爭論，在以必然而永恆的知識為純粹的理性的產物，而幾何學被了解為一種必然而永恆的知識時是重要的。但當幾何學發展至現代，於歐里德的幾何學之外，另有非歐幾里德的幾何學的建立，歐氏系統與非歐系統彼此不同，但同可以被應用以了解世界，原來以歐氏幾何學為唯一依理性的自明的原則以建立以了解世界的說法即有問題。依現代的了解所謂理性的自明並不是必然的，而可以有不同的設定。非歐氏說即由不同的設定而建立。不同的幾何學系統既可以由不同的設定而建立，則原先以幾何學原於理性或原於經驗的爭論即失去其重要性。

幾何學或原於理性或原於經驗雖有所說的不同的爭論。但以幾何學為了解空間的形構的學問則沒有爭論。其由原先作為量度地形的技術發展為表達空間的內涵的學問亦是明顯的。其既發展為空間藉以表達其內涵的學問，其即與空間的被了解結合為一。其由平面而發展為立體，空間亦由長度、廣度、深度而成為立體的三度空間說。

機械力學之所以與空間相結合，則由於其所了解的物體常在一定的空間之中。物體由一位置移至另一位置上亦顯示了物體與空間的相關連。此一了解初時與由幾何學以展示空間的了解一樣，皆不與時間相關連。從常識的想像上，為我們了解的事物不但在一定的空間上與空間結合不可分，亦在一定的時間上與時間結合不可分。但初期由幾何學或機械力學以了解空間是將空間與時間分開的。牛頓的絕對時空說，亦是將時空分立為二。

牛頓以時空為絕對的並分立為二主要為解答物體在時空上的運動有確定可測度的準則而來的說法。依牛頓的了解，沒有客觀而絕對的空間，則物體在空間上的運動即不可了解。因所謂運動，乃一物體在空間上的位置的改變或移動。若沒有一絕對的空間位，則一物體在空間上的運動即不可說。要說一物體在空間上有運動即要肯定一獨立於物體之外而作為物體運動的準則的絕對的空間。我們如承認有絕對的空間，物體在此空間中有運動，則其運動亦即應有一定的速度。即一物體於一定的時間中由一空間位置移至另一空間位置。運動有速度、速度預設時間。故絕對的時間要被肯定。因如無一絕對的時間，則所謂一定時間經一定距離或空間量的運動亦不可說。由於絕對的空間與絕對的時間的肯定，一切物體的運動速度的快慢及所經的時間的久暫，空間的長短即可以以絕對的時空為一普遍公共的準則。依此準則而將一切相對的時空運動皆互相關聯，以配成一絕對的時空運動的系統。

但牛頓此一絕對的時空說在二十世紀相對論出現之後即為相對的時空說所代替。依相對論，時空、動靜、速度及形量質量的計量皆為相對的。此相對說為現代的物理學對宇宙或物質世界的新了解。此一新了解為對傳統的機械力學的一新發展。

依傳統的物理學，物體有相對的運動，亦有絕對的運動。相對的運動乃對一物體相對於其所在的空間的移動而說。如河中的船相對於岸上而移動，或地球上的人或其他的動物相對於其所在的位置而移動。至於絕對的運動乃對絕對的空間而說。如一物體如地球上的人或其他任何一星球，在絕對的空間的某一定的位置移至另一定的位置的運動即為絕對的運動。但依相對論，我們可以不假定絕對的空間的存在，則一切運動皆為相對的運動。相對的空間是就一物所在的位置上說。一物在相對的空間上的運動可以有確定的了解。如船相對於岸而移動，地上萬物相對於地

球而移動，地球與其他的行星相對於太陽而運動。至於太陽系是否有一不動的恆星系為其運動

的絕對的準則？傳統上所謂恆星是否僅是不同於太陽系的星系而亦在移動？則是一問題。若答

案是肯定的，則其以什麼為運動的準則而可成為對絕對的空間的說明，是不易說的。又從理論

上說，在一絕對的空間中，於我與你之外另無第三者存在，則無論是我離你而動或你離我而

或我與你同時向相反的方向而動，皆無法分別孰是真正的動者。於此，我若設定我為靜則你

動，而設定我為動則你為靜。正如我在船上，設定船為靜則岸為動，在岸上設定岸為靜則船為

動。設定太陽為靜，則地球與其上的萬物皆為動。由太陽系與其他的星球相對而說。則皆可自

設定為靜者，而以他物為動者。依此說以說動之所以為動的意義，惟是二物體經一定時空，其

空間距離發生變化的意思。在物體的空間距離發生變化時，我們可以任何一物體及與之無距離

變化的其他的物體所合成的系統為一靜的系統，而以其他與之距離不斷變化的物體的系統為一

動的系統。動靜既相對，與動靜相依而呈現的時空亦即為相對。我們通常或以為時間為一直線

式的表現，而在一切不同的空間中有同一的時間，時間並可以離空間而了解。但依相對論，時

間不能離空間而了解。在不同的空間中有不同的時間。時空亦不能抽離一切物質而獨自存在。

如時空中無物質，時空即不存在無意義。

3 對歷史的事件的了解

對歷史的事件的了解是預設了時空觀念於其中的；對時空有不同的觀念即對歷史的事件有

不同的了解。

歷史的時間常被了解為一向過去、現在與未來作無窮直線式的延伸的時間。此一時間觀念

常由時鐘與日曆去表達。時鐘以秒為最小單位。積六十秒而成一分；積六十分而成一小時；積二十四小時而成一日；以一日指謂地球環繞太陽一次。日曆則積日而成週，而成月；積月而成年；以一年指謂地球環繞太陽一週，年則可以向前後作無窮的伸展。在日曆上則另選擇一準則如耶穌誕生之年以劃分此一無窮的伸展為兩段，而有公元前與公元後的區別。

此一直線式的時間觀念依牛頓的物理學的了解與空間分別為二。空間為一具有長、闊、深的三度向，而異於時間的一度向。所謂歷史事件即為發生於某一時間上與空間中的事件。個人的行為，群體的活動，國家的事務，人類文化的發展皆可以被確定於某一時間上與空間之中，或某一段時間之中與某一區域之上。

通常說歷史事件是就人的行為表現上說。但除了人的行為表現外，宇宙間其他的事物的生化亦在歷史時間之中。此如生物的進化、地質的改變，太陽系的形成等。就人的了解上說，作爲人的歷史事件與作爲其他的事物的歷史事件有明顯的不同，即人的歷史事件是中型的事件（middle-sized events），其他的事物的歷史事件則或爲巨型的（macroscopic），如天文學所了解的對象，或爲微型的（microscopic），如微生物學或化學所了解的對象。但雖有所說的不同，它們皆在人的了解的範圍內，而可以用牛頓的物理學與歐幾里德的幾何學去描述。因依相對論的理論說，對人的活動或對一般的知覺對象的了解，用牛頓的時空說與愛恩斯坦的相對的時空說去衡度是一樣的。因此在人的歷史事件上，歷史的時空說與科學的時空說是沒有不一致的。

但在歷史的時空上被選擇而加以記錄的事件則與在科學或物理學的時空上被記錄的事件有所不同。

此即對歷史的事件的選擇而加以記錄有很大的選擇性，有質的區別。對物理學的記錄則沒有如此

的選擇，而將所有的事件量化，去除了質的分別。由此一意義上說，歷史事件近於當下直接的感覺性，而遠於概念化的了解對象。

歷史事件既有高度的選擇性，對歷史事件的描述即為假設的描述。對描述的證明依於選擇的證據。人之所以注意對某一歷史事件加以描述與證明常相對於某一個人或某一時代的需要。

因此對歷史的解釋即常因個人的所見與不同時代的需要而重作解釋。

4　傳統西方哲學對歷史事件與歷史時間的不同解釋

凡屬於歷史事件在時間上都是過去了的。相對於人的認知上說，此過去了的歷史事件其真實性為何，是一爭論的問題。此一問題直接關連到對歷史時間的了解。因歷史事件存在於歷史的時間上。對歷史的時間有不同的了解即影響到對歷史事件的性質的了解。在西方傳統上對歷史事件與歷史時間有後面各種不同的解釋。

(1)　為運作的實驗的解釋（The operational pragmatic account）：此解釋以歷史敘述所具有的認知指涉只及於該敘述所指謂的遺跡。歷史事件如為我們所直接經驗的，即為我們所親知而無需解釋。所說的歷史遺跡亦可被直接觀察及。被觀察及遺跡本為散殊而無秩序的。

但其可被看為假設事件的證據而系統化。假設事件不涵有曾經發生過的意義。它們僅被看為有用的工具。對假設的事件的假定是以其為真實的，如直接經驗及的現實事件一樣。但由於大多數假設的事件不在我們的當下的經驗內，我們對其唯一有效的認知指涉只是及其所留下來的遺跡或指向它的證據。我們組織各證據成一概念的建構而用此建構作為解答在將來出現的問題的工具。

此一對歷史事件的解釋被近世所稱許的，是其不以過去了的事件當其過去了而仍然存在的吊詭的說法。此是一種本乎脈絡論式實驗主義的科學的哲學的觀點而來的運作主義的對歷史事件的解釋。此解釋將科學與歷史結合在一起。但此一對歷史的解釋亦有其困難。其困難正如我們在討論知覺的對象時所指出的運作主義的困難一樣。在那裡我們指出運作主義對成功的預測與失敗的預測的依據所在不能有解釋。在此它亦不能對有些歷史的假設能成功地解答所面對的問題，有些則不能的原因何在有所說明，尤其是對某一特殊的過去事件從事某種證據的搜集的原因所在不能有解釋。因為從運作主義的觀點上說，每一假設都有預測的成份。歷史的假設亦是如此。若不是如此，其即不是運作的。並且所有對歷史的假設的證據是需要得到科學的肯定的。因此在科學理論上運作主義所遇到的困難不可避免地在歷史的運作論中要出現。

(2)　為形式論者的解釋（formistic account）：此一解釋以一不表示時態的命題所陳述的事實具有特別的存在的地位，亦即以此事實爲潛存的事實。具有時態命題所陳述的事實爲現的事實爲眞實的事實，只時態不同而已。故歷史事件、現在事件與未來事件皆爲眞實的存在。歷史時間亦貫穿於過去、現在與未來中，而爲潛存的分別呈現。此種有時態與無時態的陳述的分別，在中文中不很明顯。但在英文及具有同類文法的語言中則很清楚。我們以英文爲例去說明：“France was invaded in 1914.”此是一對歷史事實的陳述。此事實是過去了的。此過去了的事實是否仍存在是一問題。但形式論者藉著不同語言的表達以其爲潛存事實的表現，而仍然存在於歷史的時間中。“It is a fact tha-t France was invaded in 1914.”「在一九一四年法國曾被侵略是一事實。」歷史的事

實是潛存事實的表現，仍存在於歷史的時間中。現在正在表現的事實與將來要表現的事實亦皆

為潛存事實的分別表現，亦同存在於歷史的時間中，而可以分別說成為："It is a fact

that today is sunny in Hong Kong." 「香港今天陽光普照是一事實。」"It is a

fact that a man will be landed on the Mars in the early 21th century." 「人

將於二十一世紀早期登陸火星是一事實。」

此一將存在事實相對於潛存事實，而以潛存事實為不具有時態的恆真事實，存在事實則為

潛存事實的分別表現，以潛存事實作為存在事實的依據所在的形式論者的說法原自柏拉圖。在

現代的思想界中仍有主張此一說法者。但此一說法所存的困難一直得不到好的解答。其困難即

是潛存事實與存在事實的關係為何？亦即柏拉圖哲學中的理型界與感覺界的關係為何？就表示

潛存事實的命題與表示歷史事實的陳述的關係上說，其困難在於我們究竟以此所說的歷史事實

仍保留有某種存在的意義，或其已完全不存在而只由潛存反映其存在的意義？若是前者，則不

需要以潛存去表達其真實性，歷史學者可直接描述此繼續存在的過去歷史事實。但形式論者皆

不以為歷史學者可以直接接觸過去了的歷史事實，亦很少有以歷史學者可以直接接觸潛存事實

的。若是後者，則過去了的歷史事實不再存在而僅由潛存表達。但既已不存在如何又可以由潛

存表達呢？潛存又如何說呢？此是難得到合理解答的問題。

(3) 為機械論者的解釋（mechanistic account）：此一解釋以過去了的歷史事件可以

於一涵容一切的時空中見到。在此時空中所有事實皆分別永恆地存在於一定的時空的位置中。

此是依於絕對的時空觀念而來的解釋。在常識上此絕對的時空觀念中的絕對空間說似是容易接

受的說法。作為三度向立體的容器而具有無限延伸的絕對空間與歐幾里德的幾何學並不相違。

牛頓接受此一觀念。康德亦以其為人的心靈的特殊結構表現。以絕對的時間為宇宙容器的第四度向則在常識上不如此容易接受。但它是對絕對的空間觀念的一致性的延伸。因為任何物體或事件的明確的位置不但在三度空間中需要有所確定，其所在的時間亦要有所確定。由此我們可以對世界中所有物體或事件在絕對空間中的位置所在與時間所在有確定的概念。

從歷史時間的觀念上說，此一理論最吸引人的地方在其給與歷史事件一確定的位置，永遠存在一定的時空中。歷史學家對歷史事實的探求只在尋找出此一事件在何時何地發生，以及追求歷史事件在時空的連續上所表現的因果關連。

此一理論所面對的困難是對現在正發生的事件與過去發生過的事件和未來要發生的事件沒有好的區別。對過去、現在與未來的事件作區別初看起來好似很容易。如以我們正在經驗及的事件在當下時間上的為現在的，已經驗過的事件在過去時間上的為過去的，未經驗及而要經驗的事件在未來時間上的為未來的。但問題在於對所謂過了的事件而加以重述時，則此事件是過去的或現在的？例如我陳述一我所經歷過的過去事件是過去的或現在的呢？此是一不易說明的困難。後，即八九年七月十日我重述該事件，該事件是一九八八年七月十日的事，經過一年對此一理論最大的挑戰是相對的時空說。相對的時空說不承認有離開事物而獨自存在的絕對時空，而是以時空為事物的相互關係的相對表現。

(4)　為機體論者的解釋（Organistic account）：機體論者與牛頓一樣認為有一絕對。但他們不以為此絕對即為時空，而是以之為所有經驗事物的有機的和諧表現，有時稱此表現為一至高的心靈。此心靈統攝一切有限的經驗事物。有限的經驗事物在此心靈中各得其位。有限的經驗事物只在現前出現。但其存在於現在、過去與未來中。現前的出現為絕對的一現象表現。

在絕對中所有經驗事物皆不失落。所有經驗事物在融貫的絕對的整體中有一一永恆不變的位置。因此過去了的事實得以完全保存。時間只爲現象的呈現而提供通道。此通道爲人的了解與想像的限制所在。

表面上，機體論者好似爲機械論者所不能解答的問題提供了解答。過去了的事實歸於一無所不包的絕對的永恆眞實。因此歷史學家可以以過去了的事件爲絕對在其融貫的整體中的分別表現。但機體論者對於在經驗層次上的時間如何歸入永恆不變的絕對的時間上，或對絕對的永恆所融合的片斷如何轉化而成爲變動不已的時間現象上的片斷，是得不到好的解答的。因此機體論對時間與歷史事件的解釋亦不能得到普遍的認可。

在此順便一提的是柏格森（Bergson）對此一問題的說法。柏氏以過去了的事件繼續永存不失。其存在的方式如滾雪球一樣，過去了的事被滾在其中，層層積聚，而無失落。他以人能記憶過去的事，即爲其仍存在的證明。人在記憶中可順序地回憶已發生過了的事，正如雪球內層所積累的雪一樣發生過的事仍存在於過去了的時間中。此在過去了的時間上的事正如雪球內層所積累的雪一樣❷❸。但此一說法亦有問題。因我們的記憶只能及於過去了的事件的陳跡，而不是及於已過去了的事件。在記憶中所呈現出過去了的事件，只是呈現出過去了的事件在人的惱中所遺留的影像或觀念，而不是重現爲影像或觀念所依據的事實。

懷海特（Whitehead）受柏氏的影響在他的《創造的發展》（Creative Advance）一書中以未來正在創生中。此創生雖在一定的規律中，但可有新的呈現。故對未來事件只可以有原則性的預測，而不可以完全預測。但過去了的事件則是不朽的。此不朽可以由我們對過去

了的事件的直接知覺（prehension）上見到。懷氏吸收了機械論者的絕對的時空說，因此他以對過去了的事件的直接知覺並不需以其完全呈現於現在，而只是知覺其在過去的時空上㉙。

5 選擇論對歷史事件與歷史時間的了解

以上所介述的四種有關歷史事件與歷史的時間的了解皆有問題。其間題皆與其對整個世界了解的理論有關。因此而成為一世界理論的問題。選擇論既為一不同的世界理論，故其對所說的問題即可不限於上述任何一種解釋中，而可以有新的了解，所謂時間不是獨立於事件之外而獨自存在，而是即表現於事件與事件的關係中。依照此一新的了解，所謂時間可被抽象了解為一秩序表，事件即表現於此秩序表上而分別存在。沒有不存在於時間秩序上的事件，亦沒有不依事件而呈現的時間。此一依事件而呈現的時間伸展成為過去、現在與未來。事件亦依此伸展而成為過去的事件、現在的事件與未來的事件。現在與未來仍不屬於歷史。所謂歷史的時間即為此過去了的時間。歷史的事件亦為過去了的事件。但未來不斷轉變為現在，現在不斷轉變為過去而成為歷史。時間與事件皆是如此地轉變。因此過去、現在、現在與未來的不同是就事件呈現於時間的秩序上而顯示出的一種相對的關係的不同。轉變為整個事件的活動，而過去、現在、現在與未來亦不同，其轉變亦不同。所說的整個事件可不指整個宇宙，而指在整個宇宙中所成的各系統。各系統的活動不同，而顯現的時間歷程亦不同。故每一系統的時間上說可以彼此不同。每一系統中的事件的組織活動的不同，可稱為每一事件在其所屬的系統中的不同表現。如此事件是指一有生命的個體，則其生命活動的表現與一另有生命的個體的生命活動的表現亦不同。平常我們稱此為兩個不同生命的表現。事實上此亦為兩種不同

的時間在不同的個體生命活動中表現。由此而說，一個個體生命的時間與另一個體生命的時間亦是相對而不同的。但習慣上我們不由個人的生命表現的不同上而說時間的相對，而只說此是個體生命的不同表現。時間是依個體所在的系統中的整個表現而說。如生活在地球上的人的時間是依人所在的地球環繞着太陽旋轉而說。並依此一旋轉活動的規律表現而分爲年、月、日。又將日分別爲時，時分別爲分、爲秒，而客觀化其爲一在此系統中的各事物所共同遵循的時間秩序。但此一時間秩序可以與不同系統的時間秩序不同，而彼此成相對。於各個體的活動之上有一系統的活動，依此活動而成一共同的時間秩序；於各系統的活動之上是否有一統各系統的統體活動而成一統體的時間秩序，則是一困擾的問題。宇宙統體在一活動中是沒有問題的。但如何由此一統體的活動而建立一統體的時間則成爲一問題。因所謂統體的活動是集各相對的各別系統的活動而說，各別系統的時間可相對於各別系統的不同活動而定，而所謂統體的時間如亦就各別系統的相對活動而說，則只有各別系統的相對時間而沒有統體的時間。若不由此而說，則只能採用牛頓的絕對時間的說法，以時間爲獨立於存事物之外。但此一絕對的時間說本身有問題，而爲相對說所代替。因此，我們只有相對於各別系統而說的相對時間而沒有一在此之上的統體活動所自成的時間。

時間既爲事件展現的一歷程表現，在此歷程上的事件互相關連，彼此相對而成過去、現在與未來的不同時間與不同事件，則有關各事件在此一歷程上的眞實問題可說凡在此一時間歷程上表現的事件皆爲眞實的事件。但由於在此一歷程上有過去、現在與未來的不同，在歷史時間上表現過了的事件以及在未來時間上要表現的事件與在現在時間上正在表現的事件即有不同，而應分辨地說現在正在表現的事件爲現實（actuality），而過去了的事件和未來要發生的

事件為眞實（reality）。說其為現實因其正在表現而可為我們所直接覺知到，說其為眞實因其不是假的其曾經表現過或是將要有所表現而與只是一種想像或杜撰的事件不同。此曾經表現過的事件可以作歷史上的證明，將要表現的事件可以作科學上的證明，當下正在表現的事件則不需要證明而為我們直接所覺知到。為我們直接所覺知的事件之所以不需要證明，因為證明的最後歸依正在當下的覺知。至於在歷史上發生過的事件之所以需要證明，因我們不知道它是否眞的發生過，故需要有歷史上的證明才能確定其為眞。未來要發生的事件因其未曾發生，故亦要證明以確定其是否發生。現在正在發生而為我們所直接覺知的事件為現實而為實然的。現實而被證明的過去的事件與未來要發生而可證明的事件為眞實。在其可被證明而尚未被證明時為概然的眞。眞實與現實的不同正為在時間程序上的不同的為眞實。實然眞與概然眞的不同亦反映了時間程序上的不同。於此外，概然眞亦有假的可能故當其被證明後才可稱為眞實。

歷史的事件的眞實性與未來要發生的事件的眞實性當其被證明後，皆相對於現在正發生的現實事件而稱之為眞實。其未被證明時皆稱之為概然眞。但歷史事件的概然眞與未來要發生的事件的概然眞亦有不同。此不同在於未來要發生的事件的概然眞當其經過實證的程序而證明為眞時，其即由概然眞而成為實然眞，亦由眞實而成為現實。但歷史上的事件則已成過去，其只可以由概然眞經過實證的程序後而成為實然眞。但永不能由眞實而再轉為現實。我們只可以由其被證明為眞實而推證其在過去曾經表現為現實，但永不能使其重複表現為現實。故對歷史事件的證明只是一種追定（retrodiction），而對未來要發生的事件的證明則為一種預測（prediction）。

追定與預測有不同，一為本因果律依可能有的證據以輪轄於已發生過的事件上，以確定其眞實性；一為本因果律依可能有的證據以輪轄於將要發生的事件上，以確定

其眞實性。故對二者眞實性的確定皆爲科學的。

6　對現前的了解

依選擇論對事件與時空的了解，時間既爲事件與事件相互關係的一種程序表現，而空間則爲對事件三度向的存在說明，世界爲一時空四度向的不斷活動表現，則時空不能被了解爲不可再分割的數學點；事物亦不能被了解爲被分割爲無量的極微或最小的物理點；而是以空間爲事物表現的所在，時間爲其歷程，事物則爲在所說時空之中的一現前呈現。此一現前呈現既呈現於時空之中，故其即有其一定的廣延性，而不是一無廣延的數學點或極微的物理點。故對此一現前的了解即不能純由理性思辨的進路而從事無限的分析，而是對其作一直覺式的經驗了解。如詩人或文學家對現前事物與時空的直覺了解，或心理學家對人所經驗的事物的反省體會，或就事物呈現的可能性以了解其可能的現前呈現情景。

詩人或文學家以現前的事件呈現於某一特定的時空中而具有一定的廣延性有明顯的表達。

如李白詩：

朝辭白帝彩雲間，暮宿江陵一日還；兩岸猿聲啼不住，輕舟已過萬重山。

此詩對時空、事件與事件呈現在一定的時空中，皆有清楚的表達。詩中的「朝」「暮」「一日」表達了對時間的不同感受，而顯示了時間的現在、過去與未來的意義。「白帝」城「彩雲間」「已過」「江陵」「兩岸」「輕舟」「萬重山」則表達了對空間的感受而顯示了空間

在不同位置中的一自然呈現。在所說的時空中則有自然事物呈現於其上。於自然事物之外更有人在經歷此時空，更經歷其中的轉變而回憶其經過。故在詩人了解中時空與事件融合為一整體的活動表現。在此活動表現中的事件為在不同時空中而具有廣延性與時空不可分的具體呈現。

心理學家對現前的事件與時空的關係的了解，可以由詹姆士對當下時間的描述見到。詹氏以為實際地為我們所認知的現在不是如無厚度的刀鋒一樣，而是如有一定的厚度的馬鞍一樣。由此而向兩頭延伸為時間。

正因為持續是部份的結合，一個與另一個連續關係才被知覺。我們所知覺的時間結合的單位是一持續有頭與尾—頭有所向，尾有所止。我們不是先感覺連續的一頭，繼而感覺到另一頭，亦不是由一連續而推論其兩頭，而是感覺到一具有頭尾的單位的全部。我們的感覺並不收縮為一小點。我們對感覺之流的某一部份的知識，過去了的或未來的，近的或遠的，常與我們對現在事物的知識結合在一起。對象在知覺中緩慢地消失，如當下的思想對象是ABCDEFG，次一對象將是BCDEFGH，再次是CDEFGHI。在思想的對象中拖延着的過去逐步地消失，那要來臨的將來逐步地填補那消失了的過去。那些拖延着的舊對象與那些將要來臨的新進者是記憶與期待的胚種，為時間的回顧與預期的所在。它們給與意識（知覺）的連續性。沒有此連續性意識即不能成為一意識之流。當下的呈現既逐步在消失亦逐步在增進而成一連續流走，而呈現其時間。此時間即自然成為過去、現在與未來的一結合而表現。詹氏曾以「似真的現在」（specious present）去說現在。現在如不斷在流走，則對此不斷流走的現在似乎只是一現象而沒有確定的真實性可說。故嘉理（E.R.Clay）有「虛構的似真的現在」（the fiction of the specious present）的說法。但詹氏只引用他的「似真的現在」以說現在，並不以現在僅為虛構的，故去掉嘉氏的「虛構」的字眼㉚。

對於「似眞的現在」的長度的量度是不容易的事。很明顯的它是有一定長度的。對於詹氏所說的ＡＢＣＤＥＦＧ的Ｇ的進入或Ａ的退出的似眞的現在，亦沒有確定的方法可用以量度其長度爲多少，只是我們在直接的經驗上都有此感覺。以閱讀爲例，在閱讀的過程中即不斷有新的字進入我們的視覺中，亦不斷有看過了的字退出我們的視覺之內。

心理學家曾由人一下子所接受的連續的刺激因素的多少以說此一似眞的現在的長度。此即爲對我們所注意的幅度的試驗；亦有由比較時鐘的滴答二聲或兩下閃光的持續長度以說似眞的現在的長度的。經過多樣比較研究之後，屈德周（Henry Woodrow）以心理上所認爲現在是不能有很確定的說法，而是在兩秒三與十二秒之間，而在某些情景中亦可以更長[31]。

心理的反應與生理、物理有關。心理感受的現在與物理上的精力表現有關連。米德（G. H. Mead）參考懷海特的意見而說物理對象無論是一鐵的原子或一生物有機體需要時間以表現其功能。懷氏曾說「在一瞬中沒有鐵。要成爲鐵需具有一事件的性格的表現[32]。」米德由此而以爲表現一物的功能的時間需足以「使一物成爲某一物」。對一鐵的原子的時間長度將是足以使該原子中的衆電子環繞其核心一周。一個人的似眞的現在應是足以使其成爲該個人的期限[33]，米德以「使一物成爲某一物」去說現前的確定的意義爲何不容易說。但有一意義是可以說的，即自然事物由一型式轉變爲另一型式需要有一段時間。由某一時間中的某一形狀轉變爲另一形狀表現了一時間的持續性是沒有問題的。

至於當下的空間的問題，詹姆士以所有感覺皆涵有量的成素，亦即皆有延展性。但詹氏此一說法未得到共同的承認。因爲有關聲、香、味的感覺通常是以其異於色與觸的感覺，而以前者爲沒有廣延性的，後者則有。

詹氏的見解近於由物理學的觀點以了解時空說。因由物理學的觀

點上說，所有物質成素皆存在於時空中而佔有一定的時空。詹氏注意及打雷的震度強於以鉛筆磨擦石硯的震度﹔李子所造的布丁的味道強於醋，麝香的香味亦強於蘋果或檸檬。但詹氏以我們對所說的震度或味道的量，亦即它們的空間性只有模糊的感覺而沒有明確的界限。但它們都表現了空間則似沒有問題❸❹。

古代的人已能感覺到空間。他們將感覺、觸覺和視覺混合而成一三度空間的知覺活動。此所說的三度空間即牛頓的空間。故牛頓的空間觀念是依於人的先天所具有的知覺活動而來的觀念。康德以空間為人的感性的直覺形式亦與此有相應的地方。

我們可否對當下的空間用公分去量度其界限，如以秒鐘去量度的現在一樣呢？答案是對空間可以量度是沒有問題的，但對當下的空間的量度直到現在我們尚未發展出如何量度的方式。

7 選擇論對物理時空歷史時間與現前的總括了解

選擇論對物理時空歷史時間與現前的了解有與前面所介述各家的了解相同之處，亦有不同的地方。它以物理時空是由對世界事物抽象了解而來的一抽象的假設的格式。因其是由對世界事物的抽象了解而來的假設的格式，故其可應用於了解世界的具體活動上，而世界中的諸事物由次原子至原子單細胞有機物等，皆在此一假設的格式中，亦即在四度向的時空格式中被了解。所謂事物即表現於此格式中依此格式而活動的事件。所謂物理時空即為眾多事物的活動表現而成，其即不完全脫離具體的事物被抽象把握的假設的格式。時空既為由眾事物的活動表現抽象而成，其即不完全脫離具體的事物，而常相應於具體事物。故如某一系統內的事物表現不同，相應於此不同表現的時空亦不同。

由此可了解相對的時空說與相對的事物關係說緊密關連而不離。至於所謂歷史的時間，其與物理的時間實為同一的表現而作不同的抽象了解而來的說法，即其為相應於物理的時間而作一前後的伸延而來的了解。此一了解亦正為相應於人對事物的感受所成的意識之流而來的表示。歷史的時間所包涵的過去與未來即為由對物理的時間的前後伸延而成的表現，亦為一對意識的一已成過去與將要來臨的感覺而有的表示。此一對兩頭前後的延伸或對已過去的感覺與未來的感覺而來的表示既與當下的物理時間或當下的感覺而有的表示。故其即與此當下的時間或感覺有相同的性質，而同有其真實性，而不應以之為不同性質的存在。但其既有過去與未來的分別，則其即不是現在。歷史的時間既包括過去、現在與未來，其即與就事物的活動表現而來的解的時間觀念，而不對過去、現在與未來作區別的歷史時間說不同。相關連於事件上說，在歷史時間上成為過去了的事件，其即過去了而永不再返；未來的事件則尚未呈現。故其相對於現在時間上正在呈現的事件即有此一在不同時間上的不同。但亦只是相對於時間的表現上而顯示此一不同，它們應同被視為存在於一歷史上時間之流中的真實。為了分辨在此一歷史上的時間之流中的事件有時間上的不同，我們可以以過去了的事件為真實。將來的事件亦是如此，現在正在表現的事件則稱之為現實，就事件為真正的事件而不是假的事件或杜撰（fiction）的事件的了解上說，真實與現實同義。其不同只限於一為表示過去了的或未來的事實，一為表示正在表現的事實。我們對此在時間上的表現上有不同而同為真實的事件的確定可同用科學的證明的方法，而其證明的程序亦大致相同。只是如在前面所已指出的，現實的事件可以有當下的覺知，未來要發生的事件沒有當下的覺知而可以預測，而可以有未來的證明。對過去了的事件不可以對該事件再有覺知，而只可以有追定的證明。

至於所謂現前的呈現或似真的現在，其與物理時空與歷史時間的關係，則現前的呈現正為物理時空的一具體表現。物理時空為依此呈現而作所成的了解所成的假設的格式。現前的呈現亦為歷史時間的依據所在，歷史時間由之而作前後的延伸而成歷史之流的時間觀。我們依意識而成的覺知必表現為一現前的領納。其在時間上為瞬間的呈現，而在空間上亦只表達為一有限度的廣延性。但人的意識不表現為一斷絕的獨一表現，而成為一前後之流。事件的存在亦為事件性的連續表現而成為一流行的化育。故現在的呈現即緊關連於物理的時空、歷史時間與現前的時間而成為一連貫的一體呈現。於此一體中就其相別性而有物理時空、歷史時間與現前的呈現不同的說法。我們所在的世界即是如此地呈現而可以分別地說明的世界。此一世界可能在無始以來即如此呈現。並可能在未來永遠繼續如此地呈現。但說其是如此的一個世界，並不是先驗的確定，而是依於我們對其所能有的經驗的依據的了解。依此了解上說，此一世界的呈現雖如所說的方式，但其動進不已，前有所繼，後有所生，生生不已，而可有如柏格森或懷海特的創進的發展。但此發展亦表現為一現前的呈現而延展為物理的時空與歷史的持續的形式中。

十、因果的關係

1 小引

亞里士多德由四因說以了解因果的關係。四因包括：(1)質料因；(2)動力因，(3)形式因，(4)目的因。質料因為指一物所具有的物質原料，動力因為一物之所以成為如此一物的力量表現，

形式因為一物之所以成為如此一物的樣式，目的因為一物之所以成為如此一物的要成為如此一物的最終目的。故四因說為說明一物之所以成為一物的整個表現，但對因果的關係的了解自亞氏之後有不同的發展。在此不同的發展中，因果的關係不再被了解為一物之所以成為如此一物的，而是僅就一物與其他物所引起的變化上說。若仍以亞氏的四因說為例去說明，則因果的關係只是有關動力因的事，而與質料因、形式因與目的因無關。此可以由伽利略（Galileo）以因果的關係為：「所謂因，在其出現時果即隨之而生；在其移走時果即消失❸。」的說法見到。依伽氏的了解，因果的關係是有關一物與另一物的相互影響上的事，而對所說的物的質料、形式、目的為何不再說。此一對因果的關係的了解是以十五、六世紀的機械論的觀點去代替亞里士多德的目的論的觀點以了解世界。機械論對物的解釋只說明一物與另一物的機械的關係為何，而不問其目的為何。跟隨着只由事物間的相互的影響而說因果的關係，而有休謨對此相互的影響為何的分析。休謨的分析是純由他的經驗主義的觀點上說。因此由其分析上所見到的只是事物外在的相互表現，而見不到事物的內在的連結為何；亦即我們只可以經驗到一物與另一物的相互出現；，相互消失，或一物移動隨之而有另一物的移動的現象，而不能經驗到物與物間的連結為何，或一物引生另一物的力量為何。由科學的因果觀而對自然的現象有新的了解與新的說明。但對人的道德行為與法律責任則不能有適當的解釋。故於科學的因果觀之外另有常識的因果觀，要由常識上對因果的關係加以肯定以作為道德行為或法律行為的依據所在。至於選擇論對因果的關係的了解則既符合科學的，亦符合常識的，並對二者作進一步的綜合的了解與說明。

2 現代的科學對因果的關係的新了解

現代的科學對因果的關係的了解是使科學對象藉着符合的規律而結合於邏輯的假設的推理的系統中。

邏輯的推理結果可藉着符合的規律而應用於科學對象的經驗事實上。因此邏輯的連結可成為得以證明的經驗事實的預測的說明。但邏輯的連結與經驗的連結不是一件事。因邏輯的系統除了藉符合規律而被應用之外，是未經解釋的。其是否被解釋對其地位無影響。其本身系統的關連性與命題的有效性，命題與命題間的關係，及其對系統的關係是完全獨立於任何特殊的經驗解釋上的。因此除非有不是純邏輯的考慮，邏輯系統中的邏輯連結是不給與自然界的經驗連結任何的依據的。

以邏輯系統所表現的功用是一種組織資料的方便設計為約定主義與運作主義的主要觀點。此一觀點為現代的科學家與科學的哲學家所歡迎。其之所以受到歡迎在其對邏輯與自然科學所具有的關係的了解。由此一了解以說因果的關係，因果的關係即成為事件與事件間的相互關係。於此一關係中，如邏輯的關係一樣，中間沒有任何的連結可說，而只有前後的相互關係。穆勒（ John S. Mill ）曾稱此一關係為「恆常的順序」（ invariable sequence ），而羅素則直以此為「涵蘊的關係」（ functional relation ）❸。由此一觀點以了解因果的關係，其所重視的是一般性、規律性與邏輯的系統的表現。決定其相互的關係在一共同的律則上。其相互的關係的決定既在「一共同的律則上」，故其即不重視個體特殊事物之間的連結，亦即不求個體事件與個體事件的決定既在「一共同的律則上」，如張三殺死了王五的個體事件的關係。

3　由常識上以了解因果的關係

常識的因果觀所要探求的不在於共同的律則與邏輯的關係而說科學的因果律則為何，而在就事件與事件的各別情形由常識的了解上而確定其彼此間的因果的關係。此一由事件與事件的直接的各別關係以了解因果關連，為法律學所本以判定一個人的行為責任。因由法律上探求一事件的原因即在追求使一事件之所以發生的另一事件，而不是追求其之所以發生的普遍律則。故從法律的觀點上以說因果的關係即近於常識而遠於科學。此所謂「遠於」並不是以法律的探求不需注重科學，而是說在探求一事件的發生的原因時是由一事件追溯至另一事件而由事件的因果串系上以尋求表現事件的表現者。

對具體事件的因果關連先可由普通語言所用的及物動詞所表示的意義去了解。如推倒、拉開、扭屈、打破、傷害等。此等及物動詞的主詞皆可被了解為因，而謂詞則被了解為果。如「我推倒了一張書桌」中的主詞「我」即為書桌之所以被推倒的因，而被推倒的「書桌」的謂詞則為果。此是就當下可見的兩事件的直接關連上說因果的關係。於此當下的直接關連外，亦可以有非直接的當下的，而是間接的非當下而有時空的距離的。除了由人的活動以說因果關連外，亦可以由自然事件的表現以說因果關連。如由自然的風力、水力、火力或其他的自然變動的情形以說因果關連。

人的行為與自然的表現皆有正常與非正常的分別。就因果的關係是有關一事件與另一事件的關連而起變化的觀點上說，世上所有事件皆在一因果串系之中而不分正常的與非正常的。但

由常識的觀點上說因果，其所注意的因果的關係常是非正常的因果表現。尤其有關法律上的因果問題是如此。其以此為對正常的事件程序的一種干預或侵犯；其並以此種因果的關係為因果的關係的準則。因此當常識的因果的關係說應用於法律上以對人的行為作解釋時，即特別注意分辨人的志願行為與非志願行為。以志願行為為說明一事件之所以發生的真正的原因所在，而法律的責任即歸到志願行為者的身上。

於以志願行為為一事件之所以發生的積極原因之外，亦肯定使一事件之所以得以發生的消極原因。例如一個人立心去偷竊他人的財物，財物損失的原因當歸於立心偷竊的人的身上。但如物主不小心收藏其財物而使其易於被偷竊，此「易於被偷竊」即為財物損失的消極原因。在自然的現象上，禾稻藉雨水而生長是在正常的程序上，但如因雨水不足而枯萎，則缺雨水即成為禾稻枯萎的消極的原因。

4　選擇論對因果的關係的了解

選擇論對因果的關係的了解與科學及常識對因果的關係的了解的範疇所了解事物正相應於科學的因果觀，而由性質的範疇對事物的了解則相應於常識的因果觀。選擇論由概念的範疇所了解的相應外，選擇論由兩類不同的範疇對因果的關係的了解較科學的因果觀與常識的因果觀更為細密與有系統性，尤其對常識的因果觀是如此。我們在後面即先說由性質的範疇而來對因果關連的了解與常識的因果觀的異同及其進於常識的地方；再說由概念的範疇對因果關連的了解及其與科學的因果說的關係。

由性質的範疇而來對因果關連的了解與常識的因果觀的相同處為：⑴二者皆以因果的問題

為各別事物的相互間的順序表現。如以由常識視此表現為「因果鏈鎖」，則性質的範疇即以此為「在完整的行為中的一種股份的連續顯示」，而所謂「鏈鎖」或「連續」皆由前後的事物中而見其連結。(2)二者皆重視在事物所顯示的順序中的動進的成份。此成份為常識所注視的是干預正常事件程序中的不正常的表現，為性質的範疇所注視的是表示欲望的驅使力與其所能滿足欲望的條件。(3)二者皆以志願的行為為因果的關係中的因的依據所在。常識以事件的正常程序受到干預產生於一立意干預的外來的行為；性質的範疇以志願的行為為一有目的的活動，而為解釋其他的活動的根源所在。故其為選擇論的根源的譬喻。但常識與性質的範疇皆不以因果關連的順序表現全是志願的行為表現，而只以此為一模式的說明。

由性質的範疇以了解因果的關係進於常識的地方：：(1)在於常識由志願的行為的順序表現而說因果時，不能對志願的要求與此要求所表現的程序有明確的分辨；性質的範疇則對欲望的驅使力與由此驅使力所表現的期待步驟有清楚的分辨。從性質的範疇上說，只有欲望的驅使力不能有認知的證明，亦不能有對此欲望有所改正。但就欲望與其所表現的期待步驟相連結在一起而要實現此欲望上了解時，即可以有認知的證明；因其所展現的每一期待步驟皆對事實有所改正。而可以有證明，其任何一步驟有錯時皆可以得到改正。此可改正的錯或為所採用的方法的錯，或根本沒有為其所期待的目的的錯。此可改正的錯或為所採用的工具的錯，則不能有此改正。因其不能對其所說的志願的要求與表現此要求的程序有所分辨。(2)在於常識對連結不同事件在一起而成一因果的關係中的連結的性質不能有細微的了解；由性質的範疇則對其間的性質。此即展示由欲望的驅使力與此欲望得到了滿足而寧止之間的情形。如以上可展示其間的性質。此即展示由欲望的驅使力與此欲望所表達的每一步驟的經過情形皆可以作反省的描述，上樓梯的欲望與由此欲望所表達的每一步驟的經過情形皆可以作反省的描述，如以上樓梯為例去說明，上樓梯的欲望與由此欲望所表達的每一步驟的經過情形皆可以作反省的描述，如以上

而見在上樓梯時的過程中兩足與身體的活動的因果關連。但常識不能對志願的要求與此要求表現的程序作分辨的了解。故對所說的因果關連的性質亦不能有細微的描述與休謨對因果的分析並不同。因休謨依其印象說所了解的是為其所了解的事物的分立、殊異、不相關連的觀念，而不見有觀念間的連結。故其對欲望之間的連結只作事實的敘述，而探求其間的連結性質亦完全見不到。(3)在於常識對有目的的行為亦即志願的行為之間的連結只作事實的敘述，而探求其因果鏈鎖，而對行為間的選擇表現則沒有描述。故選擇活動在常識的因果關係中甚為晦暗。但性質的範疇對有目的的行為中的選擇表現則有清楚的注視。其對行為中的因果關係不僅為一對已成事實的綜述，而同時為對將要發生的選擇行為的預測，並對行為的可能的連結亦有分別的了解。(4)為常識對因果的順序的了解，此因果關連始於一欲望的驅使力，終於此欲望之疇一樣有清楚的說明。依性質的範疇的了解的全程：它的開始、中間過程與它的終結，沒有如性質的範得以滿足。常識則對此一始點與終點不能有所說明。

至於由概念的範疇對因果的了解與科學的關係，可有後面的說明。藉著概念的範疇我們可以使由性質的範疇所反省的有目的的行為關連於整個科學了解的系統中。並使由科學的因果的關係的了解最後歸於由性質的範疇所反省到的事件的關連上。此一關連的依據所在，形式地說，概念的範疇與性質的範疇既同為由同一的根源的譬喻引伸而來，故其即為一事的兩面。因此由其所表達的亦當為一事的兩面的既相連而又不相同。除了此一形式的了解之外，在經驗事實層面上，此關連的依據所在則在於對有目的的行為的了解除了表現此行為者的個人可以有如前面所說的依性質的範疇而來的內在反省的了解之外，更發展出了依概念性的範疇而來的外在觀察的了解。此一對有目的的行為的外在觀察的了解，由對其他的動物

與人所作的觀察與實驗而建立了可信的行為的心理學。

此一依整個有機體的心理活動表現而建立的對人的行為的概念性的了解，或心理學家所說的對全體有機活動的了解，並可轉化為生理學的了解，亦即所謂對有機體中的分子的了解。此即前者可歸本於後者，而後者則與物理化學關連。由此而與整個自然科學相關連。此中相關連的各別學問，皆獨立發展為專門性的學問。但皆為依經驗而了解的學問，亦為由外在的觀察與實驗而建立的學問。其與由依性質的範疇而從事反省的了解為屬於兩種不同的進路，依於二者的連結而可使後者的了解為依前者的了解而擴大其範圍。前者因後者而歸到性質的現實表現上。其之所以如此，則在於前面「三」所說的神經中樞的同一表現。其之可以同一則因個人所感受的與其之所以如此，即個人的內省的感受的感受可以與醫生解剖開此個人的腦神經而從事概念的了解相同一。其之可以同一則因個人所感受的與醫生所觀察及的同為此個人的腦神經而關連及其身體的其他部份的活動表現，只是此表現分別為內在反省與外在觀察的不同渠道的呈現而已。

其既為由不同的渠道所呈現的事件，此事件是否是同一，本是一疑問。今斷定其為同一則為經過對後者多次反覆的觀察所得的記錄，與對前者多次反省的記錄歸納而得的結果。我們既可以獲得此一結果，則性質反省的了解與外在觀察所得的概念的了解的同一性即可成立。但此一成立是選擇論依其兩類範疇關連於常識與科學的進路而對有目的的行為從事作關連的探求而了解的結果。若只由任何一方面去了解，即僅有性質的範疇的了解或常識的了解，或僅有概念的範疇的了解或科學的了解，皆不能達到此一結果。近代科學的發展，如前面所已指出的，其對因果的問題已不重視各別事件的因果關連，而是由事件的抽象為普遍的律則的了解，轉化因果的關係為科學上的解釋與預測的說明，若以上面所說的醫生對病人的腦部的觀察為例，其所

注視的是其所觀察的對象與其所了解的生物學的律則性的關係，及其與已建立的其他的科學的律則，如物理與化學的律則的相關連，而非注視此個體事件中的各別事件性的相關連。因此個體的事件好似與科學的預測與解釋不相干。相干的是事件的普遍性與律則性，與由此而建立的演繹系統所成的概念與概念間的相關連。惟有當一抽象的概念或律則被應用於解釋事實時，才見純概念的建構與具體事實的關係，亦才見概念的了解與性質的了解的關係。並見所有性質的直接的了解惟在人的腦神經上。人由反省上以見此腦神經的活動為何，其因果關連為何。由此而尋求概念了解的依據即在其要從事解釋的性質的了解的現實上。

人所能有的直接的知覺本只有所說的性質的反省的了解。人由於適應環境以求生存的需要，而要將此了解擴充。擴充的方法即是由如前面所說的由有目的的行為的欲望驅使力而展現為實現此欲望的步驟，而對此步驟從事改正與證明。經改正與證明的行為步驟被應用以達到其行為的目的常表現出順逸無阻礙時，人即對此步驟有信心而逐漸以之為行為的準則。如此步驟顯示了順序性，則其前後的順序關連即被視為因果連結，而此因果連結亦實即為前面所說的穆勒所說的「恆常的順序」，或羅素所說的「涵蘊的關係」。此亦即由所說的連結而作的理性的建構。但其既發展為理性的建構，則其即轉為抽象而對事實不作解釋的演繹系統，在此系統中因果關係成為涵蘊的關係，亦即為邏輯上的根據與歸結的關係。在演繹系統中，各種關係自相關連，可被應用以解釋經驗的事實，但事實是否如此則需待經驗的證明，而不僅為概念間自相涵蘊的事。

由前面的說明，我們見到真正的因果的關係即為事件的歷程展示，為各別事件的相互表現。此表現可於人的有目的的行為活動上從事直接的觀察而見到。有目的的行為可說是因果的關係

的模式事例。在此模式中活動的意向要藉著選擇的作用不斷地達到。其所達到的目的可以當下
地感覺到和被觀察到。概念的了解與科學的了解由此引伸而成。當概念的了解發展為一高度的
律則性而成普遍的推理系統時，其可脫離現實的性質表現而自成系統，而有以科學的預測與說
明以代表因果的關係的說法。但當其被應用以解釋事實時，其有效的解釋即在對事實的說明上。
故科學的因果觀只在說法上與常識的就個體事件說因果的不同，而在最後的指謂與說明上皆歸
到同一的事實上。既歸到同一的事實上，此事實即有前面「九」所說過去與未來的真實與當下
發生的現實的不同。科學的因果真實或邏輯的因果真實與常識的或性質上的因果真實的不同說
法皆是如此。

十一、現實歷程中的相似性

1 小引

現實歷程中的相似性所要探討的是現實的自然或人生活動所具有的相似性的涵義。此一相
似性在現實的歷程中，亦即在自然或人生活動中不斷呈現。在西方傳統的哲學中對所說的相似
性有不同的了解。最先的了解是從實體論的觀點上以作說明。此即以此一相似性為依一究竟的
實體而來的。如依水、氣或火一種究竟的實體而來的表現；或依地、水、火和氣幾種不同
的究竟的實體而來的表現；或依無數的種子或原子的究竟的實體而來的表現。但此一由實體而
說相似性的說法發展至柏拉圖，不為柏氏所接受。柏氏是於為人所感覺及的事物之上建立一為

思想所了解的理型的系統，以由感覺所見的事物的相似性為依於思想所見的不同的理型而有的不同的表現。亞里士多德反對柏氏的理型說而建立他的形式說。依亞氏的了解事物的相似性的依據不在理型而在形式。但依裴柏的了解不是事物的相似性依理型或形式而表現，而是二者皆依事物的相似性而建立。前者為超越的形式論，後者為內在的形式論，而二者可融合而為一，如在前面第四章與第五章所介述的。

形式論為一相對地適切的世界理論。但裴柏以其對事物相似性的了解仍是有問題的。故他於他的選擇論中對事物的相似性不依從形式論的說法，而是依選擇論的了解而作如後四種不同的說明：(1)由自然事物的呈現而說自然的相似性；(2)由人的運作活動的表現而說運作的相似性；(3)由語言文字的使用而說制定的相似性；(4)由邏輯與數學的展現而說形式的相似性[37]。於此四種不同的了解中，我們將見到相似性不是一單一的概念，純以之指謂事物的實體或形式，而是有所說的四種不同的了解。在本節中我們將依選擇論的觀點對所說的前三種相似性作說明。至於(4)由邏輯與數學的展現而說的形式的相似性則留待下節再介述。

2 自然的相似性

自然的相似性為由現實歷程中自然事物所呈現出來的相同的性相，自然事物由此性相而表現出其恆常性與秩序性。自然事物皆各分別獨自存在而為散殊的個體。但於此散殊的個體中呈現了個體與個體間的相似性，而成為類的存在。此相似性與類的存在表現了其普遍性與恆常性而形成了自然事物的規律性與秩序性。此規律性與秩序性表現在自然事物的現實呈現上，而不是離現實的自然事物而自存。傳統的自然主義者對此一事實曾不斷地尋求其最後的本源所在，

而歸於自然事物所內具的遺傳性，即自然的現實歷代相傳，在動進的自然發展歷程中保存其原初所具有的模式，並使此模式不斷在表現。所說的恆常性與秩序性即依此不斷地表現的模式而呈現。

　自然的相似性一早即爲人所注意及。人由注意及此一相似性而有製作的行爲。在製作的行爲中人依一定的模式而表現其製作的相似性。此爲製作所依的模式繼續存在而顯現了其連續性，人的繼續製作活動亦有連續性，而表現了自然事物所具有的遺傳性。人依一定的模型而製作鞋，製作用具，生產日用品，建造屋宇宮殿。此等被造物皆依其所相應的模式而呈現出其相似性。被造物具有所說的模式而成爲個體物。

　自然事物的遺傳活動可了解爲個體的形成活動。在個體的形成活動中個體所具有的一一成素可被了解爲一集合的活動表現。在人的製作活動中亦有此一集合各成素而爲一整體的事物的表現。前面所說的鞋、用具、日用品、屋宇、宮殿的製造可以如此了解，現代的工廠生產更表現了一分工製作各別的部份合而成一整體的事實。此如製造機器、生產汽車、飛機等皆是如此。我們若對自然事物作分析的了解，將見到每一自然對象皆爲由集合不同的元素而成，其中有層次的表現。此層次分別爲次原子、原子、分子及不同的有機體。在原子層之後皆可了解爲集合了不同元素而成的整體表現。原子可分解爲電子、中子、質子等次原子。

所說的不同層次的表現，除了最基本的最下層外，其他各層皆有集合的表現。於此集合的表現中，同一層次的同一模式的表現皆有其相似性。但不同層次中的個體則彼此不同。各層次相對地說最低層次爲最基本的；較高層次爲由較低層次的元素結合而成。但我們不可以說作爲較高層次的一整體除了集合成爲此一整體的元素之外不再有其他，而是另有其個體性。此個體

性不能於構成其個體的較低層次的各別元素中得到。除了各別元素之外,不能有依此等元素結合而成的較高層次中的個體。但其個體性則不在各別的元素中,而是另有其融和性和突創性的出現。

個體性即融和性或突創性。若較高層的個體性,如有機性,不能完全還原於較低層的元素中,則於象較低層的元素結合成較高層的有機體即有突創的表現。此表現依其有機的特殊結合而存在。故當其解體時,其個體性即消失。但構成其個體的元素則仍然存在,而可以另有表現。

所說的表現是表現者自身在表現,而不是另有東西在使其如此表現。如表現者的究極為次原子,即次原子自身在表現,而不是於其外有使其表現者。因此,選擇論以自然的相似性為自然的究極的自身的表現性相,而不是於此外另有一如柏拉圖的理型作為自然表現的依據。故我們對前面所說自然事物依遺傳而呈現為某一形式的事物與人依某一模式而製作用具或日用品一樣的說法應當注意。人依某一模式而製作可有一於製作物之外的模式為人所依。但自然事物的遺傳則只是其本身發展動進的事,而沒有於此發展動進之外另有所遺傳。依此一意義上說,傳統上所說的自然事物之外另有一規律為其所遵循,而自然律即於自然事物的表現中。惟自然律有其普遍性可本之而了解現實的自然並解釋過去與預測未來,但其不是離自然事物而自存,而是即在自然事物之中,所謂自然的相似性亦正是如此。

3 運作的相似性

運作的相似性是由人將其所期待的觀念,應用於其所在的環境,而使環境中的事物依其期待的觀念而滿足其要求,而在此要求下所呈現出的事物的共同性。依運作主義者的了解,自然

事物皆爲各別獨立存在的特殊個體。於此各別的特殊的個體中，沒有一在各個體之上的共同性。離開人的期待的觀念應用於事物上，事物本身不能說有相似性。故事物的相似性的呈現實爲人運作所期待的觀念於事物的結果，而名此結果爲運作的相似性。由此一意義上說，運作的相似性與傳統唯名論者說共名的觀點甚爲相近。

唯名論者以只有特殊的個體存在，於個體之上並沒有如實在論者所說的普遍者。普遍者只有名言的意義，而沒有獨立於個體之上的存在意義。普遍者只是人運用其語言以指謂衆特殊個體的表示。人之所以如此運用語言是方便人生活上的需要。如人以「狗」一名指謂爲人所飼養的若干家畜，此若干家畜皆爲各別的個體，彼此不同，而皆以「狗」一名稱謂之。又如「家庭用具」一名所指謂的亦爲在家庭中所用的各別用具。於此各別用具之上並無一爲各各別用具所同具的普遍性質。我們不能說於各別的用具之外另有一在此各別用具之上的普遍者獨自存在。唯名論者此等了解正與運作主義者的觀點相合。運作主義者所特別注意的是人爲了其生活上的需要而以某一名稱指謂某若干事物。他們與唯名論者一樣皆以自然事物爲各自獨立存在的個體。於個體之上沒有普遍者。普遍者的出現，是出現於人因生存的要求而對事物作運作的表達，由此表達而顯現其共同的功能——運作的相似性，而賦與其共同的名稱。此中的先後的歷程是如在前面所已表示過的，先有由人的欲望而來對事物的期待的觀念，再以此期待的觀念應用於其所期待的事物上而有運作的證驗，再由此證驗中而顯示事物的共同功能，最後而呈現出由運作而顯現的事物的相似性。

上面所說唯名論與運作主義對相似性的了解，不但否認了於個體事物以上的普遍者，亦不承認有獨立於個體以上的共同概念，如概念論者所持；亦不承認有前面所說的自然的相似性。

運作主義者以事物的相似性只是一種運作的表現。用以說明運作的相似性的最著名的例子是由坐的運作而說座位。假如我們找尋我們房間的事物的共同性，依實在論者的見解，我們必須了解房間中各別事物的共相爲何，然後我們才可以了解其中某些事物作抽象而建立共同的概念，然後我們才可說某些事物有共同性；但依運作論者的見解，實在論者的共相固爲子虛烏有，概念論者的共同概念亦無從建立。因此，二者均不能說房中的事物何爲相似者；要說房中的事物的相似性只有依因此我們的要求而對象事物作運作功能的了解，而應用所說的坐位爲例作說明，則房子中的椅、橙、床、沙發，甚而書枱皆可以滿足坐的期待而表現了可坐的性質，而可名之爲座位。此座位不是由物的性質爲何上去確定，因所說可坐的各物的性質彼此不同。對此不同性質的各物而以其有相似性，此即爲由人的欲求而來的運作的表現上說。

運作的相似性在現代甚受重視，普遍地爲人所承認。由此相似性以了解世界，世界爲一充滿了功能而可爲人運作的世界。在此世界中獨立於個體之上的普遍者以及自然的相似性皆不存在。由人的要求而說期待的觀念，由期待的觀念的求達到而說運作，由運作而顯示事物的共同的功用，由事物的共同的功用而說事物的相似性確有其一定的意義。我們如只重視此一意義即可不問是否有獨立於個體事物之上的普遍者，亦可不問自然的相似性。例如現代的圖書編目即僅由此一意義而依作者的第一個英文字母名稱而建立運作的相似，而不問各書的性質爲何，是否有彼此的共同性。現代的科學對事物的解釋亦多依事物的關係而求其功用爲何，而不再理會亞里士多德所說的本體屬性的意義，或由對類與類的包涵的了解而說其共同性爲何。

運作的相似性確顯示了事物的一面相，而此面相爲傳統的實在論或本體屬性說所未注意及。

但究竟地說，運作主義者亦不能只說運作的相似性而對事物本身的相似性，此並不是僅

理會。此所謂究竟地說即是說當我們應用運作的相似性以使我們的期待的觀念得以達到時，亦即自然的相似性不

由運作自身而可以使運作的觀念相符合然後才能達到。因此如沒有自然事物的相似性，運作的相似性

事實與所說的期待的觀念相符合然後才能達到。而是要期待的觀念與事物有所符合，亦即有客觀的

是不能有所表現的。故運作的相似性必以自然的相似性爲依據。此依據不是要在各別的存在個

體之上說一個共相，而是所說的共相即在各別的個體中。運作主義者必需以此一共相爲其運作

的依據。若無此依據即不能有運作的表現。如再以前面所說的座位爲例去說明，則房中每一由

運作的應用而顯示其爲座位的事物，其自身必有其可坐性而與其他可坐的事物有自然的相似，

然後運作的相似性才可以應用於其上，若一事物沒有此可坐性則運作即不能應用於其上而顯

它的運作的相似性。如果所說的房中有一盤水，此盤水即沒有可坐性，它即不能由運作以顯示它

的可坐性的運作而成爲一座位。又如食物亦是一樣。我們可以由運作以顯示某些物爲食物以表明

其運作的相似性。但亦必需所說的某些物有與另外由運作而確定的物有可食的自然的相似性。因此，

然後才可以由運作以表示。我們不能由運作上使一塊石頭表示它的食物的相似性。因此，運作

的相似性的表示必以自然的相似性爲依據。我們是在一有自然的相似性的各別個體事物上由運

作以表示其相似性，而不能由沒有自然相似性的世界事物中運作而表示其相似。故運作的相

似性與自然的相似性相互爲用。離開人的欲望及由欲望而來的期待的觀念的求達

現的相似性依於自然各別事物的彼此相似性。各別獨立存在的個體事物的相似性由運作而顯現，由運作而顯

到的運作表現，自然事物獨自各別存在，無所謂相似性。自然事物的相似性是因人而顯現。但

4 制定的相似性

制定的相似性是人將運作的相似性外在化而以語言文字表達其意義的相似性。此相似性只有在人的活動上表現。因為惟有人才有文字的使用。前面所說的運作的相似性則不限於人的活動中。因為其他的動物亦有因欲望而引生的期待的觀念，由對期待的觀念的求達到而表示運作的相似性。但只有人才會用文字。故由文字的使用而表現的制定的相似性只有人才有。

此相似性既是由對運作的相似性外在化而來，故其是因應運作的相似性的進一步表現。此表現使人不同於其他的動物得以顯示。其他的動物因不會使用文字故其因欲望而引出的期待的觀念，及依此觀念而生的自然的事，及身而止，而不能留傳於後世。故其他的動物只有個體的自然生命，而不能有超個體的文化生命。但人由於對文字的發明與使用而使人由個體的自然生命而擴及於群體而建立起一廣延的文化社會。在此社會中個體的經驗藉文字的使用而傳達於其他個體與其後的個體。故人藉着文字的使用而使其個體的生命超越個體而存在。

中國古語有云：「倉頡制字天雨粟，鬼夜哭。」此正說明人發明文字的重要。文字既可將個人的經驗表達出來而超個人而存在，文字即可自成一界而可稱之為言說界。此言說界既可獨立於個人而存在而自成規律自在發展，其即成為個人了解的對象，為整個社會所要維護的產物。由此產物所顯示的相似性與前面所說的運作的相似性與自然的相似性互相關連，彼此相對而成為彼此不同的實在。

只是因人而顯現，而並不是人的產物，而是其自身自存有相似的性質而為人運作應用的依據所在。

制定的相似性因文字的運用而顯現。人創造文字原是方便於表現人的生活活動。若就人的欲望表現於期待的觀念上說，則是要使此觀念在運作的應用中得以客觀化，亦即文字化。此運作要成為真要與自然的相似性相符合。故所說的文字與運作活動與自然事實不相離。但當其自成為一表達人的活動的存在其自身成為一定的結構性的表現之後，其即可與運作活動及自然事物相離而自成一界，其自身並在生長發展而漸成為一完整的獨立體。當其成為一獨立體之後，其即成為人了解的對象。構成獨立體的成份並可與事實離異，亦即成為沒有事實的依據而只為文字言說上的事。

宗教式或文學式的語言文字與所說的運作的外在化或運作的文字化的文字的意義即不同。因其所指謂的不是依運作而表現的經驗事實，而是另有所指。我們對此即另有所指要有所分辨，若不然而以其亦為指涉經驗事實的事，而又不能有運作的證明，則其即成為「神話」或「語言文字的遊戲」。語言文字本身既自成體系，我們即對此體系可有所研究與了解。此研究與了解可以只是有關語言文字本身的事。若是如此則「神話」或「語言文字的遊戲」可以另有研究或另有了解，而不可以以之為對經驗事實的指謂。由語言文字以了解經驗事實必須通過運作的歷程而指向經驗事實。若不是如此，而僅以由對語言文字的分析的了解以代替由語言文字而通於事實的了解即忽略了事實，而成為語言文字的一種缺陷。

所謂由語言文字以指向經驗事實，即為由語言文字以表達期待的觀念，而使其於運作的應用中得到事實的證明。由此證明而得到運作的符合真理。此真理基本上是個人的期待的觀念得到運作的證明。但其不限於個人的期待的觀念的得以證明上，而可擴展為：個人的期待的觀念得到運作的符合真理的得以證明。此亦即任何具有客觀意義的命題，如科學的命題的得

十二、形式的相似性

1 小引

形式的相似性是由制定的相似性逐步發展而成。它不為任何制定的語言文字所限，而呈現

以證明。此證明仍需要有個人的運作，但所證明的則不僅為個人的觀念而是有客觀的意義的命題。故此證明不限於某一個人的運作上，而可為任何個人依於一定的方法而從事證明的運作上。由語言文字所表達的依於期待的觀念以從事運作的證明的制定的相似性，有其普遍性與恆常性。因其不限於任何個人之中。但其雖不限於任何個人之中而限於一民族文化之中，即使用該語言文字的民族文化之中。故所說的普遍性與恆常性應是有限度的。因此所形成的語言文字的民族滅亡，則其所使用的語言文字即不再使用。人類使用了多種不同的語言，創造了多種不同的文字。人類有不少的語言文字消失，不少文化滅亡。已滅亡的文化可以為使用其他的語言文字的人所了解；用不同的語言文字的民族亦可由翻譯而互相了解。但每一不同的語言文字的語言對於其他的語言文字來說既彼此不同，其自身即為有限，並可以滅亡，如個體生命的有限與滅亡一樣。雖然一民族的語言文字的生命要比個體的生命長得多。由一民族的語言文字的有限性而見由語言文字的表現的制定的相似性的有限性，此即限於某於民族的生活活動中的有限性。要通所有民族與所有人而成一無限的相似性以顯示一另如自然的相似性的永恆性，我們不能由制定的相似性上得到，而要由下節所要介述的形式的相似上去得到。

於所有制定的語言文字之中。它依不矛盾的原則而建立。它的內部的關係是純符號形式的關係。

它表現於邏輯、數學、或幾何學中。它既由制定的相似性逐步發展而成，故它與制定的相似性

有密切的關係。它亦與自然的相似性和運作的相似性密切相關。但它的性質不同於所說的任何

一種相似性。自然的相似性是現實存在的表現。但形式的相似性不是現實存在的，而是人

為的結果，只顯現於人的思想活動中，不能離人的思想活動而獨立存在。運作的相似性與制定

的相似性亦為人為的結果。但如前面所已指出的，運作的相似性不限於人才有，其他的動物亦可

以有，只是其他的動物只表現於個體中，隨個體的活動而顯現，亦隨個體的滅亡而消失。由人

所表現的運作的相似性則藉着人對語言文字的運用，由個體而擴展於群體，而成為群體的共同

概念。此共同概念藉着語言文字而顯現，而使運作的相似性與制定的相似性相配合，而二者皆

為人為的結果。但此結果與所說的形式的相似性的結果不同。因形式的相似性不但超越

個人而不限於某一個人的運作活動之中，亦超越於個人所屬的文化與由此文化所表現的制定的

相似性之中。因它不僅是由個人或一群人制定而成，而是依於所有人所循以活動的不矛盾的原理

亦即為人人所共由的理性的活動而表現。依此而建立一超各別個人，各別文化，各別的自然的

語言而成的純人為的語言符號的形式系統。此系統有邏輯的系統、數學的系統或幾何學的系統

的分別。但它們皆依人的思想而呈現，而成為一獨立於各別的個人而獨自存在的形式的相似性

——形式的真實。此形式的相似性或形式的真實與自然的相似性或自然的現實相對顯。說其相

對顯，因運作的相似性是以自然的相似性為依據，而制定的相似性則為運作的相似性的外在化

或客觀化的表現。語言文字可獨立於自然事物之外，對自然事物無所指謂，自成一界。但當其

要指謂自然事物時則其仍需歸到自然的相似性上，以顯示其與現實的相符合，否則會轉變為如

前面所說過的「神話」或「語言文字的遊戲」。但形式的相似性則不歸到自然的現象上，而其證明完全在其所依以建立的概念與概念間的關係上，而對自然現實可無所指涉；其推理的活動皆有關其自身系統中的互相關係的事；由推理而得到的斷定亦只限於其自身的系統中。故其依據不在自然現實上，如運作的相似性與制定的相似性一樣，而是在其自身所依以建立的概念與概念的關係的不矛盾上。故人對形式相似性的探求可完全為形式與形式間的關係的事，亦即概念與概念間的關係的事，而可與事實無關。由純形式的探求所得可被應用於現實的說明上。但現實與形式間的關係可以是不一致的。由於形式系統本身的獨立性，有人即依自然的現實與形式的真實的對顯此一事實，而以形式的真實為獨立於自然的現實之外的潛存真實，而以此潛存真實與自然現實分別為獨立不同的兩界。並以前者所表現的為先驗的必然性的真理，後者為經驗的偶然性的真理。此一說法在西方可溯源至柏拉圖的理型論。於柏拉圖之後的亞里士多德、實在論者與新實在論者的哲學亦涵有此一意義。但選擇論不採用此一二元對立的說法。如在前面所已指出的，形式的相似性是人為的結果。其雖然可自成系統而不歸依到自然的相似性的自然現實上，但其實為由人對自然現實的反應，由人應用其預期的觀念對自然作證驗的連作活動逐步發展而成，而不是完全獨立於人由連作活動而逐步發展出思辨活動所呈現的形式的相似性的關係，而顯的形式的相似性；亦即宇宙間並沒有一獨立於一切人的思辨活動之外而自存的獨立潛存的形式。

形式的相似性表現於邏輯、數學與幾何學諸系統之中。此諸系統如何由人的預期的觀念的求驗證而有的連作活動、語言的表達而逐步發展出邏輯、數學與幾何學的形式相似性可分別介述如後。

2 邏輯

從人類思想的發展上說，由運作的相似性而發展出制定的相似性，而再發展出邏輯而有形式的相似性的建立，曾經歷了一段頗長的時間。人是有生命欲的存在。故一開始即有預期的觀念與求此觀念證驗以成就生命的活動的運作的相似性的表現。從人說，此運作的相似性一早與制定的相似性相結合，而表達於語言之中，繼而有文字，由文字而發展出一為群體所接受的文化而形成一為群體所遵循的制定的相似性。人在依此一相似性而生活活動時，亦即生活在一為一群體所接受的語言文字中時，即有邏輯思想的表現。但此時表現在邏輯的形式的相似性與表現在語言中的制定的相似性相結合，亦即邏輯思想常藉自然語言而表達，而未能獨立於自然語言之外，而建立純形式的邏輯系統。邏輯思想所用的概念是藉自然語言而表達，而未獨立於運作所藉以進行的預期的觀念之外；命題亦是藉自然語言而表達而與日常生活中的陳述不分。推理的進行亦表現在現實生活的運作上。在西方，邏輯思想要發展到亞里士多德才有形式邏輯系統的建立。自此一系統建立後，邏輯可為純形式的事。其自身完滿自足。有關邏輯推理的對或錯，為其自身的概念與命題與命題間的關係而可與自然現實無關，亦與依自然現實而陳述的自然語言所顯示的相似性不同。但亞氏的邏輯系統仍藉自然語言而表達。亞氏並以他的邏輯為他依於他所建立的範疇論而展示他對存在現實了解的學問。故亞氏的邏輯實未完全發展為一與現實相對而存在的純形式系統。純形式系統的出現及由此系統而顯示其中的形式的相似性的不同，要由亞氏而經中古而至近代的符號邏輯系統的建立才得以完成。在符號邏輯中用以表達命題中的概念不再是固定的自然語言，而是用人為的符號去表示而成命題中的變項。表達命題中

一項與另一項的關係，或命題與命題的關係亦由原來的自然語言的使用，而代之以人為的符號，

亦即常項亦是用符號去表示；確定一命題之為全稱或偏稱亦以人為的符號去表示。因此在亞氏

系統中用自然語言以表達「凡人是有死的」（All men are mortal）此一全稱肯定命題中

的「人」與「有死的」的變項可以用a、b、或p、q去表示，而「是」此一常項與「凡」此

一邏輯的限量字亦可以用符號去表示。經發展後的符號邏輯對此一命題的符式為：（X）

$X\phi \vee \because \psi$，或寫成為：（X）〔$X\phi \vee X\psi$〕。在此一表示中X所代表的是什麼？沒有確定，

確定的是所有的X亦即X之全，即自然語言所表達的全稱命題的「凡」的意義，故以一括號（）

加以表示。只就X說，X代表什麼沒有說明，但當我們以ϕ去說X時，則X的性質即被確定為

ϕ。在這裡ϕ是什麼亦沒有說明，它亦可以是任何東西。但不管它是什麼東西，若它是ϕ則必

涵有ψ。以自然語言說即為：「在所有的X中，如X具有ϕ的性質，即涵有X具有ψ的性質。」

在此ϕ是什麼沒有確定，ψ是什麼亦沒有確定。我們若對ϕ加以確定，如以之為「人」則對ψ

亦隨之而確定而以之為「有死的」。此即成為在所有的人中，如其存有人的性質，則其即涵

有有死的性質。用普通的說法即：「凡人是有死的」的全稱肯定命題。此一用普通自然語言表

達的命題，在轉用人為的語言或符號去表示時，如前面所說明的，其中的常項（是），變項

（人、有死的）與限量字（凡）皆轉為符號。當其轉為符號後，其與原來用自然語言所表達的

意義即分離，而不限於自然語言所表達的意義中，而自具涵義。其既自具涵義，則其即超越各

別的自然語言與文化的表現，而為各別自然語言與文化所共同肯定。其在各別自然語言與文化

中的出現只有先後的不同，而沒有性質的差別；其不再是任何一種自然語言與文化的產物，而

是人類所同有的活動。

前面以一全稱肯定命題轉為由符號所表達的命題涵值只是對所說的符號

邏輯的形式作一舉例。我們如由此進而對現代符號邏輯作一了解，即會見到在現代的符號邏輯中已沒有任何有關經驗事物的陳述，而唯有符號與符號間的關係。由此而形成一不分解的假定的演繹推理的系統。由此系統中我們所見的爲一純形式的概念建構的事，而與經驗事實無關；獨立於經驗事實之外，亦與各別的自然語言與文化無關；超越於各別的自然語言與文化之上。但其雖獨立於經驗事實之外，超越於各別自然語言與文化之上而自成系統，其可被應用以解釋經驗事實，被涵於各別的自然語言與文化之中，而見其原是在一定文化中生活的人由其現實的生活中發展而成。故自其形成之後，雖自具性質，自成系統，其再可被應用到現實事實中，用自然語言加以解釋。由此而見所說的形式的相似性爲人在一定的自然語言與文化生活上從事邏輯發展所顯示的結果。其既由現實中來即可再應用到現實中去，而不是離人而與現實對立而自己存在的眞實，如柏拉圖及其後學所持的潛存的眞實一樣。

3　數　學

數學與邏輯一樣，亦爲由人的現實生活活動的表現逐步發展而成。其由人的現實生活上的計算活動，而發展爲一純形式的系統，而顯現形式的相似性，亦經歷了一段相當長的時間。其所顯現的形式的相似性具有獨立的性質，亦即數學的系統爲一自足的系統，其中的相互的關係爲純形式的相互證定，而不需現實事物的參證，亦與邏輯一樣。其爲一種超越各別文化的表現而爲各文化所共同肯定，其在各別文化中的出現只有先後的不同而沒有性質的差異亦與邏輯一樣。故當其形成爲一純形式的系統之後，其亦不再僅屬於任何一文化中，而是人類所同有的活動。

數學既為人類依計算的生活活動發展而來的結果，其所顯現的相似性亦如邏輯所顯現的相似性一樣不離人的了解活動而獨自潛存，如柏拉圖及其後學所主的潛存的真實一樣。

數學原於人的計算活動。人有計算活動的要求。計算為人的現實生活的一種表現。此表現可僅為人對預期觀念的相似性的一種記述。但此記述自始即藉自然語言而表現，故由計算所表現的運作的相似性與制定的相似性常相結合。人藉自然語言而計算，人的計算活動起初常是具體的生活活動。如牧羊人對其羊群的計算；農夫對其農具的計算或對其收成的穀物的計算，或對過往的日子的計算。此等計算必先有一類的概念以籠罩所要計算的事物，然後計算才可以進行。如所計算的為羊群必先有羊的概念以作為計算的指引。對農具穀物或日子的計算亦是一樣。但此所謂類，即先決定所要計算的為何物，然後可進行計算。人是能語言的動物，故其計算的活動先是以自然語言去表達。當人由原始的自然生活而發展出文字，在其所用的文字中即有供計算用的數目字。到底人所用的數目字需要多少？應有那些數目字？是沒有必然的說法的。故在各人天生下來有十隻手指，而手指正好是最能幫助人的計算活動的，所謂「屈指算來」。此一情形在羅馬的數目字中表現的最為明顯。由I至V表現了一隻手的不同數目，由Ⅵ至Ⅹ又表現了另一隻手的不同數目。Ⅹ以後則有以Ⅹ為基本而再加ⅠⅡ而成ⅪⅫⅩⅢ而至ⅩⅩ。ⅩⅩ以後以同樣的方法而增至ⅩⅩⅩ。由ⅩⅩⅩ經ⅩⅩⅩⅩ至五十有一特別的數字「L」去表達。五十以後至一百又有另一數字「C」去表達。由此而顯示了十進的意義。中國文字中的數目字的因人的手指而表現十的數目字由十數而發展為十進數亦很明顯，由一至十各有不同表示各個手指的數目字。十後亦以十為基本而再加上一、二、三的數目字而成十一、十二、十三等而直加至二十；二十至三十直至九十

皆以同樣的方式表現。至一百而有一特別的「百」字以表示。百以後的千、萬、億、兆亦有特別的數目字以表現十進的意義。

用數目字去計算是人類生活活動的一進展表現；與用數目字計算的同時，人曾發明幫助人的計算的工具，如算盤，此即為依人的手指的數目而發明的計算工具。算盤分為上下兩層，上層只有兩個珠代表兩隻手的手指的總數，下層五個珠代表一隻手的五個手指。故算盤為屈指而算的進一步設計。

用自然語言文字或算盤皆表示了人類現實生活上的計算活動。由此活動中自然地表現了由計算而顯示的相似性。但此等計算的相似性即與運作的相似性或制定的相似性不分離，而限於一民族文化的活動表現上。但由藉不同民族文化所表現的數目字以計算發展至為各民族文化所共同接受的亞拉伯數目字為計算的工具之後，我們在前面所說的一超各民族文化的計算活動即形成。

由亞拉伯數字的簡便化及後來零（○）的數字的使用，以及相隨而來對計算活動中的主要概念的符示化，即有超各別的民族文化的算術、代數等純形式的數學系統出現。此等系統出現後，其原先以現實事物為計算的對象的計算活動即轉而為一純形式的數字與數字的關係表現，而對一數的陳述的證明亦為其本身系統中的事，而與現實存在事物無關。故數學系統亦為一純假設的推演系統。此系統中的數為一自具特性的理解對象，其所顯現的相似性即為一形式的相似性，而與自然的相似性或運作的相似性不同。此亦即數學系統與現實的存在事物的系統不同。數學如邏輯一樣可被應用以解釋現實的存在界，但其與現實的存在界無必然的關係。

數學的概念不能與現實的概念完全相應，其間有分殊的地方。例如數學上的無窮數（∞）在現

實上即無與之相應的事物。無窮在現實上並不存在。它只是一消極的概念，我們只可以有□＋一的無窮概念，而不可以有□＋１的無窮現實。故數學界與現實界有相應的地方，亦有不相應的地方。數學所具有形式的真實的意義可獨立於現實的真實的意義之外。

4 幾何學

幾何學所表現的形式的相似性與邏輯和數學所表現的大致地相同。其亦為超各別的文化而為人類所共同理解及的事，自身亦完滿自足亦不須以現實的事物為依據，而可由其自身所表現的一致性以證成其形式的真實。其與邏輯和數學的不同，依傳統的說法邏輯是關於質的概念的關係之學，數學是關於量的數目關係之學，而幾何學則是關於量的形相關係之學。由現代的觀點上說，三者實皆為形式的科學而同為有關概念與概念或符號與符號間的關係的純形式的假定的演繹系統。故其同具有相同的形式的相似性。

幾何學亦與邏輯和數學一樣是由人生現實的生活活動發展而成。故在初時亦藉人的預期的觀念的求證驗而表現於運作的活動中而與自然語言相結合。故在幾何學的發展歷程中亦表現了運作的相似性、制定的相似性。它的形式的相似性是它最後發展而來的結果。

對存在事物有關形量的測度是人類現實與空間作幾何式的測定，亦即作點、線、面、立體、活動為依據。於現實生活中對存在事物現實生活上不能缺少的事。故幾何學亦以人生實際的生三角形、四方形、多邊形等的測定。此等測定是因應生活上的需要而來的自然活動表現。相應於此等表現而有規、矩、尺等工具的製造。人藉此等製造物以確定物體的形量以利便人生。此一利便人生的活動為人的自然生活的自然活動。此活動普遍存在於各不同文化的人的生活中。

如邏輯與數學的發展的經過一樣，幾何學亦由具體生活上的有關形量的了解而逐步發展出後來的純形式系統的幾何學。純形式的系統的幾何學一經發展形成之後，其即超各別的文化而為所有民族文化所共同承認。

上面所說幾何學的成長歷程只是以邏輯與數學為例作理論上的說法。從歷史事實上說，幾何學的成長並不是由在同一文化中生活的人逐步發展而成，而是由兩個不同文化中的人發展而成。此即先有古埃及人在現實生活上對尼羅河兩岸的土地的具體的測量活動，繼而有希臘人對此具體的生活上的測量活動作純理性的抽象理解而建立。古希臘人對古埃及人的具體生活經驗作純理性的了解的建立幾何學，據說是始於畢達哥拉斯及其門人。但真正能將畢氏及其門人以及柏拉圖的各散殊的幾何學的命題系統化而成為一嚴謹的幾何學系統者，為公元前三世紀的歐幾里德。自歐氏完成其幾何學原理（Euclid's Elements）一書之後，純形式系統的幾何學才得以建立。

歐氏的幾何學為純形式的，本應作純形式的了解。但後世並不以歐氏的幾何學為純形式的，而是以其為了解存在事物時空的形量的唯一方式。故以之為純理的先驗的，而與事實的經驗的事物對立。經驗的事物必依之而呈現其形量才得以了解。此一對幾何學的了解與亞里士多德以其邏輯與現實存在不分，而為繼他的範疇論而對現實存在界作進一步的說明有同樣的意思。邏輯要成為純形式的系統，如前面所已介述的，要至近代符號邏輯建立之後；以幾何學為一純形式的學問，其與現實存在界無關，但可以應用以解釋現實存在界亦要至近代非歐幾里德的幾何學得到較充份的了解。相對於應用以解釋現實存在界來說，不同的幾何學乃由不同的設定開展而成，各可被應用以解釋現實存在事物，其亦可以與現實存在事物分立而獨自存在。

其所表示的相似性爲純形式的相似性，不同於其所經歷過的運作的相似性、制定的相似性的涵義，亦不同於自然的相似性的涵義。

幾何學系統既獨立於存在事物之外而自成一純形式的推演系統，其所顯示的相似性爲形式的相似性，其即與現實之間無必然的關係。並且其亦與存在事實不完全相應。最明顯表示此一不相應的例子爲幾何學的點、線、面。因它們只屬於概念上的事，而不是指謂現實的事物；對線的無限分割的肯定亦與現實不符，因現實沒有可以無限分割的線的存在。

註釋

❶ Pepper, S. C. *Concept and Quality: A World Hypothesis*, pp. 1-2.

❷ Ibid., p. 1.

❸ Ibid., pp. 15-17; 28-30.

❹ Ibid., p. 15.

❺ Ibid., pp. 22-24.

❻ Ibid., pp. 28-30.

❼ Ibid., p. 2.

❽ 他們是從是否具有認知的意義（cognitive meaning）的觀點上去否定形而上學的命題，以形而上學的命題爲沒有認知的意義的；是因語言的混淆（linguistic confusion）而來的結果，是一種贋的問題（pseudo-problem）。

❾ Ibid., ❶ p. 47.

❿ Ibid., p. 158.

⓫ Ibid., p. 155.

⓬ Ibid., p. 158. 裴柏在此只是表示了此一意義而並沒有提及休謨與杜威。有關休謨與杜威對所說的問題的不同了解，我將於《西方形而上學中的超越論與存有論》中的「存有論」部份另作較詳細的介述。

⓭ 請參看 Ryle, G. *The Concept of Mind*, (New York: Barues and Noble, Inc., 1949), pp. 11-24.

⓮ Ibid., ❶ pp. 161-170.

⑮ Ibid., p. 224.

⑯ Ibid., pp. 234-236.

⑰ Ibid., p. 229.

⑱ 以「假設」為一「創造的想像」，似先由咸普勞（C. G. Hempel）提出。請參他的 Philosophy of Natural Science (Englewood Cliffs, N. J.: Prentice Hall, Inc., 1966), pp. 15-16.

⑲ Hempel, C. G. Fundamentals of Concept Formation in Empirical Science (Chicago: Univ. of Chicago Press, 1952), p. 1.

⑳ Nagel, E. The Structure of Science (New York: Harcourt, Brace and World, Inc., 1961), p. 4.

㉑ Toulmin, S. The Philosophy of Science, (New York: Harper and Bros, 1966), pp. 55; 78-79.

㉒ Ibid., p. 266.

㉓ Ibid., ⑲ p. 34.

㉔ Ibid., ⑲ p. 34.

㉕ Ibid., ❶ p. 267.

㉖ Ibid., p. 267.

㉗ Ibid., pp. 321-322.

㉘ Ibid., pp. 340-341.

㉙ Ibid., p. 341.

㉚ Ibid., pp. 358-359.

㉛ Woodrow, H. "Time Perception," in S. S. Steaeus (ed), Handbook of Experimental Psycholog (New York: John Wiley and Sons, Inc., 1951), p. 1230.

㉜ Whitehead, A. N. The Principle of Natural Knowledge (Cambridge: The Univ. Press, 1919), p. 23.

㉝ Mead, G. H. The Pholosophy of the Present (La Salle, Ill.: Open Court Publishing Co., 1932), p. 19.

㉞ Ibid., ❶ p. 364.

㉟ Ibid., p. 380.

㊱ Ibid., p. 383.

㊲ Ibid., p. 416.

㊳ 非歐幾里德的幾何學首由十九世紀的德國數學家 Gauss 想及，但沒有正式發表其想法。正式先分別獨立地發表非歐幾里德幾何學者爲蘇聯數學家 Lobachevsky 和匈牙利數學家 Bolyui。十九世紀末又有德國數學家 Riemann 和 Helmhot 分別發表了另一形式的非歐幾里德的幾何學。

附錄一

S. C. PEPPER'S CONCEPT OF METAPHYSICS AS

THE THEORY OF WORLD HYPOTHESES

by

Tu Li

CHAPTER I

INTRODUCTION

1. Two Different Kinds of Concepts of Metaphysics

There are many different concepts of metaphysics in the history of Western philosophy. The classification of them can be a problem of study in metaphysics. But related to Pepper's concept of metaphysics, which will be discussed in detail later, I shall classify them into two kinds: (1) metaphysics is regarded as something beyond the field of knowlwedge; it cannot be a science; (2) it is regarded as something within the field of experience; it has empirical meaning.[1]

By the first kind of concept I have in mind Kant's concept of metaphysics and that of those who accept Kant's idea that metaphysics cannot be a science; instances of the second kind of concept are Dewey's concept of metaphysics and Pepper's theory of world hypotheses. In order to make clear my meaning here and in terms of this clarity to relate Pepper's concept of metaphysics to the history of philosophy, I shall sketch in the next few pages the general historical development in recent centuries of certain concepts of metaphysics.

In general, philosophers before Kant, with the exception of some empiricists, believe that we can have knowledge of metaphysics based on our reason. But this idea is rejected by Kant in his *Critique of Pure Reason*. For reason is dis-

tinguished there by Kant into pure and practical. The former again is classified into sensibility, understanding, and reason. Knowledge is constructed by a cooperation of sense given through the a priori forms of sensibility and the a priori concepts afforded by understanding. That is, in order to have knowledge the a priori concepts must be applied to sense-experience which is given. We do not have any intelligible object of intuition to which the a priori concepts can be applied to construct metaphysical knowledge. As to the ideas generated from reason, they only have a regulative function. They do not have a constructive function. As to practical reason, it is concerned with the problem of morals, not with knowledge. So we cannot have any knowledge of metaphysics simply based on reason without relating it to sense-experience.

Based on this clarification, Kant declared that we cannot have a science of metaphysics. Science is concerned with phenomena established by applying the a priori concepts to the objects of experience, while metaphysics is concerned with noumena which are not objects of experience, nor can they be intuited by reason. So metaphysics is excluded from the field of cognition, and is regarded as a problem of practical reason.

Kant's clarification of the relation between knowledge and metaphysics and in terms of this clarification his exclusion of traditional metaphysics from the field of science, have been regarded as a further development of the theory of knowledge.[2] If we accept Kant's definition of metaphysics as concerned with noumena and accept his meaning of noumena, then metaphysics must be excluded from the field of knowledge, and should be regarded as a problem beyond sense-experience. And probably we would agree with him that it belongs to the field of practical reason.

Though not all philosophers after Kant accept his theory of practical reason, yet many of them agree with his concept of metaphysics as beyond the field of knowledge. For example, Schopenhauer regards the problem of metaphysics as the problem of man transcending his own contingent knowledge; Bergson speaks of metaphysics as the science which claims to dispense with symbols; Jaspers holds that

it is concerned with Being or *existenz* which is not objectifiable. These three philosophers' concepts of metaphysics are different from one another, but in the sense of regarding metaphysics as beyond the field of knowledge they agree with Kant.

In a sense, Kant's exclusion of metaphysics from the field of knowledge is also adopted by the logical positivists. As we know, what the logical positisists intend to do is not only to exclude metaphysics from the field of knowledge, but also to eliminate it from philosophy,[3] and their way of rejection is also different.[4] But in the sense of regarding metaphysical problems as noncognitive they have the same kind of concept as Kant.[5]

But Kant's way of approaching the problem of metaphysics is by no means the only way of dealing with this problem. And when he used this way to deal with the problem he tacitly assumed a bifurcation[6] of appearance and reality, or phenomenon and noumenon. Those who do not agree with this bifurcative method, however, would not regard the problem of metaphysics as one beyond our knowledge; and for them the difference between science and metaphysics is not based on the distinction between cognition and noncognition but on something else.[7]

In contemporary philosophy, the logical positivists have intended to exclude or to eliminate metaphysics from the field of knowledge or the field of philosophy. Thus metaphysical problems are regarded by them as nonsensical.[8] They do not want to have in contrast to Kant a metaphysics with cognitive meaning. Dewey was perhaps the first to have a metaphysics based on experience as a descriptive study of generic traits of existence.[9] According to Dewey, the philosopher or metaphysician cannot obtain any knowledge which is beyond the field of scientific inquiry. He does not have any special methods or insight into a realm of nature that transcends what we now know by scientific inquiry. It is the type of generality with which he is concerned that distinguishes the metaphysician from the practicing scientist.[10] So the difference between scientist and metaphysician is not a difference concerned with phenomena and noumena, but with the problem of knowledge of special fields and general features of the world.

S. C. PEPPER'S CONCEPT OF METAPHYSICS AS...

Pepper's concept of metaphysics in the sense of regarding it as concerned with the empirical is the same as that of Dewey. For he insists that the problem of metaphysics is not something beyond the field of experience; it is a problem of world hypotheses corroborated by evidence.11 He also indicates that this is not a new theory; it does not begin with Dewey; its origin can be traced back to the ancient Greek philosophers. Since Thales the problem of metaphysics has been regarded as an empirical study of nature.12 And this kind of study has been continually developed in later philosophy. Based on this point he worked out his book, *World Hypotheses*, in which he sketched four different relatively adequate world hypotheses as four existent different systems of metaphysics in the history of Western philosophy.13

Pepper's world hypotheses in some sense no doubt represent the existent schools of philosophy in the past, though whether or not the theory of world hypotheses has been adopted by the past philosophers ever since Thales is questionable. For at least one can say that before Pepper nobody claimed that his metaphysics is a world hypothesis. This is why the Milesian school and the other schools of philosophy interpreted by Pepper in terms of world hypotheses could be and have been understood by other philosophers from a different point of view. Relating Pepper's theory of world hypotheses to the history of modern and contemporary philosophy for understanding, I should rather think that this is a result of the development of modern and contemporary philosophy, or a reaction to the first kind of concept of metaphysics, and a contribution of Pepper to the problem of metaphysics.

At any rate, that the concept of metaphysics can be distinguished into two different kinds simply called cognitive and noncognitive seems clear. For what is asserted by Dewey and Pepper in regard to this problem is quite different from what Kant, Schopenhauer, Bergson, Jaspers, and some others say. With an understanding of this distinction, I shall make a general survey of Pepper's theory of world hypotheses in the following section.

2. Metaphysics as the Theory of World Hypotheses

The detailed meaning of the theory of world hypotheses will be discussed in the following two chapters. What I want to do here is just to point out some of its characerisics by way of introduction to this study.

As has already been pointed out, concepts of metaphysics can be either one of the mentioned two kinds.14 When a philosopher once adopts one of these two, he needs to consider how to deal with the problem of metaphysics and establish his theory of metaphysics. It seems that there are different ways for philosophers who have either kind of concepts to deal with the problem of meaphysics and establish their different theories. Those who regard the problem of metaphysics as beyond man's experience like Kant, Schopenhauer, Bergson, Jaspers, have dealt with this problem in different ways and through these ways have sought to establish their different kinds of theories of metaphysics. Something similar is true of those who regard the problem of metaphysics as a problem of empirical nature like Dewey and the exponents of the four relatively adequate world hypotheses interpreted by Pepper. For each of them has his own theory of metaphysics. But for Pepper's theory of world hypotheses what is important is not only to establish a system of metaphysics but also to understand what the difference and similarity of the different empirical systems of metaphysics are.15 Although this theory agrees with Dewey's in holding that metaphysics is empirical, yet it is not like Dewey's pragmatic naturalism in being concerned to develop only one system of metaphysics. This theory is a theory which can be used to interpret the different systems of metaphysics and applied to those systems. So Pepper not only rejects the first kind of concept represented by Kant, Schopenhauer, Bergson, and Jaspers as dogmatism,16 but also does not agree with those exponents of the second kind of concept who think that the empirical evidence points to a single metaphysical hypothesis. Pepper maintains that in some sense we can say that the philosophers with the second kind of concept of metaphysics can deal with the problem of metaphysics by different ways and through these ways can establish their different metaphysical hypotheses. For Dewey, Plato, Democritus, and Hegel have established their different systems such as pragmatism, realism, atomism or naturalism, and absolute idealism, respec-

tively, by different ways. But based on the theory of world hypotheses, if a philosopher regards a certain way as the only way for establishing the theory of metaphysics and cannot see what is the difference and similarity between the way adopted by him and the way or ways adopted by the other philosophers, he may assume that there is only one right system and tenaciously or dogmatically fix his belief on it without any understanding of the other systems. And when any conflict arises among the different systems of metaphysics, he may be unable to solve it and give a fair judgment to the others. He may reject the others as valueless. This creates a serious problem in understanding and evaluating the different systems of philosophy. Indeed, according to the theory of world hypotheses, a frequent outcome in the past of this procedure has been misunderstanding of the problem of metaphysics, and this is a danger still facing us. How to clear up this difficulty is an important problem for us. But since this difficulty has arisen from a misunderstanding of the problem of metaphysics, it can be overcome by pointing out where the problem is.

So, according to Pepper, though a philosopher is allowed to regard his system of metaphysics as established by a certain way which is different from the ways of the others, yet he also has to know that all empirical ways are based on experience, and there is some similarity among them. For all of them must be guided by the nature of experience. So though Pepper in some sense does not deny that philosophers in the past had their different ways for establishing the theory of metaphysics, yet he insists that "the constructive work of the past was all of an empirical nature."17 Those who have contributed most significantly to the problem of metaphysics have made use, explicitly or implicitly, of the method of root metaphors.18 From this point of view Pepper maintains that philosophers can choose different root metaphors and through them work to establish their different systems of metaphsics. But he does not think that the alternatives to the root metaphor method of establishing systems have proved to be equally fertile ways of generating new sets of categories or new world theories.19 So the meaning of different ways has to be related to the different root metaphors. So if

what we mean by ways of establishing a system of metaphysics is related to the different root metaphors, we can say that different empirical philosophers have established different systems of metaphysics by different ways. But if what we mean by the way of establishing a fruitful system of metaphysics is a matter of whether the root metaphor method or some other is to be followed, then there is, in effect, only one consistently workable way for establishing a system of metaphysics. From the former way of seeing the problem there are different systems of theories of metaphysics, but from the latter way, there is only one theory of world hypotheses based on the concept of root metaphors. This is why we say that Pepper's concept of metaphysics as the theory of world hypotheses is different from the concepts of metaphysics of the other empirical metaphysicians, and it is a special characteristic of the theory of world hypotheses. Pepper describes the root metaphor method as follows:

> So we return to the traditional analogical method of generating world theories. The method in principle seems to be this: a man desiring to understand the world looks about for a clue to its comprehension. He pitches upon some area of 'common-sense fact and tries if he cannot understand other areas in terms of this one. This original area becomes then his basic analogy or root metaphor. He describes as best he can the characteristics of this area, or, if you will, discriminates its structure. A list of its structural characteristics becomes his basic concepts of explanation and description. We shall call them a set of categories. In terms of these categories he proceeds to study all other areas of fact whether uncriticized or previously criticized. He undertakes to interpret all facts in terms of these categories.[20]

I shall discuss the detailed meaning of the root metaphor is the sixth section of the following chapter. What I want to indicate briefly here is that since all constructive systems of metaphysics are empirical in nature and are established by the method of root metaphors, they are world hypotheses. And since they are all world hypotheses, they have some kind of common characteristics related to the theory of world

hypotheses. Based on this understanding, Pepper offers us the following points as characteristics of metaphysics as the theory of world hypotheses.

(1) Since the different systems of metaphysics are all based on different root metaphors, all of them should be treated equally if they all have relatively adequate functions for understanding the world.

(2) Since one system is established with a different root metaphor from the others, the world understood by one system must be in some sense different from that of the other systems. And which of these understood worlds is the real world we cannot have any other idea than comparing the different systems one with another to see which one of them can give us a better explanation of the world.

(3) Since there are different systems of metaphysics and thus different ways of understanding the world, no one of them can be regarded as absolute. But though there is no one absolute system, a philosopher when attempting to understand the world must work in a certain system. This means that a philosopher has to adopt a certain root metaphor in terms of which to establish his system of philosophy. This will not prevent him from understanding that there are other systems also based on the theory of root metaphors; so they can also be world theories.

(4) The theory of world hypotheses is a theory which is used to interpret the different world hypotheses, but holding this theory and describing traditional views in terms of it will not prevent one from establishing some new system of metaphysics based on a different root metaphor. Pepper is a good example in this regard. In addition to applying the theory of world hypotheses to interpret the different traditional world hypotheses, he has proposed a new world hypothesis called selectivism.[21]

(5) Since each system is regarded as a world theory and cannot be regarded as absolute, each system is just accepted as a hypothesis for interpreting the world. For the one world is interpreted in different ways no one of which can claim complete adequacy; hence each interpretation in relation to the world can

only be called a hypothesis. This is one reason why Pepper calls each of the world theories which has a relatively adequate function for understanding the world a relatively adequate world theory.

(6) "Since these relatively adequate hypotheses are the best we have in the way of world-wide knowledge, we had better keep them all for such cognitive value as they contain, implying that they do have cognitive value in spite of the inadequacies."22 This cannot be denied by the argument that a metaphysical hypothesis is one that asserts about all facts; every metaphysical hypothesis in some sense is inadequate to do that; so it is useless as a metaphysical cognition. For the ground for the theory of world hypotheses to estimate cognitive value is quantitative, not qualitative.23

3. The Problem of This Study

With reference to the above understanding, this study will be mainly concerned with the following problems.

As already pointed out, there are two different kinds of concepts of metaphysics, noncognitive and cognitive, existing in modern and contemporary Western thought. Pepper's concept of metaphysics belongs to the latter kind. Though Pepper asserts that world hypotheses have existed ever since ancient times, yet what makes them clear is due to the theory of world hypotheses which, as I suggested above, resulted from the development of the problem of metaphysics in modern and cnotemporary philosophy, and is a contribution of Pepper to the problem of metaphysics. So this study in the next chapter, that is, Chapter Two, will examine in detail Pepper's concept of metaphysics as the theory of world hypotheses. This will be most concerned with its internal construction. That is, what the basic concepts of it are and how it is constructed will be discussed in detail.

Chapter Three will be most concerned with the external relation between one world hypothesis and another: that is, the problem of the application of the theory of world hypotheses. As has been pointed out earlier, Pepper asserts that

there are different empirical systems established by the traditional philosophers for understanding the world, and each system is based on a different root metaphor. Since the root metaphors are different the systems established by them are different and since the systems are different the world understood by these systems is also different. Now how can we say that the different constructed systems are all based on the root metaphor method? How is the concept of root metaphors applied to different systems?

The metaphysical problem becomes a complicated and controversial one in modern and contemporary philosophy, and we shall discuss Pepper's theory in relation to this problem in Chapter Four, the Conclusion of this study, considering such questions as the following. Can the theory of world hypotheses be asserted as a metaphysical theory? Can it meet its challenge? Can it really reject the second kind of concepts of metaphysics as mentioned before? What is the problem of it? Why does Pepper regard the problem of metaphysics as empirical rather than as something beyond experience?

CHAPTER TWO

THE BASIC CONCEPTS OF THE THEORY OF WORLD HYPOTHESES

1. An Introductory Remark

As already pointed out in the preceding introductory chapter, the meaning of the theory of world hypotheses can be understood from two aspects — internal and external. The internal aspect is concerned with its internal construction, that is, what its basic concepts are, how it is constructed, while the external aspect, its external relation, is concerned with how one world hypothesis is related to the others. This chapter is planned for discussing the former problem, while the latter will be discussed in the succeeding chapter.

Like any other theory having its fundamental concepts, the theory of world hypotheses is also constructed with, or supported by, a number of basic concepts. These basic concepts as indicated by Pepper are: (1) the distinction between science and metaphysics, (2) the rejection of skepticism and dogmatism, (3) two different types of corroboration, (4) the concept of hypotheses, (5) the concept of root metaphors. Each of these basic concepts has its function in the theory. By means of their different functions Pepper presents us with a theory of metaphysics as the theory of world hypotheses. In the following pages of this chapter each basic concept in turn will be treated as a topic of a section. I shall discuss each of them.

2. The Distinction Between Science and Metaphysics

After having asserted that the theory of world hypotheses is concerned with the problem of the empirical world and that the concept of metaphysics is the concept of world hypotheses, the first thing that comes to Pepper's mind is the distinction between science and metaphysics.24 For since the concept of world hypotheses is incompatible with the above mentioned first kind of concept of metaphysics, the distinction between science and metaphics asserted by Kant is unac-

ceptable to him. So he has to find out some other way to make a distinction between them, and in terms of such a distinction clarify the meaning of metaphysics and the relation between metaphysics and science.

What Pepper is concerned with here is also faced by Deway. For as already pointed out, Dewey and Pepper both share the second kind of concept of metaphysics. So neither of them can accept Kant's distinction between science and metaphysics. This is indicated by our explanation above that when Kant's bifurcative method is rejected the distinction between science and metaphysics is not based on the distinction between cognition and noncognition but on something else.[25] So the problem of distinguishing between science and metaphysics does not belong to Pepper alone; it is shared by Dewey and by those who subscribe to the second kind of concept of metaphysics.

As pointed out before, the distinction between science and metaphysics asserted by Kant and those who accept Kant's rejection of metaphysics as a Science is mainly based on the distinction between cognition and noncognition. For what is cognitive is phenomena, belonging to the field of science; beyond phenomena, there are noumena which are noncognitive in the sense that they cannot be known as objects of science can and they belong to the field of metaphysics. This distinction also can be called a two-way distinction between science and metaphysics: that is, the objective mode of distinction and the methodological way of distinction. The first way indicates that the object of science is different from the object of metaphysics. For the objects of science are phenomena, while the objects of metaphysics are noumena. The second way indicates that the method for science is different from that for metaphysics. The former can be simply called scientific method, and the latter, metaphysical method.

Since Dewey and Pepper both reject the method of bifurcation and regard the world just as what it is recognized by us to be, the above mentioned objective distinction is unacceptable. For to them the object of science is the same as that of metaphysics. And this is the empirical world. As to the methodological distinction,

it is also unacceptable to them, for they cannot agree to the mentioned metaphysical method. And to Dewey, the method of science is the same as that of philosophy. As already pointed out, Dewey did not think that there is any special method for metaphysics which is different from scientific inquiry.

Thus the above mentioned distinction is totally unacceptable to Dewey, and he also did not think that besides the scientific method there is any other kind of method for philosophy. This does not imply that he did not have any kind of distinction between science and metaphysics. As a matter of fact, for Dewey, there is really a kind of distinction between science and metaphysics, that is, the special-general distinction, as I should like to call it. For Dewey has pointed out that the work of scientists is different from that of metaphysicians. The scientist is concerned with a special scientific problem, whereas the mtaphysician is concerned with the problem of the generic traits of existence. So in contrast to science he calls metaphysics a descriptive study of the generic traits of existence.

Just as the empirical philosophers cannot accept Kant's distinction, the non-empirical philosophers would also disagre with Dewey's distinction. But regardless of whether they agree or not there is such a kind of distinction asserted by Dewey, and in some sense this distinction is clear to us. This is why I call it the special-general distinction. And by "special" here I mean that the scientist is concerned with special scientific problems. On the other hand, "general" indicates that the metaphysician is concerned with the generality of existence.

Pepper's distinction between science and metaphysics, in some sense, is similar to that of Dewey. For what Pepper asserted is a kind of study-field distinction. That is, the study of science is restricted to a certain field, while the study of metaphysics is unrestricted to any field. He stated the distinction as follows:

> The two books last named deal with restricted fields of knowledge and can reject facts as not belonging to their field if the facts do not fit properly within the definitions and hypotheses framed for the field. But the other

books deal with knowledge in an unrestricted way. These unrestricted products of knowledge I am calling world hypotheses, and the peculiarity of world hypotheses is that they cannot reject anything as irrelevant.26

From this quotation we can see that what Pepper calls "restricted fields of knowledge" is similar to Dewey's problems studied by special scientists, and what Pepper calls "unrestricted products of knowledge" is similar in a sense to Dewey's concept of metaphysics as a descriptive study of the generic traits of existence.

Besides the above mentioned similarity to Dewey's distinction, however, Pepper also indicates a kind of methodological distinction connected with the study-field distinction which cannot be found in Dewey's philosophy. But Pepper does not discuss this distinction separately. It is indicated in connection with the problem of corroboration and that of hypothesis. These two porblems will be discussed in section 4 and section 5 of this chapter. I think before having an understanding of the mentioned two problems, it is not easy for us to have a clear idea of the methodological distinction. So what I want to do here is just to indicate some general points of.this distinction. We shall come back to it again when we discuss the mentioned two problems.

According to Pepper, a world hypothesis is different from a special scientific hypothesis. And this difference can be understood from two aspects. The first aspect is that a world hypothesis is a hypothesis of metaphysics. It is concerned with an unrestricted field, with "whatever may come up for interpretation within our experience."27 As to the special scientific hypothesis, it is restricted to a certain field and only deals with facts belonging to that field. The second aspect is that a world hypothesis can only be a structural hypothesis with unrestricted scope corroborated by structural corroboration. As to a scientific hypothesis, it can be either a conventionalistic hypothesis corroborated by either multiplicative corroboration or structural corroboration, or a structural hypothesis with restricted scope corroborated only by structural corroboration.

The meaning of the mentioned different hypotheses and corroborations I shall

not explain here. As indicated before, it will be discussed in section 4 and section 5. What I want to point out here, in connection with the distinction between a scientific hypothesis and a metaphysical hypothesis is that the distinction between science and metaphysics, for Pepper, is not only a distinction of study-field but also of study-method. And this distinction is very important for the theory of world hypotheses, and should be called a kind of methodological distinction between science and metaphysics.

3. The Rejection of Skepticism and Dogmatism

The rejection of skepticism and dogmatism is regarded by Pepper as a necessary step both in respect to the theoretical aspect and the actual aspect for asserting the theory of world hypotheses. For as already menioned before, a world hypothesis is corroborated by evidence in terms of structural corroboration, while skepticism is regarded as a theory rejecting any kind of truth,[28] and dogmatism goes beyond cognitive grounds and thus in a sense denies evidence.[29] So skepticism and dogmatism in theory are incompatible with the theory of world hypotheses.

We might think that our knowledge has got its greatest development in modern centuries. So it is impossible for people continually to believe the utter skeptic and dogmatist. But, strangely enough, they do believe them. So Pepper feels that it is necessary to criticize skepticism and dogmatism, and regards this kinds of criticism as basic for the theory of world hypotheses. I shall discuss his rejection of these two attitudes in the following pages of this section.

(1) Rejection of Skepticism

Skepticism is rejected by Pepper from two aspects — the grounds of practical belief and that of ultimate belief. The argument for the first aspect is as follows:

By definition an utter skeptic is "one who doubts all things."[30] But, according to Pepper, if one really knows what this statement means, nobody can have this kind of attitude towards things. For what is asserted by it is different from saying that one disbelieves all facts or all statements of those facts. The latter is

not a position of doubt but of downright disbelief, while the former is intended to be one of doubt. For what is really implied by the former is that everything in front of us is believable and simultaneously disbelievable. The evidence on both sides is evenly balanced. So we cannot believe either side without hesitation. So "one who doubts all things" is equivalent to one who never believes anything nor disbelieves anything This is a position nobody can consistently maintain. For nobody living in this world can doubt all things. It is incompatible with our practical life.

The argument for the second aspect is the same as that of the first by taking the grounds of ultimate belief as its topic for discussion instead of the grounds of the practicial belief. The argument is presented as follows:

One might think that though the mentioned position cannot be maintained in practical life, it may be true when it is referred to the grounds of ultimate belief. But Pepper points out that even if it is referred to the grounds of ultimate belief, it still cannot be maintained. For, according to Pepper, what are the grounds of ultimate belief but the evidence of things on which our belief is based? If this is the case, then any one who wants to maintain the mentioned position must suppose that the evidence for any statement of things on which our belief is based is evenly balanced with that on which our disbelief is based, and "so also must be the evidence for the evidence for the statement; and so on *ad infinitum*."31 If there is any evidence of any statement which is not evenly balanced, then the position fails.

According to Pepper, there are two ways for asserting the mentioned supposition of infinite-balanced evidence. But in either way the skepticism fails to maintain itself. The first way is that it is asserted domatically without appealing to any evidence. The second way is that it is regarded as a hypothetical problem to be proved. If the first is the case, then skepticism becomes dogmatism; if it is the second, then it becomes a partial skepticism. A partial skepticism is not different from the position of the theory of world hypotheses, and so it is acceptable, while dogmatism is incompatible with the theory and thus unacceptable.

(2) Rejection of Dogmatism

According to Pepper, there are two different kinds of dogmatism, one appealing to infallible authority, the other, to certainty. The latter again is classified into two different types, one appealing to the principles of self-evidence as certainty and the other appealing to the description of immediate facts as indubitable.

(a) Rejection of authority

The way of rejecting authority used by Pepper is a way of discrediting its status by pointing out the conflict between different authorities which cannot be solved without appealing to evidence. As Pepper points out, there are many different kinds of authorities supported by different kinds of dogmas. But since dogmas are different they cannot avoid conflicting. And when they are involved in conflict, no solution can be expected without appealing to evidence. For the solution cannot be based on any criterion derived from the dogmas. So authorities are destined to lose their certainty as authority when they are in conflict. Hence, not authority but evidence provides the ultimate grounds for knowledge.

The conflicting accounts of the creation of man and woman in the Bible is used by Pepper to illustrate how the Bible loses its authority.

According to the first chapter of *Genesis,* both man and woman were created by God directly out of the earth in God's image. But according to the second chapter of the same book, God created man first out of the dust of the ground and then later created woman from one of Adam's ribs. This conflict is usually explained away, Pepper notes, by harmonizing the first account to the scond one. But this is a kind of explanation appealing to some other kind of principle outside the Bible. And since the solution of the conflict of the Bible is based on some other principle outside the Bible, the Bible loses its authority.32

(b) Rejection of the principles of self-evidence

Resorting to the principles of self-evidence, as already pointed out, is a kind of dogmatism. According to Pepper, this kind of dogmatism has gradually lost its status in contemporary history. For it has recently been abandoned by some

scientists and philosophers. And many principles once regarded as self-evident cannot really be principles of self-evidence.

The axioms of Euclidean geometry were for centuries the mainstay for claims of certainty with respects to principles. Since mathematicians have unanimously given up those claims, acknowledging that the primitive propositions of a mathematical system are not self-evident truths but only postulates for deductions which may or may not be true to fact, or true in fact, the claims of certainty for principles have in large part been abandoned.33

This is concerned with the mathematical axioms. As to the Laws of Thought, according to Pepper, their destiny is the same as that of the mathematical axioms. The principle of contradiction is regarded as the more important principle in respect to the problem of self-evidence. So it is chosen as an example for discussion. The main argument of rejection of the principle of contradiction as self-evident is as follows:

I reply, "As for conceivability, the contradictory of the principle of contradiction seems to be conceivable at least in the sense that it can be symbolized as 'A is non-A.' And as for this principle's implying a self-contradiction, what is more to be expected? There are empirical grounds for believing it to be false, but that the contradictory of the principle of contradiction should imply that self-contradiction is itself an expression of self-contradiction does not appear remarkable nor any ground in itself for considering it false or its contradictory true. The argument seems to beg the question by assuming the truth of the principle of contradiction. Moreover, the claim of self-evidence is automatically lost the moment it must be argued for. If self-evidence must find evidence for itself elsewhere, it is no longer self-evidence. When the crtainty of the truth of a principle can only be established on the grounds of the crtainty of the falsity of another principle (its contradictory), it has relegated its claim of self-evidence to its contradictory. . . ."34

This is a very complicated argument. It is not easy to follow. But it seems that Pepper does not think that the negation of the principle of contradiction is impossible is a truth of sefl-evidence. So he says "that the contradictory of the principle of contradiction should imply that self-contradiction is itself an expression of self-contradiction does not appear remarkable nor any ground in itself for considering it false or its contradictory true." He also maintains that since to claim the principle of contradiction is to argue for it, it is thus not self-evident.

Whether or not Pepper's argument is acceptable, it seems to me, depends mainly on how to understand the truth of "self-evidence." The meaning Pepper gives it in arguing against the principle of contradiction as a truth of self-evidence here, I think, is not quite the same as the traditional meaning of the truth of self-evidence. For the truth of self-evidence is traditionally understood as a concept which is directly grasped by our reason, and it does not need appealing to any other evidence.

This grasp is the function of our reason. We can recognize it by reflection. For from reflection we are aware of two kinds of activities belonging to our reason; that is, affirmation and negation. And the principle of contradiction is nothing but an indication of the activity of either function of our reason. So it can be the form of affirming A, then affirming A, or the form of negating A, then negating A. But it cannot be the form of a combination of affirming A and negating it simultaneously, for this is contradictory. And this contradiction is evident in regard to the function of reason, not in regard to anything else. So it is called self-evidence.

In terms of the function of reason, we not only can regard the principle of contradiction as self-evident, but also the principle of the excluded middle and the principle of identity. For since the functions of reason are affirmation and negation and not anything else, and these two functions are mutually excluded, then the nature of reason in this regard is nothing but dual activities; these dual activities can also be called the principle of duality. And it can be symbolized as a formula. When it is formulated, it is the principle of the excluded middle. Its

form is $A + - A = 1$. Its certainty is not based on anything else but on the reason itself, and directly grasped by reflection.

So to the principle of identity, its certainty is also only based on the functions of reason, and does not need to refer to anything else. That is if we affirm A, then A is affirmed; the latter A is identical to the former one.35

With reference to the above explanation, I think the truth of the three laws of thought should be regarded as the truth of self-evidenc. And what we mean by truth of slf-evidence here is it is grasped by reason. It does not need being referred to anything else.

Based on this understanding, therefore, I do not think that Pepper's rejection of the principles of self-evidence in regard to the Laws of Thought can be accepted without qualification.36 By now a question is raised. That is, if the Laws of Thought have to be understood as the truth of self-evidence as explained above, would it damage Pepper's claim that the theory of world hypotheses is a study of evidence?

To this question my answer is negative. The reason is that what we regard as the truth of the Laws of Thought is just a description of the functions of reason grasped by our reflection. This cannot be applied to any other truth; no other truth can have the same claim. So an assertion of this kind of truth as self-evident is no more than an assertion of the existence of the functions of reason. Thus, it would do nothing to harm Pepper's claim that the theory of world hypotheses is a study of evidence.

(c) Rejection of description of immediate facts as indubitability

What is regarded as indubitable facts includes "the claims of certainty for intuitions of content, sense immediacy, sense data, the offerings of common sense, the stubborn facts of science, or anything supposedly given."37 To the traditional empiricists all these things are immediate facts so that they are indubitable. But, according to Pepper, the assertion that all immediate facts are indubitable is dog-

matic as well as the assertion that the principles of self-evidence are certain. The reason for rejecting the descriptions of immediate facts as indubitable is given as follows:

First, description of the indubitable facts conflict with one another. Second, descriptions of indubitable facts conflict with hypothetical descriptions of facts supported by corroborative evidence. Third, when doubt is cast upon a description of indubitable fact as a result of either of the preceding types of difficulty, there is no recourse except to considerations of corroborative evidence. . . .[38]

Price's description of a tomato and that of Dewey are used by Pepper to illustrate how the same tomato described by two philosophers appears to be different kinds of indubitable facts, and to reject the claim for any kind of certainty of indubitable facts. For, according to Price's desecription of the tomato, "that something is red and round then and there I cannot doubt."[39] But, according to Dewey, what is certain is "the gross and compulsory things of our doings."[40] The gross compulsory things of our doings go behind all analyses and are incapable of being doubted. For they are not an affair of knowledge but rather "one of existnce."[41] Since what is regarded here as indubitability of a given fact by Price is different from that of Dewey, how can we say that a given fact is indubitable? And how can any one claim that his description of a given fact is certain? If nobody can have such a kind of claim, then the so-called indubitable fact is just a dogma; it has to be rejected.

The principles of self-evidence and facts immediately perceived appear to have been regarded as certainty ever since ancient times. In Greece some philosophers upholding reason insisted that what is directly grasped by reason is certain; some others impressed by sense perceptions emphasized that what is directly perceived by them is certain. In the Middle Ages most philosophers were theologians. What they upheld was theology. But in regard to the problem of knowledge in general they did not doubt the assertions of the Greeks despite in-

sisting that revelation is superior to reason. In modern centuries what is directly grasped by reason was insisted on by rationalists as certain and what is directly perceived by sense perception was insisted on by empiricists as certain. So Pepper said "The continental rationalists of seventeenth and eighteenth centuries tended to lean most heavily on the self-evidence of principles; and the English empiricists tended to lean on the indubitability of the facts given."42 This is one way of the development of the traditional philosophy.

On the other hand, as also pointed out by Pepper, "there has been a regular transition from authority to certainty and thence to hypothesis or probability as the dominant grounds for beliefs. In the Middle Ages authority was dominant; in the Renaissance, and even into the present day, certainty has been dominant; only recently and not yet by many is hypothesis or probability regarded as properly dominant."43 To consider this problem from the contemporary point of view, what is indicated by the last development is more important. For it is regarded as an indication of the great achievement of science. Contemporary philosophy is greatly influenced by science. Many contemporary philosophers appeal to the method of science for our most reliable knowledge. For example, Wittgenstein's insistence that the totality of propositions has to be identified with the totality of natural sciences is nothing but an instance of appealing to a science for assertion of knowledge;44 the classification of propositions into formal and factual insisted on by logical positivists is another instance; Dewey's regardng the theory of inquiry or he empirical method as the only way for reconstructing philosophy is one more instance.

Charles S. Peirce in his articles "The Fixation of Belief,"45 and "The Scientific Attitude and Fallibilism"46 already exemplified this tendency. There he insisted that we cannot fix our belief by means of tenacity, nor by authority, and a priori concepts. The only way which can help us to fix our belief is the method of science. That is, we cannot appeal to anything which is regarded as truth and grasp it tenaciously; nor can we appeal to any doctrine or creed which is attached to

certain authority and accept it as truth; nor can we credit our own natural preferences or a priori concepts and trust them as valuable. For all these have no permanent foundations, they are changing, and are different from one another. So we cannot fix our beliefs on them.

According to Peirce, what we obtain by means of the scientific method is just an opinion. It is not an absolute truth. It is an opinion of the settlement of our doubt. This opinion can be used as a means to extend our inquiry, and what we acquire from a further inquiry is possibly contrasted to the former one, and in turn this further opinion can also be used as a means for another inquiry. So Peirce indicated that in science we have no absolute universality; scientific knowledge is a kind of probable knowledge which is fallible. So what we fix our belief on is on the facts discovered by science in its process.

Peirce's position is quite similar to that of Pepper. However, Pepper's theory of world hypotheses is not limited to Peirce's or any other's idea in this concern. For, according to Pepper, in respect of the problem of understanding the world we cannot appeal to special science. For the study of special science is restricted to a certain field, but a world hypothesis which is a hypothetical understanding of the world, is not restricted to any field, and not based on any special science. So he wants to have a metaphysics as the theory of world hypotheses instead of regarding philosophy as a handmaid of science.

4. Two Different Types of Corroboration — Multiplicative and Structural

The rejection of skepticism and dogmatism in regard to the theory of world hypotheses is just a kind of negative work, like pulling out the grass from the wheat without cultivating the wheat. But this kind of work is important and necessary, for people always mix the grass up with the wheat. But from this section on what will be discussed in respect of the theory is not rejection but construction, not pulling out the grass but cultivating the wheat.

Before going into detail on the topic of this section let us indicate briefly why this topic is regarded as a positive contribution to the theory of world hy-

potheses and as the basic problem of the theory. The reason is that since dogmatism was rejected whatever is accepted as true is based on evidence. This is the thesis of the theory of world hypothese. But if we ask what is evidence? The answer would be that it is nothing but whatever is used to prove the truth by means of a certain way. According to the theory, this way is corroboration. So corroboration is positively concerned with the theory of world hypotheses and is a fundamental or a basic problem of the theory.

This is a most general understanding of the status of corroboration in the theory of world hypothesis. But we can also understand this problem in the following way. As will be pointed out later, corroboration is distinguished into two types — multiplicative and structural; and in terms of this distinction the difference between science and metaphysics is methodologically asserted. For the problem of metaphysics is a kind of problem which can only be worked out by structural corroboration; it is not a kind of problem with which multiplicative corroboration can deal. What multiplicative corroboration deals with is the problem of science. So the distinction within corroboration is concerned with the distinction between the problem of metaphysics and that of science.

The above is a brief indication of the importance of corroboration in the theory of world hypothesis. Now let us discuss it in detail.

The discussion will be presented systematically according to the following subheads: (a) The theory is a study of evidence, (b) A discussion of the meaning of evidence, (c) A description of the meaning of corroboration, (d) A brief comparison of the concept of corroboration with Dewey's theory of injury, and (e) Logical positivists' theory of truth and their challenge to metaphysics and Pepper's answer to this challenge. The contents of these subheads are one connected with another, and through a discussion of each of them we hope to present the whole meaning of corroboration.

(a) The theory is a study of evidence

Skepticism and dogmatism with their long history in Western thought have

been intimately connected with the problem of philosophy. But this connection is threatened when knowledge has got its further development in recent centuries. Pepper's rejection is an indication of this development.

Now a question is raised. What will follow after the rejection? The answer seems obvious. That is, since the skepticism was rejected there are things for study, and since dogmatism was rejected what is accepted as true is based on evidence. The last statement is the thesis of the theory of world hypotheses. So Pepper says that the theory of world hypothesis is a "philosophical study of evidence, fact, knowledge, and philosophy."[47]

(b) A discussion of the meaning of evidence

If the theory of world hypothese is asserted as a study of evidence, then the meaning of evidence has to be made clear. So Pepper discusses it.

Evidence is classified into two different types — uncritical evidence and critical evidence. The former is the common-sense fact which is to be criticized, and it is called a dubitandum (an item of evidence that ought to be doubted).[48] The latter is the fact achieved by criticism, that is, it is accepted not on the basis of common-sense understanding but as a result of corroboration. There are two types of corroboration — multiplicative and structural. In relation to these two types of corroboration we have two kinds of critical evidence — data and danda. Again, in relation to two kinds of proposition, data are classified into logical data and empirical data; the former are formulated in formal propositions, the latter, in factual propositions.[49]

The reason for regarding common sense as uncritical evidence is because it indicates "the sort of things we think of when we ordinarily read the daily papers" or "the sort of things we see and hear and smell and feel"[50] in our ordinary life. It is not definitely cognizable.

Any attempt to exhibit, or describe, or specify any of this material definitely in detail generally carries us out of the material. What was uncriticized fact immediately turns into criticized fact, and generally a transformation of the

material takes place as a result of the attempt.51

So it is regarded as cognitively unreliable and irresponsible.

Since common sense has this kind of shortcoming, one might think that it cannot be regarded as evidence. But though it has the mentioned shortcoming, when it is compared with dogmatism and critical evidence it indicates to us some special characteristics, and these characteristics can be found neither in dogmatism nor in critical evidence.

As already pointed out, dogmatism is against evidence. What it asserts is dogmatic without appealing to evidence. So it is incompatible with the theory of world hypotheses. But common sense is different from dogmatism. It is regarded as truth by common understanding; it is used by us as evidence for common agreement. Since it is related to common understanding or common agreement, it is uncritical and uncertain. But since it is something which is relied on by common understanding or common agreement in comparison with dogmatism, it is a kind of evidence.

As to critical evidence, since it is a product of corroboration, it is critically established, and is referred to science and philosophy. But compared with common sense, it is unstable. For it may be regarded as critical evidence by A but not by B. So what is regarded as critical evidence of the tomato by Dewey is different from what is regarded as critical evidence of the same tomato by Price. But to common sense it is never accepted by one, while it is rejected by another. So the common sense tomato is not only accepted by Dewey but also by Price. This is what Pepper means when he says that critical evidence has "cognitive responsibility without full security," while common sense is "cognitive security without responsibility."52 Since common sense in comparison with dogmatism and critical evidence has its characteristics and these characteristics cannot be found in either of them, it has its special status in the field of knowledge.

(c) A description of the meaning of corroboration

As mentioned before, corroboration is a way of obtaining critical evidence.

This is one way to indicate the meaning of corroboration. Besides this we can also say that corroboration is a method in terms of which knowledge is proved. For the meaning of evidence involves, on the one hand, how it is obtained and, on the other, what is proved by it. So what we discussed above in connection with the problem of evidence is related to the problem of corroboration, and what will be discussed later will also be related to it. But before discussing the other related problems, let us see how Pepper describes the meaning of corroboration.

As already mentioned before, there are two types of corroboration — multiplicative and structural. The meaning of each type of corroboration and the difference between the two types are described by Pepper as follows:

> There are two types of corroboration and accordingly two types of critical evidence. There is coroboration of man with man, and corroboration of fact with fact. Let us call the first "multiplicative corroboration" and the second "structural corroboration."
>
> . . . .
>
> Suppose I want to know whether a certain chair is strong enough to take a man's weight. I may sit in it myself. Perhaps I sit in it several times, taking this posture and that and dropping down in it with some force. And then, to be quite sure, I ask several of my friends to try sitting in it. If we all agree that the chair supports us firmly, we may feel justified in believing that the chair is a strong chair.
>
> Or I may use another method. I may examine the relevant facts about the chair. I may consider the kind of wood it is made of, the thickness of the pieces, the manner in which they are joined together, the nails and the glue employed, the fact that it was made by a firm that for many years has turned out serviceable furniture, the fact that the chair is an item of household furniture at an auction and shows evidence of wear as if many people had successfully sat in it, and so on. Putting all this evidence together, I

should again feel justified in believing that the chair is a strong chair.53

Whit reference to the above description of corroboration, the first thing I want to point out here is that despite Pepper's assertion that "they can be found in common sense,"54 the assertion of two types of corroboration with a distinction between them is a contribution of Pepper to the method of philosophy. The second thing is that the difference between these two types of corroboration can be understood from two aspects. The first aspect is that the difference is just concerning the ways of corroboration. That is, in order to obtain a result the corroboration can be conducted in either way — multiplicatively or structurally. This is what Pepper mainly indicated in the above quotation. So whether or not a chair is strong can be corroborated by either way. The second aspect is that the meaning of each type is related to a different kind of hypothesis for understanding. That is the multiplicative corroboration is mainly a kind of corroboration working for conventionalistic hypotheses, while the structural corroboration is a kind of corroboration for structural hypotheses. But this meaning is not clearly indicated in the above quotation; it has to be related to the discussion of hypotheses for understanding. In the discussion of hypotheses this distinction is presupposed. And this is a very important distinction. For it is concerned with the difference of hypotheses and the distinction between science and metaphysics. This will be clearer when it is compared with such other methods of knowledge as Dewey's theory of inquiry and the logical positivists' theory of truth.

(d) A brief comparison of the concept of cororboration with Dewey's theory of inquiry

Pepper's concept of corroboration is characteristically different from Dewey's theory of inquiry despite the similarities between them. It seems that the great contribution of Dewey's theory of inquiry to the problem of knowledge is that (1) it points out how an inquiry begins, (2) how it is instituted, (3) how it is classified into different working steps, (4) how we can obtain a result from it, and (5) what we can obtain from it. So he defined an inquiry as "the directed or controlled transformation of an indeterminate situation into a determinately unified one."55

And it is classified into five steps: (1) the indeterminate situation, (2) institution of a problem, (3) the determination of a problem-solution, (4) reasoning, and (5) verification or warranted assertion.

At first sight, it seems that what has been asserted by Pepper in his concept of corroboration is all implied by Dewey's theory of inquiry. For what is indicated in the corroboration can all be related to the inquiry. And Pepper's insistence that the result of a corroboration is a probable statement is similar to Dewey's idea that what is verified by an inquiry is just a warranted assertion and that there is no final or absolute truth.

But this is just a first-sighted understanding. When we get into them a little more, we shall find that there is a characteristic difference between them. This difference can be simply indicated as that Pepper distinguishes structural corroboration from multiplicative corroboration and relates them to the different hypotheses, while Dewey did not have this kind of distinction in his inquiry.

But perhaps one might think that though Dewey did not make out clearly this kind of distinction, yet it is implied by his inquiry. For, according to the meaning of step (3) of the inquiry, we are allowed to use any kind of hypothesis which is suitable to the inquiry, and according to step (5), we are allowed to adopt any way of verification which is helpful for working out the inquiry. So the mentioned distinction of two types of corroboration and their relation to two kinds of hypotheses are implied by the theory of inquiry, and what is asserted by Pepper in his corroboration cannot exceed the implicative meaning of the inquiry. So there is no difference between the concept of corroboration and that of inquiry. In some sense, this might be true. However, it must be pointed out that two important points are neglected by this kind of explanation. The first is that it overlooks the importance of the difference between implicative meaning and factual meaning. So, though we can say that Pepper's concept of corroboration is implied by Dewey's theory of inquiry, yet we cannot say that Dewey has made out a distinction between multiplicative corroboration and structural corroboration and related them to different hypotheses. And ac-

tually working out this distinction is important. The second point is that, as already pointed out, for Dewey, the method of science is the same as that of metaphysics. So from the methodological point of view, there is no difference between the problems of science and metaphysics. They share the special-general distinction between them. The problem of science treated by the theory of inquiry is the same as that of metaphysics. Based on this understanding, then, though step (3) of the inquiry allows us to use any kind of hypothesis, there is no need for Dewey to assert the two different kinds of hypotheses. And though step (5) permits us to adopt any ways of verification, again there is no need for him to assert the two different types of corroboration. But for Pepper, there is a methodological distinction between science and metaphysics. And this distinction is mainly based on the distinction between the two kinds of hypotheses. And as already pointed out, this distinction is the basis for his theory of world hypotheses. For the theory of world hypothesis is a structural hypothesis, and this hypothesis is only corroborated by structural corroboration. So in order to distinguish the problem of metaphysics from that of science, based on the methodological point of view, he has to assert two different kinds of hypotheses; and in order to assert the two different kinds of hypotheses, he has to distinguish two different types of corroboration. So, to Pepper, the distinction between multiplicative corroboration and structural corroboration is necessary for the distinction between conventionalistic hypotheses and structural hypotheses, and the assertion of structural hypotheses is necessary for the theory of world hypotheses. For they are the only hypotheses by which a world hypothesis is established. We shall come back to this problem again in the next section. Here let us be satisfied with pointing out that corroboration of the two kinds is a basic concept of Pepper's world theory which is not only related to the problem of methodology but also to the problem of metaphysics. So the differences between Pepper's concept of corroboration and Dewey's theory of inquiry are both concerned with differences in methodology and in metaphysics.

(e) Logical positivists' theory of truth and their challenge to metaphysics

and Pepper's answer to this challenge[56]

Knowledge is classified by logical positivists into two different kinds — formal and empirical. The former is formulated in formal propositions, the latter in factual propositions. The knowledge of the formal proposition is necessary because what it asserts in the consequent has already been implied in the antecedent. So its assertion just repeats what has already been asserted. So it is a kind of tautologous proposition; its value is necessary, but it does not give us any new information. The truths of logic and mathematics are of this kind of knowledge. The knowledge of a factual proposition is empirical because what it asserts in the consequent has not been implied in the antecedent; its assertion cannot be analyzed from the antecedent; it has to be verified by further experience. So its value is probable, for it can be wrong; but it gives us new information. The truth of empirical sciences such as chemistry, physics, and biology are of this kind of knowledge.

This kind of classification of knowledge is not rejected by Pepper. On the contrary, he regarded it as a way of clarification of the problem of knowledge. As a matter of fact, this kind of classification did not begin from logical positivists. It can be traced back at least in some sense to Leibniz's distinction between necessary truth and contingent truth,[57] and to Hume's distinction between knowledge of relations of ideas and that of matters of fact. And it is true that logical positivists openly acknowledge their debt to Hume.[58] Kant's classification of propositions into analytic, a priori, a posteriori, synthetic, and a priori synthetic, though it is not fully accepted by the logical positivists inasmuch as they deny the a priori synthetic proposition, yet in some sense is quite similar to the positivists' classification of propositions.

So what Pepper crticizes against the logical positivists' theory of truth is not their classification of knowledge but their regarding this kind of classification as having exhausted all kinds of truths and dogmatically, on the basis of it, rejecting metaphysical problems as nonsensical.

As already pointed out at the first chapter, Kant has denied that metaphysics is a science. But he limits his rejection to the point that a science of metaphysics is impossible. So what was rejected by him in the *Critique of Pure Reason* he reasserted in the *Critique of Practical Reason.*. Those philosophers who were impressed by Kant's idea of the limitation of knowledge also followed him in regarding the problem of metaphysics as a problem beyond the field of knowledge. So we classified them in contrast to Dewey's and Pepper's concept of metaphysics as the first kind of concept of metaphysics.

The logical positivists' way of rejecting metaphysics is not the same as that of Kant. But if we focus, not upon their different ways of rejecting metaphysics, but rather upon their agreement that metaphysics is impossible as a subject of science, then what was held by Kant is the same as the position of the logical positivists. And to consider this problem from the scientific point of view, what is rejected should be limited to the field of science. If a problem does not belong to the field of science, it cannot be rejected by science. So Kant's later view of metaphysics cannot be rejected by science. Based on this understanding, what the logical positivists can do in regard to the problem of metaphysics will be no more than Kant did. Sometimes logical positivists are aware of this problem and restrict their rejection to the problem of metaphysics with cognitive meaning. However, sometimes they exceed this boundary and want to reject all kinds of metaphysics. Our problem here, however, is not the rejection of what may be called the concept of the first kind of metaphysics but rather how Pepper can assert in contrast to logical positivism a metaphysics in the field of cognition which will not be regarded as nonsensical. That is how he can meet the challenge of logical positivists in regard to the problems of metaphysics; for they deny that there is any cognitive meaning for metaphysical problems. As to the problem of the concept of the first kind of metaphysics, it seems that Pepper takes sides with the logical positivists; he also wants to reject it. But let us keep this problem for the conclusion of this study.

As has been mentioned before, for Dewey and Pepper, the distinction between science and metaphysics is not that the former is cognitive and the latter
noncognitive. For to them both science and metaphysics belong to the field of
cognition. Now the problem is whether or not they can really have a metaphysics in the field of cognition, and at the same time have a distinction between
science and metaphysics. If they can, they overcome the logical positivists' challenge in this regard; otherwise, they do not meet the challenge.

With reference to what we indicated about Dewey's special-general distinction between science and metaphysics, it seems that Dewey did not meet the challenge of the logical positivists, or we may say that the challenge of the logical
positivists was not directed at him. For as we indicated before, for Dewey the
method of science is the same as that of metaphysics. There is no methodological
distinction between science and metaphysics. The difference between science and
metaphysics is just a kind of special-general distinction. That is, what is engaged
in by the scientist is different from that of the metaphysician. The former is concerned with the special scientific problem, while the latter deals with the problem
of the generality of existence. So the logical positivists' theory of truth is not
contradictory to him. And so their challenge to metaphysics is not a challenge
to his concept of metaphysics, and thus does not make sense to him. But although Dewey may not think that the logical positivists' challenge makes sense to
him, yet to the logical positivists, it seems that Dewey's distinction between science
and metaphysics is unacceptable. For according to their theory of truth, this is
not a real distinction. For what is regarded by Dewey as metaphysical problem
can be regarded by them as no different from a problem of science.[59] For to
their theory of truth, the problem which is regarded by Dewey as metaphysical
also has to be classified either as a problem of formal propositions or as a problem
of factual propositions. If it is the former, then it belongs to the formal truth; if it is
the latter, empirical truth. So what is regarded by Dewey as a problem of metaphysics
is actually not different from a problem of science. There is only nominal differ-

ence, no real difference; so this difference is just a linguistic problem, not a philosophical problem in the traditional sense. As to Dewey's claim that the descriptive study of the generic traits of existence is a problem of metaphysics because this does not belong to any specific science, the logical positivists, perhaps, would agree. But they still can say that though this kind of problem is not treated by any special science, yet, as a matter of fact, its result is verified or disverified by scientific method and also may be regarded as either a formal problem or a factual problem. So it is a problem of science, not metaphysics. If this is the case, then the distinction between science and metaphysics asserted by Dewey can be regarded by them as artificial.

From the viewpoint of the theory of inquiry, in regards to the distinction between science and metaphysics, I cannot see how Dewey can protect himself from the mentioned logical positivists' attack, if there is such a kind of attack. For the things being inquired about are the same. Whatever has been verified in the final step of the inquiry is regarded as warranted assertion with no difference between a scientific problem and a metaphysical problem. If this is the case, Dewey and the logical positivists in regard to the problem of the distinction between science and metaphysics do not really have conflict. The difference is just a kind of attitude towards the problem. There is no theoretical conflict. And Dewey would not take the mentioned logical positivists' idea as an attack on his concept of the distinction between science and metaphysics. That is what it is. He can still regard the problem of metaphysics as a problem of descriptive study of the generic traits of existence.

With reference to the above understanding, we can see that anyone who really wants to assert a metaphysical theory within the cognitive field and at the same time wants to make a distinction between science and metaphysics, must work out a method in terms of which to give a theoretical support to the distinction; otherwise, what he asserts is not really different from what the logical positivists maintain and cannot meet the challenge of the logical positivists.

But it seems that if what the logical positivists assert is equivalent to science

or equivalent to the cogniiive meaning, there is no way to work out a method which can support the distinction between science and metaphysics. It is very possible that the distinction is artificial and there is no real foundation for it. So now the key for overcoming this difficulty is to check whether or not the logical positivists' idea of truth is really equivalent to science or to the cognitive meaning. So to assert a metaphysics with cognitive meaning Pepper has to deal with the following two problems: first, whether or not the logical positivists' idea of truth is really equivalent to the whole cognitive truth; second, if not, whether or not we can distinguish the sciences from metaphysics in the field of cognition. To the first question Pepper's answer is negative, while to the second, affirmative.

Pepper's denial of the logical positivists' idea of truth as equivalent to the whole cognitive meaning is mainly based on his classification of evidence, for in terms of this classification he indicates some kind of cognitive meaning which cannot be covered by the logical positivists' theory of truth. As already pointed out before, evidence is classified into two different kinds — uncritical and critical. The uncritical evidence is the common-sense fact, while the critical evidence is a result of corroboration. And corroboration is distinguished into two types — multiplicative and structural. The product of multiplicative corroboration is called data, and that of structural corroboration, danda. Again, data are distinguished into two types — empirical and logical.

According to Pepper, what the logical positivists call truth of formal propositions and that of factual propositions do not cover the whole field of truth. They just indicate the truth produced by multiplicative corroboration. The formal truth is a result of logical data corroborated by multiplicative corroboration, while the empirical truth is a result of empirical data also corroborated by multiplicative corroboration. So, according to Pepper, the logical positivists' idea of truth is just an indication of those truths corroborated by multiplicative corroboration. But besides this kind of truth, there are truths of common sense and of science and philosophy, and the latter can be corroborated by structural corroboration, and its evidences are not data but danda.

The discussion of the difference between data and danda is intimately connected with the assertion of the distinction between multiplicative corroboration and structural corroboration and with the theory of conventionalistic hypotheses and structural hypotheses. The theory of hypotheses will be discussed in the succeeding section. Here with respect to the above distinctions, besides what was referred to above, we will summarize it as follows.

What the logical positivists regard as the only evidence of knowledge — namely, logical evidence and empirical evidence — are only two types of refined or critical evidence in relation to multiplicative corroboration. They are clear and certain and can be observed by different people and can be repeated at different times. So they are data.

Besides the data, there are evidential items in relation to structural corroboration. They are not necessarily observable. They cannot be repeated. They converge to support a fact or a hypothesis which is corroborated by them. So they are called danda.

Since danda are products of structural corroboration, data cannot be regarded as the only kind of evidence of knowledge. So logical positivists' idea of truth cannot be regarded as covering the whole field of truth.

That the application of data has its limitations and that danda are used as evidence of knowledge, according to Pepper, are undeniable. This is not only a matter of fact, but also in theory it is undeniable. For any logical positivist who wants to deny this fact cannot construct his argument on the basis of data which are regarded by the logical positivists as the only acceptable foundation of knowledge. For what is constructed as an argument on the basis of data cannot deny that there are danda, for danda cannot be objects of discussion in terms of the argument based on data. So if any one wants to construct any argument against danda he must construct it on the basis of some hypothetical grounds, and this presupposes the existence of danda. This presupposition by denial of danda, according to Pepper, must be faced by any argument against the danda. So danda

as evidence of knowledge are in theory undeniable. If danda have to be accepted as evidence of knowledge, the logical positivists' idea of knowledge is one-sided, and their rejecting metaphysical problems as nonsensical also loses its foundation.

As to the second problem, how to distinguish the sciences from metaphysics, we have already indicated Pepper's distinction in section 2. And in the succeeding section this problem will come up again.

5. The Concept of Hypotheses

After having an understanding of Pepper's concept of corroboration, now let us discuss the problem of hypotheses.

The hypothesis is also a very important conctpt in the theory of world hypotheses. We even can say that it is in a pivotal position of the theory. For, as has been mentioned before, with the rejection of skepticism we see that there are objects for study, and after rejecting dogmatism we realize that all knowledge is based on evidence. Evidence is classified into uncritical and critical. Despite all its characteristics uncritical evidence is to be criticized, and to become critical evidence. Critical evidence is a product of corroboration; and corroboration is working for the hypothesis. So all those preceding concepts are related to the hypothesis, and hypotheses can be regarded as pivotal in the theory of world hypotheses.

As Pepper points out, hypotheses have been used in common sense. A hypothesis is identified with "a guess" or "a hunch."60 But this is just an unsystematical use. In common sense, the function or status of hypotheses is not clear. It was not until modern centuries after human knowledge obtained its further development that we came to recognize the importance of hypotheses.

As already pointed out, a hypothesis is presupposed by a corroboration. For a corroboration is a work in terms of which to verify what is assumed or hypothesized. So what is corroborated is a hypothesis, and what is regarded as truth is the affirmative outcome of the corroboration of a hypothesis. So corroboration and hypotheses are theoretically related. But now a question might be raised.

That is, can we have a corroboration without a hypothesis? This seems a trivial question, but it has to be made clear.

It seems that in our daily life we have some kind of corroboration without consciously or intentionally formulating a hypothesis. For example, sometimes we try to sit in a chair to see whether or not it is strong enough for sitting, or try a pen to see whether or not it is good enough for writing. But when we did either one of these acts we did not consciously formulate a hypothesis such as "if p then q." That is, if the chair is strong enough, then it can bear my weight, or if the pen is good enough, then when we use it for writing it would be so and so. But to consider this problem from the standpoint of scientific study, every corroboration is conducted for a hypothesis. A corroboration without guidance by a hypothesis is regarded as a blindman's buff; no good result can be expected.

As also mentioned before, Pepper distinguishes structural corroboration from multiplicative corroboration. Now another question might be raised. That is, in relation to the mentioned different types of corroboration, can we have different kinds of hypotheses for each type of corroboration, or can a hypothesis be corroborated by different types of corroboration? With reference to Pepper's description of corroboration, answer seems affirmative. As we pointed out in the above section, one aspect of the distinction between the two types of corroboration is based on a different way of conducting the corroboration. So the hypothesis concerning the strength of the chair can be corroborated either by multiplicative corroboration or structural corroboration. But it seems that this has to be limited to conventionalistic hypotheses. For with reference to Pepper's distinction between data and danda, the products of multiplicative corroboration and the products of structural corroboration, and the different application of data and danda — the former are mainly affairs of conventionalistic hypotheses, and the latter of structural hypotheses — we shall see that a structural hypothesis cannot simply be corroborated by multiplicative corroboration. Multiplicative corroboration or the data can only be absorbed into the work of structural corroboration when a struc-

tural corroboration is conducted.

It seems that another clarification in connection with the problem of hypotheses and corroboration has to be made. That is, when distinguishing structural corroboration from multiplicative corroboration Pepper indicates that the latter method "seems to be predominantly one of observation," while the former is "one of hypothesis."61 If we do not refer this kind of distinction to the discussion of hypotheses for understanding, it is very easy to assume mistakenly that structural corroboration is guided by a hypothesis, while multiplicative corroboration is a corroboration without hypotheses. But actually Pepper means that multiplicative corroboration is a kind of corroboration of "man with man," and in this regard is "predominantly one of observation"; structural corroboration, on the other hand, is a kind of corroboration of "fact with fact," and in order to conduct a structural corroboration the different facts have to be connected by or converged upon another hypothesis which in contrast to the hypothesis of the corroboration may be called a sub-hypothesis of the structural corroboration.

What has been discussed so far is mainly concerned with the general clarification of the meaning of hypotheses in relation to the problem of corroboration. But this is not the major problem about which Pepper is concerned in his discussion of the problem of hypotheses. What he is mainly concerned about in his discussion is the difference between a conventionalistic hypothesis and a structural hypothesis, and the fact that a world hypothesis is a structural hypothesis.

As indicated by the term itself, a conventionalistic hypothesis is "a human convention for the purpose of keeping data in order."62 It was upheld by the logical positivists and orthodox contextualists.63 According to them, "it has no cognitive value in itself." "Cognitive value belongs where knowledge is. And what we know are data. A hypothesis is not a datum; it is simply a symbolic scheme for the arrangement of data, so that men can easily find and use the data they know."64 "The same data can often be organized in different systems, depending upon the postulates or primitive concepts employed. As between two

such systems, the one most economical of a scientist's thought is the best."65 So a conventionalistic hypothesis is "artificial and clearly distinguishable from the evidence it systematizes. The greater the refinement of data and multiplicative corroboration, the more unmistakable the distinction between evidence and hypothesis. The only gauges for the value of a conventionalistic hypothesis are economy of intellectual effort and aesthetic elegance — neither of them gauges of cognitive value."66

As to a structural world hypothesis, it is not a human convention. It is not a conceptual invention in terms of which to organize or to order the evidence. It is a reflection of the structure of nature and a means of describing nature; or, it is a convergence of the evidential items or a method of organizing or connecting the evidential items. So it "is not artificial; it is not clearly distinguishable from much of the evidence it organizes."67 It has cognitive value. It acquires "cognitive value in its own right, a cognitive value that is practically indistinguishable from that of the evidence it organizes."68

With reference to the above distinction between the two mentioned hypotheses, the first thing that appears to us is that what was regarded by the logical positivists as most important in regards to the problem of conventionalistic hypotheses is not so important in connection with the problem of structural hypotheses. For since a conventionalistic hypothesis is regarded as a human convention, "creative imagination" is accepted as the only way for obtaining a hypothesis,69 while from the standpoint of a structural hypothesis, since it is a description of the structure of nature, it is not a creation of imagination, it is just a disclosure of the evidences themselves, originating from common sense. This is related to Pepper's theory of root metaphors which regards a root metaphor as the origin of a structural world hypothesis. This problem will be discussed in the next section.

The second thing is that since structural world hypotheses originated from root metaphors, if we have different root metaphors, then we will have different structural world hypotheses. This is asserted by Pepper as a basis for his concept

of relatively adequate world hypotheses. So, with reference to the history of philosophy, since there are different ways of describing the structure of nature based on different root metaphors, there are different kinds of structural world hypotheses.

The third thing is that by nature a structural hypothesis develops into a world hypothesis. For the scope of a structural hypothesis cannot be limited to any special field. As already pointed out, structural corroboration is conducted in terms of sub-hypotheses which connect or organize whatsoever corroborative evidence may be found to support the guiding hypothesis which is to be corroborated, and a structural hypothesis by nature is related to whatever evidence which can be connected; thus, the reliability of a structural hypothesis is inevitably in proportion to its scope and to its precision of corroboration. And the scope and precision are mutually related. For when the evidence of a structural hypothesis is more discriminated the hypothesis is more adequate, and when the scope of the hypothesis increases, the hypothesis is more reliable. So in order to achieve a position of greater reliability the scope and the precision of a structural hypothesis will be increased as much as possible. It will not stop until it reaches an adequate precision and unlimited scope. And a hypothesis of adequate precision and unlimited scope is a world hypothesis .

Here a question might be raised. That is, can a conventionalistic hypothesis also be formulated as a world hypothesis? As has been pointed out already, a working conventionalistic hypothesis can be corroborated by either multiplicative corroboration or structural corroboration, and a structural hypothesis can be naturally developed into a world hypothesis. Now, can a conventionalistic hypothesis also be formulated as a world hypothesis? To this question Pepper's answer is that there was such an attempt.[70] But this attempt failed. A world hypothesis has never been successfully generated by the postulational method.[71] And since the application of data is limited to a certain field, the conventionalistic hypothesis corroborated by multiplicative corroboration cannot be formulated as a world hypothesis. Now, another interesting question might also be raised. That is, can

we have a conventionalistic world hypothesis corroborated by structural corroboration? Since a conventionalistic hypothesis can be corroborated by a multiplicative coroboration, now can it be a world hypothesis when it is corroborated by a structural corroboration? For as we pointed out before, a conventionalistic hypothesis can be either corroborated by a multiplicative corroboration or by a structural corroboration. It seems that Pepper did not have any full direct discussion in regard to this problem. But we can think about it. It seems to me, if we can formulate a world conventionalistic hypothesis which is corroborated by structural corroboration, there is no way, or it is very difficult for us, to distinguish it from a structural world hypothesis. Perhaps, this is the reason why Pepper did not go into this problem.

The three above mentioned points are intimately connected with Pepper's concept of metaphysics and that of science. In regard to the problem of metaphysics, they are related to our previous discussion and generally can be regarded as a further explanation of what has already been pointed out in the preceding section. As to the concept of science, it will be beyond the scope of this study to go into it in detail. What I want to point out here is that the assertion of the conventional or operational theory of science as the only effective theory is unacceptable to Pepper. He does not deny its value as a working theory in modern science, but he cannot agree that only this theory is effective. For to understand this problem from the viewpoint of the theory of world hypotheses, different world theories have their different theories of science. For example, formism has its correspondence theory, organicism has its coherence theory; operational theory is a theory of mechanism and contextualism. Besides this, Pepper also does not think that one can assert operational theory without some difficulty. For, according to Pepper, "the operational view in some form may indeed turn out to be correct. But the glaring difficulty with it is that despite the fact it so easily rides the wave of present emphasis upon 'explanation' and 'prediction' in science and disregard of description, it has no explanation for the success of some operations as against the failures of others."[72] So instead of following the orthodox contex-

tualists in adopting operational theory as a theory of science he worked out an operational-correspondence theory in his new selectivistic world hypothesis.[73]

6. The Concept of Root Metaphors

The root-metaphor theory is offered by Pepper to deal with the problem of the origin of the world theories.[74] This is a basic problem in the theory of world hypotheses because it is concerned with the origin of the world hypotheses, and so far as we know, this is one of the most promising ways adopted by philosophers to answer this problem.

Concerning the problem of formulating a world hypothesis, we have pointed out that a world hypothesis is a structural hypothesis with an unrestricted scope. A structural hypothesis can be a hypothesis with a restricted scope. That is, it can be limited to a special field to deal with a special problem. But in order to achieve its higher precision it demands to increase its scope. For its scope is intimately related to its precision, as mentioned before. When the scope is increased into one without restrictions, it is a world hypothesis.

But this is only concerned with how a world hypothesis is developed from a restricted structural hypothesis. As to the problem of the origin of a restricted structural hypothesis, this account does not tell us anything. With reference to the preceding section we know that a structural hypothesis with limited scope is not made up by man like the conventionalistic hypothesis. For it is a reflection of the structure of nature; it is not a human invention. So how can we have a kind of reflection not based on a pure conceptual invention or a creative imagination, but on something else? This is probably why the root metaphor theory is suggested.

This theory first appeared in Pepper's article, "The Root Metaphor Theory of Metaphysics."[76] It was enlarged in his book, *World Hypotheses*,[77] and asserted again in his *Concept and Quality*.[78] In basic essentials the three different statements of the theory are the same. They are just different in expression or in explanation of the central point. So I shall just quote what is stated in *World Hypotheses* for discussion:

The method in principle seems to be this: A man desiring to understand the world looks about for a clue to its comprehension. He pitches upon some area of common-sense facts and tries if he cannot understand other areas in terms of this one. This original area becomes then his basic analogy or root metaphor. He describes as best he can the characteristics of this area, or, if you will, discriminates its structure. A list of its structural characteristics becomes his basic concepts of explanation and description. We call them a set of categories. In terms of these categories he proceeds to study all other areas of fact whether uncriticized or previously criticized. He undertakes to interpret all facts in terms of these categories. As a result of the impact of these other facts upon his categories, he may qualify and readjust the categories so that a set of categories commonly changes and develops. Since the basic analogy or root metaphor normally (and probably at least in part necessarily) arises out of common sense, a great deal of development and refinement of a set of categories is required if they are to prove adequate for a hypothesis of unlimited scope. Some root metaphors prove more fertile than others, have greater powers of expansion and of adjustment. · These survive in comparison with the others and generate the relatively adequate world theories.79

From what we quoted above we can see that the meaning of a root metaphor can be simply indicated as follows: A root metaphor is a kind of analogy which is based on "some area of common-sense fact" in terms of which "to try to understand other areas." This is the key concept of the theory. The other descriptions are referred to this key statement. For example, if we ask how this can be done, the further explanations are (1) the area chosen as root metaphor will be described as best as possible; that is, the structure of the area will be discriminated as best as possible so that (2) what is described or discriminated of the chosen area can be asserted as the basic concepts of explanation and description, and be regarded as categories, (3) in terms of these categories all other areas of facts are studied and interpreted, (4) in the process of this study and interpretation the asserted categories will be qualified and readjusted to meet the impact of the new areas, (5) those cate-

gories having been developed and refined and proved adequate for a hypothesis of unlimited scope become the categories of the theory of a relatively adequate world hypothesis. According to Pepper's earlier account, there are four relatively adequate world hypotheses — formism, mechanism, contextualism, and organicism, and he worked out a new world theory called selectivism later. The first four hypotheses are presented in *World Hypotheses;* the new one, in *Concept and Quality.* I shall discuss each of them in the next chapter in connection with the problem of application of the theory of world hypotheses. Now let us come back to have some more understanding of the meaning of a root metaphor.

From what we have indicated concerning the root metaphor theory we can assert the following points:

(1) A root metaphor originates in common sense and is the origin of a world hypothesis. So though some of the results we get from a world hypothesis can be higher refinements of that theory, yet since they originated from common sense, in general, we can say that metaphysical problems as well as problems of knowledge start with common sense and can be referred to it.

(2) But though metaphysics or knowledge starts with common sense, it is illegitimate to subject the result of a structural refinement to the assumptions of common sense.80 For common sense is uncritical and is to be criticized, it is secure so metaphysics or knowledge may be referred to it, yet it is uncritical so we cannot accept any of its assumptions as certain.

(3) The categories of a world hypothesis derived from the root metaphor are indications of the characteristics of facts. The characteristics of the facts are mutually connected or constituted to be the structure of the facts. So the connection of the categories is an indication of the connection of the characteristics of the facts; that is, their structure. So one characteristic can be evidence of another or the other characteristics. They are mutually related and have intimate connections among them. So if we just look at the concrete characteristics what we see is a group or a set of characteristics of the facts; we do not see any hypothesis. A hypothesis is an abstract understanding of the relation of the structure. So it is called

the structural hypothesis.

(4) Since a structural hypothesis that is a world hypothesis, is made in terms of an abstract understanding of the structure of the facts, it is impossible to corroborate it fully by a multiplicative corroboration. For it is not only concerned with the evidences called data but also with danda. Since it is impossible to corroborate it fully by multiplicative corroboration, it is illegitimate to reject it by the standard of multiplicative corroboration.81

(5) Since categories of a world hypothesis are autonomously derived from their own root metaphors to interpret the world, it is illegitimate to combine them with the category derived from the other world theories.82 Again, it is illegitimate to assume that the claims of a given world hypothesis are established by the exhibition of the shortcomings of the other world hypotheses. Nor is it admissible to use the categories of a certain world hypothesis to disparage the interpretation of the other world hypotheses.83 A world hypothesis should be established by the development of its own categories. And any shortcoming of a world hypothesis also should be judged in regard to its own precision and scope. But one world hypothesis can be compared with the other to see which one is more adequate.

(6) In theory, the meaning of a root metaphor can be fully developed. And its categories can be fully understood, and the world can be interpreted in terms of them. But as a matter of fact, it cannot be understood within a short period. With reference to the history of philosophy, we see that it takes time to achieve its full development. So any world hypothesis has its own history of development. The later period of its development is usually more complete than that of the primitive stage. But since they are all based on the same root metaphor they belong to the same theory regardless of their developments.84

(7) Since a world hypothesis is autonomously developed from a root metaphor, what has been established is systematically organized; it cannot accept anything from the other world theories as pointed out before; eclecticism is thus incompatible to a world hypothesis.85 From the viewpoint of the world hypothesis theory, we cannot have any way to assert eclecticism. For since we can only have one kind of

world hypothesis, that is, the structural hypothesis, what we can do in regard to the problem of world theory is to establish the world theory in terms of structural hypotheses. So we cannot have an eclecticism as a world theory without confusing the problem.

(8) All categories or concepts of a world theory are an abstract understanding of the structure of the facts with a purpose of interpreting the world. They do not exist independently. So when they are used to interpret the world they must be related to their root metaphor. Any concept which loses contact with its root metaphor is an empty abstraction. It becomes a hypostatization and cannot help losing its function for explaining facts.[86]

(9) In principle, every fact can be a root metaphor. But as a matter of fact, only some of them can be expanded and refined as a structural hypothesis with unrestricted scope.[87] Most of them can only be a limited structural hypothesis and be applied to certain special problems for understanding the facts. This is the real basis for the distinction between metaphysics and special sciences.

(10) Since a structural hypothesis originates from a root metaphor, it is different from the conventionalistic hypothesis as already mentioned before.

With reference to the above understanding, especially to points (1), (3), (4), (7), (9), and (10), it seems that the relations between a world hypothesis and a structural hypothesis, and that between a structural hypothesis and a root metaphor are necessary. For we cannot have any structural hypothesis which does not originate from a root metaphor. Nor can we have any world hypothesis which is not developed from a structural hypothesis. So though Pepper said that the root metaphor theory is in a different level from structural hypotheses[88] and that one can reject the root metaphor theory even if he accepts the hypothetical way of dealing with the problem of metaphysics,[89] actually if one accepts a structural hypothesis as a way of understanding the world, one may well accept the root metaphor theory as its origin. For we have no other way in terms of which we can make a structural hypothesis. And if one accepts a hypothetical way of dealing with the problem of metaphysics, one must, according to Pepper, accept structural hypotheses.

CHAPTER III

THE APPLICATION OF THE THEORY OF WORLD HYPOTHESES

1. An Introductory Remark

As has been pointd out already in the third section of the introductory chapter and referred to in the first section of Chapter Two, the theory of world hypotheses can be understood from two different aspects — internal and external. The former is concerned with its basic concepts and how it is constructed; while the latter deals with its external relation between one world hypothesis and another, that is, with the problem of application of the world hypothesis theory. The former problem has been discussed in the preceding chapter. So this chapter will concentrate on the latter problem.

But before going into it, let us first clarify the meaning of application. It seems that Pepper does not like to say that his study of world theories is an application of his world hypothesis theory. On the contrary, he says that he wishes to study world hypotheses as "a zoologist studies species of animals, a psychologist varieties of perception,"90 and so on. If this is the case, then in what sense can we say that, in contrast to his discussion of the basic concepts of the theory, his study of the different world theories is an external understanding of the world hypothesis theory and call it an application of the latter? In the next section of this chapter we shall discuss this problem.

Again, in theory, all the basic concepts of the theory of world hypotheses can be applied to the different systems of world hypotheses for understanding. But as a matter of fact, it is not necessary to apply all of them. What we need to apply is the root metaphor. So, after clarifying the meaning of application, we shall explain briefly this problem, and this will be section 3. After that we shall discuss the problem of application of the five different world hypotheses. Sinc it will be a long

discussion, two sections are devoted to it. In section four we shall discuss the application of the root metaphor theory to formism, mechanism, contextualism, and organicism; and in section five we shall treat the application of the theory to selectivism.

2. A Clarification of the Meaning of Application

The basic concepts of the world hypothesis theory discussed in the preceding chapter are all used by Pepper to explain the meaning of the relatively adequate world hypotheses — formism, mechanism, contextualism, organicism — and his new world theory, selectivism. So it is safe to say that the study of the relatively adequate world hypotheses~and his new world theory is an application of the theory of world hypotheses. But when we say this, we must be careful not to interpret Pepper's application in terms simply of a common-sense understanding of this problem. For in common-sense understanding what we mean by applying a theory to something implies that we first have a theory and then apply it to describe or to explain some kind of things, and in terms of this application the theory gets its proof. With reference to what we have discovered about Pepper's world hypothesis theory, however, we can easily see that his study of the different world theories is not this kind of application. For to Pepper the theory of world hypotheses is not something antecedently there being applied to studying the world theories. He did not first have a theory and then apply it to his study. On the contrary, the affirmation of the theory is a result of his study of the world hypotheses. I think this is, perhaps, the reason why Pepper does not like to say that his study of world hypotheses is an application of the theory of world hypotheses, and rather prefers to say that he wants "to study world hypotheses as objects existing in the world, to examine them empirically as a zoologist studies species of animals, a psychologist varieties of perception, a mathematician geometrical systems."91 What Pepper states here at first sight seems contrary to the meaning of application. For according to this statement the study of world hypotheses is not a matter of applying any theory to the study, but a kind of objective study of the world theories. This is true. And this is why we say that we cannot interpret Pepper's study as a common kind of application of a theory. But though this statement emphasizes the

meaning of objective study of the world theories, yet it does not deny that in the process of the study when some kind of hypothesis or theory is gradually formulated this hypothesis or theory can be applied to the study. As a matter of fact, the formulated hypothesis or theory is used for the study. What is rejected is only the idea that there is an a priori theory being applied to the study. So to understand the meaning of Pepper's application of the theory we cannot understand it as an application of a conventionalistic symbolic scheme or an antecedently existing rational scheme. We have to understand it as a certain kind of concept which is abstracted from something in the process of study and then applied to that study as a guiding concept to understand it. That is, the concept is out of or derived from the study and then is used in connection with or referred to the study. And this use or reference is no doubt a kind of application. So the meaning of application does not necessarily imply that the applied concept might not be derived from the thing which is being interpreted. And Pepper's application of the theory of world hypotheses is this kind of application.

Though Pepper does not apparently say that his study of world hypotheses is a kind of application, yet sometimes he indicates this kind of meaning. For example, he says that the concept of root metaphor is offered or suggested by him as a hypothesis concrning the origin of world hypotheses; now what he wants to "offer" or "suggest" here is that he wants to apply the root metaphor theory to his study of world hypotheses. And he also says that "a world hypothesis does not hover in a vacuum. Its purpose is its applicability to this world of ours. By definition it is an hypothesis that applies with unlimited scope."92

3. Applying the Root Metaphor

After having an understanding of the meaning of application, we can go on to discuss the problem of application. But there is another problem which also has to be clarified. That is, the application discussed in the next two sections will be limited to the root metaphor alone. Since all the basic concepts of the theory of world hypotheses are derived from the different world theories, in theory, they can all be applied to them to understand them. So the problem of application is concerned

with the basic concepts of the world hypothesis theory. But what I want to do in the next two sections is not to apply all of them to discuss the different world theories, but only to apply the concept of the root metaphor. The reason for this limitation, first, is that it will be far beyond the scope of this study to have a discussion related to all aspects of Pepper's study of world theories, and the application of all the basic concepts of the world hypothesis theory to the world theories would turn out to be such a discussion. Second, in order to have an understanding of the external relation of one world theory to another, which is the purpose of our study, it is not necessary to apply all the basic concepts to the different world theories. It will be sufficient for our purposes to apply only the root metaphor. For the concept of root metaphors is the fundamental concept of the theory of world hypotheses. So a discussion of the application of root metaphors will indicate to us what the nature of a certain world theory is, what the difference between one world theory and another is, and how they are established by the same theory of root metaphors. These topics are all pertinent for the problem of the external relations of the world hypothesis theory. So in the following two sections of this chapter I shall only give a discussion of the application of the root metaphor to the different world hypotheses.

4. An Application of Root Metaphors to Formism, Mechanism,

   Contextualism, and Organicism

When discussing the concept of root metaphors in the preceding chapter, we quoted Pepper's description of this concept, and pointed out that the meaning of the root metaphor can be separated into different steps for understanding: (1) choosing some area of common-sense fact as a root metaphor, (2) describing the chosen area as best as possible in order to see what can be asserted as the basic concepts of explanation and description and be regarded as categories, (3) studying or interpreting the other areas of facts in terms of the asserted categories, (4) qualifying and readjusting the asserted categories in the process of the study to meet the impact of the new areas, and (5) developing and refining those categories to give them unlimited scope so that they become the categories of a relatively adequate world hypothesis.

These different steps are regarded as ways of establishing a world theory. According to Pepper, all the four relatively adequate world theories were established by the root metaphor method. And it can be used to establish new world theories in case we find adequate new root metaphors.

By applying the root metaphor to a world theory here we mean essentially what Pepper refers to as using the root metaphor method to establish a world theory. The difference is that Pepper is primarily concerned to make sure how a world theory is established by this method, and we are concerned here to indicate how to apply the root metaphor to a world theory and to understand it. Since the best way for understanding a theory is to follow the way by which it is established, the best way for applying the root metaphor to a world theory to understand it is to see how this theory is established. So in discussing the problem of applying the root metaphor in this section and the succeeding one, I shall generally follow the root metaphor method to see how a world theory is established, what its nature is, and how one world theory differs from the others

Making reference to the description of the root metaphor method, we can assert the procedure of application of the root metaphor to a world theory as follows:

(1) to discover its root metaphor,

(2) to see what categories are derived from it,

(3) to see how the categories are used to interpret the facts or the world,

(4) to see what the difference between one world theory and the others is, and

(5) to see what the merit and shortcoming of it are. With these in mind, I shall discuss first formism.

(1) An application of the root metaphor method to formism

"Formism" is used by Pepper to indicate "realism," or "Platonic idealism." "It is associated with Plato, Aristotle, the scholastics, neoscholastics, neorealists, modern Cambridge realists."[93] The reason for him to give all of them the name "formism" instead of calling them sparately "realism," "Platonic idealism," and so on, is, on the one hand, "to avoid issues over the names themselves,"[94] and on the

other, to relate them to their root metaphor. For, according to Pepper, all of them are established by means of the same root metaphor — similarity — although they are regarded as different schools of philosophy.

Formism is classified into immanent formism and transcendent formism by Pepper. The root metaphor for the former is similar things, such as "blades of grass, leaves on a tree, a set of spoons,"[95] and so on; for the latter, artificial plans or natural plans, such as the plan of an artisan for making different objects, or the plan of growth of natural objects like crystals or oaks,[96] Categories derived from the similar things are (1) characters, (2) particulars, and (3) participation;[97] Those derived from plans are (1) norms, (2) matter for the exemplification of the norms, (3) and a principle of exemplification which materializes the norms.[98]

Since both immanent formism and transcendent formism have their own root metaphors and derived categories, it seems that they are different kinds of world theories. But, according to Pepper, they have to be regarded as one world hypothesis. The reason for this assertion is that though the meaning implied by the similar things in some sense is different from that of the plan and different categories are derived from them, yet both of them are endowed with similarity as their central concept. So the two sets of categories derived from immanent formism and transcendent formism can be merged into one set and become immanent and transcendent categories. The discussion of the merging or the amalgamation of the two sets of categories is given in detail by Pepper, but I shall just give the result of the discussion here, that is, the immanent and transcendent categories. They are (1) forms consisting of characters and norms which may have scond-degree participation with one another, (2) basic particulars, and (3) first degree participation or exemplifications.[99] Since we can have a set of categories of immanent and transcendent formism they have to be regarded as one world hypothesis.

With reference to the above mentioned procedure of application of the root metaphor to a world theory, what we have done above is concerned with the first two steps — to discuss its root metaphor, and to see what categories are derived from it.

So the third step will be to point out how the categories derived from the root metaphor are used to interpret or to explain the facts or the world. In respect of this problem what Pepper wants to tell us is that we can have a relatively adequate interpretation of the facts of the world in terms of the categories of formism. But what he mainly points out is how the particulars exist in accordance with their forms as an indication of the meaning of the categories. So he says that according to formism, the world is full of particulars regarded as concrete existences existing in accordance with the forms, that is, with space and time. "In concrete existence no characters ever seem to appear except in the form of time or in the forms of space and time."100 The form of space and that of time are laws regulating concrete existences;101 or say, all concrete existences participate in the laws of time and space. This kind of situation, with the concrete existences participating in the laws of time and space, is nothing but an indication of the explanation of the meaning of facts of the world by the categories of formism.

Again, things existing in this world appear in causal relations. But in formism causality is nothing but "the result of the participation of patterns, norms, or laws in basic particulars through the forms of time and space."102 He explains the participation as follows:

First, a basic particular (or set of basic particulars) having certain characters; second, the participation of these characters in a law, which itself participates in time and space characters; third, the determination, by the law, of other basic particulars as having certain dates or positions and as having certain characters the same as those possessed by the first basic particulars, or different from them. Causality is the determination of the characters of certain basic particulars by a law which is set in motion by the characters of other basic particulars which participate in that law.103

So causality is just an indication of the meanings of the categories.

Furthermore, the categories not only can be employed to explain the natural world but also can be employed to interpret the problems of human society. Ac-

cording to Pepper, either "Plato's search for the perfect state or Aristotle's for several types of social structure, exhibiting a golden mean" or modern men's "for the life cycles of the several normal types of culture" presupposes the formistic categories.104

As to the problem of the difference between formism and the other world theories, Pepper is mainly concerned with formism and mechanism. The difference between these two theories is mainly due to the fact that the forms or laws of nature of formism tend to be separate and discrete from each other and from things existing in the world and cannot be identified with things. For forms or laws are regarded as the first category, and things as the second category. These two categories are distinguished from each other, so they cannot be identified with each other. For mechanism, which will be discussed later, there are no subsistent forms. Forms are not transcendent to particulars but are immanent in them. So they are not regarded as separate laws but as the structure of a cosmic field.105

The special merit of formism, as Pepper points out, is its root metaphor. For all of us can have a very clear concept of the similarity of things. And it can be applied to every thing which appears to us. So it is easy to accept categories derived from it as important means for understanding things of the world. The chief shortcoming of formism is the looseness of its categorial structure. For owing to this looseness it lacks determinateness. But though formism has this shortcoming, it will not lose its status as being a world hypothesis. For regardless of its shortcoming, it indicates one aspect of understanding the world which cannot be replaced by the other world hypotheses. So with due regard to the fact that the other world theories also cannot avoid shortcomings, formism is asserted as a relatively adequate world theory by Pepper.

(2) An application of the root metaphor method to mechanism

"Mechanism" is used by Pepper to indicate "naturalism" or "materialism" and by some others to refer to "realism." "It is associated with Democritus, Lucretius, Galileo, Descartes, Hobbes, Locke, Berkeley, Hume, Reichenbach."106 Related to the same root metaphor, all of them are called mechanism. For, ac-

cording to Pepper, though they are regarded as different schools of philosophy, they are all established on the same root metaphor.

I shall adopt the same procedure of application of the root metaphor to mechanism as in the case of formism. That is, (1) to discuss its root metaphor, (2) to see what categories are derived from it, (3) to see how the categories are used to interpret the facts or the world, (4) to see ·what the difference is between this theory and the others, and (5) to see what its merits and shortcomings are.

The root metaphor of mechanism, according to Pepper, is a machine.107 This can be a watch or a dynamo or a lever or the like. The lever is used by Pepper as an example for interpreting this theory. As in 'the case of formism, Pepper also discusses in detail how the categories of mechanism are derived from its root metaphor lever. Again, I shall not follow it in detail here. The result of this discussion is the assertion of the categories of mechanism. They are divided into two sets, the primary categories and the secondary categories. The former includes (1) field of location, (2) primary qualities, (3) laws holding for configurations of primary qualities in the field (primary laws); the latter includes (4) secondary qualities, (5) a principle for connecting the secondary qualities with the first three primary or effective categories, (6) laws, if any, for regularities among secondary qualities (secondary laws).108

According to Pepper, for the mechanists the world is nothing but things understood in terms of the above two sets of categories. The reason for dividing the categories into two sets is because they have different functions for interpreting the world. The interpretation related to the first set is directly connected with the machine, and since these categories can give us an understanding of the world as a machine, they are called primary or effective categories. The interpretation based on the second set, is related to our experienced world. These latter categories are not concerned with understanding the world as a machine as in the case of the first set, but they indicate the irreducible characters of the world perceived by us; and they are called the ineffective categories.

The primary categories can be employed either from a discrete point of view, or from a consolidated point of view, to interpret the world. The former is called discrete mechanism, the latter, consolidated mechanism. Both of them can give us a systematic interpretation of the world. The former is more related to the world view of a mechanical theory of matter. So the material model for it is a lever. The important figures are atomic materialists such as Lucretius, Democritus, and Epicurus. The latter is more related to the world view of an electrical theory of matter. The material model for it is an electromagnetic field. And it is a result of the contemporary revolution in physics.

Not all that is asserted of the world in terms of the primary categories is directly experienced by us. What we experience is described by the secondary categories and secondary qualities. In terms of the secondary categories we understand the world which is perceivable.

Since what is asserted by the primary categories of a sophisticated mechanism cannot be experienced directly by us and what is experienced is the secondary qualities, the connection between the primary structure and the secondary qualities becomes a problem of this world theory. As Pepper points out, many things regarded as secondary qualities exist in this world and they cannot be reduced to the primary elements. The traditional theory of correlation which has been regarded as the most promising theory of solving the problem of connection between the secondary qualities and the primary ones is not fully acceptable. The reason for questioning it is because in terms of the idea of correlation we cannot solve the problem of connection.[109] So according to Pepper, this is the "redoubtable mind-body problem"[110] which the mechanists never can solve. So, it becomes an important problem of *Concept and Quality,* and Pepper believes that he has solved this problem there.[111]

The world view of mechanism is quite different from those of the other world theories. As already pointed out, this is due to the fact the world is understood by mechanists in terms of different categories derived from their own root

metaphor. But what is especially singled out as a topic for discussion as a problem of difference between this world theory and the others by Pepper here, as mentioned before, is the difference between mechanism and formism in regard to the problem of laws or forms. For the laws of mechanism are resolved into the particulars or the particular — the structure of the field — and only particulars exist, or only a particular exists, that is, the field.112   As to the forms of formism, they are discrete and separable from the particulars. They operate upon the particulars or the field of the masses. So any mechanist who does not clear up this problem and tries to identify the laws of mechanism with the forms of formism will be unable to avoid the problem of categorial confusion. So does the formist who intends to identify particulars with the laws.113

As to merits and shortcomings of mechanism compared with the other world theories, it is effective in the field of the physical sciences and ineffective in the field of values. So it is inadequate in relation to scope as a world theory, and adequate in precision in respect of understanding the physical world.

(3)   An application of the root metaphor method to contextualism

"Contextualism" is used by Pepper to indicate "pragmatism." "It is associated with Peirce, James, Bergson, Dewey, Mead. There may be a trace of it in the Greek, Protagoras."114   Pepper himself is also regarded by some other philosophers as a contextualist.115   But he does not claim that he is an exponent of contextualism.116   Perhaps, when writing *World Hypotheses* he preferred contextualism to the other world theories. But after having worked out his new world hypothesis, selectivism, he became a revisionist of contextualism.117

The root metaphor of contextualism, according to Pepper, is the historic event.118   This is not a common-sense concept, but it is clear and well-known to us. The word "historic" here must not be mistaken just as "past." It is not limited to the past; it is alive in the present and is going on to the future.

Since the root metaphor is related to what is going to happen in the future, change and novelty are implied by it. In relation to knowledge, knowledge of

the future cannot be based simply on what has happened in the past. Alternatives are allowed. There is no absolute permanence or immutability to contextualism. This is just a fiction.[119] So Pepper says that in contextualism nothing shall be construed as denying that anything may happen in the world, and that change and novelty are accepted as the fundamental presuppositions of contextualism.[120]

Two basic categories are derived from the root metaphor. They are quality and texture. And three subcategories are derived from the basic category of quality. They are the spread of an event or its so-called specious present, its change, and its degree of fusion. And three subcategories are derived from the basic category texture. They are the strands of a texture, its context, and its references. And references are distinguished into four different sorts. They are linear, convergent, blocked, and instrumental.[121]

Pepper explains in detail the categories and subcategories of contextualism and in terms of this explanation he indicates how the contextualists understand the world. And how their world view is different from those of the other world theories. His explanation is full of insight, and helpful for us to understand pragmatism. But it is not my plan to go into it in detail here. I shall be satisfied with pointing out the following three points. They have been regarded as the most important ideas of contextualism and are different from those of the other world theories.

The first point I want to point out is that, as already mentioned before, change and novelty are presupposed by the root metaphor of contextualism. These two ideas are different from the ideas of absolute permanent forms and unchanging laws asserted by formism and mechanism respectively. And they are concerned with the problem of precision of contextualism.

The second point is that, on the basis of the contextualistic subcategory of the "spread of an event" or "its so-called specious present," time is taken as a qualitative present. It is not something which is absolute, or a priori, or

schematic. This kind of concept of time is not only different from that of Newton and Kant but also different from the mechanistic concept of time. For to mechanism time is taken as a schematic affair. So the mechanists criticize against the contextualistic concept of time. "The qualitative present is nothing but a confused way of saying something that is much more clearly expressed in terms of schematic points or slices along a line."122 But for the contextualists, the dimensional "time" of mechanism is a conceptual scheme useful for the control and ordering of events, but not categorial or, in this sense, real. It "distorts the qualitative fact."123

The third point is that for formism or mechanism, "it is assumed that any object or event can be analyzed completely and finally into its constituents."124 But "this assumption is categorially denied by contextualism; for according to its categories, there is no final or complete analysis of anything. The reason for this is that what is analyzed is categorially an event, and the analysis of an event consists in the exhibition of its texture, and the exhibition of its texture is the discrimination of its strands, and the full discrimination of its strands is the exhibition of other textures in the context of the one being analyzed — textures from which the strands of the texture being analyzed gain part of their quality. In the extended analysis of any event we presently find ourselves in the context of that event and so on from event to event as long as we wish to go, which would be forever or until we got tired."125

As to the merits and shortcomings of this theory, it is inadequate in precision and effective in qualitative presentation. For since the contextualistic root metaphor presupposes change and novelty, the meaning of an event is indeterminate. It is always open for new experience and new understanding; it is contrary to any definite concept of any thing. So it is inadequate of precision. It is effective in qualitative presentation, for it gives us some categories which help us to have a concrete understanding of the world. For example, in terms of the subcategory "fusion," things are presented to us as a concrete whole. Their concreteness and vividness will disappear when they are treated as analytical

objects.

(4)   An application of the root metaphor method to organicism

"Organicism" is used by Pepper to indicate "absolute (or, objective) ideal-ism." "It is associated with Schelling, Hegel, Green, Bradley, Bosanquet, Royce."126

The root metaphor of organicism, according to Pepper is integration.127   As with the historic event of contextualism, however, integration is also not an altogether safe common-sense concept; but it is also a well-known concept and is easily grasped by us.

Categories derived from this root metaphor are seven.   According to Pepper, they might be more or less, depending on how detailed one wished to be in his exposition of the theory.   These seven categories are: "(1) fragments of ex-perience which appear with (2) nexuses or connections or implications which spontaneously lead as a result of the aggravation of (3) contradictions, gaps, oppositions, or counteractions to resolution in (4) an organic whole which is found to have been (5) implicit in the fragments, and to (6) transcend the previous contradictions by means of a coherent totality, which (7) economizes, saves, pre-serves all the original fragments of experience without any loss."128

These categories can be divided into two sets — the progressive set and the ideal set.   According to Pepper,

the fourth category is the pivotal point of the system and should be included in both the progressive and the ideal sets.   It is the goal and final stage of the progressive categories and it is the field for the specification of the ideal categories.   So, categories 1 to 4 inclusive constitute the progressive set, and categories 4 to 7 the ideal set.129

The reason for the above division of the categories of organicism into two sets and calling them progressive and ideal respectively is that with reference to the root metaphor every actual event in the world is understood by the organicist

as a more or less concealed organic process. "He believes, therefore, that a careful scrutiny of any actual process in the world would exhibit its organic structure, though some of the processes with which we are generally familiar reveal the structure more clearly and openly than others."130 In order to present this understanding or belief adequately, the categories thus, on the one hand, should indicate the steps involved in the organic process (that is what the first set of categories are intended to do), and, on the other, should indicate the principal features in the organic structure ultimately achieved or realized (this is what is aimed at in the second set of categories). Since the main function of the first set of categories is to describe how each event aims at the final integration, it indicates the progressive action and is called the set of progressive categories; whereas the main function of the second set of categories is to show how each event achieves or realizes its final integration and to indicate the final, or the ideal aim, and thus this set is called the ideal set of categories.

As in the case of the categories of the other world theories, Pepper gives a detailed exposition of each category of organicism. And in terms of this exposition the organicistic world theory is indicated. But again I shall not go into it in detail here. What I want to do is to point out the central point regarded as the most special and characteristic concept of organicism.

This is the concept of an inclusive, determinative, and organic whole indicated by the ideal categories. Though this concept is in conflict with some other concepts expressed by progressive categories, yet it reveals a higher ability of man's creative imagination. Being supported by scientific evidence, it has earned a higher place in the history of cognition. The conflict of this concept with those expressed by the progressive categories is mainly due to the fact that the progressive categories disclose the process of the event as limited to a certain duration. So it is not necessarily related to the integration of the whole. But when it is connected to the integration of the ideal categories what appears as a process of an event disclosed by the progressive categories cannot be interpreted as a duration but as the integration of the whole. So the concept of an inclusive

whole indicated by the ideal categories is inevitably in conflict with those expressed by the progressive categories.

Since every event in respect of the ideal categories is related to or resolved into the integrative whole there is no isolated or discrete event. This is quite different from the concept of similarity of formism. For formism asserts events can be independent, and one event is similar to the others. Again, since the process in duration of an event is resolved in the inclusive integration, there is no independent process of events. This is different from the concept of blocking, or change, or novelty, or fusion derived from the root metaphor of the historic event of contextualism.

As to the merits and shortcomings of this world theory, its great merit as already mentioned is the creative imaginative revelation of the inclusive, determinate, and organic whole which has earned a high place in the history of cognition. But it is inadequate in scope. For many events such as suspense, distrust, longing, all forms of desire, frustration, all pain, and all pleasures of anticipation and fulfillment cannot be adequately interpreted. For these events have to be interpreted by progressive categories. But when all progressive categorial problems are resolved in the ideal categories, the mentioned events cannot be adequately treated.[131]

5. An Application of the Root Metaphor to Selectivism

So far the discussion of the application of the root metaphor to the world theories has been concerned with "the previous development of speculative philosophy,"[132] which is regarded by Pepper as "the fruitful achievements of the past,"[133] discussed in Part Two of *World Hypotheses*. Now we are going to discuss how a new world theory based on the concept of root metaphors has been worked out, or how Pepper has applied the concept of root metaphors for constructing a new world hypothesis which is regarded as a further contribution to speculative philosophy.[134]

This new world hypothesis is called selectivism by Pepper,[135] and it is pre-

sented in his new book, *Concept and Quality.* Selectivism is not used to indicate any existent philosophy as the other four world theories are used to. It is an outcome of Pepper's earlier study, *World Hypotheses,136* and is a radical revision of contextualism.137 It draws upon the new evidences of recent sciences and the new results of contemporary philosophy. So throughout the book though Pepper draws strength from Feigl, Ryle, Whitehead, Dewey, James, Gestalt and behavioristic psychologists, Austin, Nagel, and others, he speaks as a philosopher unattached.138 His discussion is simply based on the new theory and does not refer to any existent philosophy, with the possible exception of Whitehead's view.

Since selectivism is an outcome of his earlier study of world hypotheses and a further contribution to speculative philosophy, the method used in the previous study, or the way of approaching the problem adopted by the previous study might be expected to be reaffirmed by the new study. And this is the case. Pepper has made this point clear. He says that "the method consisted in originating and testing hypotheses and refining them for the clarity, consistency, and adequacy of their categories in relation to the evidence available to them." "In all essentials that earlier analysis still seems to me sound."139 He also says that "the present study takes the earlier for its point of departure."140

Perhaps we might wonder why Pepper still wants to use the same method for his *Concept and Quality,* a book worked out some twenty-five years later than *World Hypotheses.* For during this period, there had arisen on the European continent a school of existentialism and in England a school of linguistic analytic philosophy. And both of them have seriously criticized the traditional metaphysics. To this problem Pepper's answer is that he is impressed by the constructive criticism and clarification of the problem of metaphysics afforded by the two mentioned schools. But he cannot agree with their common assumption "that each occupies and completely fills the total field of philosophy to the exclusion of each other and any other movements in philosophy."141 And he does not find that either the existentialists or the analysts have offered any suitable substitutes for the perspectives and insights of the traditional, speculative empirical hypotheses.142 So he believes that his way

of approaching the problem of philosophy is still correct. "There is plenty of room for constructive speculation, and probably even for a new world hypothesis."[143] So Pepper's attitude toward these two mentioned schools is almost the same as toward the logical positivists though he did not criticize the former in his new book as he did the latter in his *World Hypotheses*. And he really did not lose his confidence in his theory of world hypotheses as the best way for dealing with the problem of metaphysics or with philosophy.

As has been pointed out already, from the viewpoint of applying the root metaphor to interpreting the world, Pepper's method of selectivism is the same as that of the other mentioned world hypotheses. Thus, the difference between selectivism and the other world theories is not a problem of methodology but a problem of finding a more suitable root metaphor in terms of which to establish a new system of world theory and through which to deal with the different problems of science and philosophy faced by the modern and contemporary philosophers. So the difference between selectivism and the other world theories in a sense provides the same kind of problem as that of the relation of any one of the mentioned world theories to the other world theories including selectivism.

The root metaphor of selectivism is the purposive act.[144] The reasons given by Pepper for choosing the purposive act as root metaphor are: "(1) that the goal seeking purpose is so highly organized an activity as perhaps to enfold most of the simpler ones there are, and thus to present an exceptionally useful sample of the processes of nature; (2) that it is an activity open to awareness of its full qualitative immediacy throughout its whole course; and (3) that a detailed conceptual description of it in behavioristic terms is available."[145]

Two sets of categories referring to the qualitative aspect and the conceptual aspect of the root metaphor are derived. They are as follows:

Qualitative Categories

A. Categories for a single qualitative strand (e.g., drive quality).

1. *Felt quality* with dynamic urge for action.

2. *Duration* of the quality yielding a continuous qualitative strand.

3. *Intensity* of quality felt as dynamics of activity.

4. *Reference* to goal felt in the dynamic quality.

5. *Blockage* from environmental strands.

6. *Splitting of dynamic reference to charge instrumental strands* with their felt references to instrumental goals towards attainment of goal of drive.

7. *Selection of instrumental strands* towards attainment of final goal.

8. Positive feeling of *satisfaction* in terminal act or quiescence pattern (and, in blockage, negative feeling of *dissatisfaction*).

B. Categories of Context of Qualitative Strand

   1. Simultaneity of diverse strands.

   2. *Articulation* of successive strands in an integrated total act.

   3. *Anticipations and apprehensions* as felt dispositions for action.

   4. *Fusion* — the merging of the qualities of diverse strands into a new distinct quality instituting a qualitative strand in its own right.

   5. *Specious present* — or field of immediacy.

C. Categories of Qualitative Range

   1. (a) *Actual present* — consisting of whole range of specious presents in action.

      (b) *Past* — *real* but not actual, as events referred to as once actual but now outside the actual present.

      (c) *Future* — *real* so far as it is an inherent potentiality of the actual present, but not actual.

   2. *Controlling environment* of strands — for any qualitative strand in action — the actuality and reality of the situation.

Conceptual Categories

A. Catgories for a single complete act of purposive behavior in "objective"

terms.

1. *Bodily action* and *tension pattern* arising from internal bodily changes, or environmental stimulation (the drive impulse).

2. *Continuity* through a period of time.

3. *Energy* of a measurable quantity observable as kinetic energy in overt action or conceived as potential energy in states of bodily tension.

4. *Vector character* of bodily energy indicating along with bodily changes conditions for dissipation of the energy or its maintenance in a steady state.

5. *Interaction* with environmental activities.

6. Vector changes due to interaction with environment, and *channeling of energy for shortest path* through response mechanisms for final discharge of energy, or for maintenance of a steady state.

7. *Selection* of response mechanisms for discharge of energy or maintenance of steady state.

8. *Quiescence patterns* of responses in reduction of energy for the drive impulse.

B. Categories of Physical Structure

1. Body of *organism*.

2. *Articulation* of behavior of organism in an *integrated* act.

3. Dynamic dispositions such as *physiological sets* available for action upon proper stimulation.

4.

5.

C. Categories of Physical Environment

1. *Space-time*.

2. *Configurations of matter in space-time*.146

These two sets of categories are closely parallel. The only marked discrepancy is the absence of categories in the conceptual scheme for B4 (*fusion*) and B5 (*specious*

present) in the qualitative scheme.

Using these two sets of categories Pepper proceeds to give us an extended discussion of the problems of philosophy. His discussion is first concerned with the problem of knowledge and then with the problem of values and that of aesthetics. It is impossible for me, and it is also not my purpose, to go into this theory in detail here. Following my procedure with reference to the other four world theories, I shall try to point out what the special characteristics of this world theory as contrasted with the other world theories are in the following pages of this section.

The special characteristic of this world theory as indicated by Pepper is the identification of felt quality with scientific concept or description, or, as Pepper puts it, the "qualitative neural identity theory."147 This identification is implied by the meaning of the root metaphor, and on the basis of the root metaphor Pepper expresses it in the derived categories.

As indicated by the above quotation, there are two sets of categories derived from the root metaphor, and both of them can be applied to interpret any purposive act. That is, any purposive act can be understood either in terms of qualitative categories or in terms of conceptual categories. Through the former the meaning of the act is felt by the person who performs the act, through the latter, it is observd and described by the scientist. And since both sets of categories are derived from the same root metaphor and are applied to indicate the same act, what is indicated by them is the same. The only difference between them is that one indicates the qualitative aspect of the act, the other, the conceptual aspect; or say, one indicates the activity of the act phenomenally, the other, conceptually.

Perhaps we might wonder why this identification is so important. For in common sense this seems very natural. Nobody would doubt that the pain described by the doctor is the pain that he felt, or that what I am afraid of can be understood by others. But strangely enough, what is obvious to common sense may become an insoluble problem in philosophy. And the identification of felt quality with scientific concept is such a kind of problem. This problem has puzzled philosophers

ever since ancient times. Since the Greeks the mind-body problem has been a controversial problem, and it is still an unsolved problem in philosophy. So to common sense, Pepper's identification of mental feeling with physical description seems obvious, but to philosophy it is not so obvious. It has to be regarded as a great contribution. For owing to this identification, as Pepper puts it, the problem of the relation of the mental to the physical which has tantalized mechanistic naturalism from Descartes down to the presnt, is resolved.[148] In Descartes' philosophy the mind-body problem is unsolvable regardless of how much effort was devoted to it by Descartes himself and his followers. In the mchanistic world theory, this is a problem of the relation of the sensory emergents (the secondary categories) to the cosmic machine (the primary categories).[149] It is also unsolvable despite the different attempts to connect the former to the latter. In contemporary analytic philosophy, it becomes a problem of the relation of physical language to phenomenal language. Many contemporary analytical philosophers have been puzzled by this problem. And it makes those who have different ideas on this problem part company.[150] But it seems that what they can do is just to indicate their different ideas in respect of this problem; they still cannot solve it.[151] But to the identity theory of this new world hypothesis, this "problem ceases to be a mind-matter problem and becomes a quality-concept problem. Not a problem of two kinds of entities with incompatible properties, but a problem of qualitative actuality and various symbolic descriptions of it."[152] So the mind-body problem or the sensory emergents-cosmic machine problem gets its answer, and "the problem of how to relate the conceptual categories in physical language with the qualitative categories in phenomenal language,"[153] is resolved also.

In *Concept and Quality* the theory of identification of mental feeling and physical description is related to the whole problem discussed in the book. It is indicated in the first three chapters, and presented in Chapter Four, and defended in Chapter Five, and then applied to the other chapters of the book for further affirmation and explanation. In Chapter 6, it is applied to the problem of dispositions, in Chapter 7, to the problem of the act of perception, in Chapter 8, to the perceptual object, in

Chapter 9, to the perceiving persons, in Chapter 10, to the scientific object, in Chapter 11, to space-time, history, and the immediate present, in Chapter 12, to causation and determination, in Chapter 13, to similarity in actual process, in Chapter 14, to logical similarity and formal reality. All of these are mainly concerned with the problem of knowledge. As to the problem of values and that of aesthetics, they are presented in Chapter 15 and Chapter 16.154

With attention to the scope of this study, I shall not discuss all of these affirmations and explanations resulting from the "qualitative neural identity theory." I shall just give some of them in the following.

As has been indicated already, for selectivism the object for philosophy is the object described by its two sets of categories. It is not only a problem of language. From this point of view the assertion of selectivism is different from that of linguistic analysis. So based on this point, Pepper gives Gilbert Ryle a serious criticism.

I cannot resist calling attention to Ryle's results as an illustration of what is likely to happen when philosophic study is restricted to linguistic analysis. A linguistic analysis is clearly useful as a preliminary study of any problem. . . . But when a philosopher is occupied with a seious problem relating to know-ledge, causality, social relations, or values, or dispositions, or the like, he cannot expect to come out with significant and reliable results if he restricts his studies to words and the doings of words and grammar. A philosopher engaged on a serious study and analysis of a problematic field of subject matter and its concepts, must keep an eye on the subject matter as intently as upon the concepts. The concepts are empty and floating wild except as they are attached to their subject matter.155

From the same position, he indicates his views on logic.

There is a gap between the concepts and structures of logic and the processes and structures of actuality. And whenever the two prove to be irreconcilable, it is not actuality but logic that has to give way. Perhaps this point is too obvious to require so much explanation. But at least the world theory of form-

ism (often called Platonism) maintains an opposite view, and there is more Platonism among us than is often realized.156

This conception of logic in some snse is similar to Dewey's view of logical form as something emerging from experience in the process of inquiry, and his notion of the ultimate subject-matter of logic as something based on experience as contrasted with the proximate subject-mattter of logic.157 But what Pepper indicates here does not simply repeat Dewey's concept of logic. As has been pointed out already, what he indicates is based on his new selectivistic world theory.

> Our thesis is that formal logical reality is dependent for its being on the processes of actuality...According to our categories, the grounds for the truth of judgments about a dependent reality should be found in the process of actuality upon which the logical reality depends.158

The above two examples are concerned with the problem of knowledge in general. I shall now give one concerned with the problem of aesthetics, and one with philosophy in general or with applying philosophy to education. The problem of the work of art was opened up in an appendix to *The Basis of Criticism in the Arts.*

> The description of the "stimulus-control object" is there worked out in great detail and has not been improved upon by me elsewhere...In the present chapter I have finally come to what I believe is a satisfactory solution of that problem. It was not possible, I now see, until I could base it on an analysis of the concept of disposition, making the crucial distinction between passive and dynamic dispositions. It seems to have required a new world hypothesis to bring this distinction clearly to light.159

This is an indication concerning the achievement of the theory of aesthetics based on his new world theory.

As to the problem of applying selectivism to education or relating it to the role of philosophy in general, he declares:

> And philosophy — under the pressures of conceptual analysis and the dogma

that scientific method as practiced in the physical sciences monopolizes the achievement of knowledge — philosophy has all but vacated its office of furthering humane cultivation and a balanced wisdom. Whole schools have gone completely irrational...Yet on our view, philosophy has a unique function in the educational sphere — that of keeping the balance between concepts and qualities. In the academic scheme, philosophy should be given a place of its own as neither one of the sciences nor one of the humanities. For its irreplaceable role is that of maintaining a comprehensive understanding of both for the enterprise of civilized living.

The foregoing comments on the application of our philosophy to education and the modern world are not a digression. They point up the central contribution of our world theory — that concept and quality are essential to each other in the understanding of our world.160

With reference to the merits and shortcomings of this world theory, Pepper has said that selectivism is a radical revision of contextualism,161 and perhaps "is more adequate than the traditional views."162 But from the viewpoint of the world hypothesis theory, selectivism cannot be regarded as the only adequate world theory, but rather just as one more relatively adequate world hypothesis. Pepper is quite aware of this. So he even says: "I do not in my more judicial moments think that the qualitative neural identity theory has necessarily quite replaced the dualistic mind and body theory associated with traditional mechanism."163

In theory, we can have a more adequate world theory if it gives us a better scope and precision than the other world theories provide for understanding the world. But we cannot have an absolutely adequate world theory. Standing inside a certain world theory we might be attempted to think that what is indicated by it is certain or absolute. But from the viewpoint of the theory of world hypotheses it can just be regarded as one more way of interpreting the world. For, besides it, there are other world theories affording us other ways of

understanding the world.

Formism, mechanism, contextualism, and organicism, as pointed out before, are regarded as relatively adequate world theories. Animism and mysticism (I omitted them in discussion) are regarded as inadequate world theories.164 As to selectivism, Pepper sometimes seems to think that it is the best world hypothesis but for the most part he refrains from that kind of thinking as mentioned above.

Whether or not selectivism is the best world theory, let it be open to the readers. But from the metaphysical point of view to understand this problem, selectivism as well as the other world hypotheses, are based on the same theory. So it can be applied to the root metaphor for understanding as well as the other world hypotheses.

CHAPTER FOUR

CONCLUSION

In the Introduction of this study, we pointed out that Pepper regards the problem of metaphysics as the problem of the theory of world hypotheses. We also indicated that with reference to the relation of this kind of concept to the history of philosophy, it is a reaction to those who regard the problem of metaphysics as beyond the field of cognition and those who regard it as nonsensical. And it is also a further development of modern and contemporary philosophy, and a contribution of Pepper to the problem of metaphysics. For, as also pointed out, since Kant metaphysics has been regarded by many as something beyond the field of science; and the logical positivists regard it as nonsensical. Thus, philosophers after Kant, if they do not wish to follow Kant's way of treating the problem of metaphysics, nor like to take the side of the logical positivists, must overcome the challenge of Kant and that of the logical positivists in regard to this problem. As also indicated in the Introduction and Chapter Two, Dewey is such a philosopher who neither follows Kant's way nor agrees with the logical positivists' rejection of metaphysics. He regards the problem of metaphysics as a study of the generic traits of existence. Pepper's concept of metaphysics is the same kind as that of Dewey. His theory of world hypotheses, however, is a further justification of Dewey's way of dealing with this problem. The problem as to whether or not Dewey has met the mentioned challenges was indicated briefly in Chapter Two, Section 4. We will not repeat it here. With reference to what we have discussed in the previous chapters I shall summarize the problem as to whether or not Pepper has met the mentioned challenges. After this, in conclusion, I shall have come comments on this problem.

This problem can be divided into the following three questions.

(1) Can Pepper really meet the challenge of Kant?

(2) Can he really meet the challenge of the logical positivists?

(3) Can he really reject from the field of metaphysics all those ideas concerned with the problem of metaphysics as noncognitive?

With reference to the first question as to whether or not Pepper can really meet the challenge of Kant in regard to the problem of metaphysics, it seems that in discussing the theory of world hypotheses Pepper does not pay much attention, if any, to Kant. No one of the four relatively adequate world hypotheses is clearly related by him to Kant's philosophy. It seems that Kant's theory of a priori concepts is regarded by Pepper as a kind of dogmatism which has to be rejected.165   But in *Concept and Quality,* Kant is referred to in discussing the problems of space-time, the scientific object, and aesthetics. In the first two discussions, Kant's ideas are rejected. In discussing the problem of space-time he disagrees with Kant's theory of intuition of space and time.166   In discussing the problem of the scientific object, he criticizes Kant's idea of a thing-in-itself which cannot be reached by science.167   Only in the discussion of Kant's idea of aesthetic value does he show some appreciation of Kant's idea of "purposiveness without a purpose."168

On the basis of the above mentioned criticism by Pepper of Kant which just occasionally refers to some aspects of Kant's philosophy, it is not easy to say whether or not Pepper meets the challenge of Kant in regard to the problem of metaphysics. But with reference to Pepper's theory of world hypotheses discussed in Chapter Two of this study, we can have some judgments concerned with this problem.

Kant's main reason for approaching the problem of metaphysics from practical reason is that it cannot be approached by pure reason. For, according to Kant, as pointed out in the Introduction, what can be known by pure reason is the phenomena of the world; besides the phenomena, there are noumena of whose intrinsic nature we cannot have any information through pure reason. So pure reason is concerned with phenomena which are the objects of science, and science

is limited to phenomena. As to noumena since they cannot be understood by pure reason, they are regarded as a problem of practical reason. Metaphysics is understood as different from science. Since science is concerned with phenomena, noumena are treated as the object of metaphysics approached by practical reason.

With this rough understanding of Kant's idea of metaphysics we can easily see that what has been mainly asserted by Kant is not accepted by Pepper in his theory of world hypotheses. Kant has asserted that besides or beyond the world of phenomena there is a world of noumena approached by practical reason. But Pepper declines to accept this kind of assertion. Pepper insists that the theory of world hypotheses is a study of evidence. Whatever was asserted which cannot be verified by evidence is rejected as dogmatism. From the viewpoint of the theory of world hypotheses, as I interpret it, since we can never experience or intuit noumena, they cannot be objects of science; thus they also cannot be objects of the study of world hypotheses. So the assertion of a noumenon as the object of metaphysics is dogmatic and illegal.

If the assertion of noumena rather than phenomena as the object of metaphysics is unacceptable, the idea of the limitation of knowledge based on distinguishing between the noumenon and the phenomenon is also unacceptable. So to Pepper, as already pointed out, the difference between science and metaphysics is not a matter of distinguishing between phenomena and noumena, but rather an affair of the restricted field and the unrestricted field, and both of them belong to this understandable world.

Now if the assertion of noumena on the basis of limitations in our knowledge is rejected, and the problem of metaphysics is not regarded as a problem of noumena by Pepper, then Kant's challenge to the problem of metaphysics is not taken as a real challenge. Perhaps this is the reason why Pepper does not take it as a serious problem in his discussion of the theory of world hypotheses.

Concerning the second question as to whether or not Pepper can meet the

challenge of the logical positivists, as indicated before, Pepper has given the logical positivists a serious criticism.169 The main theme of his criticism is based on the assertion of structural corroboration and the difference of structural corroboration from multiplicative corroboration. As already pointed out, there are two types of corroboration — multiplicative and structural. The former is "the corroboration of one observation with another, or of one man with another, where the fact observed is supposed to be exactly identical in the different observations," while the latter "is the corroboration of fact with fact. It is not a multiplicity of observations of one identical fact, but an observed convergence of many different facts towards one result."170 According to Pepper, what is asserted as truth in terms of the logical positivists' theory of truth, that is, based on the proof of formal propositions or the verification of factual propositions, is just an indication of the truth corroborated by multiplicative corroboration. For multiplicative corroboration is concerned with the evidence of refined data, and the refined data are evidences concerned with formal propositions and factual propositions.

Now if what is concerned with formal propositions and factual propositions is the refined data, and formal propositions and factual propositions are regarded by logical positivists as the only two kinds of effective propositions, then what logical positivists judge regarding the problem of truth in terms of either one of these two kinds of propositions should be limited to the field of refined data. If this is the case, then nothing except judgments based on refined data can be regarded as meaningful by the logical positivists. And, therefore, the judgment of metaphysical propositions as nonsensical asserted by logical positivists should be regarded as nonsensical. For this judgment is not based on refined data, that is, it is neither based on the evidence of formal propositions nor on that of factual propositions. So, according to Pepper, the logical positivists in regard to the problem of metaphysics are compelled into a dilemma, which can be formulated as follows:

Either the logical positivists abstain themselves from judging the problem

of metaphysics, or they give up their assertion that whatever is accepted as having cognitive meaning should be asserted in terms of the mentioned two kinds of propositions; if their choice is the first statement, then they are not permitted to judge that the metaphysical problem is nonsensical; if their choice is the second one, then they have no foundation to reject metaphysical problems as nonsensical; therefore, from either way out, their challenge to metaphysics cannot be counted as a real challenge.

As to the third question whether or not Pepper can reject those theories regarding the problem of metaphysics as noncognitive from the field of metaphysics, it seems that Pepper's answer is affirmative. As already pointed out, to Pepper, neither the challenge of Kant nor that of the logical positivists to metaphysics can be counted as a real challenge. And every constructive work of philosophy in the past "was all of an empirical nature." And ever since Thales root metaphors have been used as the effective way of understanding the world. And as a result of this use a number of relatively adequate world hypotheses have been gradually established. The theory of world hypotheses is thus not a new theory; it is not a new theory by which to meet the modern and contemporary challenge of metaphysics, nor in terms of which to revive the traditional metaphysics; it is a traditional way used by various philosophers to deal with the problem of understanding the world. So the problem of metaphysics is a problem concerned with how to understand this empirical world in terms of evidence. As to those problems without cognitive meaning, they cannot be regarded as a problem of philosophy. If evidence cannot be presented for them, they have to be rejected from the field of philosophy.

The above exposition I think is Pepper's position concerning the problem of metaphysics in regard to the third question. As to whether or not it is acceptable is questionable.

The disagreement with Pepper's concept of metaphysics and the answers to the above questions, I think, can be raised from different points of view. But

what I want to indicate here will be limited to three points. The first one is concerned with the way of deriving the categories, the second point with regarding the world hypothesis as an old theory of metaphysics ever since Thales, and the third point with the rejection of those ideas concerned with the problem of metaphysics as noncognitive from the field of metaphysics.

As already pointed out, all the categories of a certain world hypothesis are derived from their root metaphor, and the world is interpreted in terms of them. But it seems to me that though Pepper in each world hypothesis gives us a description in detail of deriving categories from the root metaphor, the only guiding principle on the basis of which to derive the categories he can shows us is that "He describes as best as he can the characteristics of this area (that is the root metaphor), or, if you will, discriminates its structure."171 This description or discrimination no doubt is based on one's experience of the root metaphor in connection with the world which one wants to interpret. Now a question is raised as to how one's experience of the root metaphor is related to the world. It seems that the description of the characteristics of the root metaphor, or the discrimination of its structure, is intimately related to one's understanding of the world. Or one can say that it is based on one's experience of the world. If this is the case, then the description of the root metaphor of one who has a certain kind of experience of the world would be different from those with another kind of experience of the world, and categories derived by them thus will be different from one another. If this is the case, then we cannot say that categories are really derived from the root metaphor, they are only cooperative productions of the root metaphor and one's experience of the world. If this is the case, it seems to me that the root metaphor loses its status as a root metaphor.

As to the second point of disagreement with Pepper's concept of metaphysics, it is that though Pepper has pointed out that ever since Thales root metaphors have been used by philosophers for understanding nature, and asserted that every constructive work in the past "was all of an empirical nature," he cannot deny that it was not

until his study of world theories that the meaning of the root metaphor became clear to us. This is why what has been treated by Pepper, on the basis of his root metaphor view, as world hypotheses such as the generating substance of the Milesian school, or the two inadequate world hypotheses, or the four relatively adequate world hypotheses, could be and has been understood differently by other philosophers. That is why we say that regarding the problem of metaphysics as the theory of world hypotheses is a contribution of Pepper to the problem of metaphysics. So in some sense we can say that Pepper's interpretation of the past philosophies in terms of his root metaphor theory is similar to Hegel's interpretation of the past philosophies in terms of his absolute idealism.

The third point of disagreement is that I do not think that Pepper can exclusively reject or say that it is necessary for him to reject those ideas concerned with the problem of metaphysics as noncognitive from the field of metaphysics. For as we know that besides those philosophies regarded as empirical in nature by Pepper and interpreted in terms of his theory of world hypotheses, there is another trend of thought which has been regarded as having an equally important status in Western philosophy which cannot be adequately interpreted by his root metaphor theory, for it is not of an empirical nature. What I have in mind of this trend of thought can be roughly referred to as the Pythagoreans' concept of the soul, Socrates' immortality, the Stoics' law of nature, Plotinus' God, or the One, the Christian God, Kant's noumena, or God, freedom, and immortality, Schopenhauer's need of life or will to live, the existentialists' Being, Transcendent, *existenz,* and so on. This kind of problem is different from what Pepper calls a problem of an empirical nature, and cannot have an adequate status or any proper significance in the theory of world hypotheses. Here the word "adequate" or "proper" is important. For, as we know, this kind of problem is presented by those who advocate it with some kind of argument supported by some kind of evidence. Since it is advocated with argument supported by a certain kind of evidence, it seems that it belongs to the field of cognition, and since it is just supported by some kind of evidence, its scope is limited and cannot be treated

widely and adequately. It is thus to be regarded as an inadequate world hypothesis. But, as a matter of fact, what they give as evidence in this concern is just a kind of indication. That is, the evidence is not regarded as something through which to verify or to corroborate what they intend to tell us, but just as an indicating sign in terms of which to help us to see what is beyond our cognitive field. What it points to is not something within the field of science, and so it is not an object of science. Since it is not within our cognitive field, it cannot be dealt with by the theory of world hypotheses, or regarded as an inadequate world hypothesis.172

But though it is not within the field of cognition, we cannot say that it is insignificant to us, or it is a dogmatism having to be rejected from the field of metaphysics. To consider this problem from the viewpoint of the theory of world hypotheses, we can say with Pepper that whatever cannot be an object of cognition must be rejected from the field of metaphysics, yet from the viewpoint of the history of philosophy we cannot deny that it is concerned with human beings and is called either a metaphysical problem, or a religious problem, or a problem of human life, or an existential problem. If this is the case, then I cannot see how Pepper can reject it exclusively from the field of metaphysics and limit the problem of metaphysics within the field of cognition. I think perhaps this is the reason why Pepper's theory of world hypotheses is just regarded by the other philosophers as a kind of theory of metaphysics, and is not accepted by them as the theory of metaphysics.173

From what we have indicated above, I think it is obvious that the problem of metaphysics cannot be regarded exclusively as a cognitive problem. But as has been pointed out before, Pepper regardless of the mentioned historical fact insists on rejecting noncognitive systems of metaphysics from the field of metaphysics. Now why does Pepper want to regard metaphysics as cognitive and reject views of noncognitivitists? Some one might be interested in asking this question. It seems that Pepper did not directly give us any reason for his insistence, and did

not argue for it. What he indicates to us in this regard as far as I can find is that he wants "to know the truth,"174 and to know the truth with evidence. With reference to Pepper's emphasis on the importance of knowing the truth, it seems that he believes that knowing the truth with evidence is the correct way to increase our knowledge and is more useful to human beings. So based on this belief he developed a system of cognitive metaphysics.

As I noted in the Introduction of this study, Pepper's concept of metaphysics as the theory of world hypotheses is an important contribution to the problem of metaphysics. But this contribution need not be based on a successful rejection of non-cognitive systems of metaphysics from the field of metaphysics. If what we pointed out above is really Pepper's basis for rejecting noncognitive systems of metaphysics, then one can argue against him by saying that Pepper's wanting to know the truth is just an indication of his empirical character which cannot be a good reason for asserting metaphysics only as a problem of cognition. For there is no sufficient reason why you want to know the truth instead of believing it, or practicing it. "To know the truth" in some sense is quite different from "to believe in the truth," and "to practice the truth." For if what one wants is to believe the truth, then the truth which is the object of belief is not necessarily known by him. He may accept any truth accepted by others as truth with no difference between cognitive and noncognitive, or known and unknown. So religious men never say that what is the truth is to be known, for the truth revealed by God cannot be known by men. Men can only accept it as everlasting truth. Philosophers who assert that the problem of metaphysics cannot be grasped by man's mind do not necessarily have the same attitude towards the problem of truth as that of religious men. But what they advocate in suggesting something like approaching Being without conceptualizing Being is in some sense like that of communicating with God not by our mind but by our heart.

"To practice the truth" is also quite different from "to know the truth." For what is regarded as truth here is not known by man either, but is just a kind of confidence guiding his action.

The reason for me to point out this kind of argument against Pepper's rejection of noncognitive systems of metaphysics is not that I want to deny the importance of the problem of metaphysics based on cognition. What I want to do is just to point out that there are alternatives in respect of man's attitudes towards the problem of metaphysics. One regards metaphysics as having cognitive meaning as asserted by Dewey and Pepper. The other regards it as something transcending man's cognition; it is supersensible; it has to be accepted by faith or to be achieved by some way which cannot be conceptualized but just immediately intuited through a period of cultivating one's mind or by a certain kind of practical action. And what is intuited is just a kind of vision which cannot be an object of knowledge.

As to Pepper's belief that knowledge is more useful to human beings, in general, this is true. But it cannot be accepted without qualification either. For, as we pointed out before, there was a kind of philosophy whose activity was not limited to the cognitive field in the past, and we can also say that there is such a kind of philosophy for the time being, and will be such a kind of philosophy in the future. So it is not easy to say without more ado that to know the truth with evidence is more useful to mankind. For it allows us to argue that the influence of noncognitive systems of metaphysics on man's life or their contribution to human culture has been and will be as important as the cognitive understanding of our world.

If the case is as we pointed out above, then there is no definite reason for a philosopher to regard the problem of metaphysics either as cognitive or as noncognitive. The answer to the question why Pepper regards metaphysics as cognitive and rejects views of noncognitivists thus is that it is due to his "personal desire to know that truth" instead of believing the truth or practicing the truth. That is, it is a problem of personal preference or a problem of temperament as William James puts it.

BIBLIOGRAPHY

Books

Ayer, A. J., ed., *Logical Positivism*. New York: The Free Press, 1966.

————. *Language, Truth and Logic*. New York: Dover Publications, Inc., 1952.

Buchler, J., ed., *The Philosophy of Peirce*. New York: Harcourt, Brace and Co., 1940.

Copleston, F. C., S.J. *A History of Philosophy*. Vols. I-VIII. London: Burns and Oates Limited, 1966.

————. *Contemporary Philosophy*. Maryland: The Newman Press, 1956.

Dewey, John. *Experience and Nature*. La Salle, Illinois: The Open Court Publishing Co., 1958 (first published in 1925).

————. *Logic: The Theory of Inquiry*. New York: Henry Holt and Co., 1938.

Drennen, D. A., ed. *A Modern Introduction to Metaphysics*. New York: The Free Press, 1966 (first published in 1962).

Hempel, C. G. *Philosophy of Natural Science*. Englewood Cliffs, New Jersey: Prentice-Hall, Inc., 1966.

Hill, T. E. *Contemporary Theories of Knowledge*. New York: The Ronald Press Co., 1961.

Kant, Immanuel. *Critique of Pure Reason*. Translated by Norman Kemp Smith. London: MacMillan and Co., Limited, 1929.

————. *Critique of Practical Reason* and *Other Writings in Moral Philosophy*. Translated by Lewis White Beck. Chicago, Ill.: The University of Chicago Press, 1949.

————. *Critique of Judgment*. Translated by J. H. Bernard. New York: Hafner Publishing Co., 1951.

Mou, Tsung-san. *Logic* (Chinese version). Taipei: Ching Chung Book Co., 1960.

Pepper, S. C. *Aesthetic Quality: A Contextualistic Theory of Beauty.* New York: Charles Scribner's Sons, 1937.

————. *The Basis of Criticism in the Arts.* Cambridge, Mass.: Harvard University Press, 1945.

————. *Concept and Quality: A World Hypothesis.* La Salle, Ill.: Open Court Publishing Co., 1967.

————. *Principles of Art Appreciation.* New York: Harcourt, Brace and World, Inc., 1949.

————. *World Hypotheses.* Berkeley and Los Angeles: Univ. of California Press, 1942.

————. *The Work of Art.* Bloomington: Indiana University Press, 1955.

Russell, Bertrand. *A Critical Exposition of the Philosophy of Leibniz.* London: George Allen and Unwin Ltd., 1964.

T'ang, Chun-i. *Introduction to Philosophy* (Chinese version). Vol. II, Hong Kong: Yulin Publishing Co., 1960.

Thilly, F., and Wood, Ledger. *A Hilstory of Philosophy.* New York: Holt, Rinehart and Winston, 1957.

Weitz, Morris, ed. *Twentieth-Century Philosophy: The Analytic Tradition.* New York: The Free Press, 1966.

Articles

Burtt, E. A. "The Status of World Hypotheses," *The Journal of Philosophy,* 42 (Feb. 15, 1945), 85-101.

Hall, E. W. "Of What Use is Metaphysics?" *The Journal of Philosophy,* 33 (April 23, 1936), 236-45.

Ha.tshorne, Charles. Review of *World Hypotheses*. *Ethics*, 53 (Oct., 1942), 73-75.

Hockstra, Raymond. "Pepper's World Hypotheses," *The Journal of Philosophy*, 42 (Feb. 15, 1945), 85-101.

Kahn, S. J. "Critical Judgment and Professor Pepper's Eclecticism." *Journal of Aesthetics and Art Criticism*, 9 (September, 1950), 46-50.

Morgan, D. N. Review of *Concept and Quality*. *Journal of Aesthetics and Art Criticism*, 28 (Winter, 1969), 243-46.

Pepper, S. C. "Philosophy and Metaphor." *The Journal of Philosophy*, 25 (March 1928), 130-32.

————. "Categories." *University of California Publications in Philosophy*, 13 (1930), 73-98.

————. "The Root-metaphor Theory of Metaphysics." *The Journal of Philosophy*, 32 (July 4, 1935), 365-74.

————. "On the Cognitive Value of World Hypotheses." *The Journal of Philosophy*, 33 (Oct. 8, 1936), 575-77.

————. "Metaphysical Method." *The Philosophical Review*, 52 (May 1943), 252-69.

————. "The Status of 'World Hypotheses': A Rejoinder." *The Philosophical Review*, 52 (Nov., 1943), 602-04.

————. "A Proposal for a World Hypothesis." *The Monist*, 47 (Winter 1963), 267-86.

Robinson, Elmo A. "Animism as a World Hypothesis." *The Philosophical Review*, 58 (Jan. 1949), 53-63.

Shields, Allan. Review of *Concept and Quality*. *Journal of the History of Philosophy*, IX, No. 1 (1971), 127-30.

FOOTNOTES

1. This kind of classification is not openly adopted by any one in his discussion of this problem. But on the basis of the recent centuries' development of the problem of metaphysics, I think this is an acceptable classification.

2. F. C. Copleston, S. J., *A History of Philosophy* (Maryland: The Newman Press, 1960), Vol. IV, pp. 57-58; 61-62.

   The Analytic Tradition, ed. M. Weitz (New York: The Free Press, 1966), pp. 207-219.

4. A. J. Ayer, ed., *Logical Positivism* (New York: The Free Press, 1959), p. 11.

5. *Ibid.*

6. F. C. Copleston, S. J., *A History of Philosophy,* Vol. IV, p. 60.

7. S. C. Pepper, *World Hypotheses* (Berkeley and Los Angeles: Univ. of California Press, 1966; first published in 1942), pp. 1-2.

8. A. J. Ayer, ed., *Logical Positivism,* p. 10.

9. John Dewey, *Experience and Nature* (La Salle, Illinois: The Open Court Publishing Co., 1958; first published in 1925), pp. 5, 71-72.

10. *Ibid.,* pp. 71-72.

11. S. C. Pepper, *World Hypotheses,* pp. 1-2.

12. *Ibid.,* pp. 92-96.

13. See *World Hypotheses,* Part Two, pp. 151-314.

14. What the reasons are for a philosopher to adopt one kind of concept instead of another is an interesting question. Perhaps this is concerned with a person's temperament. See the Conclusion of this study.

15. D. A. Drennen, ed. *A Modern Introduction to Metaphysics* (New York: The Free Prss, 1966; first published in 1962), p. 263. Drennen in his introductory remark to Pepper's "The Root Metaphor Theory of Metaphysics" indicates that "His theory, consequently, is less a theory about metaphysics

and more a theory about other theories of metaphysics."

16. In rejecting dogmatism Pepper does not mention the names of these philosophers. But he indicates that any philosophy not based on evidence is dogmatism. He defines "a dogmatist as one whose belief exceeds his cognitive grounds for belief." See *World Hypotheses*, p. 11.

17. S. C. Pepper, *Concept and Quality* (La Salle, Illinois: Open Court Publishing Co., 1967), p. 1.

18. S. C. Pepper, *World Hypotheses*, pp. 91-92.

19. *Ibid.*, pp. 89-92.

20. *Ibid.*, p. 91.

21. Pepper presents this theory in his book *Concept and Quality*, and I discuss it in Chapter Three, section 5, of this study.

22. S. C. Pepper, "On the Cognitive Value of World Hypotheses," *The Journal of Philosophy*, 33 (Oct. 8, 1936), 576.

23. *Ibid.*, 575-77.

24. S. C. Pepper, *World Hypotheses*, pp. 1-2.

25. See Page 4 of this study.

26. S. C. Pepper, *World Hypotheses*, p. 1.

27. S. C. Pepper, *Concept and Quality*, p. 8.

28. S. C. Pepper, *World Hypotheses*, p. 3.

29. *Ibid.*, p. 11.

30. *Ibid.*, p. 3.

31. *Ibid.*, p. 7.

32. *Ibid.*, pp. 19-21.

33. *Ibid.*, p. 21.

34. *Ibid.*, pp. 23-24.

35. See Mou Tsung-san, *Logic*, Chinese version (Taipei: Ching Chung Book Co., 1960), pp. 162-163.

36. In *Concept and Quality*, Chapter 14, section 4, Pepper interpreted in detail how "logical reality is dependent for its being on the processes of actuality."

But it seems that it also cannot be regarded as a successful rejection of the principle of contradiction as self-evident.

37. S. C. Pepper, *World Hypotheses*, pp. 25-26.

38. *Ibid.*, p. 25.

39. *Ibid.*, pp. 26-27.

40. *Ibid.*, p. 28.

41. *Ibid.*, p. 29.

42. *Ibid.*, p. 25.

43. *Ibid.*, pp. 17-18.

44. F. C. Copleston, S. J., *A History of Philosophy*, Vol. VIII, pp. 496-497.

45. C. S. Peirce, "The Fixation of Belief," in *The Philosophy of Peirce*, J. Buchler, ed. (New York: Harcourt, Brace and Co., 1940), pp. 5-22.

46. C. S. Peirce, "The Scientific Attitude and Fallibilism," in *The Philosophy of Peirce*, pp. 42-59.

47. S. C. Pepper, *The Basis of Criticism in the Arts* (Cambridge, Mass.: Harvard University Press, 1965), p. 3.

48. S. C. Pepper, *World Hypotheses*, p. 47.

49. *Ibid.*, pp. 51-52.

50. *Ibid.*, p. 39.

51. *Ibid.*, p. 40.

52. *Ibid.*, p. 44.

53. *Ibid.*, pp. 47-49. This description was given in *The Basis of Criticism in the Arts* in a different expression but with the same meaning.

54. *Ibid.*, p. 48.

55. John Dewey, *Logic: The Theory of Inquiry* (New York: Henry Holt and Co., 1938), p. 117.

56. In *World Hypotheses*, Pepper did not use the term "logical positivists." What he used there is "positivists" instead of "logical positivists."

57. B. Russell, *A Critical Exposition of the Philosophy of Leibniz* (London: George Allen & Unwin Ltd., 6th Impression, 1964), pp. 16-17.

58. A. J. Ayer, ed., *Logical Positivism,* pp. 4, 10.

59. R. Carnap, "The Rejection of Metaphysics," in *20th Century Philosophy: The Analytic Tradition,* p. 210.

60. S. C. Pepper, *World Hypotheses,* p. 71.

61. *Ibid.,* p. 49.

62. *Ibid.,* p. 71.

63. S. C. Pepper, *Concept and Quality,* p. 45.

64. S. C. Pepper, *World Hypotheses,* p. 71.

65. *Ibid.,* p. 72.

66. *Ibid.,* p. 82.

67. *Ibid.*

68. *Ibid.,* p. 83.

69. C. G. Hempel, *Philosophy of Natural Science* (Englewood Cliffs, N. J.: Prentice-Hall, Inc., 1966), pp. 15-16.

70. S. C. Pepper, *World Hypothesis,* pp. 87-88.

71. *Ibid.,* p. 89.

72. S. C. Pepper, *Concept and Quality,* p. 268.

73. *Ibid.,* p. 269.

74. S. C. Pepper, *World Hypotheses,* p. 84.

75. S. C. Pepper, *World Hypotheses,* p. 84.

76. S. C. Pepper, "The Root Metaphor Theory of Metaphysics," *The Journal of Philosophy,* Vol. 32 (1935), pp. 365-74.

77. S. C. Pepper, *World Hypotheses,* pp. 91-92.

78. S. C. Pepper, *Concept and Quality,* p. 3.

79. S. C. Pepper, *World Hypotheses,* pp. 91-92.

80. *Ibid.,* p. 102.

81. *Ibid.,* p. 101.

82. *Ibid.,* pp. 96, 104.

83. *Ibid.,* p. 98.

84. *Ibid.,* pp. 96-97.

85. *Ibid.*, p. 104.

86. *Ibid.*, pp. 113-114.

87. *Ibid.*, p. 91.

88. *Ibid.*, p. 84.

89. See "The Root Metaphor Theory of Metaphysics," pp. 265-266.

90. S. C. Pepper, *World Hypotheses*, p. 2.

91. *Ibid.*

92. S. C. Pepper, *Concept and Quality*, p. 9.

93. S. C. Pepper, *World Hypotheses*, p. 141.

94. *Ibid.*

95. *Ibid.*, p. 151.

96. *Ibid.*, p. 162.

97. *Ibid.*, p. 154.

98. *Ibid.*, p. 163.

99. *Ibid.*, p. 170.

100. *Ibid.*, p. 171.

101. *Ibid.*, p. 173.

102. *Ibid.*, p. 175.

103. *Ibid.*, pp. 176-77.

104. *Ibid.*, p. 179.

105. *Ibid.*, p. 184.

106. *Ibid.*, p. 141.

107. *Ibid.*, p. 186.

108. *Ibid.*, pp. 193-94.

109. *Ibid.*, p. 216.

110. *Ibid.*, p. 217.

111. See the succeeding section.

112. S. C. Pepper, *World Hypotheses*, p. 214.

113. *Ibid.*, p. 174.

114. *Ibid.*, p. 141.

115. F. Thilly and Ledger Wood, *A History of Philosophy* (New York: Holt, Rinehart and Winston, 1957), p. 654.

116. S. C. Pepper, *Concept and Quality*, p. 2.

117. *Ibid.,* pp. 2-3.

118. S. C. Pepper, *World Hypotheses,* p. 232.

119. *Ibid.,* p. 243.

120. *Ibid.,* pp. 235-36.

121. *Ibid.,* p. 236.

122. *Ibid.,* p. 241.

123. *Ibid.*

124. *Ibid.,* p. 249.

125. *Ibid.*

126. *Ibid.,* p. 141.

127. *Ibid.,* p. 280.

128. *Ibid.,* p. 283.

129. *Ibid.*

130. *Ibid.,* p. 281.

131. *Ibid.,* p. 314.

132. S. C. Pepper, *Concept and Quality,* p. 1.

133. *Ibid.*

134. *Ibid.*

135. *Ibid.,* p. 18.

136. *Ibid.,* p. 1.

137. *Ibid.,* p. 2.

138. See Allan Shields, Review of *Concept and Quality, Journal of the History of Philosophy,* Vol. IX, No. 1 (1971), p. 129.

139. S. C. Pepper, *Concept and Quality,* p. 1.

140. *Ibid.*

141. *Ibid.,* p. 2.

142. *Ibid.*

143. *Ibid.*

144. *Ibid.*, p. 5.

145. *Ibid.*, p. 18.

146. *Ibid.*, pp. 28-30.

147. *Ibid.*, p. 76.

148. *Ibid.*, p. 17.

149. S. C. Pepper, *World Hypotheses,* p. 217.

150. See T. E. Hill, *Contemporary Theories of Knowledge* (New York: The Ronald Press Co., 1961), pp. 392-93; 426-27.

151. *Ibid.*

152. S. C. Pepper, *Concept and Quality,* p. 92.

153. *Ibid.*, p. 93.

154. See D. N. Morgan, Review of *Concept and Quality, Journal of Aesthetics and Art Criticism,* 28 (Winter 1969), p. 243.

155. S. C. Pepper, *Concept and Quality,* pp. 169-170.

156. *Ibid.*, p. 484.

157. John Dewey, *Logic: The Theory of Inquiry,* pp. 1-2.

158. S. C. Pepper, *Concept and Quality,* p. 478.

159. *Ibid.*, p. 604, footnote 6.

160. *Ibid.*, p. 564.

161. *Ibid.*, p. 2.

162. *Ibid.*, p. 94.

163. *Ibid.*, p. 95.

164. S. C. Pepper, *World Hypotheses,* pp. 120-24, 127-35.

165. As pointed out before, when rejecting dogmatism, Kant's name was not mentioned. But Pepper indicates that any philosopher whose philosophy is not based on evidence is a dogmatist. See page 8, footnote 1, of this study.

166. S. C. Pepper, *Concept and Quality,* pp. 53, 321, 337.

167. *Ibid.*, p. 317.

168. *Ibid.*, p. 578.

169. S. C. Pepper, *World Hypotheses*, pp. 60-70.

170. S. C. Pepper, *The Basis of Criticism in the Arts*, pp. 6-7.

171. S. C. Pepper, *World Hypotheses*, p. 91.

172. What is indicated in this paragraph can also be presented as follows: In the history of Western thought there have been two trends of thought concerned with the problem of metaphysics. That is, there has been a mysterious trend in Western thought as well as an intellectual trend. In ancient Greek times before the Milesian natural philosophy, there were Homeric mythology and Hesiodic cosmogony. A little later than the Milesian school, there was Pythagoreanism influenced by Dionysiac religion. Even in Socrates' and Plato's thought one can find some kind of mystery. Aristotle's philosophy is more empirical, but he never openly denies that there is some kind of reality transcending man's mind. Post-Aristotelian Neo-Platonism indulges in mysticism. Stoicism in some sense cannot be exempt from mysticism either. Medieval philosophy was dominated by Christian thought. Christian philosophers accept revelation as something superior to any knowledge obtained by reason and experience. Comparatively speaking, modern and contemporary philosophers have placed more emphasis on the importance of knowledge and have been more interested in establishing the theory of knowledge. But as we all admit that obtaining knowledge is just one aspect of human life, there are questions they cannot answer just by knowledge, and the world cannot be regarded as identical with what we know without controversy; mysticism or some kind of noncognitive theory of metaphysics has its position in human history.

173. See F. Thilly and Ledger Wood, *A History of Philosophy*, p. 549; and also see D. A. Drennen, ed., *A Modern Introduction to Metaphysics*, p. 263.

174. S. C. Pepper, *World Hypotheses*, p. vii.

An Understanding of Chinese Philosophy From the Theory of World Hypothesis

Tu Li
（李杜）

I. INTRODUCTION

With reference to the basic concepts of the theory of world hypothesis,[1] an understanding of Chinese philosophy can be divided into three aspects: the distinction between science and metaphysics; the rejection of utter skepticism and dogmatism; the root metaphor theory as a starting point to establish a hypothetical understanding of the world.

Related to the development of modern Western philosophy, the distinction between science and metaphysics is important and essential. For it is a step regarded either as separating metaphysics from the field of knowledge or as asserting the theory of world hypothesis with cognitive meaning. But in Chinese tradition science never achieved its independent development, nor was metaphysics denied to the meaning of understanding the world. So the problem of distinguishing science from metaphysics did not come out as a philosophical problem. In theory this is a problem which Chinese philosophy also has to face. But nothing was ever discussed in the past.

Nor did utter skepticism come out as a serious problem in Chinese philosophy. Nobody ever tried to assert a statement like this, "One who doubts everything."[2] This of course does not mean that Chinese philosophers took every statement for granted. It only means that they did not want to assert a universally dubitable statement. To Chinese philosophers any doubt should directly point to the statement regarded as problematic. They did not think that everything is dubitable.

Nor is there in Chinese tradition any kind of dogmatism as rejected by Pepper. Religious authority like Christianity was never established in China, nor did we develop any principle regarded as self-evident — neither in logic nor in mathematics. Neither did we have the idea of indubitability of immediate facts. So what was distinguished or rejected by Pepper in the first two aspects of the theory of world hypothesis was not regarded as serious problems in Chinese philosophy.

As to the third aspect, I think, we really have a kind of analogical and hypothetical understanding of the world, though, perhaps, this kind of understanding in Chinese philosophy was not fully developed as in the West. But as in the

West, China has a long philosophical tradition. In this tradition, different schools of philosophy were produced, and different methods were used by different philosophers to understand the world. I really think that the hypothetical way of studying the world was adopted by some Chinese philosophers, though none of them apparently said that they did so.

A world theory is originated in a root metaphor. A root metaphor may be anything which is adopted as analogical understanding. When this analogical understanding is enlarged to the extent that it covers everything which appears to us, it becomes a world hypothesis.[3] It seems to me that to understand by analogy is a common way used by almost all people. Whether it is enlarged enough to become a world theory depends on what is chosen as means for analogy, and on the cultural situation in which it is used. If a culture does not mature well enough to develop a kind of intellectual understanding of the whole world, the analogical understanding will be limited to some extent, and thus no world theory can be expected. However, in China we really have a long intellectual tradition. In this tradition, several relatively adequate world theories were developed. As I roughly understand, Taoism, Liism, Ch'iism and Yin-Yangism should be regarded as world theories. So in the following sections, ˙ will have a brief discussion on them respectively.

II. Taoism

Taoism is usually understood as a school of philosophy. Its founder is Lao Tzu. But here it is not used to indicate that school. What I want to do

with Taoism is to indicate a world theory using something as its root metaphor from which are derived some categories by which to understand the world.

As we understand now, *tao* is not a concept used only by Lao Tzu, Chuang Tzu or any other Taoists. It is a common concept accepted by all ancient scholars regardless of the fact that they were not Taoists such as the Confucianists or the thinkers of the other schools.[4]

Like any other object-word, at the beginning *tao* was used to indicate a particular thing, that is road or path on which we can walk. But gradually it was developed into a general concept used to signify anything with the similarity to road or path and thus became a metaphorical or analogical term used to understand other things.

Historically speaking, in the *Book of History* and the *Book of Odes tao* already became a metaphorical term; other things were interpreted by it. But it was not until the times covered by the book of *Kuo Yü* or *Tso Chuan*[5] that it was widely used to describe the activity of man as well as the state of the world, and gradually a kind of Taoism was formulated. This kind of Taoism was not only a philosophy of Lao Tzu, Chuang Tzu or other Taoists, but also a philosophy of Confucius, Mencius or the thinkers of the other schools. Their difference does not lie in using road as a metaphor to understand other things but in what kinds of things were understood by it.[6] Thinkers after the Ch'in dynasty in general were the same as those in the Pre-Ch'in period. And thus a kind of Taoism which I propose to discuss was prevalent in Chinese philosophy.

I will not discuss in detail how different thinkers of different schools

used road as a metaphorical term to describe things here. It is impossible for me to do that in a short paper like this. I will be satisfied with a general description of this kind of understanding with reference to S.C. Pepper's theory of world hypothesis. That is to point out what the root metaphor of Taoism is; what categories are derived from it; and how the world in general is described in terms of the derived categories.

As indicated before, the root metaphor of Taoism is road or path on which we can walk. Categories derived from it as I primarily understand are: (1) particular, (2) norm, and (3) activity actualizing the norm.

These derived categories are essential but their meanings are not definite. Categories are essential because they are deduced from the root metaphor. Their meanings are not definite because they are related to what are to be understood. When the understanding is enlarged, the meaning is refined and readjusted, accompanied by the enlargement.

To Taoism everything in the world is a presentation of *tao* understood in terms of the categories. As we have experienced and as indicated by the categories, the world is full of particulars called myriad of things (萬物), which present themselves in accordance with norms. No existent thing is not present; no particular is not in a state of existence in accordance with the norm. But the norm is not only a static mode to which particular things conform; it is also a dynamic principle guiding the activity of particular things. So the activity actualizing the norm is started from the particular and guided by the norm. It is a cooperative presentation of the particular and the norm. The

norm is not regarded as something existing outside the particular, nor is it a component or a constituent of a particular. It is presented by things and is the way in which a thing is presented. The relation of the particular and the norm is a kind of co-existence and mutual dependence. Particulars exist in accordance with norms and norms are present in virtue of particulars.

Everything in the world is a presentation of particular in accordance with the norm. But as regards how many norms there are, no answer can be obtained, nor that of particulars. For they cannot be determined formally, nor can we do this by appealing to past experiences. The world of Taoists in some sense is similar to that of William James. It is in the making. Accompanied by new things, new norms continuously come out.

The world is in the making. Nobody can have a complete knowledge of it. But those that are already presented to us can be understood in accordance with some principles. According to Taoists, the world should be understood from two aspects — the natural and the mental. From the first aspect we understand different kinds of things existing in accordance with the different norms; from the second, different activities of man guided by different norms are manifested. Since different kinds of things exist in accordance with different norms, the difference of things is intimately related to the difference of norms. The variation of the former is concomitant with the latter. The change of the latter is followed by a transformation of the former. Since different activities of man are guided by the different norms, the difference of the activities of man is connected

with the difference of norms. Man has different activities. Each of the activities is guided by a norm. No activity of man is not guided by a norm. No norm of human activity is not manifested in man's activity. So the norm and the activity of man are co-existent and mutually dependent. If we understand the norm from this point of view, its relation to the activities of man is inseparable. The inseparability of the norm from the activity of man is universal. It is not true that some kinds of norms are inseparable but others are not.

What kind of norm is accepted as a guiding principle of a certain activity of man is determined by the activity. If the activity is different the norm guiding the activity is different. No value judgment is asserted. Value judgment is not something derived from the relationship of the norm and the activity of man. It is based on another criterion asserted by man. And the criterion can be different. So what is asserted by Confucianists as the criterion of value to which man's activity conforms is different from that of the traditional Taoists and the thinkers of the other schools.

From the viewpoint of S.C. Pepper's theory of world hypothesis only things with cognitive meaning are discussed. But to Taoism discussion is not limited to the cognitive world. The problem of spirit, T'ien or God is also discussed. To Pepper this kind of problem is noncognitive; no cognitive conclusion can be expected. So it is excluded from the study of the world hypotheses. But to Taoism, tao is used as a root metaphor to deal with everything which man wants to understand. Man has an aspiration for understanding the

spiritual world, so it is assumed that there is such a kind of world existing in accordance with tao though it was not given an intelligible understanding; Tsoism understood in this light, is not only a kind of metaphysics concerning this world, but it keeps a channel which is connected with the gate of the supernatural world.

III. LIISM

Li is originally used to indicate the streaks in jade or in stone or grain in wood and the like. So what is indicated by li is something which can be found in everything. Owing to this fact, I think that it is regarded as the essence of things by ancient Chinese thinkers.

Historically speaking, in the Pre-Ch'in period, li was already an important concept. But it was not until the Northern Sung dynasty that this concept was developed into a world theory and Liism was formulated. Before the Northern Sung dynasty, li was only used separately to indicate the streaks of things, "the markings of completed things," the way of argument, the principle of action, the arrangement of literary composition and so on. But after the establishment of the School of the Principle (理學) in the Northern Sung dynasty, li is accepted as something in terms of which all other things are systematically interpreted, and a world theory of Liism was produced.

The root metaphor of Liism is a jade or a stone or a piece of wood. From this root metaphor, as I primarily understand, are derived the three categories, that is (1) matter, (2) principle, and (3) relation between the matter and the principle, in terms of which the world is understood.

Compared with Taoism, Liism is more concerned with a static world. In general the world explained by Taoism is a dynamic world in which different things are presented in accordance with the categories derived from the root metaphor with active character. As to Liism, it tends to indicate a static world. In this world what appears attractive to us is the formal system of conceptual understanding.

According to Liism, things in the world as existents are a combination of the principle and the matter. Nothing in this world is a pure matter, nor is it a pure principle. Matter and principle are present in a state of combined existence. So they are objects of perception. But when the principle is abstracted from the concrete things, it is separated from the matter and becomes a pure object of thought. And when this object is regarded as fundamental, what is understood is quite different from the world regarded as a combined presentation of the principle and the matter.

A separating understanding of the principle from the matter was greatly stressed by Liists in the past. And the problem of the priority of the principle over the matter or the matter over the principle was once earnestly discussed, though without any final result. According to the Liists' understanding, this problem is insoluble. For no acceptable criterion can be found by which to answer the question. But to our understanding, both the principle and the matter are categories derived from the root metaphor. Since they are categories they are secondary concepts of Liism. The primary concept is jade or stone from which the principle and the matter are derived. So the principle and the matter are on the same level.

No one of them is prior to the other. Perhaps, we are tempted to think that since the principle is so stressed by Liism, it is more essential and should be regarded as prior to the matter. But this thinking is ungrounded. The reason is that when we understand a stone as a root metaphor of Liism both the principle and the matter are derived categories of the root metaphor. They are on the same level; none of them is prior to the other.

Whether the principle is prior to the matter or the matter to the principle is a controversial metaphysical problem discussed ever since the establishment of the School of the Principle. But what is most contributory of Liism to Chinese thought is not that metaphysical controversy but the acceptance of the principle as an abstract object of thought. Based on this acceptance the understanding of the different levels of natural world as well as cultural world was developed. And when modern Western thoughts were introduced to China, the principle of Liism became a key concept in terms of which the Western thoughts were connected with the Chinese learnings. The different systems of knowledge such as logic, mathematics, natural science, social science and philosophy are asserted in relation to the understanding of the principle of Liism, and each of the different systems is also regarded as an indication of that principle.

The difference between science and philosophy is stressed by contemporary thinkers. Those who want to understand things from the scientific point of view, perhaps, would be more interested in distinguishing science from philosophy and one of the above-mentioned systems, such as logic, from another system, such

as social science. But one who acknowledges this distinction is not obliged to reject the idea that each of the different systems is respectively an indication of the systematization of the principle of Liism. This is what Liists want to assert, and they also want to regard that the principle can be applied to every system of knowledge in terms of which the world is interpreted, and that the world is partly an indication of the principle.

IV. CH'IISM

Ch'i is originally used to indicate a state of flux of air or vapor or steam and the like. This state is not only limited to the above-mentioned things, but it can also be found in other things. I think it is because of this fact that Ch'i is regarded as something essential to all things and is used to interpret the other things. This kind of understanding might originate in ancient times. But it was not until the times covered by the book of Kuo Yü or Tso Chuan that the above-mentioned understanding was widely accepted. Since then ch'i became a metaphysical term. Ch'iism became a world theory. Chuang Tzu was greatly influenced by this theory. His naturalism is a kind of Ch'iism. After Chuang Tzu thinkers like Tung Chun-shu, in the Former Han dynasty, Wang Chun, in the Later Han dynasty, and Chang Tsai, in the Northern Sung dynasty, all can be regarded as Ch'iists. Their systems of philosophy in one sense or another were formulated in terms of ch'i, that is, they used air or vapor or steam as a root metaphor from which are derived some categories in terms of which other things are explained.

The root metaphor of Ch'iism is air

or vapor or steam and the like. Categories derived from it as I primarily understand are: (1) quality, (2) change, and (3) the law of change.

As stated above, all Ch'iists understand ch'i as something fundamental to all things, but it is not regarded as unanalysable as a Democritian atom. It can be further split up into some elements on which categories are based.

Quality is derived from air as a category of Ch'iism. This quality is the matter that is in a state of flux. So it is not static; instead it is in a state of perpetual change guided by a law. The change and the law are regarded as second and third categories of Ch'iism respectively.

The quality is derived from what air is because there is nothing prior to it, neither God nor Tao. To Ch'iism God can be regarded only as a kind of activity in accordance with the law of change, and Tao is the way of change initiated by the quality in accordance with the law. So Ch'iism is a kind of naturalism. Air is not a result of anything. Everything is coming out of air understood in terms of the mentioned categories.

Change is a change of the quality and the quality is present in a state of change. So the world understood in terms of quality and change is in a state of perpetually becoming; things in the world are dynamic; they never stand still.

The world is in a state of becoming. How does it become? It becomes in accordance with a law of change, and this law is understood as the law of nature by Ch'iists. Related to the appearance of condensation and rarefaction of ch'i, it is understood that the law of change indicates a kind of

interaction of two opposites. These two opposites are called by some Ch'iists as *yin* and *yang*. But here we must be careful not to confuse the *yin* and *yang* just mentioned with the ideas of *yin* and *yang* accepted as its root metaphor by Yin-Yangism which will be discussed in the next section. What are called *yin* and *yang* by some Ch'iists is the change of *ch'i* in accordance with the law of change presented as two opposite activities. As to Yin-Yangism, *yin* and *yang* are regarded as its root metaphor for anything with two opposite aspects or two opposite states and so on. So though the Chinese characters of them are the same, their implications are quite different; the difference is related to the different thinkers of the different schools of philosophy.[7]

V. YIN-YANGISM

Yin-yangism is usually understood as a school of philosophy. Its founder was Tsou Yen (鄒衍). But here it is not used to indicate that school. What I want to do with Yin-Yangism as with Taoism before, is to indicate a world theory using something as its root metaphor from which are derived some categories by which to interpret the world.

As we understand now, *yin* and *yang* are two general concepts widely used by scholars prior to the appearance of Yin-Yang School. Neither did thinkers in later times using them commit themselves in any way to be followers of Yin-Yang School.[8] If *yin* and *yang* are understood from this point of view, I think, it is acceptable to regard them as two common concepts not limited to any particular school of thought.

The root metaphor of Yin-Yangism

is the two opposite aspects of a leaf or any other thing with two opposite aspects such as the upperface and the underside of a table, two ends of a stick, and so on. (Originally speaking, *yin* indicates the place where no sunshine can reach, and *yang* the place the sun is shining on. But gradually, this original indication was developed; *yin* and *yang* are used to signify anything with two opposite aspects as mentioned above.)

Categories derived from the root metaphor of Yin-Yangism as I primarily understand are: (1) contrary characters, (2) mutual rejection, (3) mutual embrace, and (4) harmonious integration (or completion).

To Yin-Yangism, the world is full of things with *yin* and *yang* contrasts. They are further understood in terms of the derived categories.

Contrary characters are essential to everything. For to Yin-Yangism, everything is a combination of some elements with contrary characters. (This is true of natural things as well as of human affairs. But here the discussion will be limited to the former.) We cannot find anything in this world which is not composed of elements of contrary characters. Characters contrasting with each other reject each other. This rejection inheres in things. It is understood as the change of a thing when it increases to such a scale, that from it the transformation of that thing results. When a thing is in the state of transformation the mutual rejection is dominating that thing. But though contrary characters are essential to a thing, they are just one aspect of that thing. Opposite to this aspect there is another aspect which embraces its opposite. The whole picture is that everything with a character which is contrary to the other character

is connected with the other character. The different components penetrate and embrace each other, indicating what Lao Tzu says, "All things support the *yin* and embrace the *yang*. It is on the blending of the breaths (of the *yin* and the *yang*) that their harmony depends."[9]

Rejection and embrace are contrary to each other. But both of them indicate the relation of a thing called the relation of *yin* and *yang*. Since the relation of *yin* and *yang* not only indicates the contrary characters but also the mutual embrace, it is not only understood by the formula "A is contrary to B," but also by the formula "A is connected with B". The latter has further been interpreted recently with reference to the knowledge of modern science. For to Yin-Yangism causality is nothing but an indication of the relation of *yin* and *yang*, so are the relations of ideas formulated in mathematics or logic. Furthermore, this positive indication is not only referred to the concept of sciences but also to the philosophical relations. It is also applied to the studies of fine arts and literature.

Yin-Yangism's assertion that rejection and embrace are mutually related is well grounded. As we have experienced, things appear to us with components in contrary characters. Since one character is in contrast to the other, they are mutually rejected. But this rejection is not absolute. For it is impossible for anything to exist with an absolutely rejecting element within it. There must be something in the contrary which makes them reconciled. This something is not imposed from outside; it is in the character and is regarded as an element of embrace.

The understanding of harmonious integration is based on embrace. The harmonious integration is a further indication of embrace and is a completion of *yin* and *yang* relation. Harmonious integration can be classified into different levels related to different relations of *yin* and *yang*. The hierachical order is started from a thing understood as an individual which is the result of a combination of contrary characters of elements. With an eye to the modern understanding of things which are classified into inorganic and organic, the harmonious integration of an individual thing is understood as the inorganic integration and organic integration. The organic things are further classified into plants, animals and human beings. Conforming to this classification, the harmonious integration will be presented as the harmonious integration of plants, of animals, and of human beings. This is just one aspect of the situation. The other aspect is that the harmonious integration is not limited to the integration of individuals. It is also present in the things above the individuals. To Yin-Yangism, the social organization is an indication of the latter kind of harmonious integration. And in addition to this, the whole world is understood by Yin-Yangists as a presentation of the ultimate completion of *yin* and *yang*, which is the result of the greatest harmonious integration.

In contrast to harmonious integration, the disintegration of disharmony in theory is also asserted by the Yin-Yangists. But it is only accepted as a complement of harmonious integration just as a contrary character is regarded as a complement of the mutual embrace. Yin-Yangists' world is a world of harmonious integration with different levels in hierachical order.

When *yin* is understood as contrary

to *yang* and when the character of the former is different from that of the latter, Yin-Yangism is regarded as a dualism. But this regard is just one aspect of the theory. As the contrary characters embrace each other and are in a state of perpetual movement, the contrary characters are not absolute. To some Yin-Yangists the perpetual movement is understood as the activity of *tao*. So *tao* is also regarded by Yin-Yangists as ultimate. In this regard, Yin-Yangism is sometimes confused with Taoism by some thinkers who do not differentiate *tao* as an indication of the continuous activity of *yin* and *yang* from *tao* indicated by Taoism in terms of its categories derived from its root metaphor of road.

VI. CONCLUSION

The world theory is a theory of understanding the whole world. In contrast to special sciences, it is a metaphysical theory. Traditional metaphysics has seriously been criticized by some contemporary philosophers. What they attack most is the fact that we can get no cognitive meaning from metaphysical statements. Metaphysical propositions are nonsensical.[11] I do not want to discuss this problem in detail here. Nor can I give it a whole evaluation. What I want to do is just to point out that since the criticism is directed to the problem of cognitive meaning, it has nothing to do with the kind of metaphysics regarding the problem of understanding the world as a study of evidence as asserted by the theory of world hypothesis. For study of evidence is an empirical inquiry with cognitive meaning, and it is not contrary to the study of special sciences.

That the theory of world hypothesis cannot be attacked by those who deal with the problem of metaphysics from the scientific point of view is clear. But as indicated by modern understanding, what is regarded as a problem with cognitive meaning is limited to the field of cognition. But, as we know, there are things which cannot be grasped by cognition. That is, besides cognitive meaning there are things which are asserted not by cognition but by some other functions of man such as awareness and feeling. And in this regard what man is aware of or feels about is not something which can be conceptualized but something which is prior to the conceptual understanding such as the *Existenz* of man or the awareness of the unconditioned or the feeling of God. All these belong to the problem of metaphysics.

So in regard to the whole problem of metaphysics, what the theory of world hypothesis is concerned with is only one aspect. It is limited to the field of cognition. With this in mind we will understand that though in Formism what Pepper wants to discuss is the philosophy of Plato and that of Aristotle, yet he cannot give a proper discussion on the problem of God in Plato's philosophy and Aristotle's.[12] For the same reason, in Organicism what Pepper wants to discuss is Hegel's philosophy; he cannot give an adequate explanation to the problem of the Absolute or God in Hegel's philosophy.[13] But as we know, God or the Absolute is the ultimate end to which man wants to aspire. To the theory of world hypothesis God or the Absolute is not an object of evidence study; it has no cognitive meaning. But to philosophy as a whole God or the Absolute is

something about which we want to talk.

According to Pepper, the theory of world hypothesis is one but the world hypotheses are many. The world understood by one world hypothesis is different from the world understood by another world hypothesis. There is no absolute understanding of the world; one understanding is relative to another. Compared with what the theory does not deal with, the theory as a whole is also a relative theory. For the theory is not concerned with what is ultimately asserted by traditional philosophers, and what is man's ultimate aspiration. So if it is regarded as a theory of metaphysics, it is only a kind of metaphysics. It really gives us a new understanding of the problem of metaphysics. yet metaphysics is not limited to this kind of theory. Therefore, from the viewpoint of the theory to understand Chinese philosophy, what is explained in this paper is also only a kind of Chinese philosophy.

NOTES

1. The theory of world hypothesis was advocated by S.C. Pepper (1891-1972). This theory is mainly formulated with the following basic concepts: (1) the distinction between science and meta-physics, (2) the rejection of utter skepticism and dogmatism, (3) two different types of corroboration, (4) two different types of hypothesis, (5) the concept of root metaphor. See S.C. Pepper, *World Hypotheses* (Berkeley and Los Angels: University of California Press, 1966; first published in 1942), Part One: The Root Metaphor Theory, pp. 1-144. See also Tu Li, "S.C. Pepper's Concept of Metaphysics as the Theory of World Hypotheses," New Asia Academic Annual, Vol. XVI (Sept., 1974) pp. 223-317.

2. S.C. Pepper, *World Hypotheses*, p. 3.

3. Ibid., pp. 91-92.

4. See Tu Li, A Study of the Concept of T'ien-Tao and the Idea of God in Chinese and Western Philosophies (in Chinese) (Taipei: Linking Publishing Co., 1978), Part One, chs. III-IX, pp. 35-198.

5. The times covered by Kuo Yü: 990-453 B.C.; by Tso Chuan: 722-468 B.C..

6. See 4.

7. Etymologically speaking, *tao, li, ch'i*, or *yin-yang* is separately used to indicate something or some state of a thing. Each of them has its own originality. Each of them is used by different thinkers as root metaphor to understand the world as indicated in this paper. But this is just one aspect of the picture. The other aspect is that when these terms became metaphysical terms their original meanings were neglected and were freely used by different thinkers. So the continuous activity of *yin* and *yang* can be regarded as the action of *Tao*, and *ch'i* is also sometimes regarded as the matter of *Tao*, or *Tao* as the way of activity of *ch'i*, or *Tao* as the way of activity of *yin* and *yang*, and *yin* and *yang* can also be regarded as a way of the activity of *ch'i*, and so on, and a kind of eclecticism was thus prevalent.

8. See Hsu Fu-Kuan, *On Human Nature in Chinese History* (Taipei: Commercial press 1969), Appendix II, "A Study of Yin-Yang, Five Elements and the Concerning Material," (in Chinese), pp. 558-661. See also Tu Li, "T'ien, Tao and T'ien-Tao in the Book of Changes," (in Chinese), *New Asia Academic Bulletin*, Vol. III (1982), pp. 95-101.

9. Lao Tzu, *Tao Te Ching* (The Way and Its Power), ch. 42.
10. See 7.
11. See M. Weitz, ed. *The Analytic Tradition* (New York: The Free Press, 1966), pp. 207-219. See also A.J. Ayer, ed., *Logical Positivism* (New York: The Free Press, 1959), p. 10.
12. See S.C. Pepper, *World Hypotheses*, Part Two, pp. 151-185.
13. Ibid., pp. 280-314.

國立中央圖書館出版品預行編目資料

世界的假設裴柏與西方的形而上學 / 李杜著 -- 初版 -- 臺北市：臺
灣學生，民 79
14,366 面；21 公分
ISBN 957-15-0170-0（精裝）：新臺幣 320 元
-- ISBN 957-15-0171-9（平裝）：新臺幣 270 元

1.裴柏（Popper, S. C.）- 學識 - 哲學　2.形上學

145.59　　　　　　　　　　　　　　　　　　79000972

世界的假設：裴柏與西方的形而上學（全一冊）

著作者：李　　　　　　　　　杜
出版者：臺　灣　學　生　書　局
發行人：丁　　　文　　　治
發行所：臺　灣　學　生　書　局
台北市和平東路一段一九八號
郵政劃撥帳號○○○二四六六八號
電話：三　六　三　四　一　五六
FAX：三六三六三三四
本書局登記證字號：行政院新聞局局版臺業字第一一○○號
印刷所：淵　明　印　刷　廠
地址：永和市成功路一段43巷五號
電話：九　二　八　七　一　四　五
香港總經銷：藝　文　圖　書　公　司
地址：九龍偉業街九十九號連順大廈五字樓及七字樓
電話：七　九　五　九　五　九　五

定價　精裝新臺幣三二○元
　　　平裝新臺幣二七○元

中華民國七十九年十一月初版

16002　　　　翻印必究・版權所有

ISBN 957-15-0170-0 (精裝)
ISBN 957-15-0171-9 (平裝)